DARK AGE NUNNERIES

DARK AGE NUNNERIES

THE AMBIGUOUS IDENTITY OF FEMALE MONASTICISM, 800–1050

STEVEN VANDERPUTTEN

CORNELL UNIVERSITY PRESS
Ithaca and London

Copyright © 2018 by Cornell University

All rights reserved. Except for brief quotations in a review, this book, or parts thereof, must not be reproduced in any form without permission in writing from the publisher. For information, address Cornell University Press, Sage House, 512 East State Street, Ithaca, New York 14850.

First published 2018 by Cornell University Press
Printed in the United States of America

Library of Congress Cataloging-in-Publication Data

Names: Vanderputten, Steven, author.
Title: Dark age nunneries : the ambiguous identity of
   female monasticism, 800–1050 / Steven Vanderputten.
Description: Ithaca : Cornell University Press, 2018. |
   Includes bibliographical references and index.
Identifiers: LCCN 2017038573 (print) | LCCN 2017039896
   (ebook) | ISBN 9781501715969 (epub/mobi) |
   ISBN 9781501715976 (pdf) | ISBN 9781501715945 |
   ISBN 9781501715945 (cloth :alk. paper) |
   ISBN 9781501715952 (pbk. :alk. paper)
Subjects: LCSH: Monastic and religious life of
   women—Europe—History—Middle Ages, 600–1500. |
   Monasticism and religious orders for women—
   Europe—History—Middle Ages, 600–1500. |
   Convents—Europe—History—To 1500. | Europe—
   Church history—Middle Ages, 600–1500.
Classification: LCC BX4220.E85 (ebook) | LCC BX4220.
   E85 V36 2018 (print) | DDC 271/.90009021—dc23
LC record available at https://lccn.loc.gov/2017038573

Cornell University Press strives to use environmentally responsible suppliers and materials to the fullest extent possible in the publishing of its books. Such materials include vegetable-based, low-VOC inks and acid-free papers that are recycled, totally chlorine-free, or partly composed of nonwood fibers. For further information, visit our website at cornellpress.cornell.edu.

Contents

List of Illustrations vii

Preface and Acknowledgments ix

Abbreviations xiii

Introduction 1

1. Setting the Boundaries for Legitimate Experimentation 11

2. Holy Vessels, Brides of Christ: Ambiguous Ninth-Century Realities 37

3. Transitions, Continuities, and the Struggle for Monastic Lordship 65

4. Reforms, Semi-Reforms, and the Silencing of Women Religious in the Tenth Century 88

5. New Beginnings 111

6. Monastic Ambiguities in the New Millennium 135

Conclusion 155

Appendix A: The Leadership and Members of Female Religious Communities in Lotharingia, 816–1059 159

Appendix B: The Decrees on Women Religious from the Acts of the Synod of Chalon-sur-Saône, 813, and the Council of Mainz, 847 167

Appendix C: Jacques de Guise's Account of the Attempted Reform of Nivelles and Other Female Institutions in the Early Ninth Century 172

Appendix D: The Compilation on the Roll of Maubeuge, *c. Early Eleventh Century* 176

Appendix E: Letter by Abbess Thiathildis of Remiremont to Emperor Louis the Pious, c. 820s–840 183

Appendix F: John of Gorze's Encounter with Geisa, c. 920s–930s 185

Appendix G: Extract on Women Religious from the Protocol of the Synod of Rome (1059) 189

Appendix H: The Eviction of the Religious of Pfalzel as Recounted in the Gesta Treverorum, *1016* 192

Appendix I: The Life of Ansoaldis, Abbess of Maubeuge (d. 1050) 195

Appendix J: Letter by Pope Paschalis II to Abbess Ogiva of Messines (1107) 198

Notes 201

Bibliography 255

Index 301

Illustrations

Figures

1. Tombstone of Abbess Ruothildis of Pfalzel	2
2. Cesarius of Arles offers his *Rule* to the religious of Niedermünster	31
3. First page of the *Indicularius Thiathildis*	42
4. Hamage before and after the reconversion in the ninth century	48–49
5. The *Codex Eyckensis I*	55
6. Small reliquary from the treasury of Aldeneik	80
7. Bishop Gozelin's foundation charter for Bouxières	97
8. Church of Saint-Pierre-aux-Nonnains	107
9. Tower of the abbatial church at Epinal	123
10. Extract from the *Roll of Maubeuge*	141
11. Eleventh-century coins of Munsterbilzen	149

Maps

1. Female religious communities in Lotharingia, c. 870	60
2. Female religious communities in Lotharingia, c. 960	101
3. Female religious communities in Lotharingia, c. 1050	113

Preface and Acknowledgments

Historians today widely reject "dark age" as an accurate term for describing the early Middle Ages and the way in which its society and culture impacted on people's lives and attitudes. Almost on a weekly basis, they can be seen deploring its injudicious use in political discourse, the media, and everyday language, providing in the process ample evidence to argue its origins as a modern ideological construct. Partly as a result of the scholarly efforts to demonstrate the fallacy of this construct, over the past few decades the story of the centuries between c. 500 and the so-called Renaissance of the 1100s has emerged as a profoundly complex one, where nuanced arguments have substituted for the sweeping statements of yore.

An exception to this rule may be found in accounts of the years between c. 800 and 1050, a phase in the history of women religious that many scholars still tend to think of as a "dark age." Dark, in the sense that the realities of life in and around the cloister are difficult to access: the primary evidence from many communities is fragmented; the social, economic, intellectual, and religious context ill-understood; and research findings are scattered across a multitude of case studies. But dark also in the sense that, according to the dominant academic narrative, female monasticism in many places suffered from the physical and social isolation of its members, the progressive transfer of its institutions into the hands of the laity, and the precipitous decline—brought about by the former two factors—of women's intellectual life and spirituality.

With this study I hope to tell a more nuanced story, where the testimony of the primary evidence takes precedence over established scholarly accounts. It is a story, moreover, that dismantles the view of women religious in this period as the disempowered, at times even disinterested, witnesses to their own lives. As a running thread throughout the discussion, I highlight their attempts (and those of the clerics and the laymen and laywomen sympathetic to their cause) to construct localized narratives of self, nurture mutually beneficial relations with their social environment, and remain involved in shaping the attitudes and behaviors of the laity generally. In the following argument, the resulting multiformity in the sisters' experience of monastic life takes center stage.

I am pleased to acknowledge my debt to many institutions and individuals who made this book possible. Ghent University's Special Research Fund, by awarding me a third term as research professor, enabled me to research and write this study in a relatively short period of time. Additional support came from the Research Foundation–Flanders (FWO–Vlaanderen), by financially backing my project "Re-evaluating Female Monasticism's 'Ambiguous Identity' in the Ninth-to-Eleventh-Century West." I am grateful for the opportunities I was granted to extend my understanding of the literature, including during an invited professorship at the University of Bristol (sponsored by the Institute for Advanced Studies) in February 2017 and a visiting fellowship at the Università Cattolica del Sacro Cuore in Milan and Brescia (sponsored by the Royal Flemish Academy of Belgium and the Accademia dei Lincei) in April 2017. Finally, I also owe a debt of gratitude for the times I was given the opportunity to test the argument of this book or parts thereof at conferences and invited lectures, including at Aberystwyth, Antwerp, Boston, Brescia, Bristol, Brussels, Canterbury, Dresden, Kalamazoo, Leeds, and Namur.

While preparing this study, I published a number of preliminary findings as articles, namely "Reformatorische lichamelijkheid en de geconditioneerde emoties van twee religieuze vrouwen omstreeks het jaar 1000," in *Tijdschrift voor Geschiedenis*; "Debating Reform in Tenth- and Early-Eleventh-Century Female Monasticism," in *Zeitschrift für Kirchengeschichte*; and "Un espace sacré au féminin? Principes et réalités de la clôture des religieuses aux IXe–XIe siècles," in the proceedings of the conference *Spazio e mobilità nella "Societas Christiana" (secoli X–XIII): Spazio, identità, alterità*. A collaborative paper with Charles West entitled "Inscribing Property, Rituals, and Royal Alliances: The 'Theutberga Gospels' and the Abbey of Remiremont," published in *Mitteilungen des Instituts für Österreichische Geschichtsforschung*, lay at the basis of my comments on this manuscript and its contents. I am grateful to the anonymous reviewers of these pieces for their helpful remarks and to the editorial boards of the journals for accepting them for publication.

Karel Velle, head of the State Archives in Belgium, kindly offered to digitize the *Roll of Maubeuge*, an exceptional document Alexis Wilkin had previously brought to my attention. Eugenio Donadoni of Christie's generously allowed me unlimited access to the fabulous *Theutberga Gospels* before its sale in July 2015. Anja Neskens shared the unpublished results of her excavation work on the church of Aldeneik and later on gave me a warm welcome when I came to look at the magnificent pieces in the treasury of Saint-Catherine's church in Maaseik. Etienne Louis of the Communauté d'Agglomération du Douaisis promptly communicated the latest results of his excavations at the monastic site of Hamage and generously shared his unpublished work on the medieval written testimonies of saint's cults at Saint-Amé in Douai. Finally, Hannah Matis kindly sent me her paper on Paschasius Radbertus before it was made available in *Church History*. I also wish to extend my thanks to the staff of the Archives Départementales de la Meuse, the Trierisches Landesmuseum, the Hauptstaatsarchiv in Koblenz, the Stadtarchiv in Trier, the Geheimes Staatsarchiv Preussischer Kulturbesitz in Berlin, the Zentralbibliothek in Zürich, the Koninklijke Bibliotheek van België / Bibliothèque Royale de Belgique in Brussels, the Rijksarchief in Maastricht, and Ghent University Library for promptly responding to my queries for images, information, and consultation of manuscripts and other documents.

I consider myself fortunate to have discussed parts of my research with Albrecht Diem, Gordon Blennemann, Anne-Marie Helvétius, Rutger Kramer, Julia Barrow, Kirsty Day, Julia Smith, John Van Engen, Fiona Griffiths, Charles West, Patricia Stoop, Michèle Gaillard, Conrad Leyser, Nicolangelo d'Acunto, Kimm Curran, Giancarlo Andenna, Frédéric Chantinne, Philippe Mignot, Simon MacLean, Gert Melville, Carla Bino, Matthieu van der Meer, Ludger Körntgen, Carine van Rhijn, Emilia Jamroziak, Jane Schulenburg, and Jirki Thibaut. A special mention should go to Isabella Bolognese, who mildly—and, ultimately, helpfully—chastised me for ignoring women religious in a previous study entitled *Monastic Reform as Process*. To Susan Vincent, who helped me decide that the subject for this book was indeed a valid one and who asked difficult but pertinent questions when editing the earliest draft. And to Peter Potter, formerly of Cornell University Press, for helping me to see clearly what I hope to achieve with this and previous monographs.

I dedicate this book to Melissa Provijn, for supporting my struggles with primary sources and draft chapters with copious reading notes, countless cups of tea, and a tremendous amount of sympathy. And to my son Hugo, for keeping my study of ambiguities from becoming too ambiguous.

Abbreviations

AASS   *Acta Sanctorum quotquot toto orbe coluntur*. Ed. Johannes Bolland and others, 69 vols. Various publishers, 1643–1940.
BM   Bibliothèque Municipale
BNF   Bibliothèque Nationale de France
CCSL   *Corpus Christianorum. Series Latina*
KBR   Koninklijke Bibliotheek van België/Bibliothèque Royale de Belgique
MGH   *Monumenta Germaniae Historica*
MGH SS   *Monumenta Germaniae Historica. Scriptores*

DARK AGE NUNNERIES

Introduction

Sometime in the final years of the tenth century a woman called Ruothildis passed away. The abbess of Pfalzel, a female monastery in the German city of Trier, she had been wealthy, with a strong sense of pride in her noble origins and connections and in her position as leader of a community of women religious.[1] No doubt, she would have found the exquisitely carved inscription that subsequently adorned her tombstone very appropriate:[2]

> Here lies buried Ruothildis, spouse of the Redeemer
> but her soul rejoices upwards.
> When she was in this world, this most chaste virgin shone
> immaculate abbess of the virgin choir.
> She remained a comely canoness under the holy veil
> but in life she was a true nun.
> Having died on the Kalends of December
> she returned to the husband to whom she had piously committed herself.[3]

Today, Ruothildis's tombstone is on display at Trier's Rheinisches Landesmuseum, where it is presented as one of the highlights of Ottonian epigraphy. While visitors may marvel at the quality of the carving and the elegance of the script, for historians the epitaph presents a conundrum, even if most commentators have failed to acknowledge its significance.[4] Indeed, much of the text duly acknowledges the tropes central to clerical discourse around 1000,

FIG. 1. Abbess Ruothildis of Pfalzel's tombstone, c. 990s. Copyright Rheinisches Landesmuseum in Trier. Reproduced with permission.

referring to the status of women religious as brides of Christ; their commitment to chastity; and, more implicitly, their service to God and society through prayer and chanting. But two lines in particular—"She remained a comely canoness under the holy veil / but in life she was a true nun"—suggest to knowledgeable observers, as it would have to early eleventh-century spectators, an underlying tension in how Ruothildis was either perceived or perhaps understood herself. The passage, all the more remarkable because it was literally cast in stone, indicates that the abbess, even though she had been veiled as a canoness, had been a Benedictine nun in all but name.

Two centuries before Ruothildis's death, Carolingian lawmakers led by Emperor Louis the Pious (814–40) had established only two legitimate forms of religious life for women: a strict one for Benedictine nuns (emphasizing communal service and individual poverty) and a more relaxed one for canonesses (with the right to own private property, enjoy the usufruct of ecclesiastical properties, and have servants). This division was still in place, at least theoretically, during Ruothildis's tenure, which coincided with the beginning of a phase in Pfalzel's history where the Trier clergy, for reasons religious and political, aggressively pushed for the community to adopt Saint Benedict's *Rule*.[5] Was the epitaph, therefore, a criticism of the abbess and her sisters for not bending to the will of the male clergy? Or do these two lines reveal the sisters' resistance, claiming that the identity she had assumed on accepting the veil was irrelevant to evaluating her spiritual qualities and achievements? By making this statement, were the author or authors of this inscribed text also rejecting the notion that transitioning to a Benedictine regime would improve religious life locally?

INTRODUCTION   3

If the epitaph reflected a wider protest by the sisters to the imposition of Benedictine strictures, their opposition did little to change the position of the Trier clergy. In 1016, Archbishop Poppo forced an end to the dispute by staging an incident whereby a member of the community allegedly enchanted his liturgical slippers with a spell, causing anyone who wore them to be overcome by sexual desire. Poppo pressed for the sisters to evict the offending woman and to convert to a Benedictine regime. When several refused, he dissolved the monastery and sent those women who were willing to comply with his demands to the nearby Benedictine nunnery of Oeren; others were sent away, either to join a house that matched their former lifestyle or to abandon the life of a religious community altogether. Pfalzel was subsequently converted into a house of clerics, and the former female community quickly faded into oblivion.[6]

The basic outline of the story of Pfalzel's dispute with the archbishop of Trier is one that emerges many times over in the evidence for tenth- and early eleventh-century groups of women religious across Continental Europe. Indeed, the imposition of such reforms and heavy-handed clerical rules has informed a scholarly narrative that remained dominant until late in the twentieth century characterizing the period between the later ninth century and the middle of the eleventh as a "dark age" for women religious. The case of Pfalzel does, however, distinguish itself from other such accounts in that the sources arguably voice the position of the two opposing parties in the conflict. While the clerics' defamation strategy obviously warrants our attention for its focus on the women's alleged sexual threat, through Ruothildis's epitaph a much scarcer testimony presents itself of how a female community, or at least some of its members and associates, may have understood and expressed their identity as women religious and responded to criticism of their current behavior.

Evidence such as this suggests far more ambiguity concerning the lives of women religious during this supposed "dark age" than the scholarly narrative had allowed until very recently. From the two testimonies—the epitaph and the clerical case against the Pfalzel sisters—a remarkable disparity emerges. While the clerics ostensibly rejected the sisters' lifestyle as canonesses as inappropriate and likely to lead to misconduct, the sisters—in contrast—appear to have indicated that titles, legal status, and other such things mattered little in regard to who a woman religious really was as a moral person, as an individual devoted to Christ, and as a member of the church serving society. The distinct views on female monastic identity that are projected in these two testimonies raise an important series of questions that casts new light on the contours of life for women religious in this period. Should we regard the Pfalzel sisters' statement as cynical opportunism—an attempt to accommodate clerical preference for a Benedictine regime without giving in to the demand for a complete remodeling of the community and its institutions? Or was it an expression of a more broadly carried, "gendered" way of looking at female religious life, where formal identities were considered secondary to actual conduct? If the latter, was the subversive view that of the sisters or of the clerics?

A Fractured Landscape? Traditional Views on Female Monasticism, 800–1050

Until the 1990s, the dominant scholarly narrative about cloistered women between 800 and 1050 would have seen the epitaph as illustrative of the rotten state of female monasticism around the year 1000.[7] Having put an end to the bewildering variety of practices and regulations typical of female religious life and set two paths for women religious, Carolingian lawmakers organized both groups by means of consolidated written instructions. For nuns, there was Saint Benedict's sixth-century *Rule*, adapted for use by women; for canonesses, Louis and his bishops drafted a set of newly compiled instructions, issued at a major synod, held at Aachen in 816. The Benedictine model ended up being observed in only a small minority of institutions, singled out to represent the sovereigns' role as warrantors of Christian orthodoxy and provide prayer service and material assistance to members of the Carolingian dynasty and their closest associates. In contrast, the far more popular regime for canonesses was designed specifically to make female monasticism attractive to aristocratic women and their relatives.

Because of the supreme political and social interests represented by both forms of female monastic life, lay rulers and ecclesiastical leaders tightly controlled them, enforcing strict observance of these rules. Yet, as Carolingian royal power became increasingly compromised over the course of the later ninth century, direct oversight over female religious life became problematic. Rulers were compelled to transfer the leadership and, in some cases, the outright ownership of institutions into the hands of lay associates, many of whom took on the title of lay abbot or abbess. Monasteries soon became precious commodities in the hands of local magnates, and as foreign invasions and domestic conflicts created turbulences strong enough to destabilize the entire political system, the religious rationale behind upholding female religious communities largely evaporated. Nunneries formerly patronized to provide prayer service to ruler and empire gradually evolved into retreats for noblewomen, and their members increasingly lost touch with the religious mission.[8] Of all the accounts scholars have given of this situation, Suzanne Wemple gave perhaps the blackest of all when she wrote that "increasingly used as a shelter, a prison, an old-age home, and exploited as a source of income for princesses and queens, nunneries lost their aura of heroic sanctity."[9]

The resulting image for the period between the later ninth century and the middle of the eleventh was one of a sparse, institutionally and ideologically fractured monastic landscape, staffed by aristocratic individuals bound more by status than by a shared sense of purpose, and patronized by lay relatives interested more in claiming territorial influence and monastic wealth than in promoting divine service. With very few exceptions, female religious life appeared to scholars as mired in a state of institutional and spiritual inertia. Nor was the situation helped by the fact that the Carolingian reformers, by imposing strict enclosure and barring women religious from exercising any pastoral or sacramental duties, had removed them from the forefront of ecclesiastical and intellectual life.[10] Comparisons with earlier centuries seemed to corroborate this impression of stagnation and even decline: in these studies, women's monasticism pre-800 emerged from the documentary record as highly diverse, engaging directly with surrounding society, and exercising significant influence on contemporary developments in intellectual and spiritual life.[11] Specialists also distinguished a cultural and institutional renaissance taking place from the mid-eleventh century onward and continuing deep into the twelfth, in the course of which clerical and monastic reformers integrated women religious in male structures of monastic organization, and the rules for Benedictine nuns and canonesses were strictly enforced.[12] These reforms presumably galvanized intellectual and spiritual life in these communities, guaranteed the stability of their institutions, and created effective means of guaranteeing that the religious stayed true to their purpose.[13]

Based on this historical perspective, the answer to the question about the meaning of the curious passage on Ruothildis's tombstone seems obvious. Since ground rules had been laid in the early ninth century to create two distinct cohorts of women religious, any kind of crossover like the one suggested in the text of the inscription was counter to the official view of female monastic institutionalism and spirituality. It therefore constituted evidence of the problematic understanding that these and numerous other groups of women religious around the turn of the millennium had of their status as individuals and purpose as communities. And since the dissolution of Carolingian royal power had led to a far-going secularization of the institutions and discipline of religious women, it would seem reasonable to assume that the arguments of the Pfalzel sisters against the archbishop's proposal for reform were in fact a poor excuse for a stubborn refusal to subordinate their own comfort and their relatives' interests to reshaping a truthful reflection of the reformers' ideals.

Recent Perspectives: Acknowledging the Ambiguity of Female Monasticism

Over the last three decades, numerous corrections have been brought to the view laid out here. To borrow from Barbara Yorke's assessment of previous scholarship regarding female religious life in Anglo-Saxon England, it holds "undoubted truths, but like all generalisations . . . is in danger of simplifying a state of affairs which was in reality more complex."[14] In particular, recent work has questioned three key assumptions underlying the master narrative of female religious history in this period.

First, increased awareness of the need to investigate the discourse of medieval texts has led scholars to adopt a skeptical approach to commentaries regarding the spirituality and organizational performance of female monastic groups. Male reformers of the tenth and eleventh centuries justified their interventions in the lives of women religious by making sweeping statements regarding women's inability to organize their lives independently, their frailty when facing external threats, and their proneness to giving in to sexual temptation.[15] They also pointed out the devastating impact of foreign invasions, domestic warfare, the greediness of lay abbots and abbesses, and the encroachments of ruthless secular lords. However crass or overly dramatic some of these judgments and explanations may sound, their role in shaping traditional interpretations of the primary evidence has been significant. To many observers, the link (chronological or other) between these commentaries and actual interventions to change the observance, organization, or some other aspect of the life of women religious was sufficient evidence to accept as fact a previous state of institutional and spiritual decline. However, as we now know, the dynamics behind monastic reform in these centuries are far too complex to allow such conclusions.[16] Likewise, long-accepted views on the disastrous impact of lay abbots and abbesses, of women religious owning private property or benefices, and their status as canonesses (as if that in itself is an indication of poor conduct) have been thoroughly revised.[17] Even disruptions caused by the invasions and wars of the decades around 900 have been the subject of considerable criticism and nuance.[18]

A second point concerns the marginalization of women religious in a spiritual, intellectual, and social sense. Scholars such as Suzanne Wemple and particularly Jane Schulenburg have offered compelling evidence to argue that the situation of women religious drastically changed as a result of the enforcement of enclosure by ninth-century reformers. Women generally became less visible as authors or as participants in current intellectual and spiritual trends, were no longer invited to participate in church gatherings, and to a significant extent also physically disappeared from the public eye.[19] Yet, while the written output of lawmakers arguably did project a discourse and a policy of oppression and marginalization, this does not necessarily mean that it was completely effective, or that it was implemented with exactly the same vigor throughout the ninth, tenth, and early eleventh centuries, and in exactly the same way for all communities belonging to the (current or former) Carolingian empire.[20] Starting in the 1990s, gender historians also began to question views of the female religious experience that were either completely positive or negative. Instead, they looked to understand how women from the past navigated the tension between oppression and self-determination, and between expropriation and appropriation.[21] At present, many opportunities lie unexplored to investigate how religious of the ninth to eleventh centuries responded to changes in their status and sought for ways to remain socially relevant and spiritually influential.

Finally and perhaps most importantly, revisionist scholars also began to doubt that the reforms of the early ninth century had actually created two distinct, homogeneous cohorts of Benedictine nuns and canonesses, or that this led to a new phase in female monasticism where it was no longer (to use Jo Ann McNamara's words) "shaped by its practitioners."[22] Study of the situation on the ground confirmed suspicions that the observance and organization of female houses was in fact, with very few exceptions, ambiguously located between the two models.[23] Local contexts, the historical legacy of each community, and the expectations of their individual members as well as their patrons continued to impact on the way female monasteries were organized, how communal identities were shaped and represented, and the forms in which women's spirituality was structured. In a groundbreaking study of the 816 rule for canonesses, Thomas Schilp also showed that Carolingian lawmakers themselves probably did not even intend for female communities to follow their instructions to the letter, as long as they observed the key principles of chastity, enclosure, prayer, and service to ruler and empire.[24] This has raised questions, voiced among others by Katrinette Bodarwé, over using these written rules as a reliable means for reconstructing the realities of female religious life either in the immediate aftermath of the reforms or in subsequent decades.[25]

It seems clear, at this point, that the old scholarly consensus about the pernicious impact of heterogeneity in female religious life is in fact an inaccurate reconstruction based on an overly credulous reading of normative texts and contemporary criticisms and fails to adequately reflect the aims, ideals, and experiences of the women religious themselves, and of their associates. This observation invites us to reconsider fundamentally the primary evidence. For instance, in the case of the Pfalzel material, it is now possible to argue that the women's ambiguous outlook on monastic discipline and identity would not have been unusual at the time and that it was not their opinion, but that of their detractors, that sounded radical and perhaps even impractical. Yet so far, historians have not attempted to insert these observations into a larger model for explaining female monasticism's perplexing heterogeneity and ambiguity and, more generally, also its overall development.

There are several reasons for this lack of a new narrative. One is that the majority of recent studies concern specific institutional contexts, literate and literary practices, or individuals, leaving—by no fault of their authors—numerous questions unanswered about general patterns and processes. Another is that there exists no systematic study of the expectations of contemporaries, both insiders and outsiders, as regards the behavior of women religious and the organization of their institutions.[26] Finally, specialists remain hesitant to abandon the notion that uniformity in monastic organization and observance is essential to good spiritual and institutional performance. Thus, the question of what should replace the traditional account of the female religious landscape in this period as being a disastrously fractured and secularized one remains unanswered.

Investigating Ambiguity: Looking at Female Monasticisms

This book contributes to a new narrative of female monasticism's "dark age" in the ninth to mid-eleventh centuries by examining all forty known communities of women religious in Lotharingia, an area now covering parts of eastern France, western Germany, Belgium, the Netherlands, and Luxemburg.[27] Next to tenth-century Saxony,[28] Lotharingia in the period under review boasted the highest number of female institutions in all of Europe,[29] an observation that gains even more significance when one considers that nearly all of the forty communities within this area were hosted in two core regions.[30] For the first, the Meuse, Scheldt, and Scarpe valleys held a significant number of early medieval foundations, overseen spiritually by the bishops of Cambrai and Liège. Of the second, the modest number of female institutions in the Vosges and Lorraine regions massively expanded in the tenth and eleventh centuries, particularly in the lower Meuse and Moselle areas and around the episcopal towns of Trier, Metz, and Toul.[31] The spatial concentration of monasteries in these specific areas by default implies a large sociopolitical, economic, and cultural footprint and also a need for communities to distinguish themselves from one another. Here, female communities were also repeatedly subject to reforms and changes in patronage, leading to a situation where differences, not just between institutions but also between different generations belonging to the same institution, were a given.[32] This situation, I want to argue, led a number of female groups and their supporters to nurture a kind of religious "elasticity" that gave them the ability to respond with flexibility to changing internal dynamics and to changing expectations by outsiders from the lay and clerical worlds. As such, the region's communities of women religious constitute an ideal case study for investigating female monasticism's heterogeneity and normative ambiguity and for putting the traditional narrative of its development in these centuries to the test.

In the following six chapters, I give priority to contemporary sources over commentaries dating from the mid-eleventh century onward to reinterpret the evidence along three lines of argument. The first is that the Carolingian reformers' instructions for canonesses and for Benedictine nuns functioned, for much of the period under review, not as absolute norms for organizing religious life, but as written reference points setting the boundaries of legitimate experimentation.[33] The interpretation of female monastic life by lay and clerical rulers swung, much like a pendulum, between these hypothetical extremes on the disciplinary scale, depending on the specific political, socioeconomic, and even cultural contexts in which they operated. For their part, women religious and their male associates thought of these norms as instruments for reflection and debate and throughout the period worked toward shaping distinct, local views of monastic spirituality and organization.

The second argument I put forward concerns the perspective of historians. The attempts by scholars to objectify contemporary criticisms of female monasticism's situation and development in the ninth to early eleventh centuries have shown their limitations, as have those of feminist scholars arguing for a catastrophic oppression of women religious. Therefore, I want now to reconstruct, as much as is possible, how these women and their male associates navigated the tension between oppression and self-determination. For this they relied on what I call "coping strategies," modes of conduct and self-representation designed to retain or restore female monasticism's spiritual and social relevance in a contemporary context. To reconstruct these coping strategies, I propose an approach that explains the status and conduct of groups of women religious as the product of intersecting normative, social, economic, historical, and even geographical variables, rendering the situation of each community unique.[34] This "intersectional" identity is not something only we, as twenty-first-century observers, can apprehend.[35] It is something the religious and their associates were also aware of and actually built on to create a vision of themselves that was at the same time credible, socially relevant, and distinct. This process determined—insofar as it was not suppressed by clerical agents—the extent to which the religious were successful at avoiding marginalization, both in social and in religious terms.

Thirdly and finally, I argue that, while the women religious obviously formed the focus of attention in all the documentation that survives from female institutions, their story *as spiritual communities and as institutions* is a more ambiguous one gender-wise. Significant groups of men assisted the women in their sacramental and other needs, and at least some of these identified with the community's interests and self-understanding.[36] In turn, the agency of these men—clerics serving the religious, hagiographers writing the *Life* of a patron saint, patrons giving some of their wealth to the monastery, noblemen and rulers seeking burial at the abbatial church, and ordinary men seeking intercession from a community's patron saint—crucially contributed to the women's sense of identity and purpose. More generally, I want to argue that as social, but certainly also intellectual and even spiritual communities, the significance of female institutions at certain times far surpassed the boundaries of their cloistered dwellings, engaging with and influencing male and female members of the laity.

There will be examples for other regions that nuance some of the arguments I will be making in these pages. Indeed, it might seem more obvious, methodologically and with an eye to crafting a cohesive argument, to study the situation and perception of women religious by gathering and analyzing a carefully selected set of explicit testimonies and case studies from across western Europe.[37] But the objective of this book is not to give a general assessment of the development of female religious life in the ninth through eleventh centuries. Instead, it is to look at the flexibility of women religious in shaping their spiritual and communal identities and in responding to changing expectations as regards their role in contemporary society. As Albrecht Diem recently stated, "Quite often, the unintentional background information—the stage décor rather than the play itself—provides the most reliable insights."[38] To make it possible to include in my analysis this "background information"—evidence that is not explicit on either spiritual issues or communal identity, but that does contain meaningful information on how these communities constructed narratives of self—I have opted to concentrate on a specific region with a dense, highly diverse (in terms of size, prestige, and relations with secular and ecclesiastical rulers) monastic landscape. A welcome corollary of this approach is that it awards lesser-known communities and individuals equal significance as those whose names are routinely cited in the discussions of this period.

CHAPTER 1

Setting the Boundaries for Legitimate Experimentation

In spring 1059, Pope Nicholas II presided over a synod that is now remembered as one of the most dramatic episodes in the eleventh-century church reform. Its aim was to formulate a mission plan to establish a stronger papacy, make the ecclesiastical institutions and their officers less dependent on lay rulers, and assert the pope's and the councils' supremacy in religious matters. Its mastermind was Archdeacon Hildebrand, later to be Pope Gregory VII, and it is his voice that we hear most distinctly in the remaining documentation that records a series of epoch-making sessions held over the course of these months. In each of these sessions, he forcefully, sometimes quite bluntly, stated the priorities, criticisms, and ambitions of the reformers.[1]

On the first of May, Hildebrand addressed the issue of organized religious life, particularly that of canons regular and women religious. He first denounced the "audacity, stupidity even" of "a rule, said to be compiled . . . at the order of Emperor Louis" that excerpted canonical and patristic texts to make it seem legitimate for canons regular to own private property. He then turned his attention to women religious. Beginning in apostolic times, professed virgins or widows had no choice but to live in a monastery (rather than their own house) and had been barred from accepting stipends and benefices. Because of Louis, these principles were no longer observed. To illustrate this, he invited the bishops to consider a chapter of Louis's rule, according to which each woman religious should each day be given three pounds of bread and four measures of (alcoholic) drinks. The author of the protocol barely concealed his satisfaction at what followed:

> The holy gathering of bishops exclaimed that this decree was to be removed from the canonical institution, for it invited not to Christian temperance, but to a cyclopic stupor devoid of reverence for God or man, and that the expense seemed to suit more that of husbands than canons, or matrons than nuns, with the result that they would run—for this is how herds of pimps, lovers, easy women, or other pests fraternize—a risk to their integrity or chastity, or some other harm through temptations . . . similarly (they condemned) those chapters that allowed for ecclesiastical benefices.

In his speech, Hildebrand was referring to a set of decrees issued in the wake of another church meeting, held in 816 at Aachen, by the order of Louis the Pious, who "although an emperor and a devoted man . . . was still only a layman." His address—besides echoing a trend among church leaders to intervene in the organization and observance of women religious and to condemn the involvement of lay rulers in the legislation and supervision of religious communities—has informed the classic scholarly notion that the publication of these decrees was a turning point in the history of women's monasticism. Unlike Hildebrand, modern historians did not see the issuance of the rule for canonesses as a development that was necessarily negative. But like him, they did rely on that text and on Saint Benedict's *Rule* to reconstruct the realities of the life of religious in the aftermath of the reforms. Any evidence that spoke against strict, literal observance of these norms was taken in one of three ways. It was indicative of the women's unwillingness to comply with society's new standards for religious life, pointed to ineffective oversight, or showed that other circumstances were preventing the women from following the reformers' instructions to the letter.[2] More recently, a number of experts of women's history took these normative texts as evidence of the catastrophic disempowerment and marginalization of religious.[3] They too recognized a pattern of decline: but in their view, the new regulations dramatically contributed to this course, barring groups of women religious from ways of remaining relevant spiritually and socially.

Questions remain, however, whether Hildebrand and modern historians were right in assuming that the creation of two homogeneous cohorts of female religious communities had really been lawmakers' objective, and whether it had truly been their intention to apply the reform decrees to the letter.[4] This chapter shows that the decrees for nuns and canonesses were intended to serve neither purpose. Instead, they showed female religious, their associates, and their patrons where lay the outer boundaries of legitimate experimentation. To make these points I will consider, in order, the decrees of the Aachen reform synod of 816; the context in which they originated; their impact on subsequent prescriptive and legislative texts; and, finally, their reception in female religious contexts. These observations will allow us to reassess, in chapters 2 and 3, the concrete situation of female communities in ninth- and early tenth-century Lotharingia.

Rereading the 816 Reform of Women's Monasticism

The reputation of the Aachen decrees as foundational texts for women's monasticism derives more from the wider context of reform in which they originated than from their actual content. In the half decade following his accession as sole ruler of the Carolingian Empire in 814, Louis the Pious set up a series of ecclesiastical meetings that, considered together, form a comprehensive discussion of Carolingian religious policies. One of several focuses of the reform program concerned organized groups of religious, both male and female. For groups of monks, Louis and his collaborators - the most influential of which was Abbot Benedict of Aniane - laid out a comprehensive plan not to allow any other form of monastic discipline and organization than the one outlined in Saint Benedict's *Rule*, actively seeking to have the principle of "one rule, one custom" (*una regula, una consuetudo*) implemented in Frankish monasteries.[5]

The reformers—whom we know were far from being in agreement ideologically—advocated the principle of enclosure as key to the pursuit of ascetic perfection. In turn, ascetic perfection was key to the execution of a monastery's main function, which was to provide prayer service for the emperor and his realm and, if necessary, support the emperor both financially and through the supply of troops.[6] Because these principles were hard to reconcile with the pastoral and other tasks of clerics living communally, Louis and his associates at the Aachen synod of 816 issued the *Institutio canonicorum*, a well-conceived document in which the organization of groups of canons regular was laid out in detail. The *Institutio*'s promulgation was a watershed event, not so much in disciplinary and organizational terms—clearly much inspiration came from Chrodegang of Metz's mid-eighth-century *Rule* for canons[7]—but in indicating that it would henceforth be the standard norm for all such groups in the empire. The subsequent success of the policies outlined for monks and canons was helped in no small part by the fact that both rules (Benedictine and canonical) gave local leaders considerable liberties in shaping the finer details of communal life. Saint Benedict's *Rule* in particular represented views on purity, community, and salvation profoundly different from those held in ninth-century monastic contexts and therefore was in need of considerable, in part localized, tweaking and glossing.[8]

Because a new rule for canonesses was also issued at the same Aachen meeting, historians assumed that the objectives of this text were identical to those of the *Institutio canonicorum*, namely to create a unified cohort of canonesses as an alternative to those who observed Saint Benedict's *Rule*.[9] Certainly earlier legislation had been lacking in precision. Franz Felten's detailed reconstruction of the terminology of the royal and conciliar decrees in the second half of the eighth and the early ninth century reveals that lawmakers, despite promoting canonical communities as the alternative to those following the *Rule*, before 816 had declined to define precisely what they meant by this "canonical" alternative.[10] For instance, as early as 755, the council of Ver had decreed that veiled women were supposed to live in a monastery "under the regular order" (*sub ordine regulari*) or, with the bishop acting as supervisor, "under the canonical order" (*sub ordine canonica*).[11] While the text of this council does not explain what is meant by either of these *ordines*, contemporaries at least distinguished them from veiled women living outside of the context of organized religious life.[12] And in 796, the council of Frankfurt instructed that abbesses were either to make profession under Saint Benedict's *Rule* or to accept a status regulated by conciliar legislation.[13] Similarly, one of Charlemagne's capitularies dated around 802 states that "canonical abbesses and women religious should live canonically according to the canons, and their monasteries should be organized in an orderly fashion"; however, "regular abbesses and women religious living the monastic life should understand the *Rule* and live according to it."[14] A similar argument may be found in the decrees of the council of Mainz, held in 813.[15] In these and other instructions, "the canons" and "the decrees of the councils" remained vague notions, referring to a body of late antique and early medieval conciliar legislation and patristic texts that was by no means free of contradictions and lacunae. And often, lawmakers did not bother making explicit distinctions between different modes of life, preferring to focus on services (prayer for ruler and empire) and behaviors (obedience, enclosure, stability, observance of the basic principles of religious life) that were expected from cloistered women generally.[16]

It was such vagueness, so Emperor Louis found, that made non-Benedictine female groups particularly vulnerable to abuse and misconduct. His response and that of his reformers was to draft and promulgate as law the *Institutio sanc-*

timonialium Aquisgranensis,[17] a set of rules that would henceforth function as an objective yardstick with which one could measure the conduct and organization of women religious and that could be wielded to bring uniformity to non-Benedictine modes of women's communal life.[18] In a capitulary Louis issued in 818–19, he referred to his wish to "assemble sayings of the Fathers . . . into one rule for canons and canonesses and transmit it to canons and women religious for them to observe . . . to the letter."[19] The lifestyle the reformers proposed for the canonesses was less demanding than that of Benedictine nuns and allowed for more personal freedom.[20] Although lawmakers expected these women to carry out similar prayer and commemorative services, their instructions foresaw a more comfortable lifestyle, with individual members enjoying the benefits of private ownership (with some properties and goods being able to pass back to their relatives), in some cases living in privately owned homes within the monastic enclosure, and sometimes even wearing secular clothes.[21] Unlike Benedictine nuns, canonesses could also choose to abandon their veiled status: entering a convent essentially meant withdrawing, temporarily or permanently, from the matrimonial market, which relieved some of the pressure for single or widowed women to marry and gave their relatives more time to plan strategic alliances through advantageous unions.[22]

Later commentators imagined all kinds of scenarios in which this alternative rule for canonesses had been debated and subsequently applied.[23] Writing in the ninth or early tenth century, the author of a *Life* of Saint Odilia, the seventh-century abbess of Hohenbourg in Alsace, had her decline a request by her subjects to adopt the *Rule*, arguing that "this place is very unsuited . . . to a regular life, since water can be brought here only with great effort."[24] For his part, the fourteenth-century chronicler Jacques de Guise allegedly relied on a lost narrative called the *Deeds of Bishop Walcand of Liège* to claim that the *Institutio* had originated as a result of a standoff between, on one side, the abbesses of female communities in Lower Lotharingia (particularly Nivelles and Sainte-Waudru in Mons and others in the Cologne region) and, on the other, the bishops of Cambrai and Liège and Emperor Louis. On being presented with the reformers' plans to turn all female houses into Benedictine nunneries, the abbesses had declared that they would not accept the *Rule*; that they would be chaste but were not willing to take a vow to that effect; and that they were willing to promise being obedient to the abbess and living an honest life. Desperate to see the women live according to an established rule, the reformers issued a separate set of written instructions for secular religious (*religiose seculares*), the *Institutio*.[25]

Factually incorrect and replete with anachronisms, De Guise's account remains valuable as a testimony of how canonesses in later centuries were routinely represented as leading a religious life less sincere than that of Benedictine nuns and how biased authors tried to make sense of Carolingian lawmakers' bipartite vision of female religious life, by putting the blame for this flawed model squarely on the women themselves. Modern observers, even though they were skeptical of these accounts, admitted that the creation of the *Institutio* truly was a landmark legislative act. In their view, although the reformers had been reluctant to allow the liberties awarded to canonesses, at least the decisions of the Aachen synod had brought an end to the uncontrolled diversity in women's observance and had offered a legitimate alternative for those unable, or unwilling, to accept the rigidity and practical disadvantages of the *Rule*.[26] Thus was established a double female religious order consisting of Benedictine nuns and canonesses, each regulated by a set of written instructions.

Although the above account was the standard one in academic discussions until the 1990s, more recent studies of the decrees of the 816 synod have cast doubt on the notion that they led to a paradigmatic shift in the realities of female religious life. A first point, raised by Thomas Schilp, is that the *Institutio* for canonesses can hardly be taken seriously as a female alternative to the rule for canons, or even to Saint Benedict's *Rule*. While the prologue displays the same ambition as the other documents of the then-current church reform, the remainder is a barely cohesive compilation. More than half of the text—which in total is only one-third of the length of the *Institutio canonicorum*—consists of patristic extracts providing broad commentary on the religious life of women in general. The remainder admittedly consists of more specific instructions for veiled women, gathered from a wide range of sources, including the church fathers, canon legislation, and early medieval rules, particularly that of Cesarius of Arles.[27] Nonetheless, as a whole the text functions rather as a rambling florilegium discussing the basic premises underlying the existence of women religious, than as a foundational document for a new, well-organized cohort of canonesses.[28]

A second point further undermines the landmark status of the *Institutio*. Just three years earlier, the synod of Chalon-sur-Saône, presided over by Louis's father Charlemagne, had issued thirteen decrees to provide "women religious (*sanctimoniales*), who call themselves canonesses (*canonicae*)" with succinct "admonitions" (*admonitiunculae*) to compensate for the fact that they did not have, like those who lived the monastic life, a written rule.[29] Put briefly, the *admonitiunculae* insist on the duties of an abbess: to act as a living exemplar of righteous and devoted religious conduct (canon 52), to care for the material and other needs of the community (54), and to oversee the correct implementation of prayer service and chanting by the sisters (54, 58). Further, the decrees impose limits on the contacts an abbess can have with men, establishing appropriate contexts for any necessary exchanges with clerics and laymen (55–56) and deny abbesses the right to leave their monastery unless they have permission from the bishop or are ordered to do so by the emperor (57). The other women religious themselves are told to read, sing, psalmodize, and observe the canonical hours (59); not to converse excessively with priests (60); not to eat and drink in their own homes in the company of clerics or laymen, even if these are relatives (61); and, finally, not to leave the monastery unless they are ordered to do so by the abbess (62). Further dispositions prevent vassals and other officers of the abbess, or any cleric or layman, from entering the monastery unless absolutely necessary (63); dispose that the porter is to be chosen from among the mature and reputable sisters (64); and, lastly, delegate authority to the local bishop in deciding on matters not covered in the text (65). Reading these instructions, which take up little more than two pages in the printed edition, strikingly reveals how little originality there actually is to the second part of the *Institutio* and how its verbose rehearsal of the 813 *admonitiunculae* provides neither a vastly more comprehensive, nor a vastly different, view of female religious.

A third, more general point is that the vision the *Institutio* offers of a life for women religious, despite its authors' claims to the contrary, is decidedly ambiguous. When read separately, the first part of the text appears as if it was written not for canonesses, but for Benedictine nuns, as it insists on a hierarchical mode of communal life that strongly resembles Saint Benedict's instructions. And several sections in the second part clearly reveal that canonesses were expected to act much like Benedictine nuns were supposed to do, a fact that is already apparent in the decrees of the synod of Chalon-sur-Saône.[30] Women living according to the "canonical rule" were told to accept a cloistered life, wear a veil in public and in church, generally avoid contact with men, abandon educating boys, delegate to others the management of an institution's finances and hospital provision, accept supervision by the local episcopate, and focus a great deal more than they had done previously on the *opus Dei*, or the fulfillment of liturgical duties.[31] This, in effect, was a model for a female religious life that actually *combined* the Benedictine principles of communal living, enclosure, and strictly choreographed liturgical service, with a relatively comfortable existence and the choice—albeit made communally—between a system of communal property, one of free personal use, or personal use under the guidance of a worldly officer. Except for being able to choose to retain the right of individual property, possibly their dress, and presumably also the option of leaving the monastery for a married life, in the eyes of lawmakers little actually distinguished these religious from their Benedictine counterparts.

Contextualizing the *Institutio*

Based on these observations, it seems justified to argue that the author(s) of the 816 regulations were not interested in enforcing a clear distinction between the status of Benedictine nuns and that of canonesses. From what we can infer from the primary evidence, not a single community is on record as having transitioned to an observance precisely matching the one outlined in the *Institutio*;[32] and just one community, Remiremont, is explicitly referred to in contemporary sources as having transitioned to a regime defined by the *Rule*.[33] As Albrecht Diem has noted when discussing the reformers' intentions, "what an individual religious woman did and how a community of religious women organized itself concerned them less than the project of controlling and unifying those (mostly male) monastic institutions that were supposed to be multifunctional, supporting pillars of the Carolingian state."[34] Accepting this view would help explain why the contemporary *Annals of Lorsch* state that, at the council in Aachen, "two handbooks (*codices*) were written, one about the life of clerics, and the other of the life of nuns (*nonnae*)".[35] The author's word choice in using *nonnae* (a term that is usually taken to reference Benedictine nuns) is significant, not because it invalidates the notion that the text refers to non-Benedictine religious, but because it confirms the notion that observers at the time were not making rigid distinctions between different categories of women religious and did not attribute to the Carolingian rulers the desire to do so either.

There are several ways to explain this attitude. One would be to argue that regulating the life of women religious was low on the reformers' list of priorities and that its extensive treatment in the 816 decrees came about because of the desire of lawmakers to represent the then-current plans for a reformed Church as all-encompassing.[36] According to Johannes Fried, the background to this quest for comprehensiveness was Louis and his associates' cool relationship with the papacy and their desire to present a distinctly "Frankish" interpretation of religious and spiritual life as an alternative to the pope's vision. Making sure that this model was particularly coherent, or free of ambiguities, came second to arguing its superiority to Roman practices: thus, Frankish church leaders were in frequent disagreement on the interpretation of the base texts relied on to promulgate the reforms. Even in the case of Saint Benedict's *Rule*, opinions on how to interpret the text differed considerably;[37] likewise, prominent thinkers were not always able to explain why the texts and principles they valued above others were preferable to other options.[38] Arguably these motives and attitudes explain the *Institutio*'s ambitions as a text and the fact that it does not deliver what it promises, or what later commentators and modern historians have thought it promised.

Accepting such reasoning as sufficient to explain the *Institutio* would, however, reduce the reformers' legislative effort to a mere symbolic gesture. And while it does go some way toward explaining the timing and circumstances of the new regulations, it does not explain their content. In a second and alternative interpretation of the reformers' attitude, Thomas Schilp has argued in favor of seeing the establishment of a theoretical bipartite model of nuns and canonesses as the result of a compromise rather than a premeditated policy. Louis and his advisers resolutely favored the Benedictine *Rule* as a template for religious communal life. But because the reforms also bookended a process whereby the early medieval system of proprietary nunneries was almost entirely dissolved, there was a distinct risk that lay aristocrats would not be inclined to support institutions formerly controlled by their peers but now firmly in the hands of the sovereign or his bishops.[39] By issuing a set of regulations for canonesses, the reformers proposed an alternative model, offering noble women especially and their relatives the opportunity to retain control over their wealth and continue to pursue familial interests.[40] In Schilp's view, the Aachen synod's decisions, although far from impressive as text, reflect a pragmatism about rule making that would prove vital to female monasticism's survival in the next two-and-a-half centuries.[41] In that sense, they signal not so much a rupture with the past, but a logical extension of policies initiated under Charlemagne, where the institutional performance and long-term viability of monasteries had played an important role alongside considerations about spiritual performance and service of women religious to ruler and empire.[42]

Scholars have also noted that the *Institutio* likely systematizes and consolidates in written form a "mixed" reality already practiced in female institutions, proposing to them and others a template based on the best practices the reformers had observed in communities they regarded as exemplary.[43] Given what we know about medieval monasticism's tendency to show either small or more significant variations in observance from one institution to another, there is good reason to assume that this allowance for variety on the part of the lawmakers was based on a realistic understanding of monastic realities on the ground.[44] Arguably, the various living forms of female monasticism had been already evolving toward each other thanks to royal and episcopal interventions since the mid-eighth century, and the reformers' decrees served to guide that process in a specific, legitimate direction defined by local interests, tradition, and consensus. Within that direction, two forms of religious life, one very stringent and another one less so, emerged as viable options. Yet there existed no objective need to make these two forms absolutely distinct or to make all communities belonging to either of the two groups identical in organization and spirituality.

A third and final way of explaining the enduring diversity and ambiguity of female monasticism (by which I mean that the religious practiced locally shaped forms of religious observance resembling, but not necessarily matching, the reformers' instructions) is that making distinctions between different cohorts of women religious was simply not as necessary—and progressively became even less so—as was the case for male religious. While Benedict of Aniane had promoted a strict regime of enclosure for Benedictine monks, canons for obvious reasons had to live in different settings, if only because they were required to provide liturgical services beyond the physical confines of their community. And with the role of the priesthood growing in ecclesiological thought and practice, canons by necessity had to live differently from monks. Such a need to create distinctions based on sacramental duties was absent with female religious, given the policy of the reformers to exclude them completely from carrying out such tasks.[45] Whereas in earlier centuries there had existed a wide range of options for women to express their religious calling, including through pastoral service and active participation in sacramental acts, female religious across all disciplinary divides were now expected to provide the same basic service to society and to pursue individual perfection by the same means: rigid observance of canonical hours, prayer service, psalm singing, and other ritual tasks.

Whichever of the different explanations (or a combination thereof) one relies on to understand the reformers' motivations, it seems clear that the 816 decrees should not be taken as foundational documents that created two cohorts of women religious. Nor was it used as a yardstick against which to evaluate subsequent institutional realities, and least of all was it relied on to measure the success or failure of the reforms.[46] Arguably, the ultimate objective of the reformers was to indicate a range of legitimate disciplinary and organizational possibilities, with the *Rule* and the canonical alternative functioning as textual reference points. These textual reference points would serve as an "imagined reality" (*gedachte Wirklichkeit*), informing those involved in female religious groups regarding which boundaries needed to be observed in order not to compromise the moral reputation, social attraction, and institutional viability of a female convent.[47] Religious women, their associates, their patrons, and their direct superiors continued to enjoy a great deal of freedom, if only because it was impractical to expect each community to be organized in exactly the same manner.

The Impact on Ninth- and Tenth-Century Vocabulary, Liturgy, and Legislation

To corroborate the discussed observations, we have only to look at the immediate and long-term response to these instructions of 816. A first point of confirmation relates to the terms contemporaries supposedly used to refer to and distinguish specific categories of women religious. More than a century ago, the German historian Wilhelm Levison already showed how relying on the vocabulary of contemporary texts to distinguish canonesses from Benedictine nuns in the aftermath of the reforms is highly problematic. Nothing specific about institutional discipline and organization can be deduced from the use of words such as *monasterium*, *coenobium*, or *claustrum*; nor can we tell what kind of discipline women observed when they are referred to as *nonnae*, *ancillae Dei*, *Deo sacratae*, *sanctimoniales*, *sorores*, or *virgines*.[48] For instance, the decrees of the 813 council of Chalon-sur-Saône refer to non-Benedictine religious as *sanctimoniales* (a term often interpreted to mean Benedictine nun) "who call themselves *canonicae*"; and one of the earliest copies of the *Institutio sanctimonialium* is entitled "Rule and way of life for *sanctimoniales* who are called *canonicae*."[49] It was only in the decades around the year 1000 that *sanctimonialis* came to be interpreted, in some contexts at least, as "Benedictine nun": before that time, the term could indicate any woman religious.[50] Not coincidentally, this shift took place at a time when there was a surge in Benedictine foundations in the Empire, particularly in Saxony, and when female communities across Lotharingia and Saxony were being pressured into abandoning their ambiguous observance.[51] Perhaps the most specific term of all, *canonica* or *canonissa*, was rarely used, and in the context of the ninth and tenth centuries should be understood primarily as meaning "non-Benedictine religious." This is most likely the meaning the makers of Abbess Ruothildis of Pfalzel's tombstone wished to convey when calling her a "canoness under the holy veil."[52]

A second corroboration can be found in ritual handbooks from the period, which show no discernible trend on the part of liturgists to acknowledge a paradigmatic shift in attitudes toward women religious.[53] Looking at early ninth-century pontificals and sacramentaries from the Lotharingian area, none of these reflect the presumed drive of contemporary reformers to establish two distinct cohorts of women religious. An early ninth-century sacramentary made for Hildoard, bishop of Cambrai (d. 816), the only faithful copy we have of the one Pope Hadrian had sent to Charlemagne, contains only a few prayers for the ordination of deaconesses, women religious (*ancillae Dei*), and abbots and abbesses.[54] Revealingly, ninth- and tenth-century scribes who made additions to and corrected the manuscript did not intervene in any of these ritual scripts.[55] The same is true of the famous sacramentary of Gellone, a late-eighth-century manuscript used at Cambrai, and a pontifical made around 800 in eastern France and used in the tenth century at Sankt Maximin in Trier.[56] Likewise, post-816 liturgical manuscripts representing various Frankish interpretations of the "Gregorian" sacramentary reveal no interest in making distinctions between different forms of female religious life.[57] And when a late ninth-century scribe from the Metz or Toul regions added a formula for the benediction of abbesses to the "Theutberga Gospels," a manuscript that was presumably kept at the abbey of Remiremont, this new formula heavily relied on pre-816 templates.[58]

Tenth- and early eleventh-century manuscripts reveal a similar lack of interest in defining distinct cohorts of women religious. Explicitly defined rituals for ordaining canonesses were established in the mid-tenth-century *Romano-Germanic pontifical*.[59] That handbook provided rites for, respectively, virgins taking the veil while entering the cloistered life, virgins taking the veil but opting for a life in their own homes, deaconesses, widows taking the veil, abbesses ruling over houses of canonesses, and Benedictine abbesses.[60] But these changes, scholars have noted, do not reflect or presage a broad reform of liturgical practices, let alone handbooks.[61] A late tenth-century sacramentary made for the abbey of Saint-Vaast in Arras simply replicates the limited contents of a late ninth-century exemplar used at the abbey of Saint-Amand;[62] and an early eleventh-century benedictional and sacramentary made for use at Metz likewise holds nothing but a blessing of the clothes of virgins and widows and a blessing for virgins.[63] Only toward the middle of the eleventh century do we see distinctions between different cohorts of religious in Lotharingian pontificals; but even there, the transition is ambiguous at best.[64] Overall, for the entire period reviewed in this book, Lotharingian liturgists never made a concerted effort at consolidating clear distinctions in the relevant liturgy. This raises important questions, further discussed in chapter 4, regarding the non-religious motivations of, especially, clerical agents in Lotharingia, who, from the middle decades of the tenth century onward, began pushing for the Benedictine reform of female monasteries.

Perhaps the most decisive argument, though, against the installation of a rigid, bipartite system of female monasteries can be found in post-816 royal and conciliar legislation. What is most striking about this extensive written body is that the Aachen synod's instructions *as text* were almost universally ignored. This was either because they were not very practical or—more likely perhaps—because contemporaries recognized the origins of the *Institutio* as part propaganda in presenting a Frankish model for church reform, part compromise between the reformers' intentions regarding female monasteries and the lay aristocracy's interests, and part indicator of the desire of Louis and his associates to regulate existing trends in female monasticism. It remains difficult to establish exactly how closely these objectives tied in with Louis's situation in the later 810s, when he was at the pinnacle of his power as emperor. Nonetheless, it is telling that Carolingian lawmakers almost immediately moved away from the grandiose comprehensiveness of the *Institutio* and from paying much attention to female religious generally.

Jane Schulenburg has provided a chronology, starting somewhere in the mid-eighth century and ending with the Mainz council of 847, where Carolingian rulers and clerical leaders took measures relevant to the status and observance of women religious.[65] Her analysis, besides indicating just how limited in scope the interest of lawmakers in the female monastic phenomenon was, reveals that they made little distinction between nunneries and houses of canonesses and focused their attention on two key issues. The first of these, the enforcement of supervision by bishops, is a phenomenon closely connected (in its first stage) to the growing role of the episcopate in Carolingian ecclesiastical politics and (in a second, from the 820s onward) to the bishops' growing self-confidence in asserting their authority over ecclesiastical institutions. The policy for women religious ran more or less parallel to what was being decreed for male religious communities, even though it seems to have been somewhat stricter. The second issue concerned the strict enclosure of women religious, both in an active (removal of monastic individuals from lay society) and a passive (separation of the monastic space and community from the outside world) sense. Plenty of indications survive that the Carolingians insisted that the veiling of virgins and widows had to take place voluntarily and that the state of veiled women should guarantee a high degree of shielding from contacts with the outside world, especially men.[66] At the same time—and the *Institutio* itself illustrates this—enclosure did not imply that the status of a woman religious was permanent.[67]

Why such emphasis on (temporary) enclosure? Some scholars have suggested that in the eyes of lawmakers the growing significance attributed to the priesthood, combined with the drastic reduction of pastoral and sacramental responsibilities for women religious, reduced the need for the latter to engage with the outside world. From the 820s onward, women religious were explicitly barred from carrying out sacramental or pastoral acts, except psalmodizing and reading.[68] The council of Paris of 829 is particularly negative about women's participation in the sacraments, prohibiting them (as Charlemagne had done in the 789 *Admonitio Generalis*) from approaching the altar.[69] A telling passage may also be found in the decrees of the council of Ver from 844, where women are barred from wearing male clothes (presumably ones that made them look like clerics) and shaving their heads (presumably a reference to the tonsure) "for a religious reason that falsely seems (appropriate) to them."[70] Informed by changing views on clerical purity and notions about women's supposed weakness in resisting sexual temptation, this legislation was also taken as an opportunity to reduce exchanges between female religious and the outside world, particularly as represented by members of the clergy, and also to reduce the agency of female monastic leaders. Thus women religious were also barred from educating boys, and from staffing hospices and hospitals; just as significantly, abbesses also no longer could assume leadership over male religious or bless them, or attend ecclesiastical meetings.[71] Abbesses were even barred from consecrating new members of their own community: the 829 council of Paris indicated explicitly that virgins were to be consecrated by the local bishop, and widows by the bishop or, with the bishop's consent, by a priest.[72]

But there is likely also a connection with another of the lawmakers' sustained concerns: the abduction of *sanctimoniales*, women who had taken the veil and entered a religious community. Interest in the subject can be directly associated with the growing importance of female monasteries to the exercise of authority on the part of Carolingian rulers and their management of aristocratic networks, a process that ironically ran parallel to the marginalization of women religious in cultural, sacramental, and spiritual terms.[73] On the one hand, legislation increasingly insisted on aristocratic women marrying in their own class and on the management of political networks through nuptial union.[74] Female members of the aristocracy, whether they were formerly veiled or not, were to marry only at the end of a carefully managed, politically charged process of negotiation between different elite groups. Rape and abduction compromised the functioning of that system, with disruptive consequences going much further than a mere conflict between families.

On the other hand, female monasteries as institutions were increasingly becoming the subject of direct exploitation by Carolingian rulers for financial, political, and symbolic purposes. The first signs of this change are noticeable toward the end of the eighth century, when a system of private foundations of proprietary nunneries basically ground to a halt, and Charlemagne actively encouraged the concentration of smaller communities into larger ones, a policy that received active support from the episcopate.[75] As with male monasteries, the ultimate objective was to shape communities into efficiently functioning, viable institutions where veiled women could meaningfully invest their energies in educating young individuals, in praying and chanting for the benefit of the empire and its ruler, in providing commemorative services and possibly even a burial place to the privileged, and, finally, in generating sufficient income to support the Carolingians, either by paying taxes or providing military assistance.[76] Illicit interventions in the existence of female communities and their individual members disrupted not only the adequate exercise of these duties and services, but also compromised the relevance of their prayer service to the empire, and, indirectly, the future of the empire itself.

Such concerns about the symbolic role of women's monasteries and their growing significance in Carolingian politics as focal points for aristocratic networks became even more acute toward the middle decades of the ninth century. Simon MacLean has demonstrated that queenly involvement with female monasteries expanded significantly in response to growing tensions over the role of queenship in Carolingian society. In the early ninth century, the role of royal and imperial spouses increasingly became formalized, slowly evolving into an office that functioned as an interface between the political center and the regional aristocracies. This evolution entailed the risk that increasingly queens were considered to have an instrumental role in maintaining public order and therefore were held morally responsible for crises. Part of the response, spurred by episcopal criticism of female power as problematic and disruptive, was that queens began founding, and especially claiming, nunneries and withdrew to them when they became widows. Yet such royal women did not give up all of their former status: even after they retired to a monastery, the queenly function as political interface continued to be operative, transforming the institutions themselves into symbolic and actual meeting points for aristocratic networks.[77]

Considering the growing number of interests tied up in women's communities, especially those that stood under direct royal control, and the sharply increased scrutiny of the morality of royal wives and widows, the step toward considering abduction, and in some cases even voluntary resignation, a violation of political and moral order was a small one. In 860 or shortly thereafter, Archbishop Hincmar of Reims even published a treatise specifically devoted to rape and abduction, arguing that such offences were no longer a private matter, but an infraction of human and divine authority, necessitating excommunication.[78] Obviously, such reasoning was supported by a strong religious and ethical rationale, as can be inferred from Hincmar's arguments. But just as significant—and revealing as to the meaning of his reference to human authority—is the sociopolitical component. In fact, any action that affected either the moral reputation or material integrity of these institutions was a major offence to royal interests. And when in the middle decades of the ninth century the lay abbacy of nunneries also became a means through which

CHAPTER 1

Carolingian rulers could secure the fidelity of members of the local and regional aristocracy, the stakes only increased.[79]

In any other sense, though, lawmakers after around 830 dropped women religious almost completely from their agenda. Arguably, there was an element of institutionalized misogyny, or at the very least disempowerment, to this phenomenon: according to Andrew Rabin, there is a distinct tendency in these texts to "discount female ecclesiastics as readers of legal texts, especially royal legislation," and to ignore them as "the principal subjects of juridical action."[80] Instead, the focus lay on instructing others—particularly clerics—on how to manage communities of female religious.[81] One of many such examples are the decrees of a council, held in 836 at Aachen. In sharp contrast with what they tell us about the obligation of monks and canons to observe the rules that are available for each form of religious life, for women religious they make no such distinction and do not refer to any written rule. Instead, they simply instruct that the women "should be subjected to a discipline that is suitable to the fragility of their sex, with all diligence of religion."[82] And the decrees focus on the urgent responsibility of the women's male "custodians" (*custodii*)—presumably lay aristocrats, or perhaps lay abbots or abbesses—to maintain that suitable discipline, for "convents of women . . . in some places seem like brothels rather than monasteries, because of the negligence of leaders in providing necessities, or because of carelessness."[83]

One of the few times lawmakers did bother to provide women religious with a comprehensive set of instructions was at the Mainz council of 847. Canon 16 of the decrees of this meeting revealingly consists of a single, one-paragraph admonishment and essentially summarizes the relevant decisions promulgated at the earlier Chalon-sur-Saône synod of 813. Just as significantly, it addresses female monasticism as a single phenomenon, ignoring all institutional and disciplinary divides:

> On the life of women religious. An abbess, who has a monastery in a town, should never leave the monastery without permission of the bishop or his representative, unless she is obliged by royal order. And when she goes outside, she should take care and act vigilantly for the sake of the sisters she is taking with her, so that none of them is given the license or occasion to sin. She is (also) to appoint someone to replace her, so that she would take care of and exercise vigilance over the souls of the women religious. The abbess should apply herself to teaching that person those things that are relevant to the needs of the sisters, and to the restoration [of these things]. The sisters who are installed in the monastery should dedicate themselves to reading and singing, to chanting

or reciting the psalms. And the canonical hours, namely the matins, primes, terces, sexts, nones, vespers, and complines should be celebrated in equal measure. And all, except those who are infirm, should sleep in the dormitory, and come every day to the communal meal. And that they observe the other things that are included in the rules of sisters, and that have been decreed for them by the Holy Fathers.[84]

The message here is clear. Beyond the instructions explicitly detailed in this passage, the behavior and organization of women religious ought to be evaluated on a basis consisting of monastic rules (not just Saint Benedict's *Rule*) and the "sayings of the Fathers." Rather than arguing that this fragment indicates that women religious had to choose between two distinct forms of religious life, the decree acknowledges the wisdom of a broad range of textual resources that requires interpretation by those involved in governing these communities.

Just two decades after the allegedly epochal reform synod of 816, Carolingian bishops were only willing to recall a bipartite model for men, based on the *Institutio canonicorum* and Saint Benedict's *Rule*; for women, they simply delegated responsibility for setting up an adequate mode of life for women religious to those overseeing these institutions and counted on the fact that these people would have sufficient insight into monastic normative tradition and current expectations of female religious life. The decrees of the 836 and 847 synods are outstanding examples of these views; and when, in 853, Charles the Bald instructed his *missi* (appointed representatives from the clergy and the lay elite) to visit monasteries "of canons and monks or women religious" (*monasteria, tam canonicorum quam monachorum sive sanctimonialium*) and investigate their members' mode of conduct and observance, he apparently counted on the same understanding of normative tradition.[85] Another half century later, the 909 "reform council" of Trosly rehearsed these views, decreeing that all women religious were to act as a "holy vessel, ready to serve God" (*vasa sancta in ministerium domini praeparata*).[86] Unlike the council's pronouncements for male religious, the decrees do not make reference to the primacy of Saint Benedict's *Rule* or even to the existence of two groups of nuns and canonesses. From a spiritual view at least, making such a distinction was an exercise that bore no consequences for female monasticism's legitimacy. Moving on yet-another half century, Emperor Otto I (a ruler often referred to as a champion of Benedictine reform) ambiguously wrote to the sisters at Hilwartshausen in Saxony, indicating in one and the same document that he expected them to live "the canonical life" (*vita canonica*) and follow the "correct rule for virgins" (*recta regula virginum*).[87] As late as 1003, Emperor Henry II wrote that the to-be-elected abbess of Alsleben was to behave "regularly and canonically."[88] While this latitude as regards the observance of women religious was evidently being questioned by that time (witness the case of Pfalzel and several other instances discussed in chapters 4 and 5), old views took a long time to die.

Women Religious: Tracing the Impact on Their Self-Understanding

It is difficult to reliably assess the way in which the members of female communities and their local patrons acknowledged the instructions issued by lay and clerical rulers. The most obvious way is to look at the situation on the ground and attempt to reconstruct how the status and self-understanding of women religious evolved over the next century or so. But before moving on to this discussion—which will be the focus of chapters 2 and 3—we need to ask if there is any way of assessing their response to the supposedly foundational decrees of 816 and the relevant legislation of later decades.[89]

For a long time, scholars assumed that women religious either passively accepted the reformers' instructions or defiantly rejected them. Influential for the former were the views of eleventh-century polemicists such as Hildebrand, who postulated that all non-Benedictine religious were followers of the *Institutio sanctimonialium* and that their performance as spiritual beings could be measured by testing the moral and legal relevance of that text.[90] For the latter view, we already saw how fourteenth-century chronicler Jacques de Guise tried to make sense of the existence of the *Institutio sanctimonialium* by claiming that the religious of Nivelles and a number of other communities in Lower Lotharingia had refused to accept the strict demands of Saint Benedict's *Rule*. Looking at things in the longer term, Jacques and subsequent commentators also suggested that the supposedly worldly behavior in later centuries of many religious—particularly canonesses—was a result of their refusal to strictly observe any rules. At the turn of the twentieth century, the German historian Albrecht Hauck explained indications of the ambiguous identity of religious post-816 (or simply the absence of any evidence unambiguously showing that they were nuns or canonesses) by stating that they had "passively resisted" the reforms and that many communities ended up subscribing "to no specific rule at all." "They believed," so he argued, "that this was their good right, and were not inclined to abandon this notion."[91]

While these commentators saw no middle ground between acceptance and rejection, we now know that such a view cannot be reconciled with what the historical evidence tells us. For one, there is plenty of evidence suggesting that women religious did not strictly observe either Saint Benedict's *Rule* or the *Institutio* and that their practice always, or nearly always, occupied a middle ground between these two models. Yet, it is also clear that women religious in the ninth to eleventh centuries could not have simply said "no" to their lay and ecclesiastical lords when negotiating over matters of observance and that their observance was always subject to the supervision of clerical agents. This indicates tolerance, even expectation of ambiguity in religious observance. Second, the current understanding of the post-816 expectations of secular and ecclesiastical lawmakers is such that we must assume that these rulers were mostly content merely to indicate the fundamental behaviors expected of a woman religious and her community and make clear the boundaries of legitimate experimentation. From this we can infer that the realities of life in female monasteries must have always resulted from a process of negotiation in which the women religious, their male associates, their patrons and relatives, and their clerical supervisors were the principal participants: only from the middle decades of the tenth century did attitudes begin to change and then only gradually, as we shall see in chapters 4 and 5. Finally and most importantly, there is no longer any good reason to simply assume that the women in these communities lacked the ability or interest to reflect on their status in life and did not have the education and resources necessary to shape localized interpretations of female religious life. Although the former two points were addressed earlier on in this chapter, for the third we must go and look for scraps of information that might give us some insight into the instruments and outcomes of these reflections.

Women religious throughout the ninth, tenth, and early eleventh centuries had access to an extensive body of textual resources that revealed to them how monastic rules were not immutable, mutually exclusive normative statements. Communal libraries of female convents in Metz, Essen, and quite possibly also Maubeuge, besides manuscripts with Bible texts, hagiographies, ritual manuals, Bible commentaries, and exegetical works, also held ecclesiastical and secular law books and copies of various monastic rules.[92] Indeed, the reformers of the early ninth century had declined to suppress, arguably even stimulated awareness of, the multiform traditions from which they had shaped their decrees. The *Institutio* is replete with explicit quotations and paraphrases of the source texts from which it was compiled. And Benedict of Aniane's famous *Codex regularum*, a handbook that contains an extensive selection of late antique and early medieval monastic rules and related texts, provides a host of material relevant to the life of veiled women by Cesarius of Arles, Aurelian of Arles, John of Arles, Donatus, the anonymous *Regula cuiusdam ad virgines*, and Pseudo-Columbanus's *Regula ad virgines*.[93] The availability of this and other such collections and the refusal of reformers to obliterate the memory (and, importantly, manuscript copies) of older rules and associated texts arguably created new opportunities for reflection on the nature and purpose of monastic life.

Manuscripts made for, and used in, women's monasteries across western Europe reveal that this multiformity of monastic normative tradition was acknowledged and absorbed locally. Redacted copies of Saint Benedict's *Rule* are a good example of this.[94] From Niedermünster, an abbey in Regensburg, we have two redacted copies of the *Rule* for use by women, one from the final decade of the tenth century and another from c. 1025–44.[95] The former is of particular interest here. A sumptuous volume with several full-page miniatures, it was made for Abbess Uta, who oversaw the process of Benedictine reform at the abbey.[96] Besides a lightly redacted version of the *Rule*, it also holds a more significantly redacted copy of Cesarius of Arles's rule for women: study of the contents of that part of the manuscript shows that the women (or their male associates, or clerical supervisors) excised sections that were not relevant in a local context and added notes cross-referencing Cesarius's text with Saint Benedict's *Rule*, as well as a few interpolations deriving directly from the latter.[97] As such, the manuscript arguably reveals that the women's daily practice was neither Cesarian nor Benedictine, but ambiguously remained somewhere between the two, and that the women were unwilling to acknowledge Saint Benedict's text as the only normative standard for cloistered life. In fact, the artist who decorated the manuscript did not shy away from communicating this inclusivity (and the resulting ambiguous understanding of self) to viewers. In one full-page image, Saint Benedict is seen enthroned, holding a copy of the *Rule* sitting on his lap. In another, a standing Cesarius presents his *Rule* to two sisters. An inscription above the image identifies him as well as his text, and the copy he is seen holding reads—tellingly in the context of a reform—"You shall all live in unanimity and agreement" (*Omnes unanimiter at concorditer vivite*). If the artist felt at liberty to give such a prominent place to Cesarius's legacy in a context of Benedictine reform and also to indicate what this meant for the sisters' communal identity, then we must conclude that the mindset of those involved with Niedermünster—and with Benedictine reform generally c. 1000—was very different from how nineteenth- and twentieth-century historians imagined it. Our understanding of the situation locally is further complicated by the likelihood that the community also had access to a copy of the *Institutio*.[98]

From around the same time, we also have a number of redactions of Saint Benedict's *Rule* for use by women that were issued in the aftermath of the

SETTING THE BOUNDARIES FOR LEGITIMATE EXPERIMENTATION 31

FIG. 2. Cesarius of Arles offers his *Rule* to the religious of Niedermünster in Regensburg, c. 990s–1020s (Bamberg, Staatsbibliothek, Ms. Lit. 142, f. 65r). Copyright Staatsbibliothek Bamberg. Reproduced with permission.

famous Winchester council of the later 960s or early 970s, the meeting that consolidated the tenth-century Benedictine reforms in England. These manuscripts do not reflect the setting of a single standard for life inside these monasteries: all reveal different adaptations, suggesting that each of the redactors of these versions was thinking of one (or perhaps a few) specific institutional context(s). One of these versions actually draws its discussion of women's enclosure from the *Institutio sanctimonialium*.[99] Yet another example comes from 960s Navarra, where Abbot Salvus of Albelda created a new rule for nuns. Although Salvus wanted to see the religious living according to the spirit of the *Rule*, when composing his new text he drew heavily from Smaragdus's ninth-century commentary on Saint Benedict's original text, which had sought to make Benedict's sixth-century instructions relevant and workable in a ninth-century context.[100] Salvus also replaced several passages on penance and discipline with an entirely new chapter, prescribing the punishment to be handed out for specific offenses committed by the nuns. That part of the text derives from two treatises that may be found added to a 945 copy of Smaragdus's commentary on the *Rule* of Saint Benedict, and which derive from Saint Fructuosus's *Regula communis* (also transmitted in Benedict of Aniane's collection) and Saint Columbanus's penitential handbook.[101] Additionally to these changes, Salvus introduced elements from local liturgical practice, extended Saint Benedict's allowances for clothing, modified the profession rite, allowed for differences in the organization of manual labor, and offered considerable exemptions from reading practices.[102]

All of these case studies concern communities situated outside of the Lotharingian area. They also date from the mid-to-later tenth century, a time when clerical agents increasingly worked to impose a Benedictine identity on female religious and sought for ways to reconcile that tradition with local practices, all the while consolidating the outcome in written form. And most, perhaps all of such texts, were written by men seeking to influence women religious from the outside. Yet there is nothing to suggest that in some cases at least, Lotharingian authors, including those from an earlier period, had not been working with different rules to shape localized views of women's monasticism.[103] There is also nothing to a priori suggest that women religious were not actively involved in shaping these and earlier localized narratives of monastic identity. In a study of communities of female religious in Anglo-Saxon England, Andrew Rabin wrote that "knowledge of the law and the ability to interpret its texts offered . . . nuns, if not full autonomy, at least one route to self-definition."[104] Reliable indications of the way in which they seized that opportunity are exceedingly rare, but persuasive nonetheless. A passage in the 980s *Life* of John of Gorze suggests that, in the 920s or 930s, women at the Metz monastery of Saint-Pierre-aux-Nonnains and their male associates intensively scrutinized multiple texts from monasticism's normative tradition, and manuscript evidence from the monastery of Essen in Saxony also points in that direction.[105] Even stronger support for the existence of a living culture of comparative study of normative texts may be found in an extraordinary compilation of normative texts and related material at the end of the so-called *Roll of Maubeuge*.[106]

Apparently dating from the beginning of the eleventh century, the Maubeuge compilation—more an oddly continuous assemblage of fragments and extracts—of miscellaneous material provides exceptionally detailed insight into some of the normative texts that were available to scribes working at this abbey, not far from the episcopal town of Cambrai.[107] It consists of extracts from the *Institutio sanctimonialium* (a rare occurrence of that text generally),[108] the decrees for women religious from the previously discussed councils of Chalon-sur-Saône (813) and Worms (868), Hildemar of Corbie's commentary on Saint Benedict's *Rule*,[109] a fragment of a glossary of terms and expressions from the *Rule*,[110] a quote from John Cassian's *Conferences*, five extracts taken from an early version of a penitential handbook known as the *Paenitentiale mixtum Pseudo-Bedae-Egberti*, a fragment of a glossary to that handbook, an apocryphal appendix to a sermon *De penitentia* formerly attributed to Cesarius of Arles, and a handful of miscellaneous inscriptions.[111] The coincidence of all of these fragments being in a single document is in itself outstanding proof that individuals involved in this rural community had access to a surprisingly broad range of texts and that a highly creative reading culture continued to exist within this and, presumably, other female communities of Lotharingia. It is also quite remarkable, unique perhaps, to find direct evidence that women religious and their male associates were studying the two key texts of the early ninth-century reforms, the *Rule* and the *Institutio*, simultaneously.

The exact purpose of the Maubeuge compilation is difficult to establish. It does not contain enough of a coherent argument to suggest that it originated as part of preparations for a chapter meeting or some other form of gathering where matters of monastic identity and organization were discussed. And it certainly was not intended to be read aloud to, or (judging by its haphazard layout and the different scribes involved in its creation) perhaps even understood by, any third parties. As a whole and in its different parts, the compilation would only have been meaningful to individual readers who had deep knowledge of the study practices and texts from which the different parts were taken. This suggests that we are looking at a rare remnant of an episode of mostly oral reflection on the purpose and nature of the life of women religious, based on study of key normative texts from the past.[112] But what makes the compilation even more relevant to the present discussion is that it reveals an actual attempt to shape a locally relevant interpretation out of these traditions via a process of "uncreative writing." By using the term "uncreative writing," originally coined by Kenneth Goldsmith,[113] I want to include in the discussion indications of how communities actively, with a view to shaping localized narratives of self, disassembled and reassembled existing normative traditions. As such, the *Roll* most likely preserves a type of argument that would have been very frequently practiced in female contexts, but is nearly always inaccessible to us because of its fleeting nature.

Looking at the message of the compilation, we find that the Maubeuge religious and their male associates relied on study of consolidated normative traditions and processes of uncreative writing to speak with "double voices" or "forked tongues," in other words, relied on orthodox arguments to express unorthodox, ambiguous views.[114] Even though several of the texts referenced in the *Roll* pretend to be mutually exclusive, the view on female observance as it is preserved within that document is nondenominational. Clearly, this ambiguous view did not derive from laxity of the religious in observing one of the two rules as established by ninth-century lawmakers. Rather, it arose from rational, intense study of normative tradition, combined with a pragmatic understanding of local circumstances.[115]

Leaving aside the handful of inscriptions, the extracts can be divided into three major groups, each looking at a different aspect of life in and around the Maubeuge community. The first reveals an emphasis in local discourse on enclosure, combined with measures to delegate the sisters' pastoral work to male officers and to provide for the sustenance of these clerics while retaining control over them and over the monastery's institutions. Canon 28 of the *Institutio* orders guesthouses for the poor to be situated outside of the monastery, next to the church where the canons celebrate their liturgies.[116] An inserted passage, referring explicitly to Maubeuge, concerns the need to give tithes to the priests working at parishes belonging to the sisters and continues with the original text to detail the revenues that are due to the priests serving the guesthouse and that go toward the sustenance of the poor. An extract from the 813 decrees glosses this arrangement by indicating that priests are restricted from staying longer than needed in the women's quarters and by repeating that they are to be compensated for their pastoral services.

In the second and third group of extracts, attention shifts to the inner community. In the former, the obligations of the abbess and her role as a moral exemplar for the sisters are succinctly laid out. Canon 54 of the 813 council of Chalon-sur-Saône stipulates that the abbess is to make sure the congregation strictly observes its obligations as regards readings, offices, and chanting of the psalms. She is also to offer them an example "in all good works," and provide them with the necessary provisions to exercise their duties "so as to prevent that they would be forced to commit sin out of a lack of food or drink." In the third group, the compilers considers the sisters' duties. Women religious, according to canon 54, are to observe obligations with regard to reading, chanting, prayers, and the observance of the hours: they are also expected to sleep (with the exception of the sick) in the dormitory and attend communal meals. The Hildemar fragment, which considers obedience and hints at a master-disciple relationship between the abbess and her subjects, shifts the focus to internal hierarchy and discipline. The excerpts from the *Mixed Pseudo-Bede-Egbert Penitential* look at reporting of errors committed by fellow religious and ways to amend sinful behavior.[117] And from the 868 synod of Worms, canon 9 stipulates that veiled women who had previously received formal ordination and subsequently engaged in sexual intercourse are not allowed to relinquish their veil; in other words, they are forbidden to abandon their consecrated status.

These were the emphases of the scribes working on the Maubeuge compilation when outlining the fundamental attitudes, obligations, and ambiguous or nondenominational identity of women religious at Maubeuge and in drawing their relationship with their male associates from the local clergy. Revealingly, the scribes did not simply reproduce any of the ninth-century royal or conciliar texts—even though they come quite close to the 813 and 847 decrees—but actually assembled their own account from different contexts and traditions.[118] That someone, or some group of people, actually bothered to re-create this message from scratch is highly revealing of the intellectual setting, one in which matters of observance and institutional organization were discussed.

Two elements in the Maubeuge compilation additionally raise the question of whether the compilers of the *Roll* sought to project a message only about the identity of the religious. One clue may be found in an extract from the 868 council of Worms regarding the degrees of kinship allowable in marriage.[119] Another, formal one is the compilers' use of a rare variant of the *Mixed Pseudo-Bede-Egbert Penitential*, represented only in a single late ninth-century manuscript.[120] Presumably made in the Reims area, that volume is a compilation of conciliar legislation (including, notably, the decrees of the 813 synod of Chalon-sur-Saône and the 868 synod of Worms), penitential handbooks, sermons, and miscellaneous texts all devoted to the question of penance and the remission of sins.[121] Its connection to the *Roll* cannot be established in any other way than by pointing to the selection of texts and the distinct variants to the common tradition of at least two texts represented in both the *Roll* and the Reims manuscript. Yet whoever had access to the *Roll* in the early decades of the eleventh century also evidently had access to a handbook that looked very similar to this one, in addition to several others that contained material relating to the normative and, more generally also, literary tradition of monastic life.

Conceivably, the content matches between the *Roll* and the general composition of the Reims manuscript may be explained by the fact that clerics were involved in their production and use and that the interest in penance and marriage as expressed in both documents derives from the pastoral activities of these men.[122] But that does not exclude the possibility that women religious were also interested in this type of content. Female communities surely played a significant role in communicating to female members of the lay elite, particularly young girls, the Frankish legislators' views on subjects such as marriage and incest,[123] and it is certainly imaginable that a manuscript like this would have been kept for such purposes by the religious at Maubeuge.[124] In addition, Katie Bugyis has recently uncovered tantalizing evidence from Anglo-Saxon England to argue that female religious in certain circumstances and for certain types of sins may have acted as confessors, for individuals living within female communities as for outsiders, be they female or male.[125] Even if speculations about the Maubeuge religious providing certain forms of pastoral care are impossible to prove, we should not be hasty to conclude that the use, let alone study, of material relevant to such activities was reserved to the clerics serving the women there. Nor should we be tempted to speculate on an exclusive male or female authorship of the compilation: as I argue further in chapter 4, there is a considerable chance that we are looking at the product of an intellectual setting where the reflection on issues of religious observance and identity was carried by members of both sexes.

This chapter's observations about the attitude of Carolingian legislators to diversity and ambiguity within female monasticism invalidate former notions regarding its situation in the ninth century. The early ninth-century efforts at reorganizing female monasticism were not intended to eradicate diversity, but instead aimed to set the boundaries for legitimate experimentation. Relying on the principles outlined in these texts, the members and patrons of institutions of women religious could, without compromising the moral credibility and socioeconomic viability of these communities, establish modes of conduct and organization that best suited their situation. The resulting reality was not a homogenized, bipartite system of female religious houses, ending the diversity and ambiguity of earlier centuries. Instead, as we shall see in chapters 2 and 3, a *different* kind of diversity emerged, harnessed by a limited set of instructions that applied to all such groups, regardless of their formal status.

CHAPTER 2

Holy Vessels, Brides of Christ: Ambiguous Ninth-Century Realities

Until recently, historians told the story of female religious in the ninth century as one of rapid decline into religious and social redundancy. In their view, centrifugal and centripetal forces turned women religious into the disempowered, perhaps even disinterested, spectators of these processes. Pushing to the margins, the reformers' focus on enclosure and prohibition for women to administer pastoral or sacramental services diminished them as intellectuals, educators, and governors; broke their ability to counter misogynistic attacks; and compromised the laity's former perception of their societal relevance. However, simultaneously pulled to the center, female institutions became so intimately tied up with Carolingian power structures that they were turned into political commodities, handed out partially or entirely to aristocrats in return for their allegiance to the current ruler. Once transferred into the hands of these local and regional aristocrats, monasteries became a secure way for consolidating familial property and for offering unmarried noblewomen the opportunity to live a secluded life without missing out on any of the comforts awarded by their status.[1]

In this chapter and chapter 3, I look at what the primary evidence from the period between the reforms of the early ninth century and the 920s–930s tells us about the adequacy of this narrative of disempowerment and descent into social and spiritual redundancy. My aim is to take recent arguments about the risks of working with normative texts and the biased accounts of later commentators one step further and probe, as much as is possible, realities of female religious life as they were experienced in the ninth and very early tenth centuries. Although the source record is scattered and very incomplete—most communities emerge only once or twice from total documentary darkness—it nonetheless allows us to speculate on two phenomena. First, that the reform of individual groups of women barely had an impact on their sense of unique identity, and that monastic realities continued to be ambiguous throughout the ninth century. And, second, that women religious, even though they were confronted with measures severely limiting their freedom of action as individuals, *as communities* did not adopt a passive attitude. Because enclosure prevented them from physically reaching out to secular society, female groups and their associates reorganized monastic space, cults of saints, and liturgical routines to reinvent the female cloister as a figurative and literal focal point of lay spirituality, thus underscoring each community's distinct, historical identity. As such, they responded not just to the expectations of Carolingian lawmakers but also to changes in how monastic purity was defined and especially to how monastic lordship was evolving.

What Constitutes a "Model Monastery"? The Case of Remiremont

Older scholarship hails Remiremont as the only female institution in the Frankish empire that responded more or less immediately to the 816 Aachen synod's call for reform. Founded around 620 as a male convent by the nobleman Romaric and the hermit Amatus in the western Vosges region, it was situated on the Saint-Mont, a hill at the confluence of the Moselle and Moselotte rivers. By the turn of the ninth century, it had become a female convent, served for its liturgical and pastoral needs by a group of priests.[2] Then, in 817, the community adopted Saint Benedict's *Rule*, realizing Louis and the other reformers' vision of a "model monastery," and soon acquired the status of a royal institution.[3] The transition to the new regime was concluded by the transferal of the women from the hilltop site of Saint-Mont, situated next to a royal palace, to a more secluded spot in the valley.[4]

There are several problems with this reading. One concerns the chronology of Remiremont's reform. Michèle Gaillard has shown that, instead of transitioning to a new regime in a single, "flashpoint" event, the sisters probably did so in several steps.[5] A first, taken sometime in the years 817–21/7, was—according to the testimony of the local *Liber memorialis*—to associate themselves with "that observance" (*ista ordo*).[6] In a second, which took place either in 821 or 827, the women made profession as Benedictine nuns. Finally, in 822 or 828, the community split into two parts, one remaining on the Saint-Mont, the other descending into the valley.[7] The puzzling gaps between these different stages and the incomplete transferal of the community to the new site in the valley both suggest that the first transition—the community's association with the Benedictine "order"—did not have the straightforward significance that historians have imagined, namely, that of applying Saint Benedict's *Rule* to the members' discipline and organization.

A second problem concerns changes to the behavior and organization of the sisters once they had made profession. Previously, historians claimed to find evidence of a fundamental transformation in internal customs and institutional structure in the sisters' response to enclosure, their memorial practices, and their association with other reformed institutions. But a closer look at these changes does not reveal a radical shift. As regards enclosure, from contemporary evidence we know that the early medieval monastery on the Saint-Mont was situated next to a royal palace (*palatium*) and that Louis the Pious in particular liked to hold high-profile meetings there and also use it as a base when hunting in the abbey's wooded surroundings. Such intense secular activity arguably fitted badly with the reformers' principle of enclosure and compelled the sisters to seek a more tranquil location in the valley.[8] Yet the sisters' relocation by no means reveals a status as Benedictine nuns, for as we have seen in chapter 1, lawmakers of the time imposed enclosure on all communities of women. Furthermore, for another four decades, part of the Remiremont community actually continued to live on the Saint-Mont, belying the notion that it had broken with its former geographical identity.[9] Splitting up the community into two parts also created a situation where specific functions (particularly liturgical, but also administrative and pastoral) had to be carried out twice or at least created a need for individuals—mostly males, but undoubtedly also females in leading positions—to commute between the two sites.

Another suspected result of the transition to a Benedictine regime was the sisters' intense involvement with commemoration, presumably a response to the new regulations prescribing offices to be held on the anniversary of the dead.[10] But here again, such prescriptions were not limited to Benedictine nuns, and just as importantly, local interest in such activities had been strong before the 820s. From transcriptions in Remiremont's *Liber memorialis*, we can infer that Abbess Imma (d. before 833) or her successor Uulfrada reassembled and redrafted earlier necrologies used at the abbey.[11] Consisting of no fewer than 369 different names of abbesses and sisters who had lived at Remiremont before the *Rule*'s introduction, the new document not only revealed that liturgical commemoration of the dead was locally not a new practice but also that the community did not regard the adoption of the *Rule* as a fundamental rupture with past generations and practices.[12]

Finally, there is the fact that the Remiremont community engaged in a number of prayer fraternities, several of which included institutions belonging to the small circle of reform monasteries directly associated with royal power.[13] Between c. 822 and 862, and then continuing into the tenth century, the Remiremont sisters added to their commemorative documentation the names of individuals from Murbach, Inden, Stavelot-Malmedy, Lobbes, Schienen, Prüm, Annegray, Sainte-Radegonde, Säckingen, Marbach, and the church of Saint-Léger at Champeaux.[14] It is far from likely, though, that such associations were established specifically because of the community's acceptance of the *Rule*: as Dieter Geuenich has observed, the prayer communities that emerge after 813–16 across the Carolingian empire are distinctly "mixed" and consist both of Benedictine and canonical (and male and female) institutions.[15] This is no different for the associations in which the Remiremont sisters became involved.

Nothing in Remiremont's records suggests that the transition to a Benedictine status as such made all that much of a difference to the sisters' practices, positioning, and understanding of self. Were it not for the fact that the *Liber memorialis* includes a grand total of three references to the sisters' adoption of the *Rule*,[16] the community's "benedictinization" would in fact be impossible to infer from the community's abundant ninth-century documentation. One could, of course, argue that this is strictly because no direct information remains of how the reform had an impact on the women's existence—whether in terms of spirituality, the physical patterning and rhythms of the community, recruitment, the social and intellectual (im)permeability of enclosure, or simply at the level of an individual's daily experience of life in the cloister. But if we allow our attention to shift from a lack of sources on supposed post-reform realities to focus instead on what we can actually observe in the extant evidence, there emerges a picture of a community intent on subscribing to reformist priorities in regulating female monasticism (enclosure, chastity, and particularly prayer and other service); on adopting modes of liturgical conduct and networking that fitted the reformers' broad vision; and, above all, on pursuing and then seeking to consolidate the abbey's status as part of an elite group of monasteries closely associated with royal power.[17] For all intents and purposes, the abbey's ascent to prominence in these years had much more to do with its members' adoption of these attitudes and associations than with their newly acquired Benedictine identity.

Corroborative evidence for this may be found in six letters written by Abbess Thiathildis between the mid-920s and 940.[18] They are addressed, respectively, to Emperor Louis the Pious and his family (letters 1 and 2); Empress Judith (3); the courtier Adalhard, a relative of Thiathildis (4); an unnamed aristocrat (5); and an unnamed female community (6). These were gathered in a small collection known as the *Indicularius Thiathildis*, the only copy of which was inserted in an early tenth-century manuscript holding several letter collections.[19] Although the purpose of that volume was to provide aspiring letter writers with stylistic and formal templates, it is possible that the *Indicularius* was originally assembled to inform future local leaders, and perhaps even Thiathildis's closest aides,[20] on how to make the most of a female community's patronage and networks and how to foster a sense of mutual obligation with influential members of the elite.[21] And even if this was not the compilers' original intention, the collection lays out a rudimentary but highly informative discussion of the abbess's networking practices and of their accompanying discourse. According to the customs of the time, her missives would have been read aloud at court and therefore would have been equivalent to her public appearance-by-proxy.[22]

The first two letters, which are requests for support from the emperor, acknowledge the reformers' insistence on the moral conduct of an abbess and her devotion to her institution and its members; her role is to present herself to her community "as a holy vessel prepared for the service of God."[23] Thiathildis also recognizes the need to express her institution's special allegiance to the Carolingian rulers, and to guarantee—as was also expected from other institutions in this network—to them and to other patrons the service of perpetual commemoration and intercessory prayer. In the salutation of letter 1, the abbess declares that she and the "sisters of the community of Saint Romaric" pray for Louis's eternal glory.[24] Further on, she writes how the sisters spend their time chanting,

> All through the year and even at this moment, for your sake, that of the very honorable queen and the very amiable royal descendants, whose lengthy wellbeing we wish, a thousand psalters, eight hundred masses with offerings and very frequent litanies, so that the Lord Jesus will trample under your feet the troops of your interior and exterior enemies, and that, from now on during the prosperous current and coming time of the reign that you exercise, crowning you very generously with the diadem, for the peace of us all, he would strengthen you with the arm of his might, and that, also in the future, placing you in the choir of the saints, he offers you as a reward in heaven the crown of eternal beatitude.[25]

The letters to Louis do not specify the kind of advantages the sisters expected in return for their services, and it appears that Thiathildis sought the intercession

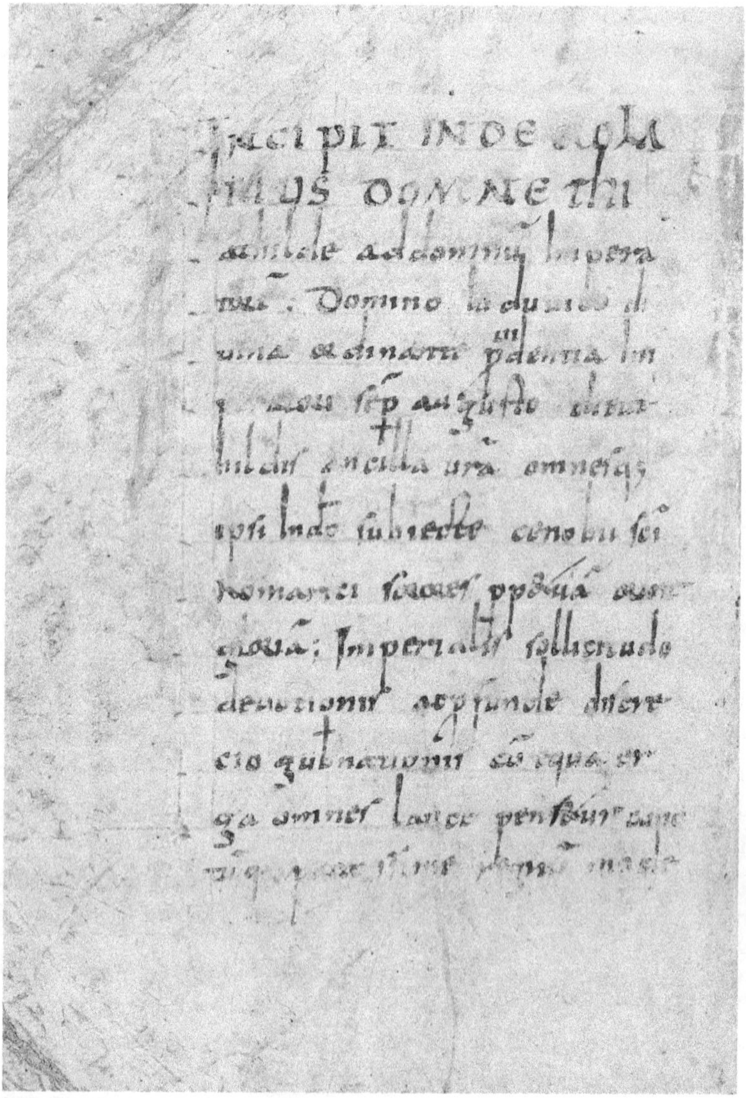

FIG. 3. *Indicularius Thiathildis*, c. 900 (Zürich, Zentralbibliothek, Rh. 131, f. 29v). Copyright Zentralbibliothek Zürich. Reproduced with permission.

of prominent members of the court to obtain specific favors. For instance, in letter 3, Thiathildis requests Empress Judith's intercession to stop royal officers from demanding to be lodged at one of the abbey's properties in the region of Chalon.[26] Illustrating her awareness of the need to gain additional support with influential courtiers, letter 4 to her relative Adalhard and letter 5 to an unknown courtier request support in anticipation of future contingencies.[27] Finally, letter 6 documents how the sisters' prayer duties became incorporated within—and allowed them access to—a network of Carolingian monasteries providing service to state and ruler. It documents part of an exchange between two communities, in this case a visit by a group of women religious and their abbess to Remiremont, which would typically have been one of the steps to establishing permanent connections like the ones consolidated in the prayer fraternities mentioned in the *Liber memorialis*.[28]

Undeniably, Thiathildis's letters are representative of what Giles Constable has described as (compared to the twelfth century and beyond) an "older and less personal current of spirituality, in which groups of men and women bound by ties of kinship and community stood together in the battle against oblivion, confident that their memory, enshrined in the prayers and masses of the nuns, would find them favor in the eyes of the almighty."[29] But even if her message about commemoration and spiritual service sounds positively traditional, it nonetheless was voiced in a context in which these ties of kinship and community by no means guaranteed that Remiremont's long-term future as a female monastery was secure. As Thiathildis was writing these letters, the liberties of women religious were continuously being eroded—as we saw in chapter 1, the 829 council of Paris was one of the most dramatic episodes in this process—and their performance, including that as providers of prayer service, was the subject of critical comparison with that of multitasking monks and clerics.

Warranting special attention in that sense is Thiathildis's omission in the letters of any reference to the clerics serving at Remiremont. This is significant, for the abbey's public image would certainly have been a mixed one gender-wise.[30] Teoderic, an individual who apparently led the local community of clerics, regularly appeared alongside Thiathildis on important occasions.[31] Indisputably a man of elevated status—a fact that can be inferred from the simple observation that he exercised this high function and that he is referred to in the sources as *dominus* and *praepositus*—Teoderic might have been one of Louis the Pious's half brothers. Drogo and Hugo, also half brothers of Louis, were abbots of Luxueil and Charroux, respectively, and it is possible that Teoderic held the same position at the male abbey of Saint-Evre or Murbach and led the clerics at Remiremont.[32] As for the clerics serving at the abbey, from a notice dating from around 850 in the *Liber memorialis* we know that their numbers were large enough to guarantee the *laus perennis* (perpetual prayer service). Based on the knowledge that at least two masses and three psalmodies a day were administered, requiring the work of at least six priests, and that daily masses were held for the deceased nuns (once in the cemetery on the hill and once in the valley), for which clerics would also have been needed, a total of at least a dozen men for (according to some estimates) eighty-four women seems realistic.[33] These men would have frequently acted as a relay between the religious and the outside world, and therefore would have been among the more visible members of Remiremont as a religious institution. Nevertheless, it would have been clear to all observers that their status was one of subordination to the community.[34]

The fact that Thiathildis ignored this mixed gender reality in her letters is potentially revealing of a desire to focus on her own leadership of Remiremont and on the sisters' spiritual achievements, rather than on presenting the monastery as an institution led by a male-female duo, and providing prayer service through the combined efforts of clerics and women religious. Presumably, it is here that we may glimpse her response to the then-current pressures experienced by female groups. Her rhetoric may reveal her need to argue that, even in a context of strict enclosure, sisters could play a valuable role in society based on their exceptional focus on prayer service, undiluted—in contrast to monks and clerics—by other duties and occupations.[35] In this context and those suggested in her other letters, making reference to the sisters' recently acquired Benedictine identity was of no particular consequence.

New Images of Female Spirituality: Organizing Enclosure

Before looking at the next phase in Remiremont's eventful history, let us first turn our attention to what the evidence for other institutions in Lotharingia can tell us about the response of female communities to reformist expectations and how this changed their members' experience of monastic space, social identity, and spirituality. If we allow, as I have done earlier on in this chapter, that female religious and their associates were able to influence the concrete execution of reformist directives, it becomes possible to interpret some of these changes as the result of strategies designed to compensate, on a communal level, for restrictions imposed on women religious. Not all such coping strategies were necessarily designed or implemented by the women themselves: limiting our view of female institutions strictly to its female membership and ignoring the actions of clerical staff and patrons would be to misunderstand how such communities functioned in a ninth-century context.

More so than liturgical reform, changes to internal discipline, or even the writing of new hagiographic narratives, the reorganization of monastic space contributed to the shaping and reshaping of what Roberta Gilchrist has referred to as "images of female spirituality."[36] Beginning in the sixth century, monastic chastity was redefined as less an individual than a collective virtue, "transforming," to use Christopher Jones's words, "the monastic enclosure into a holy place and guaranteeing the efficacy of its inhabitants' intercessions."[37] When the Carolingian reformers intervened to translate this ideal into spatial settings for monastic life, their basic attitude in making such arrangements for women religious was no different from the one they held for men; nor was it, as some scholars suggested, identifiable as either Benedictine or "canonical."[38] Looking at the reconstructed floor plans of newly built and reorganized monasteries, there was little about the principal architecture of women's conventual buildings that distinguishes them from new or reorganized male monasteries.

Rather, it was the *use* of space that contributed to the gendering of women's monasticism.[39] Our earliest reference concerns the urban monastery of Sainte-Glossinde in Metz. In 830, Drogo, bishop of Metz and half brother of Louis the Pious, transferred the relics of patroness Saint Glossinde from the sisters' church of Saint-Mary outside of Metz to their abbatial church, situated inside the city's walls.[40] Contrary to what Egon Boshof and Katrinette Bodarwé have suggested, there is nothing to indicate that the enclosure of the women and the translation of their patron saint constitute reliable evidence for a Benedictine reform of Sainte-Glossinde.[41] Drogo's translation certainly facilitated the implementation of one of the reformers' key principles—the active enclosure of women religious—for it was now no longer necessary for the sisters to leave the city, or even the monastic compound, to venerate the relics of their patron saint.[42] Yet as we saw in chapter 1, enclosure itself cannot be used as evidence for a transition to a Benedictine regime.

Nevertheless, it would be wrong to conclude that Drogo's actions were designed exclusively to remove female religious from the public sphere and to prevent them (aided by a strict policy of passive enclosure) from engaging, actively or passively, with secular audiences. By placing the saint's new grave inside their main sanctuary and by inviting laypeople to visit it there, Drogo provided visual support to the notion that the female community was connected historically to Saint Glossinde and that, through the sisters' perpetual prayers, it was making an indispensable contribution to her cult.[43] He was, in other words, compensating for the risk that urban audiences at Metz would no longer acknowledge the sisters' relevance: whereas individual contacts with the outside world were now subject to severe restrictions, indirectly the Sainte-Glossinde community probably interacted more intensively than before with its urban surroundings. Drogo's strategy was successful: by the late ninth century, Saint Glossinde had been transformed from a relatively obscure monastic saint, venerated outside of Metz's walls, into a focus of intense lay adoration. One anecdote, recorded between 882 and 900–920, highlights Saint Glossinde's growing status as an urban saint. Shortly before the murder by Norman invaders of Bishop Walo of Metz (876–82), oil reportedly began flowing from her foot. This was subsequently interpreted as an offering to secure divine protection of the city of Metz, and the oil was used for the healing of the sick and infirm visiting the saint's grave.[44]

The simultaneous promotion of the cult of patron saints, the reorganization of monastic space, and the enforcement of enclosure were not phenomena unique to the Metz monastery of Sainte-Glossinde. For several other communities across Lotharingia, nearly all that is known about their ninth-century history focuses precisely on their rearrangement of monastic space. At Sainte-Glossinde's neighboring institution of Saint-Pierre-aux-Nonnains, Drogo may have carried out a translation of the first abbess Saint Waldrada and reburied her in the abbatial church's arched entrance.[45] Beginning sometime in the ninth century, the religious also began attending the monastic liturgy in the abbatial church from an elevated tribune in the third crossing of the nave.[46] Measures like these allowed clerics and especially laypeople to attend the monastic liturgy and witness the sisters' prayer service without any risks of inappropriate contact, reinforcing the women's image as custodians of the saint's cult and fostering the notion of a direct connection between lay expressions of Christian piety and the sisters' prayer service.[47]

Similar things were happening up north, in Lower Lotharingia. At Maubeuge, in the diocese of Cambrai, patroness Saint Aldegondis's relics were given a translation to the newly constructed abbatial church (very likely the community's first), and an anonymous author redacted a new version of the saint's eighth-century *Life*, amplifying it with a section on her remains and their transferal from her original resting place on the estate of Cousolre to the main monastic site of Maubeuge.[48] This sequence of events echoes what happened at Sainte-Glossinde, in that the new setup at Maubeuge now catered for the women's need for enclosed celebration of the liturgy and visually associated lay spirituality with the sisters' perpetual service of the saint. Similarly, at Denain, Abbess Ava in the middle decades of the ninth century elevated patroness Saint Ragenfredis's remains from her grave and offered them for veneration in the newly constructed abbatial church.[49] Further to the east, in the course of the ninth century a major building campaign took place in Nivelles's funerary church, which considerably enlarged it and focused visitors' attention on patroness Saint Gertrudis's tomb.[50] This structure was part of a "family of churches" on the monastic compound, where another such building was reserved for the sisters' use; yet another presumably served the liturgical needs of the local parish.[51] And in the diocese of Liège, Abbess Ava of Aldeneik replaced the sisters' earlier wooden church with a stone edifice.[52] Following her death, Bishop Franco of Liège carried out an elevation of the community's patron saints Harlindis and Relindis, and the two bodies were reinterred behind the main altar of the new church. Then, between 855–856 and 881, a hagiography of the two saints was written.[53] Aldeneik's potential audience for these events and for the contents of the *Life* would have been large, as the monastery was located near a burgeoning settlement sustained by the production of iron, bronze, glass, and ceramics.[54]

By far the most spectacular evidence, though, comes from Hamage, a small convent in the northern diocese of Cambrai. Thanks to excavations carried out intermittently since the early 1990s, we know that toward the middle of the ninth century, the separate construction that made up the early medieval monastery was replaced with a cloister-like edifice, consisting of a wooden building holding twelve small cells and two communal rooms. This structure was attached to a new stone church dedicated to Saint Mary, which replaced the former wooden church and measured approximately 8 by 23.5 meters.[55] Like the former church, on its north side this new sanctuary featured an annex containing Saint Eusebia's grave. When discussing these modifications, Anna Lisa Taylor has argued that the building project "was associated with (Louis the Pious's) imposition of the Benedictine *Rule* on all the abbeys of the kingdom in 816–7."[56] But as we saw earlier, this interpretation does not match up with what we can now see to have been the intentions of those in authority. Nor does it bear any relation to what we know of local realities: there is no indication in the primary evidence that Hamage transitioned to a Benedictine regime. More importantly, it reduces the implications of a local building campaign to a mechanical implementation of the reformers' decrees and depicts female institutions as passive, their role limited to complying with the directives of those who made the law.

Instead, there is good reason to see strong parallels with Drogo's course of action at Sainte-Glossinde and to argue that the reorganization of monastic space and the promotion of a patron saint's cult at Hamage reveal a simultaneous attempt both to comply with the reformers' instructions on enclosure and to compensate for its possible adverse effects. Now that the sisters were barred from engaging directly with the outside world, the risk was significant

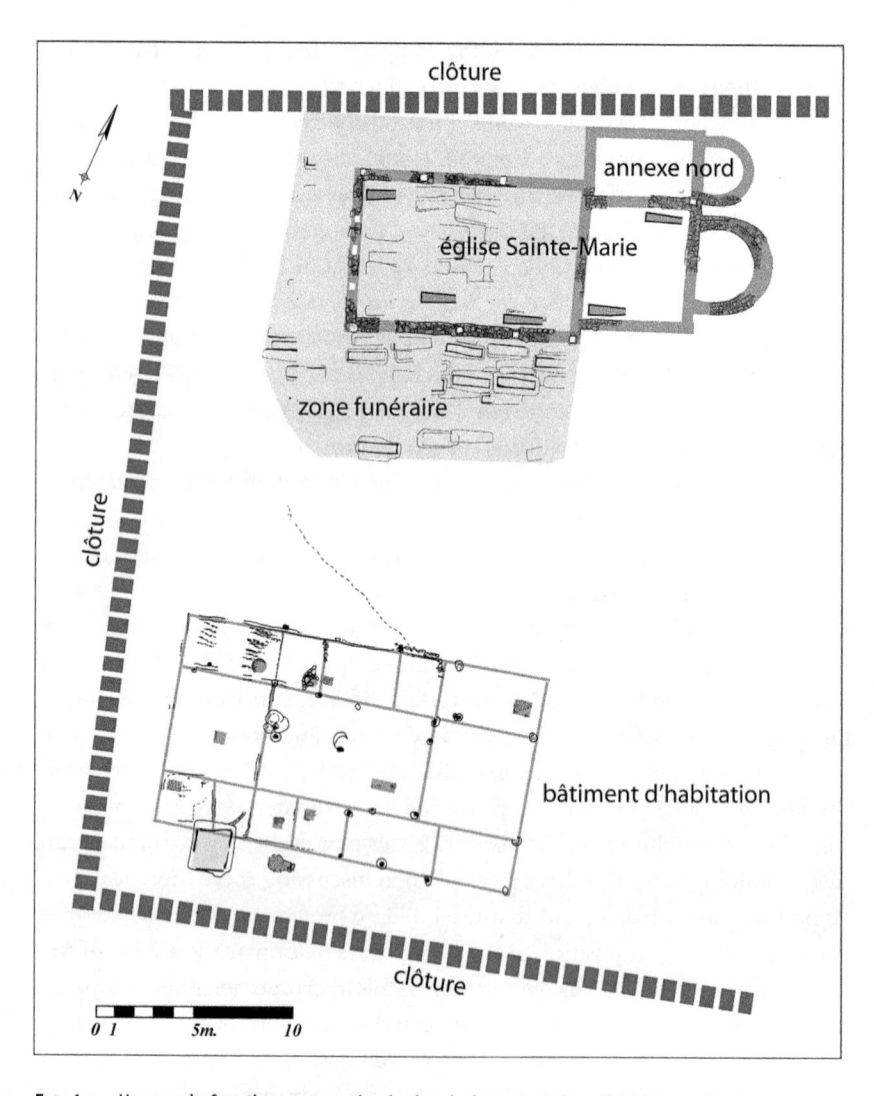

FIG. 4A. Hamage before the reconversion in the ninth century. Copyright Etienne Louis, Communauté d'Agglomération du Douaisis. Reproduced with permission.

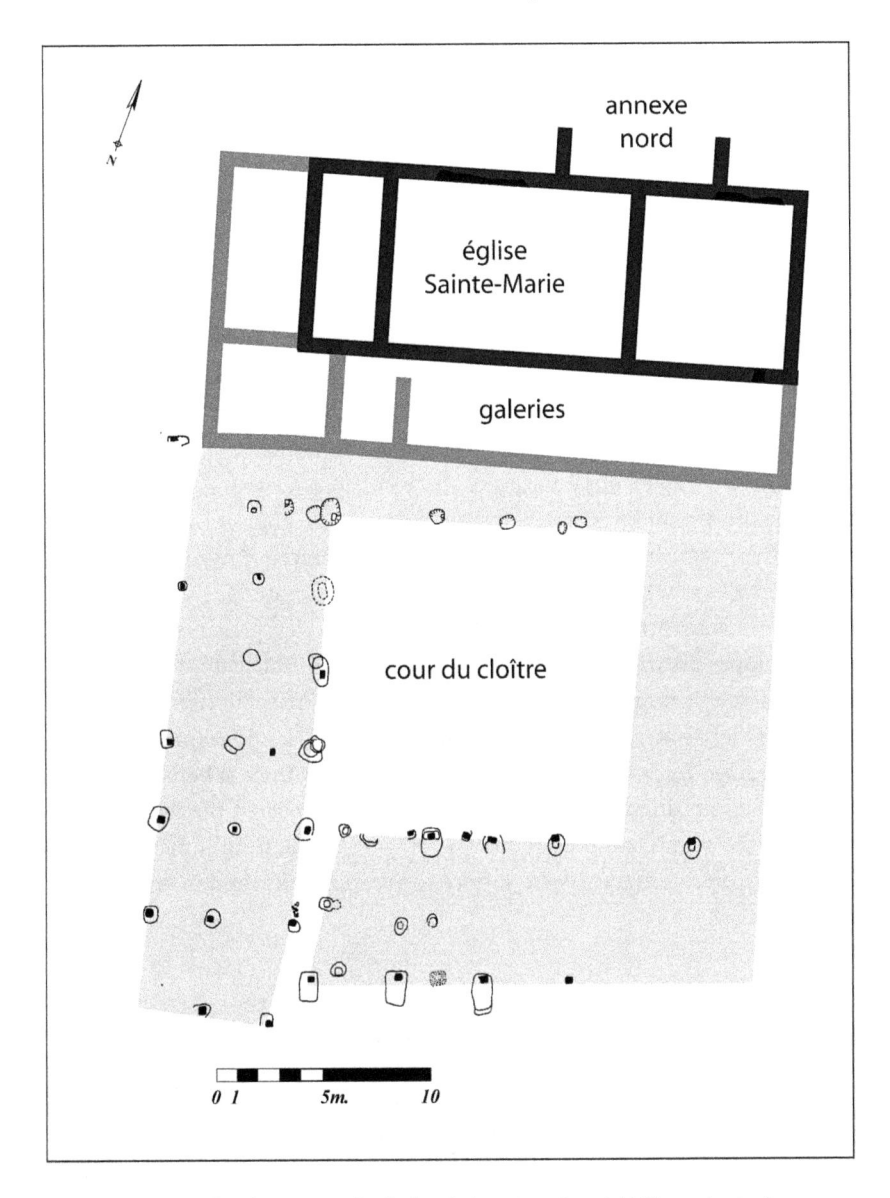

FIG. 4B. Hamage after the reconversion in the ninth century. Copyright Etienne Louis, Communauté d'Agglomération du Douaisis. Reproduced with permission.

that the clerics of the nearby church of Saint-Peter and Saint-Paul, which served them and the local parish, would monopolize lay spirituality in the area. By offering for veneration in the new abbatial church the remains of their formerly obscure patroness Saint Eusebia and by reorganizing the monastic compound so that the entry of lay visitors posed no direct risk of contact, the sisters themselves were able to create a situation whereby the monastic site and their perpetual veneration of the saint made up for their physical absence.[57]

What emerges from all of these cases is a nuanced story of female institutions adapting to lawmakers' new expectations regarding enclosure rather than a one-dimensional tale of oppression. Who exactly was behind each of these adaptations is often hard to say, but the scale and impact of the changes indicate extensive collaboration between different parties. For instance, it is unlikely that Drogo would have acted independently of the female leadership of the two Metz institutions, the local clergy, or the local secular leaders. Likewise, it seems hard to imagine that Abbess Ava of Denain and whoever was leading the Hamage community would have acted without the support of those involved in the area's secular and ecclesiastical affairs.

From the complex implications of these changes, we can also deduce that trying to draw clear lines between the actions and attitudes of reformers and those of the reformed is likely not a very useful exercise.[58] While the reform of female religious in this period had significant implications, the situation on the ground was always the result of a compromise that preserved a community's unique historical identity as consolidated in local customs and hagiographical memory and that tried to compensate for enclosure by drawing secular society's attention to female monasteries as hagiographic places of remembrance. By promoting the saints venerated at their abbatial churches, female religious and their supporters visually underscored the fact that, despite enclosure and being barred from carrying out pastoral functions, they continued to provide a very real service to lay spirituality and to secular society in general.

Hagiographic Narratives of Female Virtue

The rulers' focus on the enclosure of religious and their separation from secular society had significant implications for the women's spiritual image. All things considered, their catastrophic oppression is not something that clearly surfaces from the primary evidence. Abbess Thiathildis's letters potentially indicate that she made a conscious effort to signal the subordinate status of the clerics serving the sisters at Remiremont and the specific contribution the women were making to the empire and its ruler's good fortunes. In addition, the foregoing discussion of the spatial rearrangement of female communal life suggests that compensating mechanisms were put in place to sustain the perceived relevance of female religious communities. And women religious may not have lost all of their former involvement in sacramental and other liturgical acts after all: ninth- and tenth-century versions of the *Life, Translations and Miracles of Saint Glossinde* attest that women at the Metz institution continued to act as custodians of the main altar at Sainte-Glossinde's abbatial church and brought offerings during the eucharist.[59]

At the same time, as a result of enclosure women religious unquestionably became increasingly dependent on the men whom lawmakers instructed to provide them with liturgical and pastoral services. Because these encounters took place away from the public eye, involved a limited number of male individuals, and by necessity were frequent, they naturally gave rise to concerns over the sentiments and behavior of those involved. As we already saw in chapter 1, contemporary lawmakers acknowledged these concerns and tried to organize pastoral and other visits to avoid inappropriate situations and limit the risk of damaging rumors. It is useful to read these measures not simply as expressions of fear for the ritual purity of clerics and of skepticism about the ability of females to restrain their sexual urges. They should be seen also as sincere attempts to contain the inherent risks that came with the changing spiritual identity of women religious. Now that their contribution to society was being focused on communal prayer service (both in honor of locally venerated saints and for the benefit of state and ruler), any suspicions of individual misconduct compromised the reputation of the entire community, putting at risk its status as a societally relevant religious institution. Ritual purity was a critical condition to the effectiveness of women religious as a "prayer machine," as much as it was to clerical fulfillment of sacramentary and pastoral services.

These concerns and their impact on the spiritual image of women religious are reflected in contemporary hagiographies. Saint Aldegondis of Maubeuge's mid-to-later ninth-century *Life* in particular considers the morals of the increased intimacy of interaction between clerics and the enclosed women. Much of the text underscores chastity as the prime virtue of female religious. It argues that the memory and lives of the saints "are worth committing to one's heart: there one finds sketched out the struggle of martyrs, the steadfastness of priests, the faith of the confessors, the continence of widows, and the celibacy of virgins."[60] Saint Aldegondis, a young woman of high birth, despite pressure from her mother rejects marriage and ultimately, with the assistance of her sister Waldetrudis, chooses a chaste and contemplative life (*vita contemplativa*).[61] In return, she obtains the highest possible reward for Christian women: out of eight visions included in the *Life*, five mention the saint's status as a bride of Christ (*sponsa Christi*).[62]

None of this would have sounded particularly new when the text was first published. Earlier on in the ninth century, another hagiographer had already relied on an eighth-century *Life* of Saint Aldegondis to draft a biography of Saint Aldetrudis, second abbess of Maubeuge. It depicts the local discipline at the monastery as based on an unspecified rule (*regula*), chastity as a fundamental principle of female religious life, and the saint's status as a bride of Christ.[63] But in a development that introduces a new thematic focus in local hagiography, the new *Life* of Saint Aldegondis also thematizes the openness of Maubeuge as an institution to outsiders seeking the saint's intercession. While a chaste life presupposes an individual's seclusion from the outside world, the passage discussing the elevation of Saint Aldegondis's relics in particular indicates that Maubeuge *as an institution* did not seek complete separation from the world, and that with regard to gender its public image at least was inclusive:

> This place is replete with a flock of maidens, and full of a large number of other servants of God. The infirm are frequently healed, the blind enlightened, the lame restored, sick limbs recovered, and remission of sins granted to the imploring faithful by the intercession of the most holy and most excellent virgin (Aldegondis).[64]

The "other servants of God" passage is of particular importance here, as it alludes to the male clerics providing the Maubeuge community and lay pilgrims with liturgical and pastoral service. One of these individuals, a priest "of good reputation" who was a contemporary of Aldegondis, is described as taking the confession of a sister who had recently experienced a vision. Although the relevant passage was lifted straight from the eighth-century *Life* of Aldegondis,[65] the new version is significant for adding a brief comment that the priest had been living at the monastery, and that he had done so from childhood until reaching the "perfect age" (*perfecta aetas*).[66] This not only indicates that the author saw a need to mention that female monasteries at least historically had provided an education for boys and (presumably) girls, but that their institution's membership consisted of individuals of both sexes.

The revised passage in the new *Life* of Saint Aldegondis reads as an acknowledgment that male clergy made an indispensable contribution to life at Maubeuge and in fact were an integral part of the community—physically, functionally, and arguably even emotionally. It was they who welcomed pilgrims and other lay faithful seeking intercession from Saint Aldegondis, and thus who functioned in many respects as the public face of the institution. They also crucially contributed to the community's liturgical practices[67] and were also among the few able to interact directly with the female religious, the women in whose chastity were grounded the efficiency and relevance of the monastery's intercessory prayers. Nonetheless, through the mention in the former passage of the priest's "good reputation," we can see that the *Life* was also informed by an awareness of the risk represented by clerical involvement with a female community. As much as there was a need to acknowledge the indispensable contribution of male clerics to life at Maubeuge, maintaining an unblemished reputation both for them and the sisters was crucial to the survival of the female community.[68]

Because the precise authorship of these hagiographic texts is nearly always unknown, scholars have been tempted to explain references to the danger posed by close interactions between the religious and local clerics as the result of misogynistic sentiments on the part of male commentators. Julia Smith additionally points out that ninth-century hagiographies of female saints lay great emphasis on how these individuals fulfilled their sainthood not through public displays of Christian morals, preaching, or some other form of public leadership, but that female piety was defined as "inner, private and mystical" and that female sanctity was "safely domestic and familial," shunning audiences outside of the cloister.[69] Some commentators may interpret this as evidence of clerical interventions designed to promote and enforce a model of strict enclosure for women and of women's exclusion from pastoral and sacramental service. Yet here, as with the reorganization of monastic space, we may wonder if it really is necessary to attribute this discursive positioning entirely to outsiders and to regard the message conveyed in these texts as entirely negative. While the individual freedom of women was unquestionably curtailed in this period, in internal discourse the focus shifted toward maintaining female religious life as a communal phenomenon, and here freedom of expression may have been less limited than we might be inclined to think. Conceivably, the Maubeuge women actively participated in shaping the vision of female religiosity as it is represented in the *Life* of Saint Aldegondis, particularly in how it seeks to find a balance between the rigorous observance of chastity and enclosure, the need for close collaboration with members of the clergy, and the opening of the monastery (or at least its principal sanctuary) to laypeople seeking the intercession of their patron saint.[70]

It is important to note, also, that the second *Life* of Saint Aldegondis should not be read as an attempt to give its audience a comprehensive overview of the ideological and spiritual foundations of female religious life. Nor should it be assumed that the concerns raised in the text are those that monopolized contemporary reflections within these communities. For instance, the more or less contemporary *Life* of Saint Waldetrudis, Aldegondis's sister and also venerated at Maubeuge, omits references to this problem of chastity.[71] In contrast, it emphasizes individual poverty, a virtue passed over almost completely in the other text.[72] Possibly the two hagiographies were, at some point in Maubeuge's existence, seen as carrying complementary messages.[73] Alternatively, we may be unaware of internal developments in thinking about female religious life that, between the redaction of these two texts, shifted attention from one key virtue, chastity, to another, poverty. Our understanding of the community's spiritual and institutional evolution in these years is simply too incomplete to allow us to draw any definite conclusions from the way in which hagiographers represented the attitudes, behavior, and social profile of local saints and their associates.[74]

Likewise, the challenges involved in relying on hagiographic narratives to reconstruct the realities of life within female communities, particularly as regards the precise nature and inspiration of their observance, are considerable. No other ninth-century hagiographic text from the region illustrates this better than Aldeneik's *Life of Sts Harlindis and Relindis*.[75] Peppered throughout the narrative are allusions to Saint Benedict's *Rule*, including references to chastity, charity, prayer, and fasting as means to combat and conquer temptation. And at one point, the text claims that Harlindis and Relindis taught the new recruits of the original, eighth-century community "the regular institutions fully, and then made them implement their regular vows, and all things were communal in accordance with the rule."[76] To act according to the "precepts of the rule" (*regularia praecepta*), the two saints not only modeled the monastic ideal to their subjects,[77] but accompanied all their manual activities with the chanting of psalms.[78] Manual activity, so the author emphasizes, was the sisters' primary means of fighting idleness (*otiositas*), a "deadly plague" (*mortifera pestis*) that would inevitably lead to temptation and sin. He describes them writing and painting, sewing, weaving and embroidering.[79]

It is tempting to see in these passages a testimony to the Benedictine observance of the Aldeneik religious.[80] However, the suspected allusions to the *Rule* do not necessarily imply that their daily practices and their understanding of self were unambiguously Benedictine. Nor should we forget that the use of the words *regula* and *regulariter* in this and other texts may refer to a meaning that is more ambiguous than is often assumed: in chapter 1, we saw that an early copy of the *Institutio* had actually been entitled *Regula* and how this text carries numerous distinctly Benedictine influences.[81] And even if it truly was the author's intention to use the *vitae* of Aldeneik's saints to suggest a strict Benedictine mode of life, following Alain Dierkens's suggestion, we should not rule out the possibility that the author (possibly a monk from Echternach)[82] inserted these passages in confusion over witnessing the ambiguous status of the religious. As a result, he may have projected onto the early Aldeneik community ideals prevalent in male monasticism.[83] His repeated references of the sisters' secluded existence are at odds with local traditions about the two saints, traditions that compelled him to praise their

HOLY VESSELS, BRIDES OF CHRIST 55

actions against pagan cults in the region around Eike[84] and to mention their close interactions with visiting clerics like Saints Boniface and Willibrord.[85]

It is also far from obvious that the hagiographer's specific references to presumably common monastic occupations reflected reality at Aldeneik around 900, or that he wished to recommend these occupations to the sisters living there as part of a "domesticized" understanding of religious life for women.[86] If we look more closely at the hagiographer's references to handwork in particular, the possibility arises that—rather than looking to represent then-current practices at the abbey—he was merely trying to insert into his story mention of the material remains that the then-community presented to worshippers as having been personally made by the two saints. Such is the case for the manuscripts the saints allegedly copied and decorated. One of these, the *Codex Eyckensis I*, is an evangeliary from the first half of the eighth century and has nothing to do with Aldeneik's early history: according to book historians, it probably originated in an Anglo-Saxon monastery or, more likely, a male institution in the Meuse region.[87] Similarly, the mentions in the *Life* of Harlindis and Relindis sewing, weaving, and embroidering were informed by the presence at the monastery of several Anglo-Saxon and other textiles associated with the saints, some of which may have surfaced at, or been used on the occasion of, their elevation by Bishop Franco.[88] While women religious in this period were involved in manuscript decoration and in textile produc-

FIG. 5. The *Codex Eyckensis I*, an evangeliary attributed to Saints Harlindis and Relindis of Aldeneik. Copyright Musea Maaseik. Reproduced with permission.

tion and embroidering, none of the surviving materials currently associated with the Aldeneik monastery seems to have originated there.[89]

When presented with the finished text, the Aldeneik leadership may have found the *Life's* emphatic references to Saint Benedict's *Rule* innocuous, inspiring, or indeed reflective of their community's study of that text. Certainly the *Rule* seems to have played a significant role in the reading culture of female religious, regardless of their formal designation, and held a status higher than many other prescriptive writings.[90] However, whether the sisters recognized that text's monopoly over their communal identity and conduct is a different matter altogether.

Remiremont's Second "Reform"

From what we have seen earlier in this chapter about Remiremont and from what I have argued about the communities in other regions of Lotharingia, a view emerges of female religious and their supporters seeking to conform to the broadly defined reformist expectations and yet simultaneously taking measures to mitigate, or compensate for, the potentially disastrous effects of such changes. What is largely lacking in these analyses, however, is a temporal dimension that looks beyond a community's initial response to changing expectations. But as the preceding discussion of hagiographic narratives suggests, we should still not be oblivious to the fact that the situation of women religious could change, and surprisingly quickly.

Evidence of the fragile nature of Remiremont's newly gained status and of the sisters' proactive response to seeing their post-817 (when they presumably adopted the Benedictine *Rule*) patronage network prematurely crumble is scattered across a number of testimonies, all of which converge chronologically in the 850s–860s. Sometime between the introduction of the *Rule* and 862, likely toward the end of this period, the bodies of locally venerated Saints Amat, Romaric, and Adelphius were elevated from their graves.[91] Then, in 862, they were transferred to the valley and laid to rest in the sanctuary there. This latter event probably coincided with, or shortly followed, the definitive relocation of the entire community to the valley and the first redaction of the abbey's *Liber memorialis*.[92] The *Liber's* contents can be divided typologically into three groups: the first consists of masses for the dead (with sisters and other individuals given separate masses); the second of lists of names belonging to members of institutions involved in prayer fraternities; and the third of three calendars or necrologies, one for the sisters, another for prominent associates, and a third one for older names.[93] These three parts were subsequently augmented with over eight hundred informal records of legal transactions dating from the mid-ninth century until around 1200.[94]

Although widely recognized as a monumental record of the sisters' commemorative concerns, indications of Thiathildis's extraordinary activity toward the end of her tenure have until recently eluded satisfactory explanation.[95] The *Liber memorialis* contains a note saying that the sisters transitioned to the *Rule* of Saint Benedict "in the seventh year of Emperor Louis." While older scholarship has taken this to be a reference to the putative 821–22 transition under Abbess Imma, Michèle Gaillard proposes that Thiathildis reintroduced the *Rule* shortly before 862 and that the Louis referenced in the note is not Louis the Pious, but Louis II, king of Italy and Roman emperor.[96] Counterintuitive as this idea of a second "reform" may sound, especially in the absence of any indications of disciplinary or organizational decline, it does make sense if interpreted as a political gesture intended to dissociate the monastery from the close connection with Carolingian royalty it had established—also by means of a reform—after 816–17.

Several conditions support this interpretation. First, relations between the abbey's leadership and Carolingian royalty were at this stage significantly cooler than under Louis the Pious. Certainly, Thiathildis's connections to court circles were no longer operative in the same way following Louis's death in 840. For instance, her relative Adalhard is known as a particular defender of the interests of Louis the Pious and Charles the Bald, and therefore would not have counted Charles's rival Lothar I, who succeeded the former in Lotharingia, among his patrons.[97] Second, the politically chaotic events and moral scandal that accompanied his son Lothar II's infamous divorce from Queen Theutberga in these years also may have added to the distance between the elderly abbess and her royal lord.[98] A potent argument in support of Gaillard's thesis is the absence of Lothar in a "diptych" of Frankish rulers that was included in the *Liber memorialis* and possibly also in the note on the reform, where the obvious ruler to reference would indeed have been Lothar II.[99] Third, Remiremont's suspected demotion in these years from its status as a royal fisc—a shift that would have put the abbey at risk of being transmitted into the hands of a third party—may have been a contributing factor in Thiathildis's wish to make a statement regarding the abbey's political position.[100]

There is reason, in light of the growing distance between the Remiremont religious and their Carolingian sovereigns, to ask how heavily Remiremont's association with Carolingian royalty in previous decades had weighed on the monastic economy and whether these costs were still commensurate to the rewards the sisters and their clerics reaped from it. Earlier we saw how female royals and their associates may have enjoyed considerable parts of a monastery's income. And ninth-century legislation also indicates that an abbey's royal status carried obligations to contribute financially and (for abbesses and their retinue) sometimes personally to the crown's exercise of power. In addition, the legislation reveals obligations to provide military aid to the ruler and to offer perpetual prayer service—carried out with the assistance of numerous clerics—for the benefit of the state and its head.[101] Even in a—comparatively speaking—huge institution like Remiremont, getting rid of a preferential royal relationship when this no longer generated significant returns or specific protection was likely a sensible move on the part of the abbey's leadership. According to Gaillard's interpretation, then, the new transition to the *Rule* (something Lothar himself was not promoting at the time), the translation of the bodies of the saints to the valley location, and the definitive relocation of the community from the aristocratic site on the hill to one that was less compromised by political meaning, or at least not associated with royal ownership, should not (or perhaps not primarily) be seen as an attempt to revitalize the community or to counter internal decline. Rather, it indicates that Remiremont was seeking to claim for itself aspects of monastic identity that had been heavily imbued with references to royal service and ownership. It is also possible that the abbess took advantage of this transition to redefine Remiremont's institutional identity strictly in female terms: following *praepositus* Teoderic's death in the mid-ninth century, male leaders fade from the documentary record. While this may be an indication of the gradual transition from a clerical male leadership at the abbey to a secular one (with Count Boso first appearing as *auctor monasterii* alongside Abbess Bertha in the 920s or early 930s), it is nonetheless striking to observe that Teoderic's successors in the ninth century were not deemed significant enough to warrant prominent mention in the *Liber memorialis*.[102]

As with the previous reform of Remiremont, the primary evidence from this suspected new phase in the abbey's history tells us nothing whatsoever about the impact on life within the cloister. In fact, it seems that the religious continued to perform the non-Benedictine *laus perennis*.[103] Just as with the monastery's earlier reform, Abbess Thiathildis presumably relied on this new transition to do two things. First, make a statement not so much about the community's internal affairs, but about a fundamental shift taking place in its positioning with regard to its lordship and aristocratic connections. And, second, steer that development in a certain direction, creating more freedom for future generations of religious to negotiate a privileged relationship with their secular lordship. Arguably the 860s reform of her institutions was another coping strategy, designed as a response to the changing circumstances of her subjects. As we can deduce from a number of royal charters issued from the

860s onward and from hagiographical commentaries written in or for other female communities in Lotharingia, Thiathildis was likely not the only one to sense impending changes in the lordship and patronage of female institutions and to try and steer those changes to the advantage of her subjects.

Lay Lordship and the Royal Privileges of the 870s

In chapter 1, we saw that throughout the ninth century female religious institutions played a critical role in the efforts of Carolingian rulers to remain connected to local power networks. Often functioning as institutional relays, or conduits, for exchanges between the court and the regional aristocracy, they were also—through their prayer service for ruler and empire and through the presence of court associates—a representation of royal power, particularly in politically disputed areas. It comes as no surprise, then, that Carolingian involvement in Lotharingia's female communities was extensive throughout the ninth century.[104]

In the 870 Treaty of Meersen—an agreement between Charles the Bald of Western Francia and his Eastern Frankish colleague Louis the German to divide the Middle kingdom of the recently deceased Lothar II—sixteen female monasteries in the region are listed as belonging to the Carolingians. Of these, nine are mentioned as being the property of Charles; another seven are listed as belonging to Louis.[105] The picture of royal dominance over the female religious landscape becomes even fuller if we look at the leadership of some of these institutions.[106] For the period between the mid-ninth century and the 880s, there is a long list of Carolingian daughters, wives, concubines, and widows ruling such institutions in Lotharingia. Charles's first wife Ermentrudis (d. 869) reputedly held Hasnon; certainly their daughter Ermentrudis II (d. after July 877) was involved in the abbey's leadership, possibly as its abbess.[107] His second wife Richildis (d. 910) in 874 had founded Juvigny on her estate and presumably led that institution until her death. According to Anne-Marie Helvétius, she also held Nivelles, which not long afterwards passed on to Gisela (d. around 907), daughter of King Lothar II and the widow of Duke Godfrey of Frisia.[108] At Denain, Charles's sister Gisela and her cousin Radulph presumably acted as lay lords of that institution.[109] Not related to the Carolingian dynasty, but nonetheless highly significant in terms of royal influence, was Berno, deacon of the palace and *ministerialis*, who intervened in favor of the communities at Marchiennes and Hamage.[110] On the eastern side of the border, Lothar II's marital difficulties in the 860s resonated in the fact that his former wife Theutberga held Sainte-Glossinde in Metz;[111] in the meantime, his

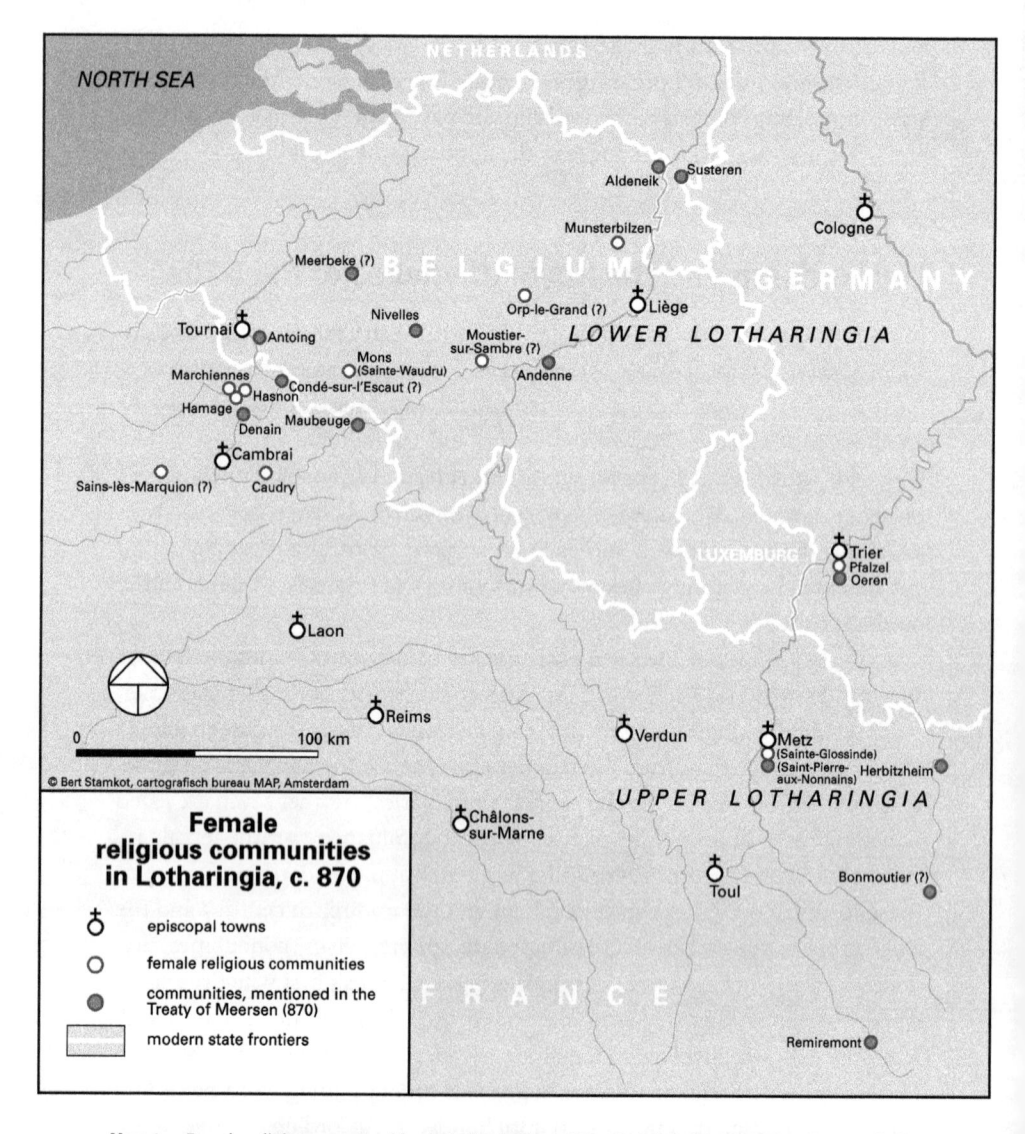

MAP 1. Female religious communities in Lotharingia, c. 870. Copyright Bert Stamkot, Cartografisch Bureau, MAP, Amsterdam. Reproduced with permission.

concubine Waldrada may have controlled Saint-Pierre-aux-Nonnains in the same city.[112]

While all of these individuals have at some point been referred to as lay abbesses or abbots, in most cases the source record does not allow us to establish exactly what position they held or what prerogatives or obligations these positions entailed.[113] Presumably, they were similar to the ones that are outlined in the two acts that Lothar I issued in 848 and 851, when he transferred ownership of the northern Italian monastery of Santa Giulia in Brescia to his wife Ermengardis and their daughter Gisela. The arrangement awarded usufruct of the monastery to the queen and, upon her death, Gisela, on condition that they maintained a community living according to the "monastic discipline" (*monastica disciplina*) and "regular institution" (*regularis institutio*). The monastery's estates were divided into two parts, one of which was administrated by the elected abbess (*abbatissa*) Amalberga, the other by Ermengardis (who is referred to as the monastery's *rectrix*).[114]

Easier to establish for Lotharingian contexts and somewhat nuancing the impression one may get of royal consorts and others siphoning off monastic wealth is the fact that several of these individuals can be observed acting as relays of royal power, simultaneously engaging with local elites on behalf of the sovereign and facilitating measures to guarantee the continued existence of the religious community there. For instance, according to the testimony of the second, late tenth-century redaction of the *Life, Translations and Miracles of Saint Glossinde*, Queen Theutberga in 858–59 or 865–69 intervened with Lothar II to formally proclaim his protection over Sainte-Glossinde in Metz, restitute lost property, and grant the monastery royal immunity.[115] Theutberga's decision to be buried at the abbey is also a potent indicator of a personal and dynastic connection to the community. And several of Charles the Bald's 877 privileges for five Lotharingian female institutions also reveal royal representatives acting in defense of monastic groups.[116] The privilege for the two institutions of Hamage and Marchiennes recounts how the aforementioned Berno had brought the brothers' and sisters' "indigence" (*indigentia*) to Charles's attention.[117] The one for Hasnon describes how Abbess Ermentrudis II obtained from her father concessions for the benefit of the local "brothers and sisters."[118] One for the "brothers and sisters" of Nivelles was granted at the request of Empress Richildis.[119] Finally, the privilege for Denain references the "repeated admonition" (*crebram ammonitionem*) by its leadership—presumably his sister Gisela and her nephew Radulph—of Charles.[120]

Charles's privileges—all of which were unfortunately interpolated or forged in the eleventh and twelfth centuries—reveal him taking measures to separate the properties and incomes of the religious from those held by third parties. He did this by installing, formally or otherwise, a *mensa conventualis*, literally a "conventual table."[121] This was a designated part of the monastic estate that was ring-fenced to provide for the community's needs. For instance, the charter issued jointly to Hamage and Marchiennes confirms the creation of a *mensa* and the ownership by the two communities of extensive properties in the region; divides the wine made at the estate of Vregay between the lord (*senior*) and the brothers and sisters of the two institutions; and grants the communities a tithe on all the abbatial *villae* (estates), regardless of the fact that these were held by the lay abbot or a lay beneficiary. If a significant deficit is to occur at one *villa*, it is to be compensated by the revenues of other *villae*, if necessary those belonging to the (lay) abbot.[122] In the document for Denain, there is also reference to the restitution of lost properties.[123] For its part, the Nivelles privilege creates a *mensa conventualis*, as well as a separately subsidized *matricula* (hospice), which is divided into two parts: one for the rich, and one for the poor, pilgrims, and travelers.[124]

It is not surprising to find that the relevant documentation in support of royal authority's claims on and protection of these institutions becomes more explicit and more plentiful toward the later ninth century, at a time when the sovereigns' stake in them was about to change. Yet, while the nature of Charles the Bald's interventions in particular is clear enough, the circumstances that led to these decisions are the subject of two distinct interpretations. According to the first, they were designed to allow the ruler to hand out the estates and lay offices of royal monasteries to his aristocratic associates without compromising the continued existence of these religious communities. For instance, for Marchiennes we know that Charles created the *mensa* one year before giving to laymen the remainder of the monastic estate as a benefice.[125] In the alternative interpretation, these measures were not taken in preparation for a controlled distribution of monastic estates and offices among different stakeholders, but to keep in check ongoing encroachment on monastic wealth on the part of local and regional aristocrats.[126] Specialists have quoted some of the sisters' own written output to support this latter interpretation. Maubeuge's so-called *Testament* of Saint Aldegondis, which purports to be an authentic seventh-century testament of the saint, records her transferring all of her properties, including the estates of Maubeuge and Cousolre, to the sisters living at Maubeuge.[127] It stipulates "no abbess or governess (*rectrix*) of this same monastery at no point in time should dare to change, rob, or alienate any of these (properties)."[128] The employment of the word *rectrix* (even though it was sometimes used for elected abbesses) alongside *abbatissa* is surely meaningful, referring to a situation where a laywoman was at the head of the institution.[129] Likewise, in Aldeneik's contemporary *Life* of its first abbesses Harlindis and Relindis, the author insists on the *haereditas patrocinii*, or the notion that the current monastic community was the rightful heir to the sisters' familial estate, which included the monastery itself.[130]

Unquestionably, charters like those issued by Lothar II and Charles the Bald created, at least in principle, greater security for communities of women religious, and some of them may indeed have originated in a context of a planned devolvement of monastic wealth, or growing pressure on monastic estates by nonroyal agents. But the rhetoric of these charters and of the previously quoted hagiographies is certainly not evidence enough to suggest a situation of acute crisis for all female communities in Lotharingia, or even for the institutions mentioned in these texts.[131] An example from Louis the German's realm illustrates this point. Sometime following the death of Queen Theutberga, Bishop Adventius of Metz (858–75) appears to have claimed significant estates belonging to male and female monasteries in the region, including Gorze, Glandière, Saint-Arnoul, and Sainte-Glossinde. Presumably to reverse these usurpations, in a series of charters issued in 875, Louis reasserted the royal status of these institutions and restituted properties to all four. Yet the charter for Sainte-Glossinde—once again a heavily interpolated document—does not reliably indicate that Adventius's action had jeopardized the female community's continued existence.[132] We also know that the bishop had previously lent his support to Queen Theutberga's intervention (previously discussed in this chapter) in favor of the sisters,[133] and it has been argued that control over the monastery may have passed to the bishop sometime in the 860s.[134] It also remains unclear whether Louis's restitutions were actually of direct benefit to the religious, or simply constituted redistribution of their wealth to the benefit of the sovereign, his allies, and the lay leadership of these monasteries. As regards Charles's privileges, it is important to remember that, ultimately, (lay) abbots and abbesses stayed in control of the management of the entire monastic estate, even following the creation of *mensae*.[135]

Even the commentaries in local hagiographies do not offer secure indications of a situation of acute crisis. Although these may echo the fear of the religious or their despair at lay encroachment on their estates, we must nuance the value of such commentary as an indicator of impending catastrophe. Firstly, one of the big unknowns is the degree to which the women relied, for their personal expenses, on privately owned endowments. Secondly, given the aristocratic interests presumably tied up in sisters' endowments and in the patronage of women's institutions generally, these claims about lay attacks and usurpations at monastic houses may refer to a broader struggle among the local and regional elite for control over economic and institutional assets. In other words, these texts may speak not just from the perspective of the religious as a community but also from that of the members' involvement in aristocratic stakeholder groups, and vice versa. Finally, despite these remarks, we should also not discount a realization on the part of these communities that they needed to become more assertive about protecting their interests, now that the lordship over monastic houses was becoming the subject of growing competition and the direct benefits of royal protection were becoming less obvious.

In contrast to this uncertainty, three things emerge clearly from these late ninth-century testimonies. First, that Carolingian royals in the 860s and 870s relied on female institutions for managing regional aristocratic networks, both directly (via royal representatives) and indirectly (via handing out parts of monastic estates as benefices). Second, that these sovereigns were looking to retain or regain a direct stake, symbolic and otherwise, in these houses via a discourse of protection.[136] Third and finally, that the religious, in voicing their concerns, did not refer to royal protection but relied on reinterpretations of local hagiographic memory, featuring particularly "virile" (in the sense of strong-willed, virtuous) female leaders.[137] This development may reveal a growing skepticism concerning the intentions of rulers and their future effectiveness as monastic lords. Perhaps it even echoes the move by the Remiremont religious from the middle decades of the ninth century onward to seek more distance from Carolingian royalty and generally to become less reliant on the benevolence and protection of specific patrons. By all accounts, late ninth-century sources do not so much suggest a situation of acute dissolution of monastic estates as one where multiple parties—royals, local noblemen, but also some groups of women religious—were positioning themselves for an impending major struggle for control over these institutions and their assets.

Study of female monastic realities between c. 816 and the 880s indicates that application of reformist directives did not result in the homogenization of female religious institutions and their observance, but rather in coping strategies that fostered distinct group identities. No doubt with the assistance of lay and ecclesiastical lords, groups of women religious developed local narratives of self that allowed them to face changes in their own condition and in society in general. Some of these changes are easily misread as straightforward implementations of the reformers' oppressive measures or as evidence of the late ninth-century pressures on female institutions and their estates. As we shall see in chapter 3, the decades around 900 would transform the monastic landscape and bring numerous challenges to women religious. At the same time, significant evidence exists of how ninth-century concepts of monastic lordship and religious identity remained functional in these decades and, in a number of cases, resulted in situations far removed from the catastrophic narrative promulgated by medieval and modern commentators alike.

CHAPTER 3

Transitions, Continuities, and the Struggle for Monastic Lordship

In chapter 2, we saw how the traditional view of the ninth century as a phase of catastrophic decline for female religious is up for revision. It is undeniably true that lawmakers imposed severe restrictions on the liberties of individual religious, and presumably the communities and their leadership faced a number of challenges as regards their institutional integrity and reputation. But contrary to what scholars previously believed, some of these women (aided no doubt by their male associates and by their lay patrons) showed a great deal of flexibility when challenged to (re)define their spiritual and institutional identities and their role in society generally. This flexibility and the traces it has left in the primary evidence invalidates suspicions of a general descent into societal and religious redundancy.

Few observers would be inclined to extend this revised narrative to the period between c. 880 and the 920s–930s. The disappearance of many communities from the source record; the rampant secularization of properties, leadership functions, internal organization, and even the conduct of individual women; the numerous references in documents from the early to middle decades of the tenth century to a need to "restore" or reform female communities; and, finally, also the depressing narratives of the current state of the church as found in the decrees of a number of synods from the later ninth and early tenth century: all of these things have been cited as indicative of a near-total collapse of monastic institutions and spirituality.[1] Julie Ann Smith paints a decidedly gloomy picture of the situation of religious when she writes that "the ongoing demands for reform and enforced claustration of female religious was paralleled by the appropriating of nunnery incomes and properties for lay purposes and the installation of laity in abbatial offices, and the incursions of non-Christian groups such as Vikings, Muslims and Magyars. In order to survive the violence of internal warfare and invasions nunneries were forced to place themselves under the protection of powerful laity who more often than not exploited their positions. . . . Nunneries were increasingly placed in the position where the conditions they were intended to be protected from were actually imposed on them. The purpose of the nunnery life was being subverted by forces they were consistently being disempowered to resist."[2]

Undeniably all was not well in Lotharingia, and many female religious presumably suffered great mental strain and physical discomfort during this half century where few people enjoyed long-term security of status, income, or even survival. But as I argue in this chapter, below a surface of change brought about by wars, invasions, and local upheavals, a more significant process of transformation was unfolding, determined by sociopolitical, institutional, and religious alterations initiated several decades earlier. Two observations are essential to understanding this phenomenon. First, the reorganization of the female monastic landscape in these decades resulted primarily from the progressive reorganization of Lotharingian regional politics. And, second, that some religious groups at least continued to rely on the coping strategies discussed in chapter 2. Far from being the fortunate survivors of processes over which they had had no control, the women in these houses and their male associates were actively involved in securing the continued existence and societal relevance of female communities.

Warfare and Invasions: Assessing the Immediate Impact

It seems hard to imagine that anyone living in the Lotharingian area would not, in some way or other, have been affected by the turbulences of the decades around 900. Domestic politics were in a constant state of flux. Almost immediately after the death of King Lothar II in 869, the rulers of Western and Eastern Francia went to war over control of the region, a process interrupted only by fragile truces and treaties too numerous to reference here in detail.[3] Foreign invasions further affected local power relations. In summer 879, the Normans carried out raids on major population centers and institutions, initially affecting the western parts of Lotharingia into the Noyon and Reims areas, and then, from 881–82, the eastern Meuse and Rhine valleys.[4] In early 882, they arrived in the Moselle valley, pushing far enough to devastate the abbey of Prüm and the city of Trier, and reach Metz. In 887, an insurrection by Arnulf of Carinthia and the Lotharingian elites against Emperor Charles the Fat eventually saw the region joined to Arnulf's newly acquired Eastern Frankish kingdom. In August 891, Arnulf decisively defeated the Normans near Louvain, and in 895, he appointed his son Zwentibold as king of Lotharingia, which the latter ruled until his death in 900. From that time and into the early tenth century, Lotharingian magnates increasingly gained control of regional politics. Internal competition among them, and between them and Eastern and Western Frankish royalty, would continue to determine the fate of regional politics for decades to come. In the meantime, the danger of foreign invasions by no means disappeared, as occasional raids would continue to impact the region. In addition to periodic incursions by the Normans, from the early decades of the tenth century, we also have reports of attacks by the Hungarians and Magyars, even though these are much less clearly documented. For instance, in 917, they invaded the Vosges region, sacked Saint-Dié and Moyenmoutier, and eventually reached as far as the Remiremont area.[5]

Traditional accounts of this period have argued for the devastating impact of warfare and invasions on religious communities and religious life in general. To corroborate this view, historians refer to commentaries from the time, indicating an acute state of disruption. In the introduction to the decrees of a synod held in 893 at Metz's abbey of Saint-Arnoul, Archbishop Radbod of Trier, together with his suffragan bishops of Metz, Toul, and Verdun, argued that

> We see fulfilled what the Lord says through his prophet, *Foreigners will devour your land before your eyes, and it will be destroyed by the enemy.* No one is in any doubt about how this has been fulfilled for us by the Normans. And we all sense that we are afflicted from all directions by corrupted Christians, as is written: *They will humiliate your people, Lord, and sell your inheritance.* We therefore must seek the piety of Christ, which the pagans now keep hostage, and decree the law of God, which the cruelest men of our people have banished through the destruction of the poor.[6]

By taking commentaries like this one as evidence of a state of chaotic disruption, historians have overlooked that these were primarily designed to allow church leaders and royals to retain the (self-) appointed legislative and executive authority of their predecessors in a changing sociopolitical environment. While the introduction to the Metz decrees evokes the psychological impact and, to an extent, the societal disruption caused by recent invasions, warfare, and lay usurpations of ecclesiastical property, the remainder of the text appears as a routine exercise in ecclesiastical governance. A good example is canon 9, which brings women religious into focus. It concerns the case of two religious of Saint-Pierre-aux-Nonnains in Metz, who had been condemned for crimes unspecified, stripped of their veils, and expelled from their community. The synod decreed that the sisters were to be given back their veils, imprisoned inside the monastery, and given "a small quantity of bread and little water" and "an abundance of the divine word" until they were able to give satisfaction.[7] In issuing this decree, the participants acted in exactly the same way as their ninth-century predecessors would have done,[8] and (even more importantly) pursued ecclesiastical policies that explicitly relied on operative hierarchies and punitive procedures within religious communities. Globally speaking, this and other measures reveal a clerical leadership working jointly with Carolingian royalty variously to maintain a moral standard within the different ecclesiastical ranks, command respect of the sacraments and other rituals, protect ecclesiastical property, and retain a strong link with royal authority. The juxtaposition of these fairly mundane measures with the dystopic tone of church leaders' overall comments on the state of the church and society is striking and hints at a shift in the discourse of justification of royal and episcopal agency rather than a reliable account of an ecclesiastical system teetering on the brink of total ruin.[9]

A second argument commonly referred to in traditional accounts is that the history of individual monastic houses in this period contains sufficient evidence to argue a state of profound disruption. According to Jane Schulenburg, the invasions "threatened the continued prosperity or even existence of many monastic communities, and consequently numerous houses were temporarily deserted or permanently abandoned."[10] While that statement holds true for a number of institutions in England especially,[11] and while many religious communities in Lotharingia were situated in areas—particularly valleys—directly hit by domestic warfare and foreign assaults, reliable reports of female institutions being directly affected in that region are exceedingly rare. In his monumental study of the impact and representation of the Norman attacks in Lower Lotharingia, Albert D'Haenens showed persuasively that the few accounts of actual devastation and disruption tend to rely heavily on literary templates, particularly biblical texts and hymns, and on hyperbole.[12] They are also almost all written by second-hand witnesses, are low on informative value, and seem to be inspired by the mental shock of the attacks more than by any kind of long-term material damage or social disruption.[13] Many testimonies from later centuries, postulating that female houses were severely damaged or even dissolved as a direct result of these disruptions, are to be read either as part of a literary strategy to claim or reclaim "lost" property or as a means to accommodate the discourse of decline that reformers of the mid-tenth century onward relied on. They can even be seen as narrative stopgaps for medieval and modern commentators confronted with a fragmentary source record for the decades around 900.[14]

The three female communities for which we do have more or less reliable references to disruptions caused by invasions and warfare reveals that even in these cases, finding out what exactly happened and what were the long-term effects is nearly impossible. The first case is that of the monastery of Oeren, in Trier, a city that in April 882 was subject to a particularly savage, three-day assault by the Normans. Although no specific memories of Oeren's fate have survived, Theresia Zimmer references archaeological evidence suggesting a catastrophic destructive event to back up her claim that it could not have escaped the attack.[15] The ensuing chaos and the wars for control over the kingdom of Lotharingia further affected the religious' position: in 906, Counts Conrad and Gerhard, vassals of King Louis the Child of Western Francia and prominent adversaries of Zwentibold, took possession of rural properties belonging to Trier's monasteries of Sankt Maximin and Oeren.[16] The second community for which we have some information is that of Marchiennes, where the religious and their clerics enlisted poet and hagiographer Hucbald of Saint-Amand to draft a *Life* of patroness Saint Rictrudis. In this narrative from 907, some two-and-a-half decades after the severest attacks on the Scheldt region, Hucbald of Saint-Amand tells us that "[the local clerics and sisters] convinced me that the things they told me [about their patroness Saint Rictrudis] had been once transmitted in writing, but that [these writings] had been lost because of the calamity of the Norman plunderings."[17] Finally, there is Remiremont. In 917, the sisters were forced to temporarily abandon their institution because of an attack by the Hungarians and to seek refuge for themselves and their relics (of Saints Amat, Adelphius, and Romaric) on the Saint-Mont. A mid-eleventh-century hagiographer recounts this event, including a dramatic passage where several of the religious nearly drowned in the swollen Moselle river while fleeing the invaders.[18] He claims that the tumult and depredations of the Hungarian invasion depleted the resources for protecting the monastery's subjects and forced the religious to use all the gold and silver from their relic shrines. Meanwhile, at least one lay lord from the region usurped some of the community's properties.[19]

Whatever the precise circumstances of presumed attacks on Oeren, Marchiennes, and Remiremont, there can be little doubt that members of these three institutions would have experienced the situation as physically threatening and psychologically distressing. But apart from the presumed destruction of buildings and property losses at Oeren, the claim by the Marchiennes sisters about losing their saint's *Life*, and the episode of displacement and reports of property losses at Remiremont,[20] we have no indications that the resources and long-term existence of these institutions were significantly jeopardized. This is significant, especially in light of D'Haenens's observation that the impressive accounts of attacks on male institutions can be counterbalanced by indications that at least some of those communities affected bounced back surprisingly quickly. Displaced urban and monastic personnel returned relatively soon after the attacks, razed buildings rose again swiftly (sometimes in a matter of mere months), and monastic domains were only affected in a limited way.[21] Organizing the reconstruction of their institutions may have been more challenging for these female communities than for their male counterparts. But as we shall see later, nothing indicates that religious life in any of them was fundamentally compromised, at least not beyond the initial phase of disruption. Oeren is on record as a functioning community from 906;[22] Marchiennes was functioning again as a religious community when Hucbald wrote his *Life* of Saint Rictrudis in 907; and for Remiremont, we have an uninterrupted list of abbesses.

In the latter two communities, we also see how the sisters actually took advantage of their plight to position themselves more effectively on the "cultic market," consolidate a specific institutional identity, and deal with a number of outstanding conflicts over property. Reading Hucbald's statement about Marchiennes's lost hagiography of Saint Rictrudis, we find that he had initially shown great reluctance to write a hagiography of this saint, on the basis that there existed very little in the way of reliable testimony. So he expresses his skepticism of the sisters' claims by saying that "I had never seen, or heard of, a reliable testimony of (Rictrudis) in writing."[23] Although he does not deny the possibility that the Marchiennes community had suffered from recent Norman attacks—around 880 several male monasteries in the region were compelled to temporarily abandon their institution[24]—he makes no attempt to disguise his suspicions that the sisters' claims were merely a ruse to force him into accepting their oral testimonies of a patron saint who had died two centuries earlier.[25] But this was not a simple case of religious who, licking their wounds after the recent attacks, were looking to transition from an oral cult to a written one. Further on we shall see that the Marchiennes leadership was likely in the process of consolidating a merger of their institution with the former house of Hamage. Arguably, Hucbald's *Life* as he published it does not reveal a community working to heal its wounds, but rather a self-confident one looking to definitively incorporate Hamage's properties and cultic identity and, in doing so, to declare the supremacy of its patron Saint Rictrudis over her daughter and Hamage's patron, Eusebia.

For his part, Remiremont's mid-eleventh-century hagiographer states that the sisters' flight to the Saint-Mont led to the discovery there of the remains of obscure Saint Gebetrudis, who immediately started performing all kinds of miracles in protection of the sisters. Thanks to her interventions and to the proactive campaign by the religious to recuperate lost property, the damage caused by recent invasions was, so he claims, quickly undone.[26] Additionally, the disruptions appear to have created opportunities for abbesses to take unusual steps for asserting their institution's rights. A particularly vivid episode, which recounts events datable to the years 917–21, tells us how the abbess of Remiremont, confronted with the theft of vineyards by a man named Walo, "against the custom of this place" sent out a few religious to approach Duke Richard of Burgundy for his assistance in solving the issue. Richard duly ordered restitution of the properties, and the religious went to one of the vineyards to order the grapes to be harvested and stored. When the usurper sent one of his men to confront the religious, one of the women threatened him with Saint Romaric's slipper and key, saying, "Take this key that you ask for, to your deepest damnation."[27] Perhaps it was a similar course of action on the part of the religious and their leadership that triggered the process leading up to Duke Giselbert of Lotharingia's restitution of several usurped properties to the religious early in the 930s.[28] Conceivably, the Marchiennes religious had not been the only ones to represent the setbacks of recent years as a catastrophe of epic proportions, using that narrative to pressure patrons and supporters to actively promote their interests.

The Dissolution of Female Institutions in Lower Lotharingia

In response to this lack of reliable evidence for the long-term effects of warfare and invasions on female religious houses, historians have referred to the definitive disappearance of a significant number of them from the source record. At first sight, the numbers do look impressive, at least for Lower Lotharingia. Out of eighteen female monasteries known to have existed in that area in the ninth century, nine apparently ceased to exist, and for several of these, later commentators have suggested that their disappearance was as a direct result of warfare and invasions, and, to a lesser extent, secularization via usurpations of monastic offices and estates. But here too, scrutiny of the evidence yields a number of observations that significantly complicate our understanding of the situation.

One difficulty is that, in most cases, later commentators and even modern historians have merely inferred the context around 900 as the most likely one for community dissolution, based on the standard narrative of profound disruption and warfare affecting religious houses. An extreme example is the female house of Sains-lès-Marquion, which disappears from the source record in the early ninth century, only to reappear in the *Deeds of the Bishops of Cambrai*, a narrative written in 1024–25, as a small sanctuary served by a single priest.[29] Likewise, the putative disappearance of Moustier-sur-Sambre and Orp-le-Grand around 900 is strictly speculation.[30] For several other institutions, we have a chronological reference point in the 870 Treaty of Meersen, but after that, most plunge back into darkness. Regarding Condé-sur-Escaut, the *Deeds* mention that the site was no longer served by sisters, but by a handful of clerics.[31] Meerbeke's post-870 fate is also unclear, except for a mention in a hagiographical text of the thirteenth century that it was destroyed by the Normans, reconstructed, and subsequently turned into a (male?) priory of Nivelles.[32] Denain and Hasnon, for their part, are last referred to in two charters by Charles the Bald from 877; but here again, the *Deeds'* claim that the two sites were abandoned as female institutions compels us to bridge nearly 150 years of silence in the documentation.[33] The only two cases where we know reasonably well what happened and when are Hamage and Antoing, discussed further on in this chapter.

A second difficulty in assessing the situation is that our understanding of the fate of these institutions is complicated by the existence of traditions—some more credible than others—that female communities that had been dissolved in the context of warfare and Norman attacks had subsequently reemerged, or possibly even continued to exist, in a different setting. For Moustier-sur-Sambre, later traditions regarding noblewoman Ermengardis's restitution of properties in 901, during the episcopate of Stephen of Liège and the tenure of an unknown Abbot Ebroin, and the subsequent restoration of the local church in 926 likely derive from mangled memories of events that took place more than a century later.[34] And reports dating no earlier than the thirteenth century state that Aldeneik, following its dissolution as a female monastery with the Norman invasions and its transformation into a community of clerics, in the 920s or 930s was restored as a female house by Bishop Richer of Liège.[35] Just as intriguing is a tradition saying that the site at Denain was not permanently abandoned and that Charles the Bald's sister Gisela died there in 898.[36] While at least the former two claims seem doubtful, accounts like these may be telltale signs that most later commentators—

for reasons legal, institutional, and perhaps even strictly related to clerical misogyny—were reluctant to accept indications that some of the female communities presumed dissolved and subsequently replaced by clerical groups had indeed continued to exist or had resumed monastic life following a brief interval. In some of these cases, it is possible that the transition to a clerical community, or a local sanctuary, took place at a later date and in circumstances removed from those of the later ninth and very early tenth century. Particularly the clerical attacks on female houses from the second half of the tenth century, discussed in chapter 5, must be taken into consideration as a possible context for the disappearance of a number of poorly documented communities.

A third complicating factor is that the information that is still retrievable for Lower Lotharingia's female institutions that certainly lasted beyond the year 900 corroborates the notion that the female religious landscape, while becoming less dense, by no means disintegrated. Some of the evidence admittedly is negative. For the eastern parts, nothing is known about Munsterbilzen and Andenne, despite later efforts to imagine a bleak picture of destruction and desolation.[37] But for others, we do have snatches of evidence that suggest a relatively healthy state of affairs. Susteren, a former male institution or possibly a double monastery until at least 870, reemerges in the source record in 891 as a women's monastery, when King Arnulf of Carinthia gave the institution and its considerable estates—an indication as clear as can be that the monastery had not stopped functioning as a viable religious and, especially, economic entity—to a "craftsman" (*artifex*) from the abbey of Prüm. The charter of this transaction refers to Susteren as "an abbey . . . where female religious provide women's divine service," also showing that it was still functioning adequately enough as a spiritual community to warrant mention in a royal document.[38] To the west, Sainte-Waudru in Mons also temporarily disappears from the written record, but reemerges in the early tenth century in the context of the Renier family's ascendance as counts of Hainaut; as we shall see, in the 930s, the sisters there would become involved in a competition with those at Maubeuge to obtain the relics of Saint Gislen.[39] Finally, at Nivelles, Maubeuge, and Marchiennes, written evidence documents their history, admittedly with intervals, throughout the 870s–930s, in the former case through charters that demonstrate the monastery as a viable institution and in the two latter through evidence relating to the promotion of local saints' cults and to ongoing reflection on monastic discipline and organization.

The image yielded by these observations seems paradoxical. Admittedly, a number of female monasteries did disappear definitively sometime after circa 870, and the few among these that reemerged in the tenth century did so as male dependencies of other ecclesiastical institutions. Speaking of the dissolution in the late ninth century of Antoing, Jacques Nazet argued that this was, in fact, "the normal outcome of a crisis."[40] Yet for at least half of the ninth-century female institutions, including several that were situated in regions most hit by warfare and Norman attacks in the ninth century, this "normal outcome" apparently did not apply. This discrepancy between two categories of female communities compels us to look for more complex mechanisms behind the dramatic numerical shift in female houses, particularly in densely occupied Lower Lotharingia. When comparing the institutions presumed dissolved to the surviving ones, one cannot but be struck by the fact that the former were all comparatively small communities that—as much as can be reconstructed—appear to have held small estates; had a comparatively underdeveloped local saint's cult or none at all; and, perhaps most significantly, are almost imperceptible in ninth-century documentation.[41] In contrast, those communities that did survive overall seem to have held more significant endowments, had been promoting local cults since the mid-ninth century, and are mentioned with varying degrees of frequency in ninth-century sources. The persistent combination of these factors in the two groups arguably suggests that the long-term existence of the former had been far from secure even prior to the turmoil of the late ninth century.

Conceivably, the monasteries' new lords in some cases decided that institutions were no longer sustainable in their current form.[42] Hamage is a good case in point. Charles the Bald's 877 charter issued jointly for that institution and the nearby monastery of Marchiennes reveals that, although formally separate, the two communities at that point were strongly interconnected, particularly as regards their leadership.[43] As the lesser institution in terms of size and wealth, Hamage's buildings were subsequently abandoned and dismantled, or, as some scholars have suggested, destroyed as a result of invasions: from that point onward, the site contained nothing but the former abbatial church, surrounded by a cemetery.[44] We may speculate that it may have seemed redundant to whoever was controlling the two institutions in the late ninth century to waste considerable resources by letting enclosed groups of women religious live on two sites situated so closely. Moving the community of Hamage to Marchiennes—which is likely what happened in these decades—may also have been a sound decision considering the threat of warfare and invasions at the time.[45] In other cases, particularly those institutions with estates barely sufficient to sustain a religious community, it was more convenient to relocate the religious and transfer the modest properties of a moribund community to some institution or individual with the means to exploit these efficiently. A monastery would thus turn into a center of agricultural production, with the former abbatial church becoming a parish church, served by a handful of clerics. Thus Antoing in very late 870s or early 880s was transferred to the ownership of the bishop of Liège and in the middle of the latter decade was acquired for the male monastery of Lobbes.[46] We have no idea for how long the site subsequently continued to be occupied by women religious, but by the mid-tenth century it appears to have housed a small community of secular canons.[47]

Dissolutions and institutional mergers like these would hardly have been unexpected; nor would they have been considered controversial as a principle. As early as 789, Charlemagne had decreed that smaller communities should be brought together; and in 829 the Frankish bishops expressed their concerns about the survival of smaller communities;[48] we can also see mergers happening in tenth-century England.[49] However, if it is true that some of these early medieval aristocratic foundations were unsustainable, this raises the question of why the Lower Lotharingian female religious landscape remained so dense until at least the final decades of the ninth century. References in the 870 treaty of Meersen to several very minor institutions suggest that at least some of these communities were kept alive as territorial demarcations, helping rulers to retain control over local aristocratic networks. Through the prayer service repeatedly performed by their membership, these institutions further deepened their representation of the sovereign and the state.[50] This may be part of the explanation—besides concerns over the spiritual service offered by religious—why Charles the Bald in a set of 853 instructions to his *missi* ordered them to make sure that "monasteries of canons, and of monks and women religious," if their membership was too low, should be augmented.[51] However, once royal lordship over these houses was effectively replaced by that of territorial rulers and ecclesiastical lords, financial and other support for these smaller houses evaporated. For these new overlords, holding a controlling stake in one or at most two female communities in a specific region and replacing other, less prominent or viable ones by small communities of clerics would have been a sensible thing to do, from a political, symbolic, and financial point of view.[52]

Such interventions, often hinted at in the evidence but never explicitly stated, certainly seem to have been less about reorganizing a monastic landscape devastated by recent invasions by foreigners or about lay warlords laying their own greedy hands on the valuable assets of these defenseless communities. Rather, they seem to have been more to do with taking a number of rational decisions that reflected the changes in how aristocratic and clerical power were negotiated and maintained regionally. It would, therefore, not be surprising at all to find that Hamage and Antoing represent just the tip of the iceberg as far as the deliberate reorganization of the female monastic landscape is concerned. Technically speaking, such putative actions amounted to what historians have referred to as the complete or partial "secularization" of monastic estates; however, the negative connotation commentators from later centuries have given to this process may not be warranted by institutional and economical realities around 900.

The Struggle for Monastic Lordship

For the communities that disappeared, it may have been the end of a female monastic identity artificially sustained by royal interests or quite simply the end of a continuous struggle to remain economically viable and attractive to patrons. But for those that remained, despite the transformation of the female monastic landscape, the symbolic and general political significance of women's monasteries remained as strong as ever. Seeking to extend their predecessors' monastic policies, King Arnulf of Carinthia and his son Zwentibold of Lotharingia went to great lengths to retain a position of prominence in the affairs of female communities and, by doing so, gained symbolic prestige and the control of local power networks. When Arnulf in 891 donated the royal monastery of Susteren to Siginand, a "famous craftsman" (*illuster artifex*) from the abbey of Prüm, an institution closely tied in with Lotharingian royal interests, he undoubtedly did so to avoid losing control of Susteren to local aristocrats.[53] When Arnulf subsequently gave the crown of Lotharingia to his son Zwentibold, the latter, now lord over a much smaller territory, took additional measures to consolidate his ownership of the monastery. In 895, following an intervention by the archbishop of Trier, Zwentibold confirmed that Siginand was entitled—likely also strongly expected—to transfer ownership to the abbey of Prüm.[54]

The reason for Zwentibold's eagerness to keep Susteren specifically out of lay hands became evident when, in August 900, he was defeated and killed in the war against Louis the Child and was buried at the monastery. According to the testimony of the thirteenth-century chronicler Aegidius of Orval, three of Zwentibold's daughters were also veiled at Susteren. Relindis—note the homonym with the saint venerated at Aldeneik—would later become a recluse at Flémalle; Benedicta and Cecilia, both still children at the time of their father's death, according to local tradition would later lead Susteren as abbesses.[55] This is suggestive of an attempt around 900 to turn Susteren into a sanctuary, supervised by the monks of Prüm, for the newly established, ultimately short-lived royal house of Lotharingia. Certainly there was an impact on local institutional identity. Although Zwentibold generally was not well remembered, his memory and that of his two daughters at Susteren remained positive throughout the monastery's existence: all three were inserted into local hagiographic traditions.[56]

Royal interest in female institutions was not always strictly personal, and certainly not limited to Susteren. In a charter for Nivelles dated 897, Zwentibold elaborated on Charles the Bald's creation of a *mensa conventualis* by adding tithes to the brothers'—presumably the clerics serving the women—and sisters' *mensa* and granting new incomes to the monastery's hospice. At the same time, royal abbess Gisela herself benefited from the remainder—a very substantial part in fact—of the abbey's incomes.[57] Jacques Hoebanx sees evidence in this arrangement for calling Gisela a "parasite" and has speculated that her lay associates held a substantial part of the lay abbesses' assigned estates and rights.[58] But we have no indication that the religious at the monastery struggled because of this—even though we have no idea how extensive the private benefices or prebends of the religious were, these need to be taken into consideration—and unlike other monasteries in the region, direct control was never devolved to these associates. A key passage in Zwentibold's charter that has been overlooked by scholars—and yet may reveal some of the reasons for his and later rulers' interest in the monastery—makes reference to the abbey's ownership of relics of their patroness Gertrudis, sister of the Merovingian king Dagobert I.[59] The fact that Nivelles had been founded on a royal fisc, and by a Merovingian royal made the institution of exceptional significance to the struggling Carolingians of the late ninth and early tenth century and to their German successors. Gisela's successor was Mathilde, wife of King Henry I "the Fowler" of Eastern Francia, and as late as 972, Otto II gave the monastery to his future wife Theophanu as part of her dowry.[60]

From Zwentibold's insistence on retaining Susteren and Nivelles, we can infer that the memory of his Carolingian predecessors' reliance on female institutions for political and memorial purposes was still very much alive, and remained—symbolically at least—crucial to the representation of the current rulers' claims to sovereign power. In other cases, having the ultimate authority over female institutions allowed these rulers to use them as a conditional benefice for their faithful associates, particularly in the context of royal successions and elections. So Arnulf in the mid-890s gave the abbeys of Oeren and Saint-Pierre-aux-Nonnains to Counts Gerard and Matfrid, both prominent members of the regional aristocracy, as a means to secure their allegiance to the new King Zwentibold.[61] Soon afterwards, in 896, several individuals including Gerard, Matfrid, and Archbishop Radbod of Trier rebelled against Zwentibold's authority. In response, Zwentibold (also in 896) conquered Trier and distributed the lands of his adversaries among his faithful servants. Regino of

Prüm in his chronicle tells us that the only two conquests not included in this generous gesture were Oeren and Saint-Pierre-aux-Nonnains.[62]

In fact, it is difficult to see much difference between these transferals to laymen and other royal associates and those that occurred between late Carolingian royals and ecclesiastical leaders. In 908, King Louis the Child issued a charter to confirm the episcopal church of Liège's ownership of—among other estates and rights—the male abbeys of Lobbes, Fosse, and the female house of Herbitzheim. The text reflects quite clearly the contemporary value of monastic institutions as political commodities: Lobbes had been given by King Zwentibold to Count Sigohard; Fosse had previously been an acquisition of his relative Gisela, daughter of Lothar II, and also lay abbess of Nivelles; finally, Herbitzheim had been owned by a certain Count Gerhard *proprio iure*, but had been transferred into the king's hands after Gerhard's betrayal. Judging the imperial church of Liège a far more secure beneficiary, Louis lumped all these properties together in one donation, giving it into the control of Bishop Stephen, "for as long as he always remains faithful."[63]

However, regardless of these policies, in many cases Carolingian royalty did in fact lose much of its grip on female monasticism in the years around 900, a process accelerated no doubt by the rapid succession of dynastic crises. The dominating figures that emerge in the documentation of the early tenth century reflect a redistribution of territorial power in the Lotharingian area to the benefit of regional magnates. At Susteren, Arnulf and Zwentibold's attempt to keep the abbey out of aristocratic hands ultimately failed: despite the family's enduring presence, after his death Zwentibold's enemies seem to have quickly claimed the abbey, and in 916 the Prüm monks had to have the matter of its ownership tabled at the royal meeting of Herstal.[64] Who exactly came to control the abbey is unclear, but the Prüm community would continue protesting against the loss of Susteren until at least 949, in vain.[65] Likewise, also following Zwentibold's death in 900, the Matfrid clan claimed Oeren and Sankt Maximin in Trier, only to be convinced to abandon its claims by Count Conrad in 906.[66] In other cases, the transferal of an abbey's lordship simply occurred when regional power holders were given it as a benefice or as compensation for their support in the election of a new ruler, even though the precise circumstances and chronology always elude us.[67] One such individual was a certain "noble and very powerful" Gotfrid, who apparently controlled the abbey of Pfalzel near Trier in the late ninth century.[68]

This process of transferals into the hands of regional and local aristocrats becomes even more evident if we move into the tenth century. At Saint-Pierre-aux-Nonnains, we see a Count Ricuin of Verdun acting as the abbey's secular lord in a notice issued in 918 to confirm a donation by a *Deo sacrata* named

Remlindis and her son Teilalf made in exchange for a *precaria*, an annuity or money rent.[69] Gordon Blennemann is likely correct in assuming that Ricuin had received control over the abbey in return for supporting the royal election of the Western Frankish king Charles the Simple.[70] Another relevant figure is Heribert II, Count of Vermandois, whose emergence as lord of Maubeuge in the late 920s or early 930s may well be the result of being given the abbey as a benefice or simply the outcome of a successful attempt at expanding his territories.[71] The abbey of Mons, a future competitor of Maubeuge, also re-emerges as a benefice or property of Renier of Hainaut, ancestor of the future counts there.[72] But perhaps the most significant figure of all and certainly the best documented is Giselbert, later known as Duke of Lotharingia. Originally an ally of Charles the Simple, who was king of Lotharingia from 911 to 923, in 925 Giselbert sided with King Henry, and married Henry's daughter Gerberga.[73] As early as December 929 and again in 936, Giselbert turns up in the documentation of Aldeneik, apparently acting as owner of the abbey's benefice.[74] In the mid-930s, we can see him holding a dominant stake in the government of Remiremont.[75] In 939, he would lose everything when he stood up against his master Otto I and was subsequently slain on the battlefield, a rebel: but for a short while in the 920s and 930s, he had been the most powerful agent in Lotharingia.

The effects of these developments on groups of women religious are difficult to verify. As we saw in chapter 2, hagiographies and royal charters from the time have been interpreted as indicators of significant problems, with local lords trying—against the interests of the women—to alienate parts of the monastic estates. Yet there is little to suggest that such usurpations and brigandage permanently destabilized the surviving monastic economies: in fact, most of what we know about such incidents comes from documents issued by members of the higher elite seeking to restore or justify their controlling stake in female institutions, as Carolingian rulers had done in the later ninth century.[76] Much more clearly represented in the sources are the interventions of several of these lords to retain the viability and societal relevance of female institutions. For instance, at Pfalzel, the aforementioned Gotfrid, his son, and his granddaughter Abbess Ratsindis donated considerable properties to the monastery.[77] Ricuin of Verdun oversaw at least one donation to Saint-Pierre-aux-Nonnains (which in 918 counted at least twenty-four members), and Giselbert of Lotharingia restituted to Aldeneik and Remiremont properties formerly usurped by his own beneficiaries.[78] And Heribert of Vermandois at Maubeuge chose to consolidate his presence there by having the church of Saint-Peter (which belonged to the local clerics) rededicated to Saint Quentin, the patron of Heribert's other institution of Saint-Quentin.[79]

FIG. 6. Small reliquary from the treasury of Aldeneik, c. 900. Copyright Musea Maaseik. Reproduced with permission.

None of the evidence just surveyed accords with the traditional narrative of disempowered women being catastrophically harassed by greedy laymen and plunging into a state whereby their very subsistence, let alone their organized devotional life, was barely guaranteed. Instead, we see a female landscape emerging in which the presence of women religious was less tied to royal political and representational interests and where their institutions were the subject of an ongoing competition over their material and symbolic resources. Of the key players in this competition, though, several promoted women's communities as a valid form of religious communal life, even if they may have acknowledged that the female monastic landscape needed thinning out. The question, then, is if these developments had any impact on how the female religious understood themselves, their communities, and their role in society.

Continuities and Adaptations in the Identities of Female Religious

A striking development in contemporary documentation is that the patronage links of women religious become more diffuse, a phenomenon that possibly reveals a somewhat distant, perhaps even diffident, attitude of the religious to their current lords and associates. Consider the example of Remiremont, where the entries of donations from the 860s onward become significantly less informative on social context, and do not even allow us to understand with any clarity which lay lords owned the monastery and for how long.[80] No doubt a certain Count Boso, son of Duke Richard, in the second decade of the tenth century saw it as a major recognition of his lordship over the abbey when the religious referred to him as "promoter of the monastery" (*auctor monasterii*).[81] But this reference is unique; and among the dozens of other members of the regional elite mentioned in the abbey's documentation, none is awarded special prominence.[82]

To explain this phenomenon, Eduard Hlawitschka refers to the loss of a direct connection with Carolingian royalty and the devaluation of the community's former prayer service for ruler and empire, speculating that this led to a significant loss of prestige.[83] Yet as we saw in chapter 2, it may well be that the Remiremont religious, despite assiduously recording their patronage network in the local *Liber memorialis*, deliberately adopted a discourse of communal identity that was less reliant on explicating privileged associations with specific elite individuals. In other communities, the rapid turnover of elite individuals assuming a controlling position over their institution may likewise have deterred the religious from nurturing such close links. Whatever the undoubtedly complex motivations behind this attitude, though, the apparent urgency with which the religious promoted themselves as focal sites of saints' cults reveals an attempt to remain relevant to as broad a cross section of society as possible and to develop a cultic identity more stable, and perhaps also more reliable, than their institution's lordship.

As we saw earlier, the leaders of female communities and their associates in the early to mid-ninth century had attempted to compensate for the consequences of the reformist emphasis on enclosure and the suppression of the sisters' pastoral tasks by promoting female monasteries as significant destinations for popular devotion and as *lieux de mémoire* for saints' cults. By the look of things, women religious and their associates around 900 tried with renewed energy to compensate for the gradual loss of relevance of the sisters' prayer service for ruler and empire (and perhaps also the fickle support of new lords). Instead, they again focused attention on their communal service of both venerating and offering for veneration their patroness saints' remains and emphasized their status as the rightful successors of that saint and his or her original followers.[84] For instance, at Metz, the late ninth- or early tenth-century first redaction of the *Life, Translations and Miracles of Saint Glossinde* echoes the mid-ninth-century emphasis on female institutions as spatial focal points of cultic devotion, particularly in an urban context. In it, the author emphatically refers to the fact that women seeking intercession from the saint are allowed access to Saint Glossinde's grave, behind the altar in Sainte-Glossinde's abbatial church.[85] Around the same time, the religious at Maubeuge acquired a *Life* of Saint Madelberta, according to tradition, their third abbess.[86] That text, which is written in a rustic style,[87] heavily relies on the first and second versions of the *Life* of Saint Aldegondis and the early ninth-century *Life* of Aldetrudis and was evidently intended to initiate a local cult focused on Madelberta's grave.[88]

Competition between communities for the favors of patrons and pilgrims might have fueled additional interest in hagiographic cults. If we are to believe a hagiographer from the monastery of Saint-Ghislain, sometime in the first decades of the tenth century the sisters of Maubeuge and those of Sainte-Waudru in Mons attempted to steal the relics of the monks' patron Saint Gislen. Apparently the Maubeuge women were initially successful, though were quickly made to return the relics by Bishop Stephen of Cambrai (909–34).[89] Another example is the drafting of the first *Life* of Saint Rictrudis of Marchiennes by Hucbald of Saint-Amand.[90] Hucbald's refusal to make a secret of his skepticism with regard to the testimony of the local sisters about their patron saint is a clear indicator that he felt more or less forced into fulfilling their request for a hagiography.[91] The reason behind the women's insistence becomes clear enough when one looks at the main part of the text and sees its attempts to reflect the new institutional situation in a newly invented hagiographic tradition. It notably emphasizes the subordinate position of Hamage and its patroness Saint Eusebia to Marchiennes and Saint Rictrudis, respectively. In an unusual passage, Rictrudis compels her daughter, still an adolescent, to abandon her leadership of Hamage and come to Marchiennes to live under her mother's tutelage. Clearly a reference to the recent merger of Hamage and Marchiennes, it reveals an attempt to claim definitively the cult of the two saints and prevent the Hamage community (and, significantly, its estates) from being separated from the main institution at Marchiennes.[92]

While these messages about the societal role of women religious and about institutional identity were clearly connected to ongoing transformations, other ideas, particularly those that concerned the inner objectives of monastic life, remained very much like those attested in earlier hagiography. In fact, they contain ambiguous elements that run directly counter to the notion in older scholarship that a former majority of Benedictine houses—a majority that, as we saw in an earlier chapter, never existed—turned into ones for canonesses. Maubeuge's *Life* of Saint Madelberta, like the earlier, second *Life* of Saint Aldegondis, insists on Madelberta's mystical marriage with Christ and her observance of virtues inspired by the rule (*regula*).[93] The aforementioned hagiography dedicated to Saint Glossinde equally mentions the saint's status as a bride of Christ, emphasizes her chastity, and traces the abbey's original estate back to a donation made by the saint's relatives. Here too, the original community is represented as "instructed according to the rule" (*regulariter instructam*).[94] And in Hucbald's *Life* of Saint Rictrudis, the saint is represented as being humble, obedient, patient, chaste, prone to fasting, vigils, and continuous prayer; she displays equanimity, softness, modesty, and kindness, and in every way she reminds us of Saint Benedict's notion of the ideal monk.[95] Yet the lack of references to individual poverty indicates that this depiction is by no means enough to argue that the Marchiennes community was committed to strictly observing the *Rule*: in all likelihood, an ambiguous regime, ever evolving and heavily reliant on local circumstances, remained in place.[96]

All three hagiographies of Madelberta, Glossinde, and Rictrudis suggest an increased need around the year 900 to promote the cult of local saints, arguably as an acknowledgment of another shift in the societal role of female communities. Yet the solutions these texts offered were in fact not very different from those proposed in the mid-ninth century; and in regard to their ideological message, they clearly belong not specifically to the early tenth century, but to a much longer timeframe beginning in the middle decades of the ninth. This compels us to be much more cautious than before in arguing that this phase in Lotharingian history marked the secularization of the observance or self-understanding of female religious. Still, some scholars have cited as evidence of such a shift a passage in Remiremont's *Liber memorialis* concerning Ida, who led the female community in the 920s or 930s: she is referenced as "abbess and deaconess" (*abbatissa et diaconissa*).[97] Eduard Hlawitschka has interpreted the double designation of this individual and the appearance of the title *domina* in some notices making reference to female members of the monastery as a clear signal of the abbey's shift to a secularized regime, marked in particular by the emergence of prebends (designated parts of the monastic estate) intended for the subsistence of each individual sister.[98] Franz-Josef Jakobi has extended these observations to paint a picture of an age where the Benedictine observance at the abbey collapsed, the monastic economy was plagued by massive losses of property, and the abbey essentially became a proprietary institution of local Count Boso.[99]

Several objections can be formulated against these speculations. First, as Michel Parisse has noted, to rely on the terminology in the single notice commemorating Ida to infer a shift from a Benedictine to a canonical regime at Remiremont is to ignore the fact that we do not actually know that the religious identified as Benedictine nuns in the decades around 900. Furthermore, in all likelihood, monastic realities were situated somewhere between the two models anyway. Certainly, the term *diaconissa* in itself is not a reliable reference to a canonical regime because we do not actually know if the religious themselves or outsiders considered such a title to be in opposition to a regime inspired by Benedictine principles. Second, local evidence suggests that a shift toward a regime where the incomes of the abbess and the community were divided only took place toward the middle of the tenth century, long after Ida's tenure as abbess.[100] Third and most importantly, this reading by Hlawitschka and other scholars ignores the possibility that, instead of indicating a community "in need of reform," the reference to Ida as a *diaconissa*—a title suggesting some form of pastoral or sacramental activity—may signify that Remiremont was a place where monastic traditions and activities were being enriched by clerical practices.

The evidence to support the latter possibility is indirect but nonetheless significant. In a roughly contemporary order for the benediction of abbesses in the *Theutberga Gospels*, a manuscript presumably owned by the religious at Remiremont, we find inserted passages taken directly from orders for the consecration of male clerics.[101] Earlier we already saw how the *Life, Translations and Miracles of Saint Glossinde* makes reference to religious at Sainte-Glossinde in Metz acting as custodians of the main altar in the abbatial church.[102] And in a mid-eleventh-century hagiography from Remiremont, we find a miracle roughly datable to c. 920 that apparently involved a religious "standing before the step of the altar," a part of the abbatial church where (according to ninth-century lawmakers at least) the women were not supposed to go.[103] Compelling evidence from Anglo-Saxon England (discussed by Katie Bugyis), from Catalonia (by Jonathan Jarrett), and from Italy (by Mary Schaefer) additionally reveals that tenth-century women religious in other parts of Europe were carrying out sacramental or pastoral duties. For England, there are indications of such individuals acting as confessors for outsiders, female and male.[104] For Catalonia, a 924 charter refers to Abbess Emma of Sant Joan de les Abadesses as "preacher and *praetor* and bride of Christ in the face of God."[105] Although Emma is likely to have preached primarily to her subjects, the fact that the author of the charter saw it fit to mention that aspect of her agency is suggestive of a growing appreciation of the pastoral implications of her leadership. Finally, in tenth-century Rome, widowed founders of monastic institutions may have been ordained as *diaconae*, and several individuals at the monastery of Santa Maria in Via Lata are on record as abbesses and deaconesses.[106] Closer to Ida's own region, anchoress Wiborada of Sankt Gallen (d. 926) owned a chalice, paten, and linen cloth for the communion bread and self-administered the consecrated host outside of Mass (*extra missam*).[107] Although it remains impossible to say which one of these activities would have applied to Ida, it is clearly incorrect to frame her status as a *diaconissa* as a sign of decline in the sisters' religious observance.

Early Calls for Reform?

For all the reasons cited in the foregoing discussion—invasion, changes in overlordship, and so on—conditions in and around Lotharingian monasteries around 900 at times must have been less than ideal, and the future certainly must have looked uncertain to the religious and their leadership. Nonetheless, there is no objective evidence to support the notion that female monasticism's internal and external situation in this period was indeed catastrophic or that all communities were affected by internal and external decline in roughly the same manner. This compels us to review some of the arguments scholars have made about female monasticism's precarious situation in these decades.

In a similar fashion, it is worth revisiting what historians have identified as one of the earliest concrete attempts to "restore" female religious life to its former glory. Remiremont's *Liber memorialis* contains a notice referring to an event that apparently took place in the years 931–36, when Giselbert, joined by a number of prominent Lotharingian aristocrats and bishops as well as by Queen Gerberga of Western Francia, restored alienated properties to the abbey.[108] In Hlawitschka's understanding, this event signifies a broader action for reform that aimed, among other things, to stop the secularization process that had begun with the progressive degradation of the community's Benedictine observance and had ultimately led to the early tenth-century Abbess Ida being, in the same *Liber memorialis*, named "abbess and deaconess."[109] To support this interpretation, he referenced the restorative nature of the transaction and the fact that Giselbert's intervention coincided chronologically with his reformist actions at the male institutions of Saint-Ghislain, Sankt Maximin, Moyenmoutier, and Stavelot.[110] He also cited the involvement of Bishop Adalbero of Metz, his colleague Gozelin of Toul, and Archbishop Ruodbert of Trier, all three of whom were notably involved in the reform of monastic institutions.[111] Based on a comparative study of reformed monasteries in the region, Hlawitschka concluded that Giselbert's Remiremont "reform"—now no longer a hypothesis but an established fact—signaled a significant reduction of the power wielded by lay abbots, the reorganization of the monastic estate, and a transition from a canonical to a more recognizably monastic discipline. Building on this reasoning, Jakobi went one step further by postulating that the Remiremont intervention signaled the introduction there of the monastic practices of the nearby male house of Saint-Evre, "restored" in the mid-930s by Gozelin.[112] The implied conclusion was that Remiremont at this point in time was subject to an intervention by major proponents of a then-current, sweeping movement for Benedictine reform.

There are many problems with this reading of the evidence. Hlawitschka's and Jakobi's speculations about Remiremont's late ninth- and early tenth-century history as being a time of rampant usurpations, violent incursions, and the progressive "secularization" of internal discipline are based on a relatively thin layer of evidence. In addition, a restitution of property like the one documented in Giselbert's notice does not make a reform; nor does the mere attested presence at the transaction of individuals subsequently involved in the reform of monastic houses. And, like her predecessor in 917–21, the local abbess herself may have started the restitution process, by requesting the intervention of a powerful lay lord. Finally and perhaps most importantly, for the decades immediately after the notice of Giselbert's restitution of property was recorded, we simply have no information about changes to Remiremont's internal discipline, organization, or management. It would, in fact, take at least another fifteen to twenty years before the first evidence of truly intensive changes emerged, once again in a context unconnected to an alleged—and doubtful—reintroduction of the *Rule*.[113] All the while, secular lordship over the abbey remained firmly in place, as it would do for decades to come: but then we can be confident in thinking that the possibility of abolishing it never even crossed Giselbert's mind.

The only certainty about the entire transaction is that the gathering recorded in the notice helped consolidate a recent political alliance. On the one hand, it replaced Count Boso's former lay lordship of the abbey, and on the other, it shaped a group of Upper Lotharingian aristocrats, a group centered on the figure of Giselbert as Duke of Lotharingia and bound by explicit expressions of faithfulness to Eastern Frankish King Henry.[114] Rüdiger Barth adds to this interpretation the notion that Giselbert wished both to demonstratively express his self-assumed status as heir to the Carolingian rulers in their role as protector of monastic institutions and to rely on this status to establish symbolically his dominant position in Lotharingian elite circles.[115] More generally speaking, Giselbert's interest in becoming so closely involved in monastic affairs was likely motivated by a triple ambition to claim lordship over these wealthy institutions, demonstrate how, in his understanding, the dominant political paradigm had shifted from the royal exercise of power into the hands of territorial lords like himself, and express his quasi-regal ambitions by demonstratively protecting religious institutions, establishing them as representations of dynastic power, and generally also promoting monastic service.[116]

If we consider things from this perspective, the need to argue a reform of Remiremont vanishes and parallels with other, nonreformist interventions become evident. In December 926, Giselbert had asked Henry I to issue a charter to restitute to the abbey of Aldeneik nineteen *mansi*.[117] That Giselbert in fact owned the abbey's benefice is made clear in a 936 charter of King Otto I, which informs us that one of the former's vassals had taken away property destined "since very old times" for the maintenance of the women (designated in the text as *sanctae moniales*), in other words for the *mensa conventualis*.[118] Although Giselbert's course of action at Aldeneik is similar in many ways to his behavior years later at Remiremont, no scholar has ever thought of associating his earlier interventions with a putative reform. Likewise, no one would ever think of framing Duke Richard of Burgundy's aforementioned intervention for the sisters in 917–21 as a part of a sweeping campaign to restore the observance of the religious and their institutions.

The conclusion of this chapter must be, then, that the notion of a "darkest hour" of female monasticism between c. 880 and the 920s–930s needs considerable nuancing. Admittedly, a significant number of institutions disappeared, some probably in these decades, and all of them situated in the regions that were hit hardest by Norman invasions. But the ones to survive did not do so merely because they escaped the worst effects of the wars and invasions of the late ninth century or were spared the worst effects of the secularization of their estates and offices. They did so because they had already established themselves as the strongest of the pack and subsequently were able to rely on mechanisms of self-promotion grounded several decades earlier. By all accounts, this yields an image far removed from the traditional narrative of destruction, displacement, and organizational and disciplinary decline. Some of that narrative is rooted in the commentaries of reformers from the middle decades of the tenth century: their actions, and how they related to female monastic realities, are the subject of chapter 4.

Chapter 4

Reforms, Semi-Reforms, and the Silencing of Women Religious in the Tenth Century

In the middle decades of the tenth century, a number of communities of female religious, particularly in the Upper Lotharingian dioceses of Metz and Toul, became involved in the efforts of ecclesiastical and lay rulers to instigate disciplinary and organizational reform in monastic contexts.[1] Until late into the twentieth century, historians hailed these episodes as necessary to restore a monastic order plagued by internal decline and external attacks and as the beginning of an incremental process of reform that culminated in the "revival"—in one scholar's view even "feminist revival"—of Benedictine life for women in the middle decades of the eleventh century.[2] In reality, the need for, and supposedly beneficial effects of, these interventions are difficult to establish. In chapter 3, I have already argued that the statements about a near defunct, almost completely secularized monastic life for women c. 900 is much harder to corroborate than historians have previously assumed. And as I show here in relation to the reformist interventions themselves, it is similarly difficult to establish whether the situation inside the communities actually warranted a complete or partial renewal of spiritual and institutional life.

Emerging much more clearly from the primary evidence are three phenomena. First, that bishops in particular relied on reform as a way of expressing specific claims to religious and political authority and of rearranging the lordship and patronage of female monasticism to their own benefit and that of their associates.[3] Second, that the installation of, or the (supposed or verifiable) "return" to a Benedictine regime by no means heralded a greater degree of freedom from the interventions of clerical and lay rulers.[4] And finally, that these interventions have rendered obscure a "pre-reform" culture of reflection over the purpose and organization of female communal life and also a great deal of experimentation. Instead of reversing a situation of terminal decline in female spirituality and monasticism generally, the reforms marked the beginning of clerical intolerance toward the "ambiguous" observance of women religious and the end of a state of relative intellectual and spiritual autonomy. They created a qualitative distinction between the strict Benedictine and traditional, hybrid models that sowed the seeds for a fiercely "antiambiguous" rhetoric, the echoes of which reverberate, up until the present day, into scholarly discussions.

Pre-Reform Trends in Female Religious Spirituality

The idea that female spirituality reached its absolute nadir in the early tenth century is at best a gross generalization. Although the relevant evidence is scarce and difficult to contextualize, it does suggest the existence in some communities of a reading culture and likely also a culture of debate, where the women and possibly also their male associates critically reviewed different normative models for female religious life. In chapter 1, we already saw how the community at Maubeuge assembled an extensive library of legal, penitential, and other handbooks, some of which were subsequently excerpted for inclusion in the early eleventh-century *Roll of Maubeuge*. And for that institution, but also for Marchiennes, Nivelles, and Sainte-Glossinde, chapters 2 and 3 suggested that local hagiographies reveal subtle shifts in the representation of monastic life, some of which resulted from the responses of women religious and their associates to changes in the lordship and patronage of female communities. Belying scholarly notions about the secularization of female observance and spirituality, several of these narratives reveal a strong interest in Benedictine principles of monastic life. Such testimonies should be read not as evidence of forgotten reforms in these communities, but rather of a culture of comparative study of monasticism's literary traditions.

It should not surprise us, then, to find that indications of women's spiritual and intellectual reflection continued into the mid-tenth century, that some religious at least were keenly aware of contemporary politics and ideological trends, and—most importantly perhaps—that clerics and monks paid considerable note to what these women had to say.[5] Surely the most striking of these

CHAPTER 4

is a passage in John of Saint-Arnoul's *Life* of John of Gorze, one of the most prominent monastic agents of the tenth century. Written in the 980s but set five or six decades earlier, it recounts how John, in his capacity of *hebdomadarius* (priest charged with weekly liturgical and pastoral services) of Saint-Pierre-aux-Nonnains in Metz, regularly held private conversations with the sisters.[6] One of these sisters, a young woman named Geisa, was special. Her aunt, Fredeburga, had arranged for her to be educated separately from her fellow novices. The result was that Geisa's behavior was distinct from that of the rest of the community in that she followed a stricter mode of religious observance. During one of their conversations, John suddenly noticed that she was wearing a hair shirt (*cilicium*) under her monastic robes. He reached out to touch it—causing great embarrassment to her—and asked her why she wore it. Geisa was initially reluctant to respond to John's questions, but did say that it seemed appropriate to her for a woman religious to dress in this ascetic manner. According to the biographer, John was deeply impressed by her discreet protest against her fellow sisters' conduct and by her determination to live a different life. He also realized that an understanding of the foundations of monastic life came in the first place through study.[7] Together with the sisters, he immersed himself in reading a wide range of books from the conventual library, including the Bible, ritual handbooks, computistic manuals, canon law collections, penitentials, ecclesiastical and secular law books, homiletic texts, commentaries, and hagiography. The *Life* relates that he subsequently managed to persuade the majority of the community members to change their behavior in accordance with Geisa's example.

John of Saint-Arnoul's testimony is significant. To begin with, his credentials in recounting the situation at early tenth-century Saint-Pierre-aux-Nonnains are good. His subject, John of Gorze, as a member of the community's *familia* at the estate of Vandières, had been associated with the monastery from birth. Once ordained a priest, through his connection with Count Ricuin of Verdun—the abbey's lay lord in the late 910s and early 920s—he obtained income deriving from a church in his home village and was made the monastery's *hebdomadarius*.[8] John of Saint-Arnoul himself was also familiar with female monasticism at Metz: scholars have speculated that he likely also authored the second version of the *Life, Translations and Miracles of Saint Glossinde*.[9] Furthermore, his account of Fredeburga's presence at the monastery is corroborated by the subscription of a charter Ricuin issued in 918.[10] All of this makes it unlikely that he was free to invent a story about Geisa and Fredeburga's preference for a more ascetic mode of life or the opportunity John had grasped to perfect his knowledge of the written foundations of religious life. A second indication of the passage's significance is that it confirms suspicions regarding the ongoing interest of women religious in exploring their spiritual identity and particularly in relying on bodily austerity to authoritatively express their views. Indeed, Geisa's demeanor reminds us of a number of prophetic women living outside of strictly enclosed communities, such as anchoresses Liutbirg of Wendeshausen (d. 865) and Wiborada of Sankt Gallen (d. 926)[11] and the three young visionaries who, according to the early to mid-940s *Visions of Flothildis*, criticized the Reims clergy for their lax and lascivious conduct.[12] And from the later tenth and early eleventh centuries, we also have several examples of abbesses relying on their bodies to express their critical views on then-current practices in women's monasteries.[13] If Geisa's conduct is described more or less accurately, she was not acting in an ascetic or spiritual void, but had adopted a specific method for self-empowerment.

Remarkably, although he clearly self-identifies as a Benedictine author, John of Saint-Arnoul does not argue that either Geisa or her aunt Fredeburga were promoting a Benedictine reform of the community. Rather, through the education of young novices and Geisa as a living exemplar, they seem to have been working toward a *shift* in local observance to a more ascetic form of monasticism inspired, but not necessarily determined, by the *Rule*. Yet frustratingly, the biographer remains vague about what Fredeburga and Geisa objected to in the lives of their fellow sisters. One possible point of discussion is the practice of bestowing *precaria*, or return gifts, on individuals who donated their properties to the monastery. Especially contentious might have been the practice whereby individuals actually became members of the monastic community. One such case is that of Remlindis and her son Teilalf, documented in Ricuin's 918 charter. In the document, Remlindis is referred to as "dedicated to God" (*Deo sacrata*), a title indicating a state of withdrawal from the world. Although it is unclear if she actually joined the core community of religious at Saint-Pierre-aux-Nonnains, the nature of her *precarium* (an annual rent in return for her donation to the monastery, which Ricuin augmented with a few extra properties) and her son's involvement in the transaction may have riled those who found themselves drawn to Saint Benedict's principle of communal property and individual poverty or who simply objected to the fact that these *precaria* and prebends encroached on the community's endowment.

Another connected issue that might have stirred the minds of religious at the time was the status of women after they took the veil. In the revised edition of the *Life, Translations, and Miracles of Saint Glossinde*, John of Saint-Arnoul recounts an incident that recalls one of several issues debated in female communities of the early tenth century. It concerns a notable inhabitant of Metz, a man named Adelmann, who had given his daughter as a very young child to the monastery of Sainte-Glossinde. When the girl had reached adulthood, she fled the monastery and married someone against her father's wishes and without his knowledge. After a while, though, she returned to Metz to visit her friends and relatives. Once there, she was struck by a debilitating paralysis of her limbs. Her father had her carried back to the monastery, where she accepted her veil again, and repeated her vows.[14] This anecdote, although obviously cast to celebrate Saint Glossinde's intercessory powers, may recall differences of opinion at the monastery on whether women religious, particularly those who had entered the convent in childhood, were free to abandon their religious state to enter into matrimony.

Presumably, the debate over women's observance at Saint-Pierre-aux-Nonnains touched on issues more diverse and spiritually profound than return gifts and the permanent status of veiled women. But the above testimonies are sufficient indications to argue that, among female communities, there likely existed different expectations with regard to the behavior and status of women religious. In fact, John's account in the *Life* of John of Gorze invites us to read in a different light reports of clashes between women seeking to enter a religious life and clerical agents. In the *Deeds of the Bishops of Toul*, we read that Bishop Gerard of Toul (963–94) attempted to found an urban monastery in the city, but failed because of the refusal of the women to observe the vow of chastity.[15] Instead of simply accepting that these women had been unable to contain their sexual urges, we should at least consider the possibility that they had refused to accept the bishop's instruction to consider their veiled status as permanent, not wishing to renounce definitively any future outside of the convent. Alternatively, the dispute may have revolved around issues of the sisters' property rights, which clashed with an episcopal push for a system of communal property. In either scenario, we should definitely not discount the possibility that the sisters resisted the bishop's initiative not because of personal preferences, but because of an informed opinion they had acquired through study and debate on how to organize religious life for women. Certainly Gerard and his clerics were not the only ones to use accusations of sexual misconduct to dismiss objections voiced by women religious who opposed the rigid views of reformist bishops.[16]

These episodes, even though they offer highly fragmented views of female spirituality in this period, reveal the falsehood of the notion that women religious in the early decades of the tenth century lacked the interest or ability to either explore their own spirituality or critique the behavior of other female monastics. In fact, we know that the intellect and views of some of these women—several of whom did not belong to Benedictine institutions—were highly valued by a number of male reformers. John of Gorze, for instance, considered his exchanges with Geisa and the collaborative study with the sisters of Saint-Pierre-aux-Nonnains of equal importance in shaping his future identity as reformer and abbot as were his exchanges with hermits, monastic leaders, and other male associates. Further on in John's *Life*, John of Saint-Arnoul mentions how his hero, after having left Metz, frequently returned to visit a number of individuals with whom he engaged in spiritual conversation. He then goes on to cite several of these by name, and the first two mentioned are Geisa and her aunt.[17] The biographer also indicates that other individuals from John's circle likewise established meaningful spiritual relations with women. In the town of Verdun, the hermit Humbert retreated into a cell (*cellula*) from where he engaged with two pious anchoresses living in a nearby cell and with at least two other women seeking his spiritual advice. Out of the latter two, one later moved to Bouxières and subsequently became—according to the author of the *Life* at least—the first abbess of the monastic community there.[18]

Through the link with Bouxières, we encounter a number of women exploring different, nonmonastic options for leading a life devoted to religious pursuits.[19] Bishop Gozelin of Toul's 938 foundation charter of a Benedictine nunnery near the village alludes to a prior settlement of female recluses, initiated or at least facilitated by a woman named Hersendis, who had donated some of her own properties in the early 930s.[20] Likewise, the attempt of Gozelin's successor Gerard to found an urban monastery at Toul may have been designed to contain an emerging urban phenomenon of unveiled women exercising some form of ascetic withdrawal, either living in their own houses, a cell, or a communal building. As we shall see in chapter 5, in 960s Verdun there were a number of "wandering women" (*gyrovagae*) who subsisted on part of the revenues of a number of properties belonging to a local hospice. And the late tenth-century foundation of Sainte-Marie-aux-Nonnains in Metz may have originated as a spontaneous settlement of "handmaidens of God" (*ancillae Dei*) serving a hospice (*xenodochium*), until Adalbero II of Metz (984–1005) or, less likely, his successor Thierry II (1005–47) turned it into a Benedictine monastery.[21] Presumably some of these women had not merely been exploring an unconventional lifestyle, but had also been looking to have a different kind of impact on society from individuals living in a cloistered regime. Since ninth-century lawmakers had explicitly prohibited the involvement of women religious in charitable tasks, confrontations with the local clergy were inevitable.

Bishops and other members of the male ecclesiastical establishment feared that new models of religious vocation for women would pose a serious competitive threat to veiled religious or even entirely replace them, as appears to have happened in contemporary Anglo-Saxon England.[22] Surely these concerns were based on fears of losing control over the female religious phenomenon, and as we shall see further, in some cases clerical agents deliberately spread rumors of misconduct to prevent women from taking such initiatives. It is far from certain, though, that all of them held a negative view of noncloistered forms of religious life. But even those who looked at these women in a positive light would have been concerned about their reputation and the potentially damaging effect of bad rumors on the reputation of female religious generally. In the *Life* of John of Gorze, we find a passage regarding his interventions in communities of women religious. Revealingly, it begins with a discussion of women's housing arrangements:

> He ripped the housings of the religious from the bite of all evil suspicions, for he badly suffered that they were thought of as inferior not based on facts, but on rumor; and imposed on them the same institutions as that of the monks and precisely the same conduct corresponding to the strength of their sex.[23]

We have no way of telling where the source of these rumors lay. But the text is clear enough in indicating that detractors relied on a discourse that explicitly associated the alleged lack of strength of women religious in pursuing an ascetic life, their ambiguity in organizing it, and their supposedly lax observance of regulations for enclosure. At the same time, the text reveals that an experimentation with permeable forms of physical and spiritual enclosure was more general than the handful of cases mentioned in the primary evidence suggests.[24]

Given these indications of an ongoing reflection on women's spirituality inside and outside of monastic contexts, it should not surprise us to find evidence of communication and even significant overlap between the two. Such is the *Passion* of Saint Maxellendis of Caudry, a narrative written between around 925 and 940–45 and recently studied by Anne-Marie Helvétius.[25] According to the hagiographer, Maxellendis, a young noblewoman, suffered martyrdom at the hands of her husband, who was unwilling to accept her decision to dedicate herself entirely to the service of God. The text emphasizes the saint's ability to resist the temptations of the world through study and prayer and to behave as a living exemplar of female lay virtue. So she visits church daily, devotes herself to fasting and prayer, distributes alms to the poor, visits the sick, and cares for orphans and widows "who are real widows." She does not wear ostentatious clothes, participate in banquets, or have a retinue of female servants, and generally avoids the company of men, particularly young ones. Maxellendis is a special saint in that, unlike many other female subjects of contemporary hagiography, she is not an abbess or even a woman religious; nor is she particularly celebrated for her martyrdom. Instead, the hagiographer prefers to focus on the image of a laywoman seeking—and arguably achieving—perfection through study and prayer without having made monastic vows. Hers is a life worthy of imitation: the text repeatedly insists on the need to follow Maxellendis's example and the benefits that will certainly come from doing so.[26]

While the prologue addresses itself to "brothers"[27] and the main text is directed to "the order of ministers of both sexes, namely clerics and women dedicated to God, so that they accomplish in this place the required office until the end of time,"[28] it is likely that the intended audience of the *Life* was mixed, both monastic and lay. Helvétius has reasoned that the description of Maxellendis's virtues indicates that the women at Caudry—presumably widows and virgins living communally but in close interaction with the world—at the time of writing were behaving in inappropriate ways for members of a religious community.[29] But the point of the text is precisely that Maxellendis does not belong to a religious community and therefore is not acting differently from other women formally devoted to a religious life but from other women living in the world. Although the notion that hagiography could fulfill a normative or corrective function in religious communal settings is surely correct,[30] in this case such reasoning may not be entirely justified. In particular, it overlooks the fact that behind the primary monastic audience of the text potentially lay a much larger one, consisting of the young girls receiving education at the monastery, of the female relatives and patronesses of the religious, and arguably of other parties too. To this second audience, the text offers a template for the achievement of Christian perfection while remaining a part of secular society.

This highly dynamic and highly diverse religious culture for women was brutally suppressed—but not extinguished—in the mid-tenth century. Looking for means to bring monastic institutions under their control (or that of their relatives) and monopolizing moral judgment over the conduct of the religious, bishops in particular radically drew the card of a single, rigidly observed model for organizing women's observance: Benedictinism.

"Women Religious Wandering Like Sheep": Episcopal Reform in Toul

Bishop Gozelin of Toul (922–66), a former secretary of King Charles the Simple, in the mid-930s became active as a reformer at the male house of Saint-Evre, where he called monks from Fleury, then from Gorze, to instruct the community on Benedictine principles of monastic life.[31] Almost immediately, he also moved to establish a female Benedictine presence at Bouxières, a small settlement overlooking the confluence of the rivers Moselle and Meurthe, a few miles from the town of Nancy. In the 938 foundation charter of the monastery, Gozelin describes the site as consisting of nothing but a nearly ruined church, visited by pilgrims seeking the Virgin's intercession for their ailments. The passage describing his intervention there is worth citing:

> Through the foresight of God, we found some women religious, wandering like sheep but looking for the pasture of eternal life, fervent in the love of God and wishing to serve Him in a remote location. Deeply moved with compassion, having consulted the aforementioned Abbot (Archenbald) and our other God-fearing faithful, we gave them the aforementioned small cell as a place to live, and made one of them, namely Rothildis, their abbess, so that she would reign over their lives.[32]

As we saw earlier, the charter's reference to the "women religious, wandering like sheep" likely disguises the existence from around 930 of a religious settlement for women consisting of *mansiunculae*, small dwellings situated in proximity to the local sanctuary.[33] The preserved summary of a lost charter Gozelin himself had issued at the beginning of the decade mentions a few small houses, a cemetery, and tithes belonging to a church dedicated to Saint Martin.[34] And according to Bouxières's charter record, before 938 Hersendis donated allodial property on three different occasions, presumably because she intended to withdraw there or because she wished to support the women already living at the site.[35] Of these, two were the previously mentioned associates of the hermit Humbert.[36] One of them was a noblewoman named Rothildis, Gozelin's first appointee as regular leader of the community.[37] Another driving force behind the foundation, the recently widowed Countess Eva of Chaumontois, later on was buried in the sisters' abbatial church.[38]

Gozelin's role as principal patron of Bouxières and his self-attributed prominence as founder has been explained by the influence of a "reformist élan" at the nearby male house of Saint-Evre.[39] Yet, even though there is good reason to believe that Gozelin's admiration of the Benedictine *Rule* (and a simultaneous drive to contain spontaneous initiatives by women religious) was sincere,[40] that alone is not sufficient. It explains neither his apparent urge to erase the memory of the community's prefoundation history, including the difficulty of discerning the precise role of Hersendis and Eva in the early community, nor Gozelin's desire to establish his own towering prominence in the community's affairs.[41] Instead, we need to understand these interventions in light of an attempt to create an institution focused on himself and his relatives, which, furthermore, was to have an identity distinct from the diocese's other female monastery of Remiremont. With that institution now tied up in Giselbert's

FIG. 7. Bishop Gozelin's foundation charter for Bouxières, 938. Copyright Österreichische Nationalbibliothek. Reproduced with permission.

ascent as duke of Lotharingia, Bouxières represented for Gozelin and his close relatives their claim on a preeminent role in regional politics.

Gozelin and Giselbert had both risen to prominence because they had chosen opposite sides in the political struggles of previous decades. In the later 910s, Count Ricuin of Verdun and Giselbert had rebelled against King Charles the Simple, setting in motion a process that eventually led to the latter's removal from the Lotharingian political scene and in 919 to Giselbert's proclamation of his allegiance to the German ruler. For his part, Gozelin, a member of the noble family of Bassigny and a possible relative of Bishop Gozelin of Langres (922–31), had not forsaken his loyalty to Charles: he is attested as the king's secretary until at least 922.[42] He and his namesake were subsequently compensated for their enduring loyalty by receiving episcopal seats. The choice of dioceses was appropriate because both Toul and Langres belonged to the Western Frankish realm, but things quickly took a turn for the worse when, in 922–923, Charles was definitively overthrown, and Lotharingia was lost to the Western Frankish throne. In 925, Giselbert submitted himself to Eastern Frankish King Henry's authority, and Toul became a part of the Lotharingian/ Eastern Frankish realms. Gozelin quickly gained the Ottonians' favor and obtained from both Henry and his son Otto I several privileges and the transferral of several monasteries to his bishopric's ownership and was likely also awarded the county of Toul. Even so, lingering rivalries remained between Gozelin's relatives and the group of aristocrats who had rebelled against Charles, now seeking, under Giselbert's aegis, to establish themselves as the dominant aristocratic players in the Toul region.[43] Bouxières's foundation consolidated, in an institutional form, the enduring tension between the two factions.

Fracture lines in the Upper Lotharingian aristocratic landscape thus became formally represented in the ownership, patronage, and, arguably, also the discipline of local monasteries. In his rivalry with Giselbert's faction and in implementing his plans to consolidate it institutionally, Gozelin had found a welcome ally in Bishop Adalbero I of Metz (929–62). In 935, Adalbero agreed to Gozelin's suggestion of transferring ownership of the local parish at Bouxières (which belonged to Metz) to Gozelin's own diocese.[44] Adalbero's compliance, aside from a shared interest in Benedictine reform, was likely grounded in the notion that his family too had been politically short-changed over the preceding two decades. Adalbero's father, Wigeric, had been a palatine count of Charles the Simple (and previously a local count under Zwentibold and Louis the Child) and in 915 had succeeded Renier I of Hainaut as the principal military leader in Lotharingia. On Wigeric's death (c. 916–19), Adalbero's mother Kunigunde married Count Ricuin of Verdun, and following Ricuin's death in 923, Giselbert essentially took over Wigeric's duties, assuming a position that would ultimately make him the first nominal duke of Lotharingia.[45]

Even though Adalbero was subsequently able to forge a lustrous ecclesiastical career as bishop of Metz, clearly his aristocratic relatives had lost much of their political prominence. This sparked a series of aggressive countermeasures. In 923, he called on his ally Count Boso to assassinate his mother's new husband Ricuin, presumably to stop the latter from further encroaching on the properties of Adalbero's relatives.[46] And as we shall see further in his dealings with the abbeys of Hastière and Saint-Pierre-aux-Nonnains, Adalbero was evidently partial to the notion that one way to reestablish some of his family's former status was to claim, as bishop, the ownership of female institutions and implicate his relatives in their government and patronage.[47] The transferral of the parish at Bouxières, while a minor transaction in economic terms, should therefore be categorized as an act of major political significance.

Underneath Gozelin's image as founder of Bouxières ran a complex web of aristocratic alliances and rivalries. As John Nightingale points out, Bouxières's patronage in the middle decades of the tenth century represents continuously shifting alliances, driven by different aristocratic clans with their own political agendas, as surely would have been the case at Remiremont.[48] Yet Gozelin made sure that his own and his relatives' involvement in Bouxières was and remained the focus of this institution's public image. For instance, of Abbess Rothildis we know that she was related to the region's highest elite and likely belonged to the prominent Bosonid family, whose involvement in Bouxières's patronage is well established.[49] But this status is not reflected in her documented agency as abbess. Even though she is mentioned in numerous charters from the late 930s onward, during Gozelin's lifetime we never see her engaged in any legal activity,[50] and the only document to describe her as anything but a passive participant in the abbey's government dates from 966, the same year Gozelin died.[51] Local memories of Bosonid and other donors also pale in comparison to those of the tightly knit, interconnected group of people, most likely relatives of Gozelin, belonging to what Robert-Henri Bautier has referred to as the "Frambert clan."[52] Thus the fact that Hersendis was not completely erased from Bouxières's prefoundation memory is likely due to the fact that she was related to Gozelin and the Metz cleric Odelric, who is first attested in the charter evidence in 959–60 and subsequently came to control the monastery.[53] As for himself, Gozelin expected a place of distinction in the commemorative practices of the religious. In his foundation charter, he asked, in return for his efforts and for the liberty of electing their own abbess, that the sisters daily recite the psalm *De profundis* and a prayer for his benefit. After his death he was buried in the abbatial church.[54]

In the early 960s, Gozelin's twilight years, his relative Odelric obtained the lay abbacies of Bouxières,[55] Remiremont, and Saint-Arnoul in Metz, before taking the archiepiscopal throne of Reims.[56] His ascension marked a temporary victory for an aristocratic clan that had been marginalized in regional politics since the rebellion against Charles the Simple and had been seeking to reestablish itself ever since.[57] Odelric's assumption of control over Bouxières and Remiremont was undoubtedly of particular significance for him and his relatives, as both monasteries were situated in the *pagus Calvomontensis*, an area politically dominated by Odelric's father and brother.[58] Particularly after Abbot Archenbald of Saint-Evre—another institution closely associated with Gozelin and his relatives—obtained confirmation of Bouxières's properties from Pope Stephen VIII, the monastery's estates grew considerably, not in the least because Odelric himself and his mother Eva, countess of Chaumontois, had made significant donations of their own.[59] In a charter Odelric issued in 959, he accordingly speaks of the monastery's community as "a considerable number of maidens."[60] And in another from 966, Duke Frederic of Lotharingia (959–78)—Bishop Adalbero of Metz's brother—referred to Bouxières as "the place where the solicitude of holy virgins tirelessly toils in the veneration of the divine."[61] It is possible that by then, Frederic had replaced Odelric in his dominant position at Bouxières. But more than likely, Frederic would have identified himself as the abbey's lay advocate, a position now increasingly recognized as a meaningful and politically attractive alternative to the lay abbacy.[62]

Such intertwining of aristocratic rivalries with the interests and management of female monasteries made communities of women religious vulnerable to shifts in their patrons' situation. When Gozelin died, his successor Gerard was recruited from a Rhineland family by Archbishop Bruno of Cologne and for obvious reasons showed no inclination to continue Gozelin's familial politics.[63] It is possible that he, like Gozelin, tried to mark this power shift by founding his own female monastery: hence, maybe, the attempt previously discussed to found a nunnery next to a new urban church at Toul dedicated to Saint Gengulph.[64] Over the next decade-and-a-half, Bouxières's group of donors changed completely. Bautier has identified among the new patrons of the monastery several faithful allies of King (then Emperor) Otto I, who, along with Bishop Gerard, donated significant properties in the area to the religious as a means of getting rid of estates situated in a peripheral region of the Empire.[65] A revealing document of Bouxières's marginal position politically is a charter from around 978, where the widow of a Count Folcuin declares that her donation of a property in Bouxières's vicinity will remain valid "whoever God may select to be the king there."[66]

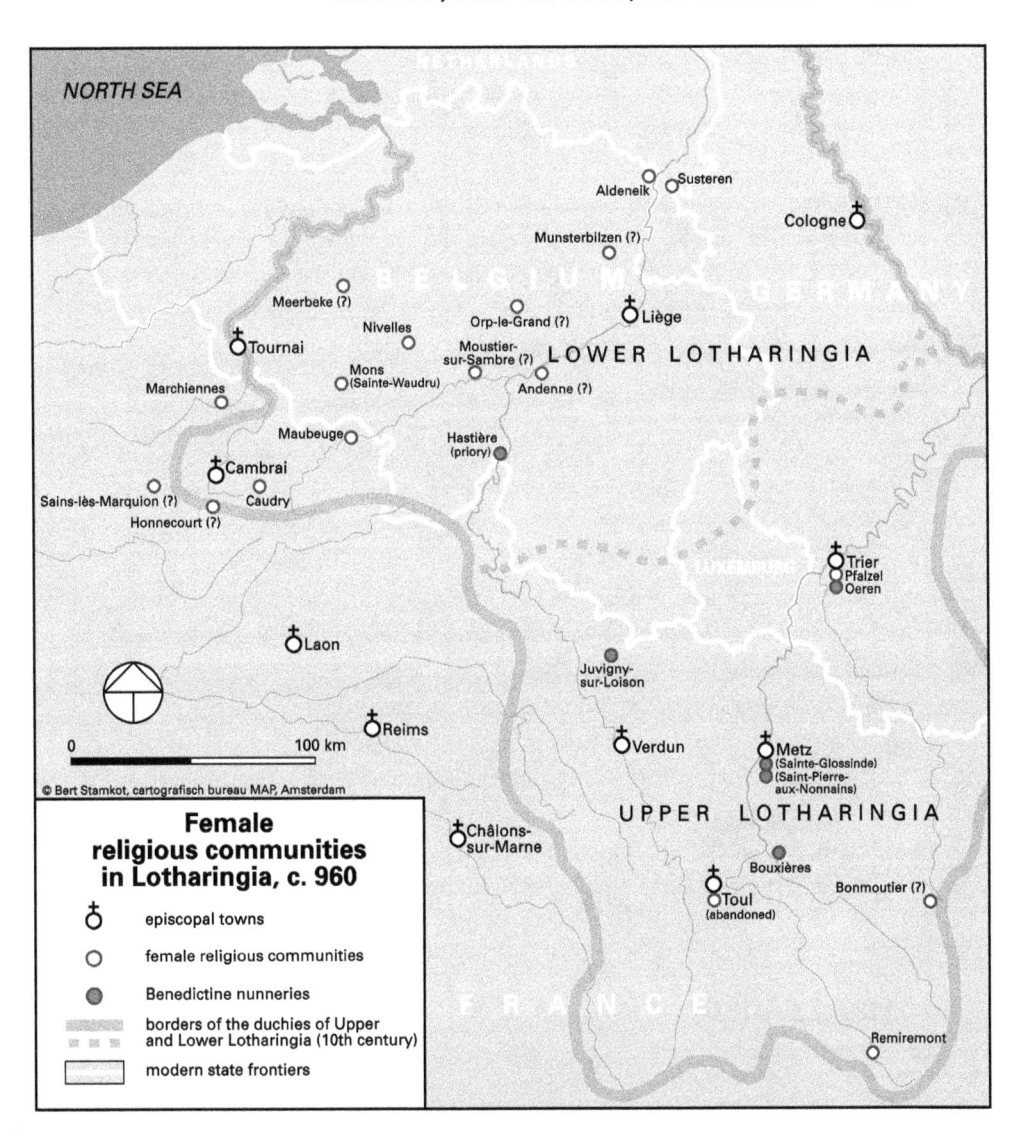

MAP 2. Female religious communities in Lotharingia, c. 960. Copyright Bert Stamkot, Cartografisch Bureau, MAP, Amsterdam. Reproduced with permission.

In Bautier's understanding, the concerns of these new donors lay less in establishing long-term links with and through the monastery than in offloading (in return for the sisters' prayer service) properties situated in a region they considered politically unstable, and therefore insecure. But then he may be painting too cynical a picture of their motivations. Heinrich Sproemberg has observed that the Ottonian rulership—either Otto I himself or his brother,

Archbishop Bruno of Cologne—were still actively involved in Lotharingian institutions as a means of securing authority in the region.[67] In 963–65, Otto gave the religious of Bouxières considerable properties, requesting that they yearly celebrate his ordination by having a "very plentiful" meal, that they pray for his sake several times a month, and, following his death, celebrate his obit and offer a meal to at least twelve poor people.[68] Meanwhile, the community was also still recruiting new members. As late as 960–65, Count Teutbert gave property to the abbey for the burial of his wife and the oblation of his daughter Rotlindis.[69] And in 966, a woman named Ermenaidis gave property for the benefit of the community, whose members at that time included her two daughters.[70]

Still, it is true that none of these individuals (including Bishop Gerard) achieved or sought to obtain prominent status as the abbey's principal benefactor. By 966, the documentation also shows glimpses of disputes with donors' heirs, who felt short-changed by grants that had been made to the monastery by their female relatives.[71] And whatever the second-generation donors had been aiming to achieve, their patronage was limited and short-lived. From a charter issued in 1027 by Conrad II at the request of Bishop Bruno of Toul, later Pope Leo IX, we can infer that the later 970s marked the end of the abbey's second and final phase of expansion. For the entire period 979–1026, we have the record of one solitary donation, by Bishop Berthold of Toul.[72] Bouxières's flame had shone brightly for a good three decades: for the next eight centuries, the religious there would subsist on little else than the material and symbolic legacies of that first flourishing.

A Family Affair: Reform in Metz

Likewise revealing is the body of evidence that relates to institutions reformed in the same decades by Adalbero of Metz, namely Saint-Pierre-aux-Nonnains and Sainte-Glossinde, both in Metz, and Hastière, in the diocese of Liège. A charter of 945, although it was tampered with in the late 1130s,[73] is valuable in giving us Adalbero's version of what happened to the latter two institutions. It claims that he first obtained permission from the emperor to transfer ownership of the estate of Hastière and its monastery to Sainte-Glossinde. Then he proceeded to reform Sainte-Glossinde, previously "defamed through bad actions" (*in malibus actibus diffamatum*). Warfare, "the violent inundation of tyrants" (*violentia tyrannorum inundatione*), and general incompetence on the part of the abbey's leadership had depleted the monastery's resources, with catastrophic consequences for the spirituality and conduct of the religious. To remedy these problems, Adalbero decided "to restore (the women's observance) to the norm of Saint Benedict, as it used to be practiced there, and to make our niece Himiltrudis the leader of the sisters living in God in this life."[74]

Fifteen years later, in 960, Adalbero and his brother Frederic of Lotharingia approached Emperor Otto I to confirm the bishop's recent intervention at Metz's other female institution of Saint-Pierre-aux-Nonnains. Otto, who since Giselbert's revolt of the late 930s had been seeking ways to integrate Lotharingia definitively into his realm, responded favorably to these and other requests to assert his lordship over monastic institutions.[75] Again available only in an interpolated form,[76] his charter expresses support for Adalbero and Frederic's efforts to "make possible, through the authority of our corroboration, that the sisters of the aforementioned monastery would fight, according to the institutions of the holy father Benedict, under the *Rule* and an abbess." The charter continues by stating the emperor's protection over properties obtained before the introduction of the *Rule*, "to make sure that the nuns would be able without grave labor to fight for the Lord, and intercede joyfully for ourselves and our successors." It also awards the sisters the right to freely elect abbesses and lay advocates.[77] Thus a reform project, pursued over the course of fifteen years, appeared completed: Adalbero had halted the moral decline of the Metz female religious, intervened in the negligent leadership of the monasteries, restored observance of the *Rule*, and—partially with Otto's assistance—stemmed the tide of lay attacks on these communities and their estates.

Neither the Sainte-Glossinde nor the Saint-Pierre-aux-Nonnains evidence allows us to verify the extent to which Adalbero's claims about a crisis occurring at these institutions is at all accurate. When drafting his charters, he evidently relied on a fairly generic discourse of reform, the best account of which may be found in John of Saint-Arnoul's *Life, Translations, and Miracles of Saint Glossinde*:

> He committed himself ... to retrieve the soul of monasteries ... that for many years already had fallen, inside and outside, in their spiritual and bodily works.... The first of his spiritual works was the monastery of Gorze ... with Lord Einold who had been promoted to his post because of his great virtues, and a very large number of religious coming together there, and spiritually conspiring in the beatitude of the poor to (follow) Saint Benedict's *Rule*. In accordance with this example, he also organized the other monasteries, as regards inside and outside affairs, of men and women, including those known as canons.[78]

And as with Gozelin's foundation charter for Bouxières, Adalbero's 945 charter, along with Otto's 960 privilege, presents readers with a distorted view of the nature and context of these interventions. The former claims that Adalbero has "restored" Saint-Pierre-aux-Nonnains's former Benedictine identity, a statement that justifies the new regime by shaping an invented past for that institution. The latter ignores previous, indigenous efforts by the Saint-Pierre-aux-Nonnains religious and their *hebdomadarius* John to reform the local observance.[79] Allegedly, the introduction of a rigidly observed Benedictine regime had not only solved all of the problems these communities had been facing, but had also rooted out their underlying causes. Adalbero's rhetoric postulated the *Rule*'s objective superiority over all other interpretations of the monastic ideal and implicitly rejected the need for religious to shape their own views through study and debate.

Exactly why Adalbero adopted this radical stance is difficult to say. It is possible that he sincerely thought the religious would benefit from his ending both lay ownership of the monastery and the practice of bestowing members of the community and patrons with benefices and especially *precaria*, such as the one Ricuin had bestowed on Remlindis and her son in his 918 charter. But as far as we can tell, the abolition of the lay abbacy did not signify a fundamental shift in elite secular control over these institutions. Far more certain, however, is the fact that there were significant political benefits to the transition. Increasingly, Benedictine reforms were becoming the strategy of choice by which lay and especially ecclesiastical rulers could both remove rival aristocratic clans from a controlling position at monastic institutions and prevent the lordship from being disputed every time a lay abbot or lord resigned or died.[80] Like kings and territorial lords in earlier decades, Adalbero relied on a discourse of protection and restitution of usurped properties to claim a lordship position over these monasteries. But he added to this another powerful argument: by the introduction of a Benedictine regime and its concomitant abolition of the lay abbacy, he was able to reject any present and future claims by the bishops' lay rivals to a controlling stake in monastic institutions. Even if the future election of regular monastic leaders would remain potential arenas of political conflict, any elected candidates would henceforth be subject to the approval of the bishop.

Adalbero was confident that adoption of this strategy would secure, not just for the bishopric but especially also for him and his relatives, long-term control over these highly significant institutional assets. The 945 charter's focus on transferring the estate of Hastière to the religious of Sainte-Glossinde and its timing are very revealing in this respect. Hastière had been founded around 900 as a female monastery by Adalbero's father, Count Wigeric. In 912–15, Wigeric gave Hastière to the church of Liège, but immediately received it again as a benefice for himself and his wife. Adalbero came to inherit the benefice and apparently considered it his private property. In 945, he took advantage of a vacancy on Liège's episcopal throne following the death of Bishop Richer to give Hastière to the religious at Metz.[81] But he also took care to prevent the transaction from benefiting anyone but himself and his relatives, by initiating a Benedictine reform of Sainte-Glossinde. From now on, no lay lord from a rival family could claim a controlling stake over this episcopal monastery.[82] By appointing his niece Himiltrudis, Adalbero also clearly indicated that, for him, the boundaries between episcopal ownership of the monastery and his familial interests were indistinct at best.[83] At Saint-Pierre-aux-Nonnains, a similar pattern of action is revealed through Otto's 960 charter. As it turns out, this document was issued just one year after Otto and his brother, Archbishop Bruno of Cologne, had appointed Adalbero's brother Frederic as vice-duke of Lotharingia.[84] Despite the fact that his position in the Ottonian hierarchy of power would be considerably lower than that of previous dukes of Lotharingia, Frederic likely took the position of lay advocate of Saint-Pierre-aux-Nonnains, as he would do at a number of other Lotharingian institutions, male and female.[85] His and Adalbero's intervention effectively blocked a return of the relatives or associates of Sainte-Glossinde's former lord, Count Ricuin,[86] or the ascent of any other rival family through a claim to the monastery's lay lordship. Their subsequent move to formally profess their protection of the sisters' interests and to have this sanctioned by Otto crowned the campaign of the two men to regain, at least symbolically, a position of regional prominence.[87]

It really is no surprise to find that episcopal interventions at these and other institutions met with considerable skepticism, particularly from individuals in the so-called group of Gorze reformers. John of Gorze and his peers were all too aware that Adalbero's original support for the 934 Benedictine reform of Gorze, although undoubtedly informed by sincere religious motives, conveniently removed the rival Matfrid clan from the lay abbacy.[88] Even more damningly, Adalbero was known to have no objections to claiming Gorze's properties when this suited his private interests.[89] Given John's personal connections to Saint-Pierre-aux-Nonnains and its membership, he may have also resented the bishop's involvement in the murder of the community's (and John's) former lord Ricuin and likewise the unfair dismissal of the sisters' behavior and spirituality. As for the women religious themselves, we can only wonder how they responded to these episcopal interventions. Certainly, they would have been aware of the fact that, in other regions of Lotharingia, the support of rulers for women's monasticism did not necessarily make them secure champions of the interests of specific communities. In 936, Otto I in a solemn charter had confirmed Giselbert's restitutions of usurped properties to the community of Aldeneik, stating the need to provide "the women religious serving the Lord there honorably and devotedly" with adequate resources.[90] But a mere sixteen years later, he transferred ownership to the church of Liège. In the document that formalizes this transaction, he simply referred to Aldeneik as "a certain monastery called Eiche," as if to indicate that its relevance here was strictly as a commodity.[91] Whether or not the lack of mention of the religious was deliberate cannot be established: but the document does support the notion that rulers, be they ecclesiastical or secular, could be quite ruthless in their dealings with monastic groups that had formerly enjoyed their attention and patronage.

Inner Realities of Reform

Despite the reformers' claims that they were restoring proper observance at female communities, sanitizing monastic institutions and economies, and rooting out lay abuse of monastic offices and incomes, little concrete information can be extracted from the sources regarding the impact of their interventions on the sisters' lives. Admittedly, the privileges awarded in these decades to reformed institutions look considerable and almost certainly boosted the communities' incomes. Otto I's 953 charter for Oeren, an institution recently turned into a Benedictine nunnery,[92] split the abbey's estates into two parts: one that was to serve the community's needs, and another that could be given to laymen as a benefice; the latter was also designed to cover the expenses of military service to the sovereign.[93] And his 960 privilege for Saint-Pierre-aux-Nonnains, discussed earlier in this chapter, likely freed resources needed for reconstruction of the abbatial church. Similar impulses were felt at Sainte-Glossinde, where Adalbero's intervention led to renewed promotion of the patron saint's cult. In a new version of the *Life, Translations, and Miracles of Saint Glossinde*, we read that Abbess Himiltrudis was beset by an "immoderate desire . . . to restore the mother of this place" and informed Bishop Adalbero of her intentions. Adalbero, assisted by Himiltrudis, and Abbots Einold of Gorze and Ansteus of Saint-Arnoul, then proceeded to elevate the saint's relics.[94] In a next phase, the abbatial church was extensively remodeled, which compelled the religious to temporarily abandon strict enclosure. It was also around this time that the community changed its patronym from Saint-Sulpice to Sainte-Glossinde.[95] The miracles added to the *Life* strongly insist on pilgrim interest in the saint and the urban character of Glossinde's cult, much as the older version of that text had done. But this time, there is also mention of men visiting the actual site of her grave—an indication, perhaps, of deliberate attempts to further broaden the appeal of her popular veneration.[96]

By contrast, we have no clear understanding of whether the free election of abbesses made much of a difference to the principle and practice of female monastic leadership. In a charter issued in 1012 by Benedict, abbot of Saint-Arnoul in Metz, and Abbess Hermentrudis of Sainte-Glossinde, there is no mention of a lay lord overseeing Hermentrudis, but an unidentified Count Gerard is mentioned among the list of witnesses, as is an advocate named Fulmer.[97] Lacking any further documentation, it is impossible to assess precisely the power relations between these individuals. Nor do we know whether the transition to the *Rule* had a decisive impact on the sisters' reputation and agency. At Saint-Pierre-aux-Nonnains, Abbess Hadewidis's (attested 960s–970s) exemplary behavior apparently warranted mention in the early 980s *Life* of Saint Caddroë, a narrative written at Caddroë's former institution of Saint-Felix, also in Metz.[98] And in a charter by Otto III from 993, which also mentions her successor Irmintrudis, she is remembered as "the venerable cultivator of religion."[99] It is worth noting, though, that a contemporary of Caddroë's

FIG. 8. Abbatial church of Saint-Pierre-aux-Nonnains, late tenth century. Copyright Joop van Meer. Reproduced with permission.

biographer, John of Saint-Arnoul, in the same years fondly remembered both women's "ambiguous" predecessor, Fredeburga. This suggests that Hadewidis's memory was positive for other reasons than that she simply observed and enforced the *Rule*, and that commentators were less concerned than we might think with religious' strict observance of that text. From the same time period, we also have a charter from the abbey of Saint-Evre in Toul that casually refers to a *sanctimonialis* who owned a property nearby. If Frank Hirschmann is correct in speculating that this woman came from Bouxières, there is a possibility that the observance practiced there was not a strictly Benedictine one.[100] If that were to be the case, the charter would be prime evidence to support the notion that not all male ecclesiastics—even those who are considered to be among the main promoters of Benedictine monasticism—objected in principle to such arrangements in female houses. In contrast, the memory response to Benedictine Abbess Himiltrudis of Sainte-Glossinde was muted,[101] perhaps because of her association with Adalbero and his brutal treatment of Saint-Pierre-aux-Nonnains. Despite her prominence as a monastic leader and John's fond remarks in the *Life, Translations, and Miracles of Saint Glossinde*, her name is notably absent from any necrologies originating from monasteries involved with the Gorze group of reformist abbots.[102]

Another good reason for us to be cautious in speculating on the possible beneficial effects of Benedictine reform—as opposed to those benefits that accrued through the active support of leaders who were seeking to gain prestige and power from their interventions—is the fact that we can see much the same transitions taking place at a number of institutions that were not formally subjected to the *Rule*. Perhaps in the 960s, the lay abbacy at Nivelles was transformed into a joint leadership of a lay proprietor (from 972 onward Empress Theophanu) and a "regular"—but not Benedictine—abbess.[103] Ottonian charters of the time also show rulers heavily promoting this royal institution, awarding market rights in the emerging trade center of Lennik, consolidating the sisters' ownership of distant properties, and awarding them the right to choose their lay advocate.[104] Following Theophanu's death in 991, the government of the abbey devolved exclusively onto the elected abbess. These arrangements, which Jacques Hoebanx awkwardly describes as a "semi-reform,"[105] had concrete implications that were not much different from the ones carried out at the Metz abbeys, and at Bouxières.

A second community for which we have evidence of significant change is Remiremont, like Nivelles an institution where historians have identified a semi-reform in the middle decades of the tenth century. More or less coinciding with Giselbert's restitution of usurped properties in the early 930s, scribes working on the *Liber memorialis* became more active in committing donations to written memory, now also filling up blank pages in a ninth-century gospel-book.[106] Shortly afterward, the nature of the notices also changed, offering more legal information, such as penal clauses, names of witnesses, and dates.[107] Overall, the liturgical purpose of the *Liber* retreated to the background, which raises strong suspicions that the community at that point began to rely on a second, now-lost codex for commemorative purposes.[108] Then, around 965, there followed a comprehensive new description of the abbey's properties, in a document described alternatively by scholars as a *censier* or a rent book.[109] Owing to a lack of comparative material from earlier periods, it is impossible to assess exactly how the monastic estate had changed and what exactly led the sisters to revise a putative older, similar document.[110] Possibly the purpose of this reorganization was the systematic allocation of certain incomes to specific institutions and offices within the monastery.[111] Another objective may have been to delegate to lay agents the collection of rents and other incomes in the more distant estates.[112] Notable in the diplomatic output of the religious are the increasing mentions of lay advocates.[113]

In reconstructing or understanding any of these transformations taking place over the course of the second half of the tenth century, speculation about a semi-reform will help us very little. Odelric—who, as has already been said, in the early 960s acted as lay abbot of both Remiremont and Bouxières and was a relative of Bishop Gozelin of Toul and an associate of his colleague Adalbero of Metz—must have favored the institutional model that was being implemented at Bouxières and the two Metz abbeys.[114] But all of this hardly constitutes solid evidence for a Benedictine reform at Remiremont.[115] Just as we saw for Nivelles, other factors were playing a significant role: interventions by lay and ecclesiastical lords seeking to create an advantage over their rivals, sincere efforts on the part of the abbey's secular lordship to reorganize community finances and institutions, and maybe even the sisters' own initiatives to secure the long-term future of their monastery. In particular, the growing prominence of advocates may well be indicative of a decision to formalize a network of lay associates consisting of prominent local power holders and to assist the religious in protecting their legal and financial interests, perhaps as a consequence of the disappearance of a single episcopal or secular lord powerful enough to assume these responsibilities. Creating additional pressure on the abbey's leadership was the continuing threat of foreign invasions. Thus we have a notice from the mid-tenth century with seven names "of those who died for the faith of Christ, killed by the pagans"; a further one mentioning a woman and her children who had been abducted by the "Huns" and subsequently redeemed; and another notice from the 970s–990s, halving the service due from an estate at Liézey following a "pagan" act of slaughter.[116]

Both at Remiremont and Nivelles, the growing prominence of local and regional lords around the year 1000 led to a shift in the abbey's lay lordship, as we shall see in chapter 5.

This chapter has followed a number of female institutions in the middle decades of the tenth century as they transitioned into new constellations or forms of ecclesiastical and lay lordship. Although parts of this process—influenced no doubt by an undercurrent of men and women sincerely pursuing different ways of organizing the life of women religious—arguably benefited the situation of some of these communities, the benefits came at a significant price. In the dioceses of Toul and Metz, bishops—wielding an official reformist rhetoric—willfully rejected the typically ambiguous discipline of women religious and dismissed their attested capacity to reflect on and debate the purpose of religious life. Although harder to distinguish in the primary evidence, nontraditional forms of female religious life were also brutally channeled, and their memory suppressed. These tactics would continue, with increasing violence and in a larger geographical area—and now focusing on institutional forms of ambiguous life rather than merely on informal initiatives—throughout the later tenth and early eleventh centuries. In fact, much of what we know about women religious in that period concerns these conflicts between rulers and ambiguous communities of women religious, while ordinary Benedictine communities almost entirely fade from the documentary record.

CHAPTER 5

New Beginnings

The decades between 970 and the middle of the eleventh century were a time of simultaneous expansion and contraction for women's monasticism in Lotharingia. From a purely quantitative perspective, the growth of female institutions is undeniable: lay and especially clerical rulers founded or reformed numerous communities, which they explicitly subjected to Saint Benedict's *Rule*. The picture becomes more complex, though, if we try to correlate this growth in numbers with changes in the socioeconomic and spiritual footprint of women religious. Overall, the endowments of the new foundations were modest, raising questions over whether founders and patrons were actually interested in expanding female monasticism as a spiritual and intellectual phenomenon. Possibly as a result, the new Benedictine nunneries appear as a localized, for the most part silent, cohort, leaving few traces in the documentary record with regard to their spirituality, understanding of self, and even their interactions with society at large.[1] Meanwhile, leaders of ambiguous communities, facing growing clerical criticism and encroachments, fiercely defended their subjects' interests. As part of this reaction, they can be observed reactivating some of the coping strategies discussed in earlier chapters.

This chapter reviews the evidence for these simultaneous processes of expansion (in numbers) and contraction (in terms of agency of the religious and their means of expression). It investigates, in order, the mechanisms and outcomes of a revived interest on the part of aristocratic agents in founding dynastic sanctuaries served by women religious; the more complex involvement of bishops in the creation of specifically Benedictine nunneries; and, finally, episcopal (and to a lesser extent also lay rulers') dealings with ambiguous monastic communities. From these discussions emerges a picture of an aggressive attempt on the part of clerical agents to insert female religious groups into ecclesiastical structures of power (underpinned by the aristocratic factions controlling key clerical posts) and equally aggressive moves to suppress the women's control over their own spiritual identities and material destinies. As we shall see in chapter 6, these interventions did not cause ambiguous modes of religious observance and identities to disappear. But they were key to shaping a discourse that denounced non-Benedictine forms of religious observance for women as unsuitable and to legitimizing a mode of conduct on the part of male reformers that increasingly disregarded the interests and opinions of the religious themselves.

Aristocratic Expansions

After almost two centuries of control by rulers and bishops, the progressive reorganization of secular power resulted in members of the regional and local aristocracy moving away from the customary practice of sending their daughters to established houses and renewed their interest in creating dynastic sanctuaries. As in Eastern Francia of the same period, to some members of these elites "female monasteries constituted . . . the sacred basis of familial power":[2] in these institutions, the intercessory prayer and commemorative practices of the religious would be primarily focused on the founders, their relatives and associates.[3] But for all three examples of proprietary foundations (Eigenklöster) reviewed in this chapter—that of Vergaville in Upper Lotharingia; several foundations by Pope Leo IX's relatives in the same region; and, finally, Thorn in Lower Lotharingia—the founders' endowments neither created a solid basis for the long-term survival of these communities nor allowed for any spiritual and intellectual activity beyond the bare minimum expected from small groups of women religious.[4]

For Upper Lotharingia, the vast diocese of Toul emerges as a first focus of aristocratic foundations. In the 960s, Bishop Gerard failed in his attempt to create an urban monastery for women in the city of Toul, allegedly because of the sisters' unwillingness to remain chaste.[5] But an aristocratic player was more successful. Around 966, Count Sigeric and his wife Betta founded the monastery of Vergaville on allodial lands in the extreme eastern parts of the diocese,

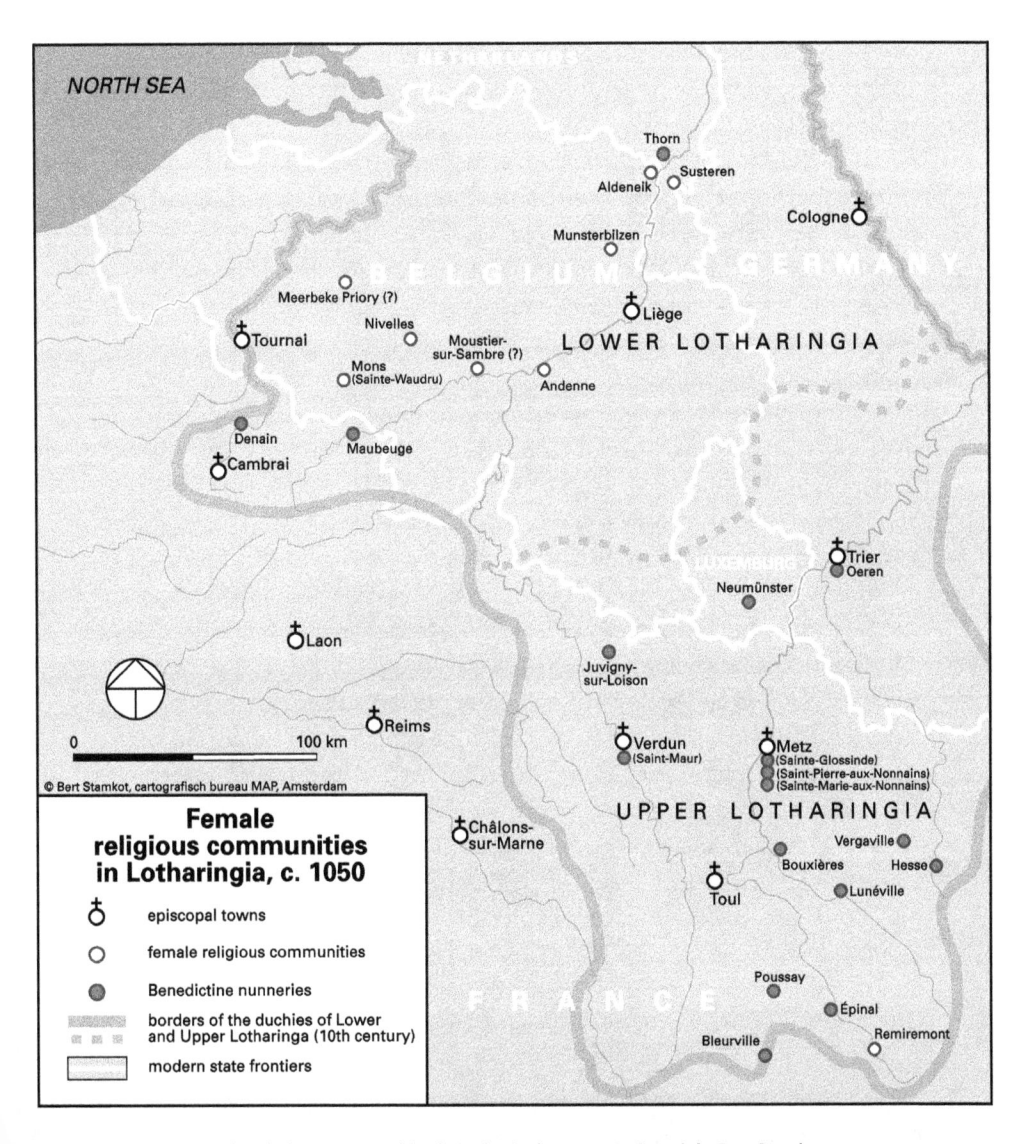

MAP 3. Female religious communities in Lotharingia, c. 1050. Copyright Bert Stamkot, Cartografisch Bureau, MAP, Amsterdam. Reproduced with permission.

in a swampy region known as Saulnois.[6] Sigeric belonged to the noble house of Salm, and according to the monastery's foundation charter, which unfortunately was tampered with at a later time, was able to transfer properties in the counties of Sarrebourg, Destry, and Mortagne and to claim lay lordship over the new community. Presumably—but far from certainly—the couple was sympathetic to the recent trend for founding Benedictine nunneries: the charter has Sigeric proclaim that "we built this monastery in honor of Saint Mary and all the saints, and we have sent there women religious, to converse in habit, under the *Rule*."[7]

Vergaville's geographical position, compared to the other female institutions of the diocese of Toul, was remote. The nearest was that of Bouxières, situated some fifty-five kilometers to the east; Remiremont was more than a hundred kilometers away. It therefore may seem like the foundation was only of marginal importance to other patrons and religious communities in the diocese. But appearances are deceptive, and in social terms the monastery was anything but marginal. The Salm family belonged to one of the most prominent aristocratic houses of Upper Lotharingia and is likely to have been associated with the palace mayor Godfrey, nephew of Emperor Otto I, and Ermentrudis, daughter of King Charles the Simple.[8] The family's involvement in monastic patronage networks also indicates that members systematically relied on these networks to sustain a position of prominence in the region's political elite. In the half decade leading up to Vergaville's foundation, Sigeric and Betta had given to the abbey of Bouxières, controlled at that time by Odelric, properties in Sotzeling and a village in the county of Destry.[9] The couple and their children also appear in Remiremont's *Liber memorialis*.[10]

Recently, though, both Bouxières and Remiremont had fallen into Odelric's hands. This must have sparked concerns over the fact that aristocratic interests and wealth tied up in these institutions were now controlled, to a greater or lesser extent, by the members of one family. Sigeric and Betta, having ostensibly reached a level of wealth and influence that allowed them to create a modest dynastic sanctuary served by nuns, undoubtedly also used their new foundation at Vergaville as a way of retaining for themselves and their relatives control over their ancestral estates. By creating a monastery on their own lands and controlled by their own relatives, the Salm family was henceforth able to reap the spiritual benefits of patronizing a religious institution and at the same time invest their wealth in the safest possible way.[11] Such tactics did not, however, inspire other members of the regional elite to join the family in investing in Vergaville. As with a development Karl Leyser has observed for early eleventh-century Saxony, local aristocrats may have become increasingly reluctant in these decades to bestow wealth on an institution in which they did not have a controlling stake and even wary of letting their female relatives pour their own resources into women's monasteries in general.[12] In fact, the lack of response was such that, for the remainder of its existence, the monastery relied heavily on Sigeric and Betta's original endowment.

A second, less extensively documented case study concerns the creation of several Upper Lotharingian institutions by relatives of Bishop Bruno of Toul.

Hesse, in the diocese of Metz, was one of the key sites representing the ascent of the counts of Dabo. Count Louis's daughter and her husband founded a new nunnery there;[13] meanwhile, Louis's grandson Bruno in 1026–27 was made bishop of Toul and in 1049 was elected as Pope Leo IX (1049–54). One year later, Leo issued a bull protecting the interests of the Hesse community and, at the request of his sister-in-law Mathilde and her son Henry I of Dagsburg-Egisheim, visited the nunnery and its abbess (his niece Gerberga) to dedicate three altars in the abbatial church.[14] Previously, Leo had already placed under the authority of the Holy See the nunnery of Heiligenkreuz, which his parents had founded and where they lay buried; in his privilege for that institution, he also referred to his own relatives as the abbey's rightful advocates.[15]

Leo's willingness to give priority to the aristocratic interests underlying the foundation of female institutions is further revealed when he supported Bleurville, a nunnery the counts of Toul founded shortly before 1050. His privilege for that institution dictated that the founding family of the counts of Toul would henceforth serve as a recruitment pool for the community's abbesses and lay advocates.[16] Yet it also stipulates that, should there not be a suitable candidate for the abbatial office among the members of the founding family, the abbess should be recruited from Remiremont, an institution that may have followed the *Rule* in some form or other, but would not have been unambiguously Benedictine in its practices.[17] None of the communities in which Leo was involved enjoyed particular efforts on the part of its founders or himself to broaden the community's appeal to aristocratic donors and the lay population generally.[18] Such an attitude rendered the long-term future of the religious precarious, and their overall impact on society in sociopolitical, cultural, and presumably also spiritual terms, modest at best.

A third example, that of Thorn in Upper Lotharingia, further illustrates the precariousness of aristocratic foundations and their presumably modest contribution to women's spirituality in the decades around the year 1000. Situated in the Meuse valley only a few kilometers northeast of Aldeneik, the monastery's origins are shrouded in mystery, as a key charter purporting to date from 992 has been unmasked as a sixteenth-century forgery. But the document does seem to hold value in identifying as founders Hereswint (also Hilsondis), countess of Stryen, and her husband Ansfrid II, Count of Louvain and Huy.[19] Ansfrid was a prominent member of the Lower Lotharingian elite: he owned properties in the Meuse region, Brabant, and Gelderland; was close to Otto I; and for a time was a part of the ruler's direct entourage, attending Otto's imperial coronation in Rome. On his return from that ceremony in 966, he married Hereswint. Between 975 and 995, the couple founded the monastery at Thorn and dedicated it to the Virgin Mary.[20]

Speaking from a juridical viewpoint, Thorn's status is unknown: the false charter of 992 claims the new monastery was created on Hereswint's allodial land, while a local tradition going back no further than the thirteenth century indicates that the site was actually a benefice given to Ansfrid by the bishop of Liège.[21] But in practice, Thorn's status was that of a proprietary monastery, much as had been the case for the vast majority of female monasteries before the interventions of Carolingian rulers in the later eighth and early ninth centuries. According to Hartwig Kersken, the couple aimed to state its membership of the Ottonian elites by imitating their Saxon peers' prolific founding of female "house monasteries." Additionally, the couple may have founded Thorn specifically in light of the absence of male offspring, and by doing so, have aimed to perpetuate their own memory and that of their direct relatives and provide a secure future for their daughters.[22] Indeed, local traditions claim that Hereswint entered the monastery at the end of her life and at her death was buried in the *secretarium* (perhaps an exterior crypt adjacent to the abbatial church)[23] and that two of her daughters were the first and second abbesses.[24] This reminds us of practices previously documented for Carolingian royalty—King Zwentibold's involvement with Susteren comes to mind—and for Merovingian aristocrats. According to Alain Dierkens, the name of the first abbess, Benedicta, indicates that the Thorn sister's observance was Benedictine from the beginning.[25] However, the earliest surviving mention of her name is in Aegidius of Orval's thirteenth-century chronicle, a fact that renders Dierkens's argument moot. Like that of many other communities from this period, the Thorn sisters' observance likely was ambiguously situated between different normative templates.[26]

The family's control over the monastery did not last long. Ansfrid in 995 was made bishop of Utrecht, and roughly a decade following Hereswint's death, he abandoned ownership of Thorn. In one interpretation, Ansfrid was pushed out of Thorn's ownership—as he had also been with the county of Huy—by an Ottonian rulership fearing too much concentration of power in the hands of one individual and seeking to transfer worldly authority over the region as much as possible to the bishop of Liège.[27] In another, he transferred ownership of the abbey in order to secure its immunity and royal protection and perhaps also to secure the future of his three daughters there.[28] A third and final one is that the now elderly Ansfrid was planning to be buried in his other foundation, the male monastery of Hohorst near Amersfoort, and had lost interest in managing the affairs of this female community.[29] Whatever the true circumstances, in 1007 Bishop Notger of Liège requested and received formal confirmation from Henry II that his bishopric owned the monastery.[30] Presumably the transfer and its formalization was rendered urgent by the fact that the nearby institution of Munsterbilzen was emerging as a major domain of the dukes of Lower Lotharingia. Attesting to Munsterbilzen's significance is the high aristocratic birth of its early eleventh-century Abbesses Ermengardis of Lutzelburg and Cunegondis of Chiny; the existence of locally struck silver *denarii*, imitations of the type of coins bearing the name of Otto III;[31] and the interment at the abbatial church of Gozelo, duke of Upper and Lower Lotharingia (d. 1044).[32] Certainly, the Liège clergy would have been aware of that the actions of Gozelo's relatives (the Verdun-Ardennes) in supporting female houses were politically significant. In a move perhaps similar to that of the bishops of Liège in the Meuse region, Gozelo's relatives had also taken over the Toul nunnery of Lunéville.[33] Gozelo's niece Oda, a former religious from Remiremont, was made abbess there by her brother, Bishop Adalbero III of Metz (1047–72).[34]

Ansfrid's removal from Thorn's lordship, besides indicating how volatile political power was on the local and especially the regional level, deprived the recently established community of its original purpose, which was to commemorate members of Hereswint and Ansfrid's family and presumably also represent their significance to the region's aristocratic networks. Yet it was probably a sound move for the community's long-term prospects. Indeed, the fact that Henry's privilege of 1007 mentions that Bishop Notger had given the sisters the incomes from three churches is indicative of a need to enlarge the community's estates in order to make the monastery viable.[35] We may wonder to what extent Thorn's founding couple had taken steps to ensure that there would be continuity in the monastery's patronage beyond their own and their daughters' deaths. Speaking in competitive terms, in the absence of Ansfrid and his relatives. Thorn's situation as a potential magnet for lay donors must have been far from rosy: with three prominent female institutions (Aldeneik, Munsterbilzen, and Susteren) already present in the region, broad interest in the new community was hardly guaranteed. Furthermore, the lack of a saint's cult, or some other reason that gave the site popularity as a destination for pilgrims, rendered even more problematic the Thorn community's long-term survival.

Henry's privilege for Thorn granted control over the local market, toll, and all instruments of juridical power that fell under its *ban* (right to exercise justice).[36] Although it is not mentioned in the charter, there is also evidence of a mint at Thorn, and at least one known coin is thought to date from the abbacy of Gerberga in the second quarter of the eleventh century.[37] All of these things brought in revenue that was presumably high enough to sustain a small community. Individual members may also have enjoyed the rewards of individual endowments or prebends, as did their peers at Remiremont, Epinal, and possibly also Bouxières.[38] And in an early 1040s hagiographic narrative written at Saint-Ghislain in Hainaut, there is also reference to the fact that the local abbess—possibly the aforementioned Gerberga—owned a *geneceum* (or *gynaeceum*), most likely a manufacture where female serfs worked to produce textile. If the testimonies regarding other *genecea* in the Rhine region and their production are anything to go by, some of the textiles made at the Thorn manufacture were sold on the open market.[39] Still, the costs of maintaining a female community were high: and as we shall see in the next chapter, soon the sisters would be looking to establish a local saint's cult.

Episcopal Foundations

Tied up in the same aristocratic networks but playing with political and representative stakes even higher than their lay peers, bishops were just as active as secular aristocrats in creating new female institutions. Investigation of episcopal foundations in both urban centers and rural areas reveals the extent to which these were designed not to promote the female religious phenomenon generally, but to achieve certain specific ends: the exercise and representation of episcopal authority, the strengthening of secular power networks focused on the bishop, and the enforcement of a specific view of religious life for women. The situation of the religious themselves and their impact in social and spiritual terms came a distant fourth to these concerns.

Illustrating this interplay of religious and nonreligious motives are developments in the episcopal town of Verdun. Up until the beginning of the eleventh century, the diocese of Verdun constituted a blank on the female monastic map, and initially Bishop Haimo (988–1024), like his predecessors, showed no interest in filling that gap. Then, in the 1020s, he founded the urban nunnery of Saint-Maur.[40] The reasons for this break with local tradition warrant close investigation and turn out to be threefold: the first (and most hypothetical) relates to current trends in female religious life, the second is political, and the third concerns personal or familial interests.

Turning first to Haimo's religious motivation, we find it likely matched the phenomenon, discussed in chapter 4, of women pursuing forms of religious life outside of the traditional institutional paradigms. In a similar fashion to what Julia Crick has suggested for Anglo-Saxon England, local lay elites may have withdrawn some of their support from a female monasticism controlled by the episcopate and instead made private arrangements for women seeking to pursue a religious life or simply withdraw from the matrimonial market.[41] Becoming a recluse or anchoress was the most obvious, widely tolerated answer to these objections. For instance, in the middle years of the 1010s, the widowed mother of Poppo, future abbot of Stavelot in the Ardennes region, followed her son to Verdun when he was recruited there by Abbot Richard of Saint-Vanne. There she became a recluse living alongside the monks.[42] Individual women may also have felt dissatisfied at the kind of agency open to them within the context of a cloistered community and looked for other ways of expressing their vocation. As we already saw in chapter 4, some recluses successfully claimed an authoritative public voice in matters spiritual and to some extent were able to influence the local church's male leadership. In the late 1040s, the monk Bertarius of Saint-Vanne wrote that around 1004 the townspeople of Verdun had been amazed to see an anchoress, after having spent many years in solitary confinement, abandon her cell to urge Abbot Fingen of Saint-Vanne to accept Richard (his future successor) and Frederic (count of Verdun) into his community.[43] Whether the episode happened as Bertarius describes it (or at all) is far less important than the fact that he expresses no surprise that such women make an impact on—indeed, have a say in matters that lawmakers had wanted to make the exclusive territory of male ecclesiastics. Some women may also—as anchoresses were wont to do—have offered aid for the local poor and sick, something that only became a problem when the success of such a lifestyle led to the rise of informal urban groups of women providing such services. A 971 charter by Bishop Wicfrid of Verdun (959–83) refers to "women dedicated to God" (*Deo sacratae*) who were leading a life of "wandering women" (*gyrovagae*) and "dishonestly and uselessly" receiving incomes from the properties associated with a—possibly preexisting—hospice.[44] While this document fails to clearly answer whether these *gyrovagae* had been personally caring for the needy and sick, it may nonetheless offer a glimpse into a reality where groups of women who had dedicated themselves to the religious life were pursuing active forms of charity.[45]

The 1020s creation of the nunnery of Saint-Maur may well have been Haimo's answer to an informal group of women seeking to become actively involved in Verdun's burgeoning urban society while living a life devoted to religious pursuits. But the foundation also coincided with a phase in diocesan politics where the bishop was struggling to retain control over his principal male monasteries, particularly that of Saint-Vanne, which had grown rich and influential under Abbot Richard (1004–46) and his powerful aristocratic patrons, the family of Verdun-Ardennes.[46] Saint-Vanne, technically an episcopal institution since its foundation as a Benedictine monastery by Bishop Berenger in 952, built much of its reputation on the fact that its abbatial church housed the graves of many of Verdun's earliest bishops, and that these were presented for veneration as saints. Over the course of the 1010s and 1020s, though, the monastery slipped from Haimo's control, as Richard and his aristocratic associates took hold of the city's sacred landscape. His foundation of Saint-Maur and its subordinate male chapter of Sainte-Croix (dedicated to Verdun's second bishop) have been explained as a move to mitigate Saint-Vanne's radiance.[47] A late 1040s charter by Bishop Thierry of Verdun also mentions miracles taking place at the sanctuary for Saint Maur, suggesting that by then there was already some lay veneration of the saint, or at the least that members of the bishop's circle were attempting to drum up interest in Maur's cult.[48] Episcopal tension with male communities in the town of Verdun may also explain why Haimo apparently recruited German monastics to help organize the newly founded community, even though highly trained, knowledgeable individuals were available at nearby Saint-Vanne. Suggestive in this sense is a twelfth-century testimony from that institution, which tells us that the early community at Saint-Maur was aware of saints venerated at Sankt Pantaleon in Cologne and had imported some of its liturgical routines from there.[49]

Bishop Haimo's third motive, which reminds us of Gozelin of Toul's foundation of Bouxières in the 930s, was personal. Although we are ill-informed on the abbey's early patronage, the fact that Haimo was buried there is indicative of a personal link between himself and the community and of the bishop's conviction, widely shared at the time, that the prayers of women religious were particularly suitable for ensuring an aristocratic individual's perpetual commemoration.[50] The presence of a separate but subordinate community of twelve canons at the nearby church of Sainte-Croix guaranteed that this commemoration would be executed in appropriate liturgical settings.[51] Still, Haimo's personal interests were but part of the story. A bull issued by Pope John XIX in 1028 shows that not Haimo himself, but his successor Rambert brought the foundation to its completion;[52] and an 1130 mention of a member of the noble Apremont family as the abbey's advocate reveals that others also associated themselves intimately with the monastery's interests.[53] Clearly, new foundations like these were an arena where different players from the region's ecclesiastical and secular elite vied to gain hold of key positions and played these out against each other. Lacking a rich archive like the one for Bouxières or extensive narrative testimonies like those for the Metz monasteries, further insight into such interactions will continue to elude us.

The case of Saint-Maur brings perspective to lesser-documented episcopal foundations from neighboring regions. Of all his peers in the later tenth and early eleventh centuries, Bishop Adalbero II of Metz (984–1005) was undoubtedly the most actively involved in reshaping the region's female monastic landscape. As a member of the aforementioned house of Verdun-Ardennes, Adalbero belonged to a faction in Lotharingian politics that was in ascendance from the 980s onward, and his actions cannot be seen separately from those of his relatives.[54] His foundations reflect an ambition to increase episcopal control over key locations in his own diocese and that of Toul and to manage all forms of religious organization according to his own purposes and views.[55] One example is the abbey of Sainte-Marie-aux-Nonnains, which was situated in the center of his episcopal town of Metz. According to Michel Parisse, Adalbero founded the new monastery to accommodate the surplus of religious from the abbey of Saint-Pierre-aux-Nonnains.[56] Although there are indications of a strong connection with the latter (and with the nearby male monastery of Saint-Symphorien), the new monastery also ended the existence on that site of a hospice (*xenodochium*) that may or may not have been run or staffed by women. All we know is that, at one point, Adalbero stepped in to dissolve the hospice and refound it as a Benedictine nunnery, where the inmates were subjected to a regime of strict enclosure and prayer service rather than the duties of hospitality and care for the sick.[57] Constantin of Saint-Symphorien's account, written not long after Adalbero's death, may echo some of the contemporary rhetoric against women who resided and worked at the site before the nunnery's foundation:

> There was a very small place in the town of Metz, a hospice that was very poor, and very vile, apart from the fact that it was dedicated to the blessed Mary, eternal virgin. That he restored the splendor of its buildings, assembled material wealth, and ordained that women religious should perpetually celebrate the Creator of all, is an indication of his love of Christ and the Mother of Lord Christ.[58]

Like Gozelin and Gerard of Toul before him, it is likely that Adalbero was trying to channel the spontaneous initiatives of women looking for different means to express their religious devotion. Unfortunately, in contrast to Haimo's foundation of Saint-Maur in Verdun, we have no insight into other motives that might also have contributed to the foundation of this new institution.

Adalbero also created two rural settlements, both of which made a great deal of sense strategically and politically. Neumünster, in a far eastern part of the Metz diocese called Bliesgau, had originated in 871, at the initiative of Bishop Adventius, as a small community of canons serving the cult of Saint Terentius, one of Adalbero's distant predecessors.[59] With no symbolic markers of episcopal presence in that part of the diocese to speak of, Adalbero intervened to transform the community into a house of Benedictine nuns, awarding it in the process a significantly enlarged—but still fairly modest— estate.[60] As elsewhere, he sought, and obtained, Henry II's approval.[61] And at Epinal, next to the episcopal palace in the diocese of Toul, he founded a

Benedictine nunnery to serve the remains of Saint Goëry, according to hagiographic tradition, the nephew of Saint Arnoul, patron of Metz.[62] Situated in the Moselle valley, on the border of Lotharingia and Burgundy, the site had originated as a fortress (founded presumably to defend against attacks by brigands coming from Burgundy), which had a market (including, perhaps, a mint) and a port.[63] The nunnery's foundation was preceded, in 974, by Bishop Thierry's translation from Saint-Symphorien of Saint Goëry, and possibly by his or Adalbero's installation of a small community of clerics.[64] Upgrading the collegial chapter to a nunnery, a significant investment, signaled Adalbero's intention of remaining closely involved in the site. It also consolidated the presence of the Metz bishops both in this strategically, economically, and symbolically important upper valley of the Moselle,[65] and more generally in the vast diocese of Toul, where they held many properties.[66] In 1003, Emperor Henry II confirmed the foundation of a nunnery, granting free election of the abbess and various immunities.[67]

Thanks to the presence of relics of Saint Goëry, Epinal became the only female institution in Upper Lotharingia that boasted a significant drawing power for pilgrims from the wider region.[68] Its surprisingly large church, although rebuilt in later centuries, still bears traces of the politically charged context in which the monastery was first established.[69] The west tower retains some of its resemblance to a typical westwork, a double-towered type of construction extremely popular in Lotharingia in the early eleventh century.[70] In this case, however, the tower was more than a mere symbolic statement of the regional elites' allegiance to the empire, as it was likely built for real defensive purposes or at least made to look as if it could serve that purpose.[71] This martial function overlapped with a spiritual one, as the women attended monastic liturgy from the balcony of the same tower.[72] There was no mistaking that spiritual representation and military presence played equally important roles in Adalbero's creation of the monastery.[73]

Finally, Adalbero's rural foundations bear strong similarities to the one at Poussay established by Berthold, bishop of Toul (995–1010).[74] Even though remote, Poussay, like Adalbero's foundation at Epinal, was situated in a densely populated area and occupied a strategically important site on a hill overlooking the valley of the Madon river. Nothing much happened until Berthold's second successor, Bruno (later Pope Leo IX) in 1036 carried out a translation of Saint Menna's relics, previously venerated at a local hermitage, and formally approved the foundation of a nunnery.[75] Judging by Pope Leo's bull from 1049, though, this new institution's estates only allowed for a small community.[76] The representative significance of having a monastic community there outweighed any concerns about creating a suitable environment

ÉPINAL. - Eglise St-Maurice, la Tour carrée

FIG. 9. Tower of the abbatial church at Epinal, early twentieth-century postcard. From the author's collection.

for female religious life to prosper institutionally, but also spiritually and intellectually.

Transformations in Ambiguous Monasticism

The expansion of the female monastic phenomenon from the later tenth century onward tends to obscure the fact that, beginning in the same period, quite a few older communities of women religious were struggling to sustain themselves and that a number of these actually ceased to exist. Part of the reason for these difficulties may have been economic, or partly related to a downturn in luck in attracting aristocratic patronage; or perhaps they were facing the adverse effects of increasing competition with newly founded institutions. But in a number of cases at least, secular and especially episcopal agents, assisted sometimes by local clerics, deliberately sought to diminish ambiguous female communities or even do away with them entirely. Before considering the dealings of these bishops, a comparative look at the known cases where secular lords intervened allows us to at least glimpse the thinking of these individuals. Through the response of the women religious, we likewise catch sight of their motivations too.

As earlier discussions in this book have already made clear, the interventions of lay aristocrats in female communities between around 900 and the middle of the eleventh century need to be understood within the ambitions of local and territorial rulers to build up "competitive lordships."[77] In some instances, the factor driving this competition was not only the possibility of creating new dynastic sanctuaries but also of claiming lordship and, to an extent, the properties and rights of existing institutions. Nivelles in Lower Lotharingia is a good case in point. Over the second half of the tenth century, Ottonian rulers had been very generous to the abbey, acknowledging its historical legacy as a royal foundation and turning it into one of the region's wealthiest female institutions.[78] As revenues from its estates and the expanding local market were pouring into the abbey's treasury, the community also became more of a free agent. In 978, Otto II granted the abbess the significant liberty of choosing the abbey's advocate;[79] and when Empress Theophanu died in 991, the system of a shared—lay and monastic—leadership at the abbey came to a definitive end. Then, in 992, Otto III issued a charter to protect the sisters' collective endowment.[80] Finally, in 993, the newly reconstructed abbatial church of Saint-Paul was dedicated.[81] But these tokens of the sisters' newly gained liberty were deceptive. Instead of signaling the definitive emancipation of the Nivelles community from lay lordship, the Ottonian's retreat as agents directly involved in the monastery's affairs reflected a shift in who controlled politics on a regional level and who would henceforth claim the title of lay lord of the institutions of the wider Brabant area.[82]

Possibly the situation remained unclear for a considerable period of time around the year 1000. A document purporting to be from 1011 claims that Abbess Oda received a significant donation from Arnulf, probably the son of Godfrey of Florennes, one of the more prominent players in regional politics, and this may or may not be indicative of attempts by him or his relatives to become the monastery's de facto lord.[83] In 1015, however, Count Lambert I of Louvain was buried at the abbey following his death on the battlefield against Godfrey's allies.[84] From that period onward, the counts of Louvain became established as the monastery's secular lords, assuming the title of lay advocate, and by the early 1040s Nivelles and its surroundings were incorporated into their territories. The counts, eager to capitalize on the economic assets of the religious, in later decades would often side with the local population—particularly the townsfolk of Nivelles demanding more freedoms—against the sisters' interests.[85] In one incident, documented in two charters issued in 1040 and 1041 by the German King Henry III, Count Otto invaded Nivelles, claimed the market, levied tolls, took over the mint, controlled breweries and mills, and infringed in other ways on the sisters' rights, including those of jurisdiction.[86]

On this and other occasions, the religious fiercely resisted the counts' and the townspeople's claims: as we shall see in chapter 6, their specific course of action (appealing to the Salian rulers for support and aggressively promoting their patron saint's lordship) reveals a lucid awareness of the conflict's stakes. In response to their appeals, Henry III created a zone of noninterference, where the abbey and its *familia* could enjoy freedom from the incursions of lay advocates.[87] Henry denounced Otto's crimes, and later underscored the institution's royal affiliation by visiting the abbey's new *basilica*—which replaced the community's former funerary church—before its dedication in 1046.[88] But he was unable to remove the count from Nivelles's affairs. His charters confirm the abbess's right to choose Nivelles's advocate, but acknowledge that the title was de facto a prerogative of the current territorial lord.[89] This arrangement reveals how the advocacy was becoming dissociated from the old obligation of protecting the interests of the religious and how it was gaining importance as a marker of a local lord's claim to former royal prerogatives over female institutions.[90]

A similarly aggressive course of action on the part of secular lords can be observed for Remiremont, which over the course of the early eleventh century evolved into a family institution of the house of Alsace. Beginning in the 990s,

Count Gerard of Metz emerged in the monastery's documentation as the institution's lay lord; his sister had married the future emperor Conrad II, and his daughter Buxinda became abbess.[91] His son, also named Gerard, became involved in the monastery's affairs as his relatives were able to claim the title of duke of Lotharingia following Gozelo's death in 1044. Shortly afterward, his position had become such that he was able to strike a deal with Henry III, which formally awarded Gerard the title of advocate of Remiremont.[92] Thanks to a notice dated 1069–70, we know that his control over the abbey extended beyond the mere lordship and that it involved direct ownership of twenty-five of the abbey's properties, two of which he had given to underadvocates as a benefice.[93] His daughter Gisela also became the abbey's sacristan (*sagrista*) and would eventually succeed her aunt Oda as abbess.[94]

The Remiremont religious do not seem to have protested against Gerard's ascendancy with anything resembling the vehemence displayed by their peers at Nivelles. A probable reason for this, besides the fact that their abbesses were his relatives, is that they were experiencing considerable pressure from the local bishop. In a move that reveals his political pragmatism, Pope Leo assisted Gerard's ascendancy by means of a privilege that severely limited the bishop's authority over Remiremont.[95] In 1049, Leo also carried out a translation of the remains of Saints Romaric, Adelphius, and Amat, an event that was commemorated in a new hagiographic narrative;[96] and in 1050, he dedicated the new abbatial church.[97] A *Life* of Saint Romaric, also written around this time, illuminates the context in which these events took place. Three times longer than its eighth-century predecessor, the strongly exegetical text complements earlier tradition by detailing how Romaric installed seven *coenobiola* of twelve women religious each to ensure the *laus perennis*, thereby conveying a message about the sisters' service to society similar to the one found in ninth-century texts from the abbey. The *Life* also emphasizes the community's right of free election, based on a papal privilege; indicates that the bishop's power over the abbey is limited; and claims that part of the abbey's estates came from the original legacy of Saint Romaric.[98] All of this reveals a defiant attitude toward the local episcopate, backed up by the contemporary production of two forged papal charters purporting to be issued by the seventh-century Pope John IV, taking the abbey under the protection of the Holy See and freeing it from the authority of bishops.[99] In later years, Abbess Gisla would seek and find intercession with Pope Gregory VII, once again in an attempt to keep the episcopate at bay.[100]

Pope Leo's relaxed attitude to supporting lay lordship of female houses and to allowing (as we saw for Bleurville) crossovers between Benedictine and non-Benedictine institutions is a clear reminder of the priorities of contemporary rulers in dealing with female monastic communities. Evidently, a consensus was growing that the most perfect form of observance for women religious was indeed Saint Benedict's *Rule*.[101] As we saw in chapter 1, just half a decade after Leo's death, Archdeacon Hildebrand at a reform synod held in Rome condemned Emperor Louis the Pious and his bishops for having issued a written rule for canonesses, thereby officially sanctioning a mode of religious life vastly inferior to that of Benedictine nuns. Reportedly, the attending bishops at the synods were scandalized when they heard about the rules allowing the canonesses a generous diet and the right to own private property.[102] But it would be wrong to take the similarities between Hildebrand's criticisms and the pro-Benedictine, antiambiguous rhetoric in Lotharingian sources from the later tenth and early eleventh centuries as evidence that the region's clerical elite were relentlessly and indiscriminately pursuing the total benedictinization of the female monastic landscape. Echoing the reforms of the 930s–960s, in episcopal dealings with ambiguous communities, the *Rule* was first and foremost a trump card drawn to leverage an agenda bearing numerous similarities to the competitive lordships their lay peers were trying to build.

Evidence supporting this interpretation is found in equal measure in instances where the clerical elites sought to install a Benedictine regime in formerly ambiguous communities and in those where they did not. A good starting point for the discussion is the case of Pfalzel. Out of a lack of documentation emerges, in the 980s, Abbess Ruothildis, according to one tradition a recruit from the prominent abbey of Essen and possibly a personal appointee of Archbishop Egbert (977–93). Relations between the two leaders seem to have been cordial, despite the community's status as canonesses, and Egbert is said to have heavily sponsored the community, promoting artistic activity and the manufacture of liturgical vestments for the archbishop's use.[103] In the later tenth century, the abbatial church (a former Roman basilica) was enlarged with side choirs and vaulted ceilings in the arms of the transept.[104] A charter Ruothildis and her brother issued in 989 donating several tributaries to the monastery further indicates the stature of the abbey and its leader.[105] Yet as we saw in the introduction, in the volatile political climate around 1000, things could quickly turn against the religious. Ruothildis's assertive epitaph, drafted sometime near the turn of the millennium, already hints at tensions with the local clergy.[106]

Not coincidentally, trouble for the Pfalzel religious had begun around the same time that Archbishop Egbert finally succeeded in forcing the nearby Oeren community into submission. In 953, Oeren had received a charter from Otto I, confirming its status as a royal institution and its Benedictine identity.[107] In 966, Otto transferred ownership of the monastery to Archbishop Theoderic

(965–77).[108] Although the documentation is extremely fragmented, this transaction appears to have sparked decades of strife between the monastery's leadership and successive archbishops.[109] Between 973 and 1000, monks at the male abbey of Sankt Maximin in Trier produced a series of forged charters, allegedly issued by Kings Dagobert (633), Pippin (760), Charlemagne (772), Zwentibold (895), and Louis the Child (902), all of which confirmed the Trier church's ownership of Oeren.[110] In response to this attempt to claim ownership of the monastery for the archbishops' distant predecessors, the Oeren community itself also forged or obtained forged charters from Otto II (973) and Otto III (993 and perhaps also 997) reversing Otto I's 966 decision.[111] Undeterred, Archbishop Egbert included Oeren in the procession, first held in 983, around different parts of the archiepiscopal *ban*.[112] And in 1000, Egbert's successor Ludolph obtained from Emperor Otto III formal confirmation of his ownership of the abbey, presumably ending the dispute. Otto compensated the Oeren community by awarding it free election of abbesses and the rights to a public market with toll, minting, and juridical rights.[113]

With the nunnery of Oeren now definitively subordinated to the archbishop's authority, relations between the Pfalzel religious and the local clergy quickly deteriorated. For at least four decades, such trivial issues as the sisters' presumably ambiguous observance had not stood in the way of a close relationship with the archbishop. Now it apparently became a major issue, as revealed for the first time in Ruothildis's epitaph. A sincere clerical preference for the *Rule* should certainly not be rejected as a possible reason for the dispute, even though it is difficult to establish precisely in what sense the Pfalzel sisters' observance was distinct from a strictly Benedictine one. Perhaps they held prebends or owned benefices; and perhaps they also retained a mode of dress and a diet that reflected their standing in the world, as did their fellow sisters at the abbey of Vilich near Bonn.[114] However, a clear motive also emerges in the fact that Pfalzel had become associated, through its links with the nearby male house of Sankt Paulin, with one of several families in Trier who, around 1000, were vying for the archiepiscopal see. At that time, Sankt Paulin was controlled by the provost Adalbero, a member of the house of Ardenne-Luxemburg and brother of Kunigunde, wife of Emperor Henry II. Adalbero was elected archbishop of Trier in 1008 and, despite Henry's objections, held on to his see until 1015, when he was finally compelled to resign in favor of his rival Poppo.[115]

With Poppo ascending the archiepiscopal throne, neither Sankt Paulin nor Pfalzel could look forward to his benevolence or generosity. Years earlier, members of the two religious houses had already anticipated a backlash: this is revealed in Ruothildis's epitaph, which presumably dates from the final decade of the tenth century, and from the fact that, shortly after 1000, a canon at Sankt Paulin drafted what is known as the *Libellus de rebus Trevirensibus*. This text functions, besides other things, as a pamphlet against Poppo and his associates, arguing in favor of Pfalzel's existence by referring to the abbey's age and its association with Merovingian royalty.[116] It would all be to no avail. During Poppo's tenure, Sankt Paulin presumably lost some of its properties because of his intervention.[117] Pfalzel, for its part, suffered far more catastrophic consequences, falling victim to a smear campaign focusing on the sisters' sexual threat to clergymen and their inferior observance. The first suggestions of trouble are in Ruothildis's epitaph, which as we saw in the introduction indicated that the abbess, even though she had been veiled as a canoness, in practice had behaved as a true nun. The naming of the Pfalzel religious as canonesses is the first known such reference for a specific community in all of the surviving documentation from the Lotharingian area, and as such indicates that clerical agents were pushing to impose unambiguous normative categories on the religious.

Shortly after the epitaph was drafted and published on Ruothildis's tombstone, the conflict intensified, and clerical attacks became more focused on the women's sexuality.[118] According to a section added to the contemporary *Gesta Treverorum*, Poppo asked one of the sisters who was "living a canonical life" to make him a pair of slippers from a seam of his liturgical cape.[119] "Desirous to make him part of her impudence," the woman enchanted the objects, and when Poppo tried them on, he was struck by carnal desire. He quickly discarded them and had one of the bystanders try on the shoes: that person experienced the same effect, as did the town's prefect. Poppo responded by threatening that he would dissolve the community if the sisters refused to accept the black habit and "commit themselves to a stricter life," in other words, accept Saint Benedict's *Rule*. When the sisters failed to reach a consensus, the offending nun and several of her fellow sisters were chased from the abbey. Others, who accepted Poppo's proposition, were transferred to the Benedictine nunnery of Oeren, and some left to join communities where their mode of life was still being practiced.[120] Perhaps because of clerical indifference to the interests and preferences of Trier's women religious, following these events the newly constituted community at Oeren fades from the documentary record.

Another region where female religious were particularly hit by clerical interventions is the diocese of Cambrai, where we have evidence for incidents and conflicts in three separate cases. The most extensively documented is that of Marchiennes. According to the 1024–25 *Deeds of the Bishops of Cambrai*, the *ordo* of women religious at some point had strayed from the right path and made the local observance progressively decline. With the support of Bishop Gerard and Count Baldwin IV of Flanders (987–1035), Abbot Leduin of Saint-Vaast in 1024 intervened to "throw out" the depraved women and replace them with Benedictine monks "who would serve better and more religiously God and the aforementioned virgin (St Rictrudis) who rests there."[121] Jean-Pierre Gerzaguet has speculated that, following the 1024 reform, the sisters were moved to the former female monastery of Denain, last mentioned in Charles the Bald's 877 charter for that institution, and since then turned into a small sanctuary served by a few clerics. But the *Deeds* mention that Count Baldwin, with the aid of Gerard and Leduin, "restored the abbey (of Denain) to its original state" by installing a group of Benedictine nuns.[122] This makes it unlikely that the Marchiennes community simply moved to Denain. For one, the sisters at Marchiennes more than likely were not Benedictine nuns and therefore would have needed extensive guidance, preferably by individuals already educated in a Benedictine context. And second, the fact that the Marchiennes sisters were not Benedictine nuns also meant that they were, in principle, free to return to the world. Like their fellow sisters at Pfalzel, some of the religious may well have done so, out of fear of the significant consequences of such a transition for their personal situation. Whatever the true circumstances and outcomes of the dissolution of the female community at Marchiennes and the restoration of that at Denain, it is clear enough that women religious in the Cambrai region would henceforth have to make do with considerably fewer resources and continue their existence (if they retained their veiled status) in a considerably less auspicious institutional environment.

A look at the background of the Marchiennes reform reveals that relations between the monastery's leadership and the local bishops must have been tense for several decades. In contrast with Pfalzel, however, we have no idea about the aristocratic interests that may have been involved. According to a later tradition, Abbess Judith was related to the family of Landas, local noblemen who in the later eleventh and early twelfth century would act as advocates for the reformed monastery of Marchiennes and would cause the local monks a great deal of trouble.[123] It is possible that Judith, via her family connections and through her actions, represented a faction in regional politics that opposed the then-current bishop's interests and was more inclined to support the Western Frankish than the Ottonian cause. In 976, through the intercession of Queen Emma, she obtained a privilege from King Lothar (954–86) of Western Francia, restituting some of the monastery's lost properties.[124] Judith's approach to Queen Emma must have qualified as a highly significant political gesture. At the time, Lothar was holding a military campaign to restore royal influence in the southernmost parts of Flanders and Hainaut and to reestablish his direct authority over the region's monasteries. One of his principal adversaries was Bishop Theudo of Cambrai, an isolated representative of Ottonian power in Western Frankish territory.[125] The abbess's intervention, which took place as her bishop was being attacked by the Western Frankish sovereign, would hardly have warmed the local episcopate to the cause of the Marchiennes community.

Besides aristocratic rivalries, we get glimpses in the evidence of other dynamics that potentially influenced Judith's confrontational stance. Recent excavations on the site of Hamage—an institution absorbed by Marchiennes in the late ninth century—suggest that in the tenth century extensive reconstruction of the local church was carried out. According to Etienne Louis, this points to intense liturgical use of the site in the context of the veneration of Saint Eusebia's remains.[126] Then, around 1000, two hagiographies dedicated to Saint Eusebia of Hamage were published, the contents of which, according to Anna Lisa Taylor, constitute evidence of a late tenth-, early eleventh-century case of "hagiographic warfare."[127] Indeed, in portraying Rictrudis and Eusebia's mother-daughter relationship both texts take a markedly different position from Marchiennes's hagiographies of Saint Rictrudis, including a metric *Life* that was issued around this time.[128] This latter rehearses the relationship between the two saints and their institutions as it was portrayed in Hucbald's 907 *Life* of Saint Rictrudis. By contrast, those dedicated to Eusebia champion the saint as a righteous leader, portray Rictrudis as an "adversarial parent," and emphasize the nature of Hamage's original foundation as a community consisting of both men and women. A possible explanation for these hagiographic discrepancies is that the clerics serving the sanctuary at Hamage were seeking to undo its subordinate position to Marchiennes and perhaps even looking to establish an independent, male community of clerics in place of the latter. Alternatively, it might have been the women themselves who, sensing that they were losing control over their institution and the cult of their main patron saint, were looking to establish a new monastery at Hamage.[129]

A contributing factor to these tensions and responses was the fact that the Cambrai episcopate was actively intervening in Marchiennes's arsenal of tutelary saints. One notable episode, which unfortunately cannot be dated, took place when the Marchiennes community was made to give away some of the remains of their patron Saint Rictrudis's son, Mauront. In 996–97, Bishop Erluin deposited them at the newly rededicated collegial church of Saint-Amé in Douai:[130] the Marchiennes religious were left with just enough relics to house in a small reliquary, and the knowledge that they now had to compete with the canons at Saint-Amé for pilgrims' favors.[131] Erluin's move would have created a great deal of resentment, and as late as the 1160s, local hagiographer

Andreas recollected that the relics of Saint Mauront had at one point been "furtively stolen."[132] Judith's elevation of the remains of first Abbot Saint Jonat, celebrated in a narrative specifically drafted to kick-start his cult, may have been carried out in direct response to all this.[133]

Although we have no further information on the tensions that underlie these events at Marchiennes, the sisters were surely also looking at what was happening to other communities of the region. At Caudry, the Cambrai episcopate had intervened, as it would do at Marchiennes, to dismantle the community's cultic identity. Following the drafting of the aforementioned *Passion* of Saint Maxellendis from c. 925 to 940–45, two translations of the saint's relics were carried out. The circumstances of the first, in 955, are unclear: but the second, which took place during the tenure of Bishop Rothard (979–95), permanently transferred the relics to a sanctuary dedicated to Saint Martin in Cambrai. Such an intervention would not have come as a surprise. The original *Passion* of Saint Maxellendis already insisted on the primacy of the local bishop and the interests of the local church of Saint-Martin and also on the notion that the two local communities, male and female, were sustained by an estate given by the saint's repentant murderer to a church of Saint Martin in Cambrai.[134] Once deprived of its patron saint and, crucially, the support of pilgrims and patrons, the monastic community at Caudry faded into obscurity.[135] Another case is that of Maubeuge, where the canons serving the local church of Saint-Quentin pulled no punches in laying claim to the sisters' estates. From the end of the tenth century, we have a forged charter, issued allegedly by the Merovingian King Childeric, to confirm Saint Aldegondis's bequest to the monastery.[136] Even though it relies on the late ninth-century *Life* of the saint, the text omits any mention of a female community and claims the entire *mensa conventualis* for the canons.[137] As we shall see in chapter 6, this may have been the spark that set off the fierce statement of autonomy as expressed on the *Roll of Maubeuge*. What the Maubeuge clerics may not have realized is that their own situation could be affected in equal measure as that of the women religious. In Caudry, they disappear from the source record along with the female community; and at Hamage, the clerics' presumed efforts at creating their own community were dismissed by an author writing in 1024–25 for Bishop Gerard, who described the sanctuary as "badly decayed because of secularity."[138]

As the Cambrai clergy were aggressively intervening in the existence of female communities, in the diocese of Liège a process of subordinating female institutions to episcopal power also appears to have taken place. Here, however, we have no trace of Saint Benedict's *Rule* being imposed on ambiguous female communities or of such communities being dissolved, in all likelihood because bishops were able to gain control over these institutions, their networks, and their assets by means other than a drastic reform. Surely the most important of these was the active support of the Ottonian and Salian rulers. In 952, Otto I gave Aldeneik, which in the 930s had belonged to Giselbert of Lotharingia, to the Liège episcopate,[139] and in 969, Hastière's link to Sainte-Glossinde was successfully dissolved, and the former institution was converted into a priory of the male monastery of Waulsort.[140] We already saw how King Henry formalized Thorn's transferral to the bishops' control by a privilege from 1007, and at Susteren, archaeological excavations have revealed that the years around 1000 marked the complete reorganization of the monastic compound. The disorganized early medieval layout (consisting of small, free-standing buildings, a well, and a few wooden edifices) was replaced with an actual monastery, which featured a rectangular floor plan.[141] The most likely person to have commissioned and perhaps also funded these works—which for the first time allowed enclosure to be implemented effectively—was the local bishop. Both here and at Thorn, the bishop likely also oversaw the rebuilding of the abbatial church, in both cases to reflect the region and its leaders' imperial allegiance.[142]

There are indications that the Liège bishops intervened to the benefit of these female monasteries. Earlier we saw that Notger gave several properties to the religious at Thorn, and it may have been from him also that the religious at Aldeneik obtained a tenth-century gospel book known as the *Codex Eyckensis II*, which bears a resemblance to a similar manuscript used at Aachen cathedral.[143] Yet, despite these suggestions of episcopal patronage and a less interventionist attitude toward the women's spirituality, none of these institutions was about to enter a glorious phase of its existence. Thorn was destined to remain a minor player, and after 1007, information about the community becomes scarce. Much the same is true for Aldeneik, Susteren, and Gozelo's former institution of Munsterbilzen, of which we hear next to nothing until the late eleventh or early twelfth century. But at least none of the communities was forcibly evicted, and none was made to give up its ambiguous identity.

Two phenomena characterize the situation of female religious in the decades around the year 1000. The first is a profound change in the region's female monastic landscape, brought about in part by the emergence of a regional elite keen to create dynastic sanctuaries, and in part by an episcopate looking to consolidate religious, ecclesiastical, and familial interests through the foundation and patronage of female institutions. It is striking, even given the general scarcity of primary sources from this period, that we hear so little about the newly founded and reformed houses; equally striking is the less-than-straightforward attitude to Benedictine observance on the part of these founders and reformers. The second phenomenon is that ambiguous communities were increasingly facing competition from female institutions and groups of clerics offering the same or at least very similar services to society. There was also a tendency for the region's territorial and ecclesiastical rulers to intervene drastically in their affairs and possibly also a slump in aristocratic interest in patronizing female houses. As we have witnessed in this chapter, some of these women religious fiercely defended their ambiguous views and tried to create legal, cultic, and ideological defenses against the attacks of lay and ecclesiastical rulers and, in some cases, even against the clerics serving at their institutions. In chapter 6, I will explore how these communities continued to nurture their ambiguous spiritual identity and sought for ways to sustain themselves in a social environment marked by growing competition, hostility, and perhaps also indifference.

CHAPTER 6

Monastic Ambiguities in the New Millennium

Following the turn of the millennium, clerical attitudes toward ambiguous groups of female religious hardened. Ninth-century lawmakers had sought to discourage any initiatives that fell outside of the legitimate boundaries set in contemporary legislation, while promoting modes of ecclesiastical government that placed women religious in a subordinate position to the clergy. From the second quarter of the tenth century onward, bishops in particular began promoting Benedictinism as the preferable monastic observance: but they pursued this ideal only in contexts where such a move was likely to yield politically advantageous results and generally seem to have maintained good relations with non-Benedictine communities. Then, beginning in the final decades of the tenth century, some—not all—of their successors began rejecting the legitimacy of a female religious life outside of the strict boundaries of the *Rule* and actively persecuted ambiguous forms of observance and organization.

While chapter 5 revealed how this final wave of interventions was triggered by circumstances largely or entirely unrelated to women's observance, it nevertheless prepared clerical minds for a full-on assault in the second half of the eleventh century. Taking at face value Archdeacon Hildebrand's ringing cry for reform at the 1059 synod in Rome, historians have concluded that by the early eleventh century ambiguous communities had become thoroughly secularized and that women's monastic spirituality had declined to the point of being almost nonexistent. In reality, objective evidence of such a decline is exceedingly difficult to find. Instead of attempting to find arguments for or against the classic narrative of disastrous secularization in these communities, this chapter will focus on what we know about how these women expressed and positioned themselves. My aim is to make three arguments. First, that there still existed a significant culture of reflection and perhaps also debate and that this culture nurtured the shaping of ambiguous monastic identities based on comparative study of the written legacies of the monastic past. Second, that there is considerable evidence to argue that a number of abbesses and their associates deployed a range of coping strategies to secure the long-term future of ambiguous communities in light of both increased competition among ecclesiastical institutions and increasingly volatile relations with the region's elites. Third and finally, I look at the newly created community of Denain to find that the transition to a Benedictine regime by no means spelled a better future for its members as regards their social relevance, resources, and impact on public religion than that of their sisters who practiced an ambiguous observance.

Narrating Ambiguity and Inner Tensions at Maubeuge

Accessing the self-understanding and self-representation of ambiguous groups is difficult, as the few fragments of evidence that have come down to us are difficult to interpret, let alone contextualize. Take, for instance, the eleventh-century *Life* of Saint Berlendis of Nivelles, which insists on the saint's asceticism—wearing only one *cilicium* "over her naked body," resting her head at night on a stone, and caring little for food and drink—yet also on her service to the sick and the poor.[1] We can only wonder if the author was seeking to reconcile in her persona the monastery's multiple, historically grown (contemplative and charitable) functions, or if he was seeking to express an opinion in the context of ongoing reflections regarding the Nivelles sisters' observance and their involvement in charitable tasks.

Likewise, scattered evidence from Remiremont offers a view of spiritual culture that is just too incomplete to detect any specific emphases. Monique Paulmier-Foucart and Anne Wagner have attributed to the abbey's collection two florilegia. The former contains the so-called *Collectiones seu florilegium diversorum patrum*, a standard assemblage of sayings from the church fathers.[2] The latter consists of various readings on the gospels; a sermon by Saint Augustine; Bede's *De laude caritatis*; a letter by Hilary of Poitier to his daughter Abra or Avra; a treatise on the eight cardinal vices; various homilies on Gregory's *Moralia in Job*; and a significant number of saints' *Lives*.[3] More so than the inclusion of material relating to female Saint Avra, the presence in this manuscript of the *Life* of Symeon in Trier (d. 1032) holds particular interest. This text, which was written by Abbot Eberwin of Tholey, represented contemporary developments in thinking about the relationship between cloistered life and eremitism and originated from the circle around Eberwin and his noted reformist colleague, Richard of Saint-Vanne.[4] As such, ownership could potentially reveal an awareness by the religious of Remiremont of new trends in monastic spirituality, and perhaps even a trend towards a flexible attitude to individual sisters' enclosed status. But even if the manuscript could be securely attributed to the abbey's library in the middle decades of the eleventh century, we would still not know how it ended up there, who actually made or acquired it, and for what readership it was intended. Manuscripts like these circulated widely in the region's monastic contexts, and it is far from certain that all of their contents applied, in some form or other, to their putatively female recipients. What is more, we should not forget that Remiremont as an institution consisted of a sizeable community of clerics, who might have acquired this manuscript for their own purposes only.

Less ambiguous in that sense is the evidence from Pfalzel and Maubeuge. For the former, Ruothildis's epitaph (as we saw in the introduction and in chapter 5) arguably emerges as a vocal rejection of the Trier clergy's attempt to award spiritual and organizational merit according to the formal status of the religious as nuns or canonesses. It is, by all accounts, one of the most compelling—and tangible—examples of supportive evidence for the notion that ambiguous communities continued the ninth- and tenth-century tradition of absorbing monasticism's written legacies to shape unique, local views on religious life for women. But the sixty-five-word inscription represents all we know about the Pfalzel view on female spiritual identity or the intellectual and spiritual culture that presumably lay beneath it.[5] By comparison, the evidence from early eleventh-century Maubeuge seems plentiful, even though, in reality, it raises more questions than it answers. The first and best-known commentary on the situation of the religious in the early decades of the eleventh century is a passage in the anonymous *Life* of Abbot Thierry of Saint-Hubert (d. 1087), a follower of Richard of Saint-Vanne and in his own right a significant agent of ecclesiastical reform. In the first few pages of the text, the biographer sketches a fanciful picture of Thierry's childhood years, followed by a remarkable account of how his parents sent him as a young boy to Maubeuge, where his sister Ansoaldis was then abbess (1012–c. 1050), to learn the basics of reading and to memorize the psalter, before moving to the nearby male monastery of Lobbes to complete his training.[6] Untroubled that Thierry as a young boy had been admitted to a female community,[7] the author notes that "it seems appropriate here to insert a few words on (Ansoaldis's) virtues and life, as way of praising Christ's name." Then follows the single surviving biographical account of a Lotharingian abbess for the entire period between 816 and 1050.[8]

Only five hundred words long, Ansoaldis's brief life description does not offer a great deal of concrete information. It begins by saying that, sometime at the end of the tenth century, a noble couple from the village of Leernes (now in the Belgian Ardennes) offered their daughter Ansoaldis, still a small girl, to the monastery of Maubeuge. The narrative then switches to a description of her qualities that relies heavily on hagiographical commonplaces and misogynistic prejudices. So it describes how, soon after her admission, she began exhibiting signs of a particular devotion to modesty and prayer, and abstained from "the lasciviousness or negligence typical of girls." In later years, her conduct served as an inspiring example to some of her fellow sisters and as a frightening one to others, and the text dwells on her softness of manner, patience, humility, forgiveness, charity, and chastity. She also abstained completely from the "disputes and conflicts and battles of women"; practiced a stringently ascetic diet and deprived herself of sleep; punished her body for any libidinous feelings; and spurned baths and washing, "teaching that no-one could be polluted on the outside, unless he or she was soiled on the inside by the pleasure of sin." In a third and final part, the text switches back to reporting concrete events of Ansoaldis's life. With the approval of Bishop Gerard of Cambrai and Count Renier V of Mons (1013–39), she "corrected the order of monastic religion, which had nearly been destroyed in that monastery and restored it so that it was better than before." The narrative concludes by saying that she suffered from cancer for the last seven years of her life and died a chaste death.

Ansoaldis's asceticism raises a number of questions. On the one hand, her austerity and mortifications are particularly grueling, especially given that they are represented within a monastic setting, and as having been undertaken by someone who was in office as abbess.[9] Her conduct is also distinctly at odds with ninth- to eleventh-century hagiography, whose ideal abbess is an aristocratic mother figure, promoting domestic values to her subjects.[10] But Ansoaldis is the only abbess for the entire region and period covered in this study to receive a proper narrative treatment of her life, and both the tone of the text and the textual borrowings from earlier hagiographies (particularly Sulpicius Severus's *Life* of Saint Martin) strongly suggest that the author was looking to promote her not as an exemplar for female monastic leaders or their subjects, but as a saint or, at the very least, a saintly figure.[11] The most convincing approach to achieve that objective, so it seems, was to shape her memory to resemble that of some of the ascetic abbesses and female martyrs encountered in pre-800 saints' *Lives*. On the other hand, her stated reliance on using bodily austerities to express a specific view on religious life (and a criticism of that held by others) does echo accounts of the lives of ninth- to early eleventh-century anchoresses and ascetic religious, such as Liutbirg of Wendeshausen (d. c. 865), Wiborada of Sankt Gallen (d. 926), Geisa of Saint-Pierre-aux-Nonnains (920s–930s), and Abbess Adelheid of Vilich (d. c. 1015).[12] In this respect, the *Life* provides support for Geoffrey Koziol's tentative argument about the physicality of women's spirituality in this period, a phenomenon that is usually thought to have subsided post-800 (and reemerged post-1200).[13] Ansoaldis's case may be an extreme example of this, heavily informed as it is by hagiographic commonplaces: but there is sufficient evidence to argue that some women religious of the period used their bodies to express dissatisfaction over their situation, and to represent a different spirituality than the one they routinely encountered.

In contrast, Ansoaldis's biography is sorely lacking in information that seems essential for an understanding of Ansoaldis's concrete acts as the community's leader. So her promotion of the cult of the local patron Saint Aldegondis through an elevation of the saint's remains in 1039—surely an event that was of crucial significance to the sisters of Maubeuge—is passed over in silence.[14] Also unmentioned are the personal connections between Thierry and herself, which, according to A. J. Theys and Joseph Warichez, probably extended to clerical and monastic individuals in high positions—several of whom were involved in promoting the *Rule* in male institutions—both in the dioceses of Liège and Cambrai.[15] Another connection on which the hagiographer is silent is that of Thierry's link, via his 1020 transfer to the newly reformed monastery of Lobbes, with Richard of Saint-Vanne, a noted agent of reform and an associate of Bishop Gerard.[16] But perhaps most importantly, the text does not actually provide any concrete information on Maubeuge's pre-reform situation, besides alluding to differences of opinion among community members about the types of conduct that were appropriate to their standing as women religious. Of particular note is the biographer's silence on the exact status of Ansoaldis's peers, as well as regards their specific conduct and attitudes. Likewise missing is information on the precise nature of the reform, which scholars have consistently imagined as a transition to a Benedictine regime.

The key testimony taken as corroborating the notion that Ansoaldis had been pushing for a new, Benedictine observance at Maubeuge is the fifth version of the *Life* of patroness Saint Aldegondis, written some ten to fifteen years after the reform, which presumably took place in the mid-to-later 1020s.[17] This new text, which may have been authored by Ansoaldis's brother Thierry, contains several allusions to Saint Benedict's *Rule*,[18] and as such has been interpreted by all commentators as evidence of the reformed community's Benedictine character. Certainly Bishop Gerard was in favor of such transitions, as witnessed in his creation of the community at Denain, discussed further on in this chapter. Yet although we can assume that Maubeuge adopted a Benedictine identity following interventions by religious and secular authority, there is no evidence that Ansoaldis had promoted such a radical transition in the sisters' observance before her appeal to Bishop Gerard and Count Renier. Even if it turns out she had, there is still no guarantee that the other religious were not pursuing their own journey into discovering the ideal mode of cloistered life. The earlier, pre-reform *Roll of Maubeuge* gives us plenty of things to consider regarding the sisters' (and possibly Ansoaldis's) ambiguous attitudes before Gerard and Renier's intervention.[19] As we saw in chapter 1, the compilation at the end of the *Roll* contains hard evidence of the availability and use at this institution of diverse normative texts relating to the organization of life in women's monasteries. As such, it reminds us of contemporary Niedermünster in Regensburg, where a copy of the *Rule* was read and used in conjunction with a tweaked, benedictinized version of Cesarius of Arles's rule for women religious.[20] Likewise, the Pfalzel tombstone of Ruothildis also more than hints at the sisters' intimate knowledge of the *Rule*, even if they subsequently declined to transition to a strict Benedictine regime.

Arguably the best indication we have that the Maubeuge religious, although well aware and appreciative of Benedictine tradition, rejected calls to adopt the *Rule* is found in subsequent, but possibly still pre-reform, interventions on the *Roll*. Aware of the recent semantic shift in words such as *monasticus/ca* and *sanctimonialis*—formerly meaning "monastic" and "woman religious," but now apparently "Benedictine" and "Benedictine nun"—local scribes expurgated passages that might have invited unwelcome interpretations. For instance, wishing to avoid the implication that the sisters' spiritual ancestors, Aldegondis and her relatives, had been Benedictine nuns, the author of a new, third *Life* of the saint (the first text featured on the *Roll*) substituted "canonical life" for the original "monastic life" in his source text, the early tenth-century *Life* of Saint Madelberta.[21] And in two passages taken from the 813 council of Chalon-sur-Saône in the compilation at the end of the *Roll*, a scribe erased the—*monialis* part of the previously neutral term *sanctaemonialis*, ostensibly again to avoid the idea that the quote was intended to apply to Benedictines instead of women religious generally.[22]

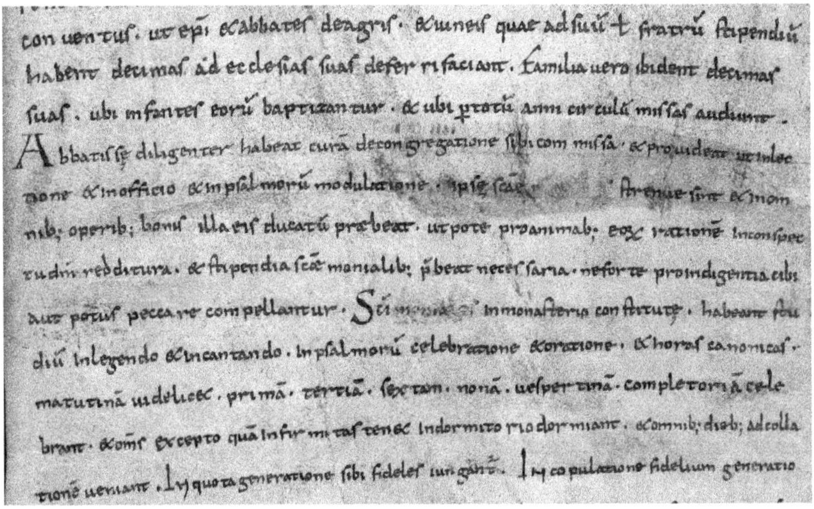

FIG. 10. *Roll of Maubeuge*, fragment showing erasure of part of the word *sanctaemoniales*. Copyright State Archives of Belgium. Reproduced with permission.

Contrary to what some scholars have thought, though, these revised passages do not objectively show the sisters identifying themselves or their spiritual forebears as canonesses. Far from labeling the religious in a particular sense, the interventions in the texts avoid precisely this. Leaving open or ambiguous the women's precise normative identity was a tactic designed to preserve the culture of comparative reading discussed earlier in this book and to reject clerical pressure to conform to rigid normative views on female observance.

Considering the turmoil in which the *Roll* presumably originated helps us to reflect on the sisters' motivations for making this statement about *not being Benedictine nuns*.[23] The most likely context, reconstructed in large measure by Anne-Marie Helvétius, was one of conflict over Maubeuge's institutional integrity. By the time the *Roll* was compiled, Saint Aldegondis's material and spiritual legacy had been a bone of contention for more than a century and a half and involved a number of different parties. A key text in the discussion had been the forged *Testament* of Saint Aldegondis,[24] which appears to date from the late ninth century and claims that the saint had bequeathed all of her properties to the religious community at Maubeuge (a statement made, so we may assume, to exclude a lay lord from that proprietary constellation). It is featured prominently on the *Roll* and is preceded by the aforementioned third *Life* of Saint Aldegondis.[25] This latter, which according to Helvétius was conceived specifically for inclusion on the *Roll*,[26] consists almost entirely of unaltered fragments from the saint's ninth-century second *Life* and the tenth-century *Life* of Saint Madelberta.[27] The two documents combined essentially reaffirm the claims of the Maubeuge religious to Aldegondis's spiritual and material legacies and represent the sisters as the legitimate successors of the monastery's original community.

The third and fourth parts of the *Roll* reveal the pressing nature of this reaffirmation at the beginning of the eleventh century. The former is a description of properties at the estates of Solre-Saint-Géry and Cousolre.[28] The fact that this description was appended to the previous two texts suggests an effort to claim for the religious community these specific parts of the monastery's total estate, indicating that there had been a conflict over their ownership. Shedding some light on this claim is the existence of a roughly contemporary fourth *Life* of Aldegondis that insists on a local cult of the saint at Cousolre.[29] According to Helvétius, this fourth *Life* may be the product of a group of former sisters of Maubeuge who, having refused to accept the transition to a Benedictine regime, were attempting to set up an independent monastery at Cousolre.[30] Alternatively, it may also be the product of a group of clerics living there, seeking—like the ones Anna Lisa Taylor assumes to have been active at Hamage—to lay the foundations for an independent male institution.[31] Because Cousolre was known in local tradition as Aldegondis's burial site, such an attempt would not only have jeopardized the economic future of the community at Maubeuge but also its cultic identity. A rival claim may have already been attempted via the recent forgery of a charter allegedly issued by King Childeric (the fourth document featured on the *Roll*), which confirmed Aldegondis's *Testament* but claimed all of her inheritance for the male clerics of Maubeuge.[32]

Presumably, the attempted takeover of Aldegondis's spiritual and financial legacy (which occurred at roughly the same time as the "hagiographic warfare" at Marchiennes/Hamage) was still a going concern when the *Roll* was drafted. The conspicuous references to the sisters' ownership of their parishes and the compensation that was due to the priests serving these may be a pointer to such tensions.[33] It may even have been one of the triggers of a crisis that took place during Ansoaldis's tenure and that was resolved after Gerard and Renier's intervention. Telling in this sense is the fact that the post-reform fifth *Life* of Aldegondis ignores these issues, suggesting that the dispute over Cousolre was no longer troubling the abbey's leadership.[34] We also have the testimony of Ansoaldis's 1039 translation of Saint Aldegondis's remains—possibly from Cousolre to Maubeuge itself—which likewise suggests a victory over the community's adversaries.[35]

The question, then, is how the spiritual message of the *Roll*, embedded in the third *Life* and the compilation, relates to Ansoaldis's campaign for reform.

According to Sylvie Joye and Paul Bertrand, a connection between the two is ruled out by the fact that several parts of the *Roll* indicate that the community had unambiguously chosen a canonical lifestyle.[36] Yet as I noted earlier in this chapter, it is important to realize that we do not know for certain that a reform to a Benedictine regime was really what Ansoaldis had been pursuing before involving Bishop Gerard and Count Renier. Like Geisa and her aunt Fredeburga at early tenth-century Saint-Pierre-aux-Nonnains, she and her supporters may have advocated disciplinary change for various reasons. But reform to these women and their leader Ansoaldis may not have necessarily meant a radical transition from one, ambiguous regime, to another where their identity would be unambiguously Benedictine. Local discourse, instead of centering on such a transition, instead looked to represent an ideal vision of specific aspects of observance and organization and of monastic leadership in an ambiguous fashion, much as we find in the compilation at the end of the *Roll*.

This evidence leads to the following, strictly hypothetical, reconstruction. Ansoaldis (or one of her predecessors c. 1000) initially relied on an ambiguous discourse similar to the one conveyed on the *Roll* to promote internal changes, all the while trying to block the clerics. Fearing that a Benedictine reform under the supervision of local rulers would compromise her community's material and spiritual autonomy or even lead to the sisters' eviction,[37] or because she suspected that the bishop and his entourage had been involved in the local clerics' efforts to claim the sisters' endowment, she and her associates rejected such a reform. But unable to end the institutional crisis, increasingly caught up (through her brother Thierry) in the reformist circles around Bishop Gerard, and maybe also acknowledging the bishop's recent (1024) move of dissolving the female community at Marchiennes and perhaps also of relocating those religious to the decidedly more modest institution of Denain, Ansoaldis eventually saw no other option but to call on Gerard and Renier to resolve her problems and thus secure the long-term survival of her community. The trade-off of this alliance was to accept a Benedictine reform after all, taking a significant loss of autonomy as part of the deal.[38] Perhaps the aforementioned fourth *Life* is a faint echo of the fact that, in the wake of that event, several women had relocated (as their fellow sisters at Pfalzel had done just a decade earlier) to Cousolre, in the vain hope of creating a new ambiguous community. Whatever exactly happened and whatever direct control over properties, governance, or self-determination the Maubeuge religious may have lost, at least post-reform they avoided the pitiful, humiliating fate of their former neighbors at Caudry and Marchiennes or the equally sorry destiny of their more distant peers at Pfalzel in Trier.

Looking for Prestige by Association

All across Lotharingia, but particularly in Lower Lotharingia, ambiguous communities of women religious sought a buttress against reform-minded clerics and expansionist territorial rulers and attempted to generate new incomes, popularity, and prestige. The coping strategies they deployed when facing these challenges and the discourse they relied on to justify these strategies show significant similarities—but also significant differences depending on context—with those I discussed earlier on for groups of women religious of the later ninth and early tenth centuries.

In these early eleventh-century communities, the focus lay on recalling and, when possible, reviving associations going back many decades, sometimes centuries. In chapter 5, we already saw how the embattled religious at Nivelles continued to request and receive privileges from the Ottonian and Salian rulers throughout the later tenth and eleventh centuries. Even if the authors of these privileges increasingly acknowledged that local power was entirely in the hands of the emerging counts of Louvain, the symbolic importance of these charters as indicators of a royal connection going back to the abbey's foundation on a royal fisc cannot be underestimated.[39] In a similar fashion Abbess Judith of Marchiennes's acquisition of a charter by King Lothar of Western Francia revived an association with Carolingian royalty going back to the early ninth century and reaffirmed the abbey's continuing—but for the most part inoperative, politically and otherwise—status as a royal monastery.[40] There can be little doubt that rulers welcomed such opportunities to assert their lordship over these institutions, especially in a context of ongoing conflict over territorial power with local and regional lords.[41] To bring home this point, some of their privileges relied on an overcharged language of destruction and chaos, as is the case in Henry III's 1040 privilege for Nivelles:

> The abbey or church of Nivelles was lessened by such fluctuations, crushed by such calamities . . . it was squashed by such oppression, that the benefice of the count (of Louvain) extended to the cloister, and that there was no place where the most sacred virgin Gertrudis, who rests there, could be given the appropriate veneration, even though she ennobled this place with her own hands.[42]

Like some of the late ninth- and early tenth-century royal charters for female institutions,[43] this and other documents also tend to overstate the harmonious nature of relations between the women and their royal lordship. The point of these statements was less that of creating or documenting the objective fact of royal protection than of erecting symbolic palisades against a common adversary. Simultaneous with this promotion of former patrons, religious communities at Maubeuge, Nivelles, and Marchiennes also revived, and in some cases fundamentally revised, local hagiographical traditions. In a clear echo of a number of hagiographies written around 900, these texts insist on the fact that the religious at these communities were the rightful heirs to the endowments of patron saints. As we saw earlier, Saint Aldegondis's ownership of the original estate of Maubeuge resurfaced as a key argument in disputes over control of the monastery's institutions, economy, cultic practices, and even its gendered identity. And at Nivelles, Henry III's charter of 1041 refers to the community's estates as the "legacy of the virgin" (*hereditatem virginis*) Saint Gertrudis.[44]

But here as in Marchiennes, the religious realized that such arguments about the legal status of certain endowments and the long-distance support of the Ottonian and Salian sovereigns would mean little in the absence of more immediate measures of self-defense. In response, they introduced into hagiographic discourse references to saintly supernatural powers of protection and the status of patronesses as divine avengers. Count Arnulf's 1011 charter for Nivelles—the authenticity of which remains uncertain—invokes the wrath "of the almighty God and Saint Gertrudis" against whoever felt the need to undo Arnulf's donation.[45] Similarly, King Lothar's more secure charter for Marchiennes indicates that usurpers of the properties he restituted to the religious would incur "the wrath of the almighty God and the blessed Rictrudis and all the saints."[46] Such passages are not particularly noteworthy if we compare them to similar texts from contemporary male institutions: but they do indicate a remarkable shift in female hagiographic discourse around the year 1000.

The analogies with coping strategies of a century earlier also extended to moves to emphatically match the sisters' communal identity with the memory of specific individuals or, better still, the cult of a locally venerated saint.[47] Munsterbilzen's hosting of the burial site of Gozelo, the last holder of the combined duchies of Upper and Lower Lotharingia,[48] revived memories of King Zwentibold's burial there and may even have led to the initial development of a cult in the late sovereign's honor.[49] At Bouxières, we are in the dark as to the precise scope of the cult of the founding bishop Gozelin. But we do know that, in addition to his grave at the abbatial church, his memory was locally consolidated by the sisters' preservation of a large number of objects associated with him. When the eighteenth-century historian Dom Calmet went to the abbey to investigate the original of Gozelin's 938 foundation charter, he found that it was kept there as a relic, housed in a black box lined with blue silk.[50] Other objects, several of which are now in the treasury of Nancy cathedral, include relics of Gozelin's head and arms, a liturgical comb in ivory, a chalice, a paten, a liturgical veil and ring, and a gospel book with ornate binding.[51] In addition to being a place of remembrance for Gozelin in its entirety, the monastery and its nearby village of Bouxières also held smaller sites of significance: in later centuries, the religious showed to visitors a small tribune or tower as the place from which Gozelin used to preach to the faithful; and a subterranean chapel of the abbatial church was known to later generations as his original burial site.[52] The community at Vergaville likewise came to celebrate as a saint their founder Sigeric, also buried at the abbatial church. In a similar course of events as with Eva of Chaumontois at Bouxières, Sigeric's female cofounder and wife, Betta, was omitted from this quasi-hagiographic commemoration.[53] In contrast, the Thorn religious only had the body of foundress Hereswint, not that of her husband Ansfrid: she was therefore singled out to become the subject of a local cult from at least the early twelfth century onward.[54]

We may wonder to what extent the cult of these local founders and patrons initially found success with the laity and how quickly their cult as saints or quasi saints was actually promoted following their death. A remarkable anecdote regarding the introduction of the cult of Saint Gislen may reveal the Thorn sisters' search for additional "cultic capital." According to a mid-eleventh-century addition to Rainer of Ghent's *Invention and Miracles of Saint Gislen*, the Thorn religious at one point received Abbot Heribrand of Saint-Ghislain and several of his monks, who were on their return journey from a visit to the court of Emperor Conrad (1027–39).[55] Heribrand gave the religious a copy of the saint's recent *Life*, a gift they acknowledged by including the saint's feast day in their liturgical calendar.[56] In a revised version of the same text, written not long after the first one, we get a glimpse of how the women subsequently went one step further by incorporating the saint into their institution's cultic identity. When one of the abbess's servants—one of the women working in her *gynaeceum*, discussed in chapter 5—experienced a difficult pregnancy, the abbess ordered the copy of Gislen's *Life* to be laid on the woman's belly, and the servant was healed.[57] Ostensibly, the Thorn religious were desperate enough to add the cult of a new saint to their roster to trivialize the absence of a historical connection between Saint Gislen and their institution or the absence of his relics locally.

At institutions that did have an established patron, we can observe a notable emphasis on the materiality of their saint's cult, and on the availability of the saint's remains at the abbatial church. Arnulf's charter for Nivelles states that the locals "rejoice because of the very frequent reports of the rewards of miracles,"[58] and Olbert of Gembloux's roughly contemporary *Miracles* of Saint Vero of Lembeek confirm pilgrimage to Gertrudis's grave in Nivelles's abbatial church.⁵⁹ As the eleventh century progressed, the Nivelles religious would further encourage identification of their institution with the saint: at least two types of locally struck *denarii* are known with inscriptions referring explicitly to Saint Gertrudis.⁶⁰ As I have observed for the hagiographies written around 900, this propaganda was not exclusively aimed at drawing in the faithful: the sisters themselves were encouraged to connect strongly with the cult of the saint and especially with the veneration of her material remains. In the mid-eleventh-century *Life* of another saint venerated at Nivelles, Berlendis of Meerbeke, we find much emphasis on the significance of saints' relics, their shrines and tombs, and the need to show appropriate veneration. Berlendis, besides showing all the virtues ninth- and tenth-century hagiographers had already considered appropriate for a woman religious, is described as personally handling Gertrudis's relics and developing a very tactile relationship with them.⁶¹ This focus on the materiality and liturgical use of saints' cults is also apparent in the cases of Andenne and Sainte-Waudru in Mons. For the former community, patroness Saint Begga turns up in the early eleventh-century calendar of the abbey of Saint-Laurent in Liège, and a certain Giselbert wrote liturgical chants in her honor, suggesting an intensified veneration.⁶² For the latter, we know that the religious, assisted by Count Renier, organized a translation of the relics of Saint Vero. In the second decade of the eleventh century, Olbert of Gembloux wrote a report of this event, and a new version of the ninth-century *Life* of Saint Waldetrudis.⁶³ The late eleventh-century chronicler Sigebert of Gembloux explains that at Count Renier's request Olbert wrote further texts celebrating Waldetrudis's memory.⁶⁴ It was perhaps in the context of this intensification of Waudru's cult that the religious also acquired a textile that became known as the "shroud of Saint Waudru."⁶⁵

All of these measures can be interpreted as attempts to create (by legal and hagiographic arguments) homegrown means of self-defense: by reaching a broader group of potential pilgrims and donors, communities sought to become less reliant on specific patrons and patronal families from the local and regional elites. Yet these interventions, especially in cultic practices and traditions, may conceal more complex dynamics. Take, for instance, the striking shift in several institutions to a cultic focus on male patron saints. In chapter 5, we already saw that the Remiremont religious in the early to mid-eleventh century promoted the cults of Saints Romaric, Adelphius, and Amat.⁶⁶ And at the end of the tenth century, Abbess Judith of Marchiennes had already given the spotlight to the obscure first abbot Saint Jonat, by carrying out an elevation of his relics and including them in a shrine together with those of patroness Saint Rictrudis and another male saint, Rictrudis's son Mauront. The omission of Rictrudis's daughter Saint Eusebia from the ceremony reveals an intentional focus on these male individuals and perhaps also ongoing tensions over the status of Hamage.[67] Finally, at Munsterbilzen, the shift was even more radical. Saint Landrada, whose relics reputedly were no longer kept at the monastery,[68] faded from local cultic activity in the decades around the year 1000 and was replaced by her confessor Saint Amor. By 1040, the abbey's *patrocinium* referred to Saint Amor, and his relics were offered for veneration in the new abbatial church.[69] From the eleventh century, we also have two types of *denarii* struck at the local mint. On the first, only an inscription AE may refer to the saint (as *Ameur*); on the second, however, from the latter part of the century, he is physically portrayed and explicitly identified.[70] A mid-eleventh-century *Life* of the saint by Egebert, presumably a deacon from Liège, completed this effort at reshaping the abbey's hagiographic identity. Perhaps significantly, the text is dedicated to a nobleman named Rotbert.[71]

On first consideration, all four cases seem to point to a strategy for encouraging the interest of potential male patrons and pilgrims. Perhaps this was in response to a drop in female patronage of women's institutions;[72] or maybe it was simply to broaden the appeal of monasteries as centers for public veneration. But we should not discount the possibility that this move shows an underlying power struggle, or at least a shift in the balance of power, between the women at these institutions and the clerics serving them, some of whom might have enjoyed the support of the local episcopate. In chapter 5, we found that there are indications—some conclusive, others less so—that some of these local clerics tried to claim the cultic identity of female communities in order to gain institutional control. This development, if our reading of it were to be proven accurate, would have been one of the ways via which ambiguous communities that outlasted the wave of Benedictine reforms in this period were integrated into male narratives of (saintly) power, losing in the process some of their spiritual and institutional autonomy.[73]

Even if these cases only reflect the attempts of the religious to become less dependent on the fickle support of powerful lords and founders, positive outcomes remain difficult to perceive in the source record. At high-profile institutions like Nivelles and Remiremont and smaller but long-established ones like Marchiennes, the beneficial effects appear limited, and for much of the eleventh century the history of female religious houses in Lotharingia is one marked by conflict, declining socioeconomic fortunes, and a marginalized position in spiritual and ecclesiastical affairs. By the time of Hildebrand's devastating speech at the synod of Rome, communities of women religious with few exceptions were becoming a fringe phenomenon in the church and contemporary religious life. Clearly some kind of intervention was in order: but contrary to what critics at the time argued, the need for this derived not from

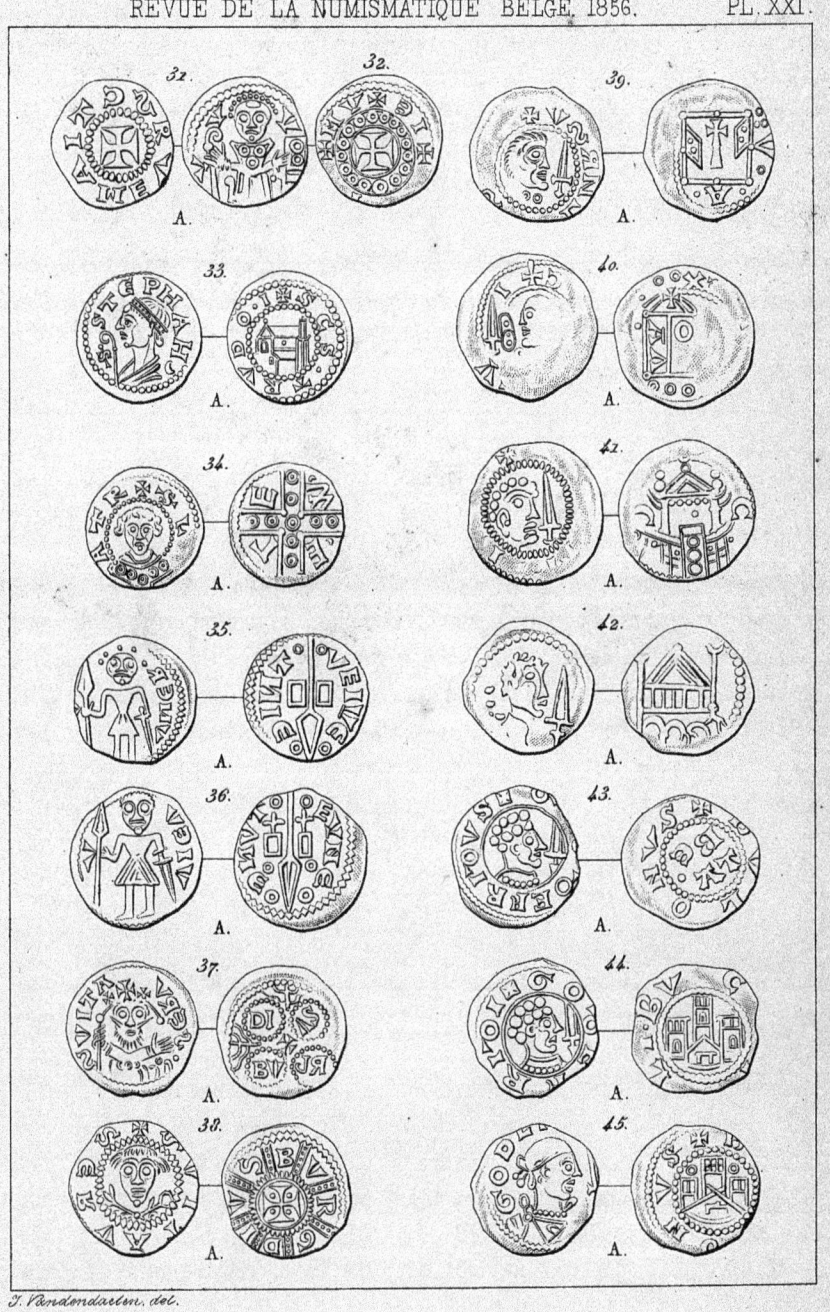

FIG. 11. Eleventh-century coins of Munsterbilzen (top left, numbers 31–32), showing Saint Amor. From De Coster, "Trouvaille," plate XXI.

the sisters' luxurious lifestyle or because of the ill-advised instructions of ninth-century reformers. Instead, it was caused by clerical and lay rulers: their erosion of the societal and religious relevance and the spiritual and institutional autonomy of women religious.

Benedictine Realities

While the strategies used to secure institutional viability described previously are most commonly encountered in ambiguous contexts, newly established Benedictine nunneries also struggled to become an established part of the region's ecclesiastical landscape. As we saw in chapter 5, communities like Thorn, Poussay, and Vergaville, while supported by high-ranking rulers, neither enjoyed ownership of extensive estates, nor made much of an impact, either in society or in a religious sense. Many new and reformed nunneries were, so it seems, deliberately kept small, and their religious deliberately kept away from the exercise of much direct influence.

A case in point is Denain, a monastery we encountered in chapter 2 as one of the beneficiaries of Charles the Bald's 877 charters. Following the late ninth century, it fades from the documentary record, to reemerge again in the 1020s, when it was (in the words of the *Deeds of the Bishops of Cambrai*) "restored" as a Benedictine nunnery by Count Baldwin IV of Flanders and Bishop Gerard of Cambrai, possibly to receive the religious from the recently dissolved community of Marchiennes.[74] Yet despite the involvement of these prominent lords, the first Abbess Ermentrudis had to pursue a prudent economic policy. According to Jean-Pierre Gerzaguet's reconstruction, her monastery had lost about a third of its property from the approximately 2700 hectares mentioned in Charles the Bald's charter. Possibly Baldwin and Gerard were aware of this older document, or at least a version that preceded the interpolated one currently available for study, but neither took action to remediate the former community's losses.[75] Nor do we know of efforts to establish Denain as a prominent cultic center. Marchiennes's former saintly patrons remained firmly in situ, and the new Denain community and its sanctuary did not have any relics of local patroness Saint Ragenfredis to offer to pilgrims. The chances of generating much interest from these and other potential benefactors therefore must have been low.

Things only began changing when, c. 1039, Fredesindis succeeded Ermentrudis as abbess. The description of her tenure in the later *Miracles of Saint Ragenfredis* reminds us of contemporary events at Thorn and generally attests to the desperation with which abbesses of recently founded, ill-funded institutions were seeking to establish a cultic identity for their communities and looking for ways to compensate for their limited landed wealth and lay appeal. According to the *Miracles*, Denain's young leader built a new church, traveled extensively in support of her institution's renewal, and recovered the relics of patroness Saint Ragenfredis, lost since the tenth century. On her way to the archiepiscopal court in Reims, she had made a detour to visit the local castellan's castle at Neufchâtel-sur-Aisne. While reading the psalter there she noted that Ragenfredis's name was rubricated in red and immediately appealed to the castellan's wife. Realizing that the castle held the relics of Denain's patron saint, Fredesindis demanded them back. An older nun named Emma stepped in to reassure the young abbess, promising to return to the castle at a later time and recover the relics. Eventually, Emma stole a satchel containing Ragenfredis's remains, and brought them back to Denain.[76] But these successes, although they must have raised great hopes within the community, did not exactly transform Denain's fortunes. Nothing that Fredesindis is reported as doing (including the dramatic recovery of Ragenfredis's relics) was enough to spur the customary bout of hagiographic activity; nor do we hear anything about a significant turn in the community's financial fortunes.

That the pull of the relics of Ragenfredis was less than expected, and that there was nothing locally that could be done about this, can be inferred from what happened once Fredesindis was recruited as the first abbess of the nunnery of Messines (or Mesen) in 1065. A personal foundation of the count and countess of Flanders, Messines was by all accounts a much wealthier, prestigious, and better-connected institution than Denain.[77] No doubt mindful of her former community's precarious situation, Fredesindis commissioned the aforementioned *Miracles of Saint Ragenfredis*.[78] It was probably also under her supervision that the Messines scriptorium produced the interpolated version of Charles the Bald's charter.[79] This new document emphasized the origins of Denain's landholdings in patroness Saint Ragenfredis's private estate, alluded to efforts to recover some of properties presumed lost from that original endowment, and stated that the local lay lord was obliged to finance the maintenance of the monastery's churches and buildings.[80] It is telling that the religious at Denain had to wait for their leader, clearly a very energetic and capable personality, to be headhunted by wealthy and powerful lords before their local cult could achieve a written hagiography, or their archive new institutional "memories." In themselves, such strategies of self-defense and self-promotion were hardly surprising, as communities all over Lotharingia were resorting to them.[81] But it is revealing of Denain's situation that these strategies were only within reach of its sympathetic leader once she had access to the resources and expertise that were available at or from Messines.

Denain's subsequent fate is emblematic, if not exactly representative, of the struggle faced by smaller ambiguous communities in subsequent decades. By the end of the century, the religious faced competition from the recent foundation of Etrun, a nunnery that benefited from its proximity to the burgeoning town of Arras and appears to have recruited among its population.[82] At local synods, the abbess of Denain would henceforth be ranked behind her colleague from Etrun, indicating that the latter institution was held in higher regard by local elites and presumably also enjoyed more robust institutional and economic health.[83] Underlying this shift in regional prominence—if prominence is indeed the right term to describe Denain's former situation—was probably also clerical criticism of the sisters' mode of life. In an 1153 letter to the bishop of Arras, Pope Eugenius III complained that the Denain sisters had almost completely forgotten what they had vowed and instructed him to organize their return to a more appropriate mode of life so as to reverse a situation of material and spiritual decline.[84]

Some of that criticism may have originated with the sisters' declining interest in a strict Benedictine observance. Indeed, Jean-Pierre Gerzaguet has speculated that there might have been an earlier attempt to reform local discipline, using Etrun as a model.[85] But it is also possible that the Denain religious had not so much strayed from their Benedictine identity (and become, as some commentators suspected, canonesses), but were rather living according to an interpretation that no longer matched clerical expectations. Early eleventh-century reformers had matched the women's conduct, in spirit at least, against Saint Benedict's instructions: but in the eyes of observers c. 1100, the result of that exercise may have been far too ambiguous.[86] Two points of contention that immediately come to mind are the sisters' putative ownership of individual benefices or prebends, and the possibility that they occupied separate houses (or otherwise lived separately) on the monastic compound. A good point of comparison is available for Messines, where, just half a century after its foundation, Abbess Ogiva faced similar criticism from Pope Paschalis II. In a letter dated 1107, he admonished her to enforce the principles of individual poverty and enclosure and called on her to generally establish a communal life conforming to the *monastica religio*.[87] Rather than simply assume that Ogiva had allowed internal discipline to lapse, we need to at least allow for another possibility. Maybe, in the mid-eleventh-century context of a high-profile, noble foundation like Messines, strictly enforcing poverty and communal life had been undesirable for all parties involved and probably also detrimental to Messines's future success as a religious institution and a focal point of aristocratic networks.[88] For comparison, of the nuns at Epinal we know that in the later eleventh century they held prebends on properties of Remiremont, and vice versa.[89] Hardly an arrangement that easily aligned with Saint Benedict's ideals, it was nonetheless widely accepted as a reasonable, effective way for supporting female institutions, their members, and their respective aristocratic networks. And for a small monastery like Denain, it might have been one of the ways to sustain viable recruitment numbers and allow the community to fulfil its duties while working with a limited budget.

Globally speaking, what we can observe are not direct testimonies of the misconduct of female religious, but the fact that the ambiguity (i.e., adaptability to local circumstances and patronal expectations) of their lifestyle increasingly riled clerical observers. In contrast, local aristocrats would have been fairly unconcerned about women religious not following the *Rule* to the letter. At Sainte-Waudru in Mons, Count Renier in the early eleventh century actively supported the religious, despite intervening, along with Bishop Gerard of Cambrai, to turn Maubeuge into a Benedictine monastery.[90] And in 1020, Ermesindis, wife of Count Albert I of Namur, donated the estate of Gerpinnes to the ambiguous community (later canonesses) of Moustier-sur-Sambre.[91] In addition to the material benefits that could be expected from this transfer, Moustier-Sur-Sambre, lacking a prominent patron saint of its own, also obtained the relics of eighth-century Saint Rolendis, whose remains are currently still kept at Gerpinnes's parish church.[92] In later centuries Rolendis became the subject of a regional cult, bringing pilgrims to visit her grave in the late eleventh-century crypt.[93] Finally, as late as 1096, Countess Ida of Boulogne, the mother of Count Godfrey of Lower Lotharingia, issued a charter that not only significantly endowed the Munsterbilzen community but also stipulated that the revenues from certain donated goods could be divided equally as daily allowances (*prebenda*) among the sisters.[94] These arrangements reveal an awareness of how communities of women religious could be kept viable institutionally. They may also demonstrate how different the perception and self-understanding of groups of women religious were from those of their male counterparts. Around the same time of her gift to Munsterbilzen, Ida also became one of the earliest champions of Cluniac monasticism in the Low Countries, when she invited monks from the Burgundian monastery to assist with the foundation of male monasteries at La Capelle (c. 1090) and Le Wast (c. 1096).[95] No doubt she was aware that Cluny also offered a new model for women, as practiced at the "glorious prison" of Marcigny:[96] but clearly, she did not see that alternative as applicable, or perhaps even acceptable, to the Munsterbilzen community.

For a very long time after Hildebrand's irate speech at the 1059 synod in Rome, many women religious and their supporters continued to think in an ambiguous sense, even if their identity was now being judged against an unambiguous model.[97] Their reasons for doing so varied, ranging from the practical to the theoretical, and merit further investigation going beyond the chronological scope of this book. And communities that fell foul of clerical approval did not necessarily lose their self-confidence, especially when they enjoyed the continued support of local patrons and the benefits of a thriving saint's cult. A potent testimony to this is the pride that is expressed through a bilingual commemorative inscription in a Munsterbilzen manuscript from the early twelfth century. Found at the end of a list of the community's members and their male clerics, it expresses confidence in the standing of these women and men and in their spiritual achievements:

Tesi samanunga was edele unde scona et omnium virtutum pleniter plena.

This community was noble and handsome, and full of all virtues.[98]

In chapter 5, we discovered that ambiguous groups of women religious in the late tenth and early eleventh century suffered a new wave of interventions. Looking at the response of the women to these pressures and at the scarce indications of debate and perhaps even reflection on female observance and organization, it becomes clear that the communities of the time were not working in auspicious circumstances. Indeed, they were essentially waging a war against forces much stronger than themselves. At the same time, this chapter has argued that some of these women were aware that they had little to gain—in fact, that they had a great deal to lose—from giving in to clerical pressure to convert to a Benedictine regime. The coping strategies they relied on to confront these dangers and remain societally relevant—reorganizing communal memories, promoting associations with ruling dynasties past and present, and reinventing hagiography—reveal striking similarities with those adopted by female communities in the late ninth and early tenth centuries. For some ambiguous communities, the effects of these later efforts were modest at best: with some exceptions, the tide of ecclesiastical renewal was simply not going in their favor. To add insult to injury, clerical critics were now accusing them and their former patrons of bringing the female monastic phenomenon to a state of near-redundancy. However, other communities thrived, thanks in no small part to the persistence of a mode of ambiguous thinking with lay patrons and the religious themselves.

Conclusion

Researching the history of female religious between the beginning of the ninth century and the middle of the eleventh is very much like listening to a badly tuned shortwave radio. Clear, reliable information comes through in short bursts, alternating with long stretches of silence and "white noise." In the past, specialists of religious history have tried to get around this by relying on normative commentaries by reformers of the early ninth century and on the criticism penned by clerical agents from the mid-tenth century onward. Yet as chapter 1 has shown, uncritical use of these sources has fundamentally distorted our view of the social and cultural role played by female monasteries from that period. It has also hidden any sense of what might have been the expectations of contemporaries in this regard and obscured the view of what forms of religious life insiders and outsiders thought of as legitimate for women or, indeed, simply workable. More specifically, the historiographical reliance on the normative voice has led us to interpret "ambiguity" in the observance and organization of women religious as being an indicator of a situation of mismanagement and spiritual decline. It has also brought scholars to regard indications of the disempowerment of religious (in a spiritual and a legal sense) as signs of a catastrophic decline in both the quality of female monasticism and its relevance to society.

Over the last two decades, both specialists of monastic history and gender historians have challenged these views, arguing that comparing the ninth to early eleventh centuries unfavorably to the preceding and following periods is to project anachronistic notions of spiritual and institutional merit onto the women religious of that period. But these studies have done little to correct a standard approach that continues to regard heterogeneity in the organization and spirituality of a female community as essentially inferior to adherence to consolidated rules. Taking as my case study a group of forty female communities in ninth- to eleventh-century Lotharingia, I have argued that this period's heterogeneity and normative ambiguity in female monasticism derived from three factors. First, the specific expectations of patrons and the need to adapt communal identities to changing sociopolitical circumstances caused the patronage of these institutions to change. Second, in a landscape where numerous religious institutions vied for the favors of patrons and pilgrims, there was a need to distinguish between them and also to argue the continued relevance of female monasticism as a whole. And third, there was a largely forgotten female culture of reflection and debate over monastic organization and observance, where written rules served as sources of inspiration rather than as templates for organizing the life of women religious.

This triple hypothesis opens the door to a fundamental reinterpretation of the textual and material remains of female monastic communities. In chapters 2 and 3, I demonstrated that female religious and their associates of the ninth and early tenth centuries developed "coping strategies" in response to (in a first phase) the directives of Carolingian reformers and to (in a second) changing sociopolitical circumstances. These coping strategies were designed to sustain the perceived relevance and viability of their institutions in particular and of female monasticism generally. By reorganizing monastic space, reimagining the local cult of saints, nurturing strategic alliances with Carolingian rulers and secular lords, and heavily promoting communal prayer service, some communities flourished. It is these institutions that survived the turbulent decades around 900 and reemerged at the beginning of the tenth century as highly prized symbolic and political trophies for the region's political elite. Here we can also observe, particularly in the early decades of the tenth century, glimpses of a culture where the male and female members of monasteries actively studied and debated different options for organizing the sisters' observance and spirituality. Significantly, the relevant evidence indicates two things. One, that the development of female monasteries as institutions, but also as religious and perhaps even emotional communities, was the product of an effort by members of both sexes. And two, that the sacramental and pastoral roles of women religious once again were the subject of reflection and, in some contexts, perhaps even a change in practice.

CONCLUSION 157

Aristocratic rivalries form the background against which attitudes toward ambiguous observance by women religious began to change. Chapter 4 showed that many of the "reforms" and "semi-reforms" of the 930s to 960s were not—or certainly not in first place—about remediating a community's poor spiritual and institutional performance or restituting lost property, but about creating representative strongholds of ecclesiastical and secular power. Although it seems beyond question that some reformers, particularly bishops from Upper Lotharingia, were sincerely convinced of the superiority of Saint Benedict's *Rule*, its application in concrete contexts suggests that we read such assertions as demonstrative acts of absolute authority over the life of women religious and as ways of claiming a stake in the region's high politics. We can only wonder if the beneficial effects of these interventions outweighed the suppression of local traditions of debate and reflection on ways to pursue a religious life, and the restrictions on the agency of local leaders, particularly abbesses.

As a wave of Benedictine foundations and reforms took place in the second half of the tenth century, the remaining ambiguous communities experienced increasingly fraught relations with clerical and sometimes even secular lords, none of which can be securely attributed to problems with the sisters' conduct or their presumed failure to manage their institutions. As chapters 5 and 6 made clear, beginning in the later tenth century and continuing throughout the early eleventh, women religious were facing challenges that were arguably many times more detrimental to their unique spiritual and institutional identity and much more restrictive to their individual freedom than the reforms of the early ninth century. There is evidence to argue that "nonreformed" female communities responded fiercely to the attacks by clerical and lay detractors, relying on coping strategies that are strongly reminiscent of those used by their ninth- and early tenth-century predecessors.

Overall though, the tone was set for a century's worth of increasingly turbulent clashes with clerical reformers and for the shaping, toward the middle of the eleventh century, of an enduring image of the period between 800 and 1050 as female monasticism's "dark age." Several ambiguous institutions also paid dearly for their defiant attitude and their continued insistence on their locally shaped identity. No doubt, abbesses and other religious were aware that they were fighting against adversaries who were much stronger politically and legally, who were continuously working on refining an antiambiguous rhetoric, and who had a public voice that was much louder than that of their own. But they presumably also realized that the stakes of the conflict reached far beyond the question of their individual autonomy or, indeed, their institution's continued existence—it would have been evident that many recently founded or reformed nunneries now existed in marginal conditions, culturally and socioeconomically. The silence of Benedictine nuns in the decades around the year thousand may have sounded almost as loud to contemporaries as it does to us as modern observers.

Critics might argue that this book's reading of the evidence reduces the female monastic phenomenon to an amalgam of discrete, independently evolving communities, with nothing in common but the fact that they consisted of groups of veiled women. But my aim was to argue that what makes female monasticism in this period a cohesive and relevant object of study is precisely its diversity and flexibility in the face of changing, frequently challenging circumstances. This diversity and flexibility was challenged, with increasing intensity, from the mid-tenth century onward. Although the effects of this shift were surely beneficial in some respects, in light of what we have seen in this study, they emerge as catastrophically limiting in others. Nonetheless, it is a testimony to the resilience and creativity of female religious in later centuries that ambiguity in observance (in the sense of not strictly observing a specific, written rule) continues to be evident in the primary evidence. Whereas previously historians have seen in these indications evidence of misbehavior, laxity, or catastrophic oppression, we should at least allow for the possibility that they were, in fact, the product of decisions based on rational consideration by these women and their male associates of what life suited best their worldly and spiritual objectives.

Appendix A

The Leadership and Members of Female Religious Communities in Lotharingia, 816–1059

Abbreviations

AbF = abbesses
AbM = abbots
AV = lay individuals identified *explicitly* in contemporary sources as advocate
LABM = lay individuals identified *explicitly* in contemporary sources as abbot
OFF = other female monastic officers
OFM = other male monastic officers and personnel
fl. = active
(*) = mentioned only in post-1059 sources

Institutions where no relevant information could be recovered from the primary evidence or the secondary literature are Andenne, Antoing, Caudry, Condé-sur-Escaut, Hamage, Hastière, Herbitzheim, Honnecourt, Meerbeke, Moustier-Sur-Sambre, Neumünster, Orp-le-Grand, Sains-lès-Marquion, Sainte-Marie-aux-Nonnains (Metz), and Toul.

Aldeneik

AbF	Ava (fl. mid-9th century)[1]
Other members	Saliga (fl. early 9th century)[2]

Bleurville

AbF Leuchardis (daughter of Count Renard of Toul, fl. 1050)[3]
AV   Founding family of Fontenoy-le-Château and Bleurville[4]

Bonmoutier

AbM/LABM   Doddo (*abbas*, fl. 816)[5]

Bouxières

AbF Rothildis (possibly a granddaughter of Charles the Bald and Richildis, and daughter of Count Hugo of Bourges and his wife Rothildis, abbess of Chelles, fl. 932–65/77)[6]
Ermengartis (fl. 977)[7]
Other members Rotlindis (oblate daughter of Count Teutbert and his wife Iuditta, fl. 960–65)[8]
(?) Emma (daughter of Frambert, fl. before 965)[9]
(?) Thiedrada (daughter of Frambert, fl. before 965)[10]
Alphaidis (daughter of Ermenaidis, fl. 966)[11]
Doda (daughter of Ermenaidis, fl. 966)[12]
(?) Helvidis (fl. before 973)[13]
LABM Odelric (*abbas*, before June 960/2)[14]

Denain

AbF Ermentrudis (c. 1025–39)[15]
Fredesindis (1039–65)[16]
Other members Ava (fl. 840s [?])[17]
Emma (fl. c. 1039–65)[18]

Epinal

AbF (*) Dietburhc (fl. 1003)[19]

Hasnon

AbF   (*) Alpaidis (fl. second quarter of the 9th century [?]; ruled one year)[20]
(*) Algintrudis (fl. second quarter of the 9th century [?]; ten years)[21]
(?) (*) Ermentrudis (I) (wife of Charles the Bald, lay abbess [?], fl. c. 860–9 [?])[22]
Ermentrudis (II) (daughter of Charles the Bald and Ermentrudis, fl. 860 [?]–after July 877)[23]

AbM   (*) Hrotfrid (d. 816/21?; ruled twenty-six years)[24]
(*) Waltoarius (fl. early 820s; one and a half years)[25]
(*) Amadeus (fl. early 820s; two and a half years)[26]
(*) Audulf (fl. 820s/830s, seven and a half years)[27]

Hesse

AbF   Serberga/Gerberga (niece of Pope Leo IX, fl. 1050)[28]

Juvigny

AbF   (*) Bertendis (from the abbey of Aude, fl. 870s)[29]

Lunéville

AbF   Adheleidis (fl. 1034–c. 1052)[30]
(*) Oda/Uda (daughter of Frederic of Ardenne, fl. c. 1052–1100 or later)[31]

AV   (*) Godfrid (count of Metz, fl. late 1040s–d. in or shortly after 1052)[32]

Marchiennes

AbF   Judith (fl. 976)[33]

Maubeuge

AbF Theodrada (fl. 930s [?])[34]
    (*) Ansoaldis (1012–50)[35]

Metz—Saint-Pierre-aux-Nonnains

AbF
: (?) Fredeburga (fl. 918–930s)[36]
  Hauwidis/Heluuidis/Hadewid (fl. 960–77)[37]
  Irmindrudis (fl. 993)[38]
  Odilia (fl. late 10th or early 11th century)[39]

OFM
: Hugo (*prepositus*), Berner, Theodonius, Askerius, Ansold, Hageric, Andreas, Botland, Privat, Ermenard (presumably clerics serving the female community, fl. 918)[40]
  (*) Johannes (*hebdomadarius*; John of Vandières, 920s/930s)[41]

Other members
: Berta, Gerlindis, Hildebordis, Ava, Tecla, Gerlindis, Berta, Betta, Heraidis, Herant, Magnifinda, Doda, Theksinda, Blida, Hartruldis, Lisinia, Gerindis, Brima, Gerlindis, Osanna, Vicluta, Agila, Angilinoldis, Ermona, Buchrudis, Rotholdis (presumably community members, fl. 918)[42]
  Geisa (niece of Fredeburga, fl. 920s/early 930s)[43]
  Eremberga, Tekardis, Rilindis, Aldegundis, Geila, Adelbulgis, Richildis, Adelbulgis, Ida, Liutcardis, Vuerenburgis, Fastrada, Geila, Hildegardis, Conegundis, Hersindis, Ermentrudis, Odilia, Geila, Berta, Matfridis (possibly a member of the Matfrid aristocratic clan; listed as sister of Berta), Anna, Ermengardis, Liutgardis, Adelaidis, Hitta, Hildegardis, Engeleua, Gertrudis, Adheburgis, Heluidis, Hathuidis (fl. late 10th or early 11th century, during the time of Abbess Odilia)[44]

Metz—Sainte-Glossinde

AbF Hi(m)miltrudis (niece of Bishop Adalbero I of Metz, fl. 945)[45]
    (*) Voda/Oda (fl. 977)[46]
    Hermentrudis (possibly a sister of Bishop Thierry II of Metz, fl. 1012)[47]

Mons—Sainte-Waudru

AbF (*) Doda (fl. c. 820 [?])[48]
 (*) Oda (fl. early 10th century [?])[49]

Munsterbilzen

AbF (*) Ermengardis (member of the Lutzelburg family, d. 986)[50]
 (*) Cunegondis (member of the house of Chiny, d. 1017)[51]
 (*) Richza *de Ara* (d. 1060)[52]

Nivelles

AbF (*) Iduberga (c. 820 [?])[53]
 (*) Tadepeuga (d. 871)[54]
 Kisla/Gisla/Kisala (daughter of Lothar II, fl. after 896–907 [?])[55]
 Adalberina (fl. 966–before 992)[56]
 Voda (fl. 992)[57]
 Alhedis (fl. 1003)[58]
 Oda/Goda (fl. 1011)[59]
 (*) Athais (fl. 1030s)[60]
 Richece (fl. 1040)[61]
OFM Frederic (provost, fl. 1003)[62]
AV Unidentified count of Louvain (*advocatus*, fl. 1003)[63]
 Lantbert (*advocatus*, count of Louvain, fl. 1011)[64]
 Henric (*advocatus*, count of Louvain, fl. 1018)[65]

Oeren

AbF (*) Geba (fl. 1000)[66]

Pfalzel

AbF (*) Warendrudis (sister of Archbishop Hetti of Trier, fl. 810s–850s, ruled forty-two years)[67]
 (*) Ratsindis (from a local family of important patrons, fl. 935)[68]

	Ruothildis/Rothildis (may have been educated at Essen, fl. 988–89)[69]
Other members	Hulindis (sister of Abbess Warendrudis, d. before c. 850)[70]

Poussay

AbF Berenna (fl. 1049)[71]

Remiremont

AbF Imma/Ymma/Emma (fl. 810s–before 833)[72]
Uulfrada I (fl. before 833)
Thiathildis (related to seneschal and courtier Adalhard, fl. before 833–after 862)
Asprin (dates unknown)
Adeluuis (?) (fl. 880s/890s)
Uulfrada II (fl. 900s/910s)
Ida (*abbatissa et diaconissa*, fl. 920s/930s)
Berta (fl. 940s/950s)
Adelsindis (fl. 940s/950s)
Ermentrudis (fl. c. 965)
Uulfrada III (fl. c. 965/70 [?])
Gisla I (fl. 970s/980s)
Haduidis I (fl. late 10th–early 11th century)
Uilleburga (fl. early 11th century)
Berscinda (daughter of Count Gerard of Metz and his wife Eva, of the house of Luxembourg and a relative of Leo IX, fl. early 11th century)
Oda (possibly daughter of Count Frederic of Moselgau and sister of Adalbero III of Metz, from the house of Luxembourg; fl. before 1045–c. 1065/70).

OFF Uulfrada (*preposita*, fl. before 833)[73]
Adelaedis (*preposita*, fl. 940s/950s)
Ermentrudis (*sacratista* [?], 940s/950s)
Berta (*sacrista*, 960s/980s [?])
Judith (*sacrista* [?], 970s/980s)
Haduidis (*sacrista* [?], late 10th century)

	Berta (*preposita*, fl. early 11th century)
	Beatrice (*secretaria*, fl. 1048–70).
OFM	Teoderic (*prepositus*, fl. under Imma and Thiathildis)[74]
	Albold (chancellor/secretary; fl. c. 895–900)
	Lambod (*prepositus*, fl. middle of the 10th century [?])
	Landald (chancellor/secretary, fl. second half of the 10th century)
	Macher (*prepositus*, fl. late 10th century [?])
	Ingluin (*prepositus*, fl. late 10th–early 11th century)
	Uolbert (*ebodomadarius*, fl. late 10th–early 11th century)
	Hugo de Candida (*hebdomadarius*; fl. before the late 1040s)
Other members	A large number of individuals from the ninth, tenth, and (to a lesser extent) eleventh centuries are listed in Remiremont's necrologies, lists of community members, and notices.[75]
LABM/AV	Odelric (*abbas*, fl. 962)[76]
	Ravenger (*advocatus*, fl. 960s)
	Lizer (*advocatus*, fl. 960s/970s)
	Benno (*advocatus*, fl. 980s/1000s)
	Arbert/Albert (*advocatus*, fl. late 10th century)
	Gerard (*advocatus Vosagi*, fl. late 10th century)
	Gerard (*advocatus*, duke of Lotharingia, fl. 1048–70)

Susteren

AbF	(*) Benedicta (daughter of King Zwentibold, fl. early 10th century)[77]
	(*) Cecilia (daughter of King Zwentibold, fl. early 10th century)[78]

Thorn

AbF	(*) Benedicta (daughter of Count Ansfrid II [?], fl. late 10th century-no earlier than 1010)[79]
	(*) Hildewardis (sister of Benedicta [?], fl. early 11th century [?])[80]
	(*) Halduinde/Hilduina (daughter of Count Ansfrid II [?], fl. early 11th century [?])[81]

Gerberga (fl. second quarter of the 11th century)[82]
(*) Hildegardis (fl. 1044 [?])[83]

Verdun—Saint-Maur

AbF   (*) Sara (fl. 1039)[84]
(*) Maria de Bussy (fl. 1043)[85]
Alix (fl. 1047)[86]
(*) Eva/Ava/Adalberga (fl. c. 1049–57)[87]
(*) Berverga (fl. c. 1050 [?])[88]
(*) Girberga (fl. c. 1060–1103)[89]

Vergaville

AbF   Aemilia[90]
Cunigunda[91]
Petressa[92]

APPENDIX B

The Decrees on Women Religious from the Acts of the Synod of Chalon-sur-Saône, 813, and the Council of Mainz, 847

1. The Decrees from the Synod of Chalon-sur-Saône, 813

Latin text taken from *Concilia aevi Karolini*, ed. Werminghoff, 2/1:284–85.

> 52. Monasteriis sane puellaribus tales praeferri debent faeminae et abbatissae creari, quae et se et subditum gregem cum magna religione et sanctitate custodire norint et his, quibus praesunt, prodesse non desinant. Sed et se et illas ita observent utpote vasa sancta in ministerio Domini praeparata. Talem enim se debet abbatissa exhibere subditis in habitu, in veste, in omni convictu, ut eis et ad caelestia regna pergentibus ducatum praebeat et sciat etiam se pro his, quas in regimine accepit, in conspectu Domini rationem redditturam.

Monasteries of women religious should put forward and create as abbesses those women, who are dedicated to guarding themselves and the flock subject to their authority with great religion and holiness, and do not neglect to pursue the well-being of those individuals they supervise. They should take care of themselves and those under their supervision like a holy vessel prepared for the service of God. The abbess should present herself to her subjects through her habit, vestment, and her whole demeanor in such a manner that she acts as a guide to those who are also on a journey to the celestial kingdoms, and know that she will have to justify herself before God for the things she received during her tenure.

53. Libuit namque huic sacro conventui quasdam admonitiunculas breviter eis sanctimonialibus scribere, quae se canonicas vocant, quoniam hae, quae sub monasticae regulae norma degunt, totius vitae suae ordinem in eadem, quam profitentur, regula scriptum habent.

It pleased this sacred gathering to address a few brief admonishments to those women religious who call themselves canonesses, for those who live under the norm of the monastic rule have the complete order of their lives inscribed in the rule on which they made their profession.

54. Abbatissa diligenter habeat curam de congregatione sibi commissa et provideat, ut in lectione et in officio et in psalmorum modulatione ipsae sanctaemoniales strenuae sint, et in omnibus operibus bonis illa eis ducatum praebeat utpote pro animabus earum rationem in conspectu Domini redditura et stipendia sanctimonialibus praebeat necessaria, ne forte per indigentiam cibi aut potus peccare compellantur.

The abbess should diligently take care of the congregation committed to her and see to it that these women religious strenuously apply themselves to reading, celebrating office, and modulating the psalms, and be a guide to them in all good works, for she will have to justify herself before God for their souls. And that she provides them with the necessary income and stipends, so they shall not be compelled to sin for a lack of food or drink.

55. Abbatissa cum viris, clericis sive laicis, horis incompetentibus non loquatur, sed quicquid cum masculis, clericis sive laicis, de rebus necessariis peragere debet, a prima hora usque ad vespertinam peragat, et hoc non cum singulis, sed coram pluribus.

The abbess should not talk to men, be they clerics or laymen, at inappropriate hours, and can only discuss necessary subjects with males, clerics or laymen, from prime until vespers. And she should do this not with single individuals, but in the presence of many.

56. A vespere usque ad primam neque abbatissa neque aliqua sanctimonialium cum quibuslibet masculis ullum colloquium habeant, ni forte talis fuerit occasio, quam evitare non possint; et si necessitas incubuerit, id coram testibus facere debebit.

Neither the abbess nor any woman religious should converse with any male, whoever he is, from vespers until prime, unless specific circumstances make it inevitable; and if there is a necessity, it has to be done in the presence of witnesses.

57. Abbatissa, quae in civitate monasterium habet, nequaquam de monasterio egrediatur nisi per licentiam episcopi sui aut qui eius vicem obtinet, nisi forte aut imperialis iussio eam cogat aut prolixitas itineris id facere minime permittat. Et si quando foras pergit, de sanctimonialibus, quas secum ducit, curam et vigilantiam habeat, ut nulla eis detur peccandi licentia sive occasio. Sed et cum pergit, in monasterio talem in vice sua constituere debet, quae de sanctimonialium animabus curam et vigilantiam habeat.

An abbess, who has a monastery in a town, should never leave the monastery unless she receives permission from the bishop or someone in his place, unless an imperial order or the difficulty of the journey does not allow it. And when she goes outside, she should take care and be vigilant that the women religious whom she takes with her are not given license or opportunity to sin. And when she goes, she should also appoint someone in her place who cares and acts vigilantly about the souls of the women religious.

58. Habeat etiam abbatissa studium aut in aedificando ea, quae ad sanctimonialium necessitatem pertinent, aut in restaurando.

The abbess should commit herself to build or restore those things that pertain to the needs of the religious.

59. Sanctimoniales in monasterio constitutae habeant studium in legendo et in cantando, in psalmorum celebratione sive oratione et horas canonicas, matutinam videlicet, primam, tertiam, sextam, nonam, vespertinam, completoriam pariter celebrant et omnes, excepta quam infirmitas tenet, in dormitorio dormiant et omnibus diebus ad collationem veniant.

Female religious should apply themselves in their monastery to read and chant, to celebrate or pray the psalms, and celebrate the canonical hours, namely matins, prime, terce, sext, nones, vespers, compline, all in equal measure. They should all, with the exception of she who is kept by illness, sleep in the dormitory and every day come to participate in the communal meal.

60. Non debere presbyteros amplius in monasterio puellari immorari, nisi donec missarum sollemnia celebrent aut aliquid ibi de Dei servitio et suo ministerio expleant.

Priests should stay in women's monasteries for no longer than the time needed to celebrate the solemnities of Mass or other things that derive from their service to God and their ministry.

61. Non debere sanctimoniales in propriis mansionibus cum aliquibus masculis, clericis sive laicis, consanguineis sive extraneis, bibere sive comedere, sed, si quando id agendum est, in auditorio agatur; et ubi auditorium deest fiat. Et cum nullo masculo eis colloquium habere liceat nisi in auditorio et ibi coram testibus.

Women religious should not eat or drink in their own homes with men, be they clerics or laymen, relatives or strangers; and when these things need to be done, they should be done in the auditorium; and where there is no auditorium, there should be one made. No male should be permitted to talk to them unless in the auditorium and in the presence of witnesses.

62. Sanctimoniales, nisi forte abbatissa sua pro aliqua necessitate incumbent mittente, nequaquam de monasterio egrediantur. Hae vero, quae famulos aut famulas non habent ad exercenda negotia, ad mediam portam monasterii perveniant et ibi coram testibus negotium suum exerceant.

Women religious should never leave the monastery, unless they are sent by the abbess for some necessary matter. Those who have no male or female servants to handle their business should come to the middle gate of the monastery and do it in front of witnesses.

63. Nullus vassus abbatissae nec minister aliquis nec clericus nec laicus claustra ancillarum Dei ingrediatur, nisi forte quando necessitas operandi incumbit.

No vassal of an abbess, or any minister, cleric or layman, should enter the cloister of the handmaidens of God, unless it so happens that there is a need for him to carry out a certain task.

64. Portaria non eligatur, nisi quae aetate matura sit et testimonium habeat bonum et vitae probabilis sit.

Only those individuals should be elected as porter who are of mature age, good reputation, and exemplary conduct.

65. Quicquid in his capitulis minus est, ab episcopo suo abbatissa perquirat et ita illi in omnibus oboediens sit secundum canonicam Institutionen, sicuti iustum et rectum est.

The abbess should enquire with her bishop about those things that are lacking in these decrees, and thus be obedient to him in all things, in accordance with the canonical institution, as is just and right.

2. The Decree from the Synod of Mainz, 847

Latin text taken from *Die Konzilien der Karolingischen Teilreiche 843–859*, ed. Hartmann, 169–70, c. 16. The translation of this decree may be found in chapter 1, at n. 84.

16. De vita sanctimonialium. Abbatissa, quae in civitate monasterium habet, nequaquam de monasterio egrediatur, nisi per a licentiam episcopi sui aut qui eius vicem obtinet, nisi forte regali iussione cogatur. Et si quando foras pergit, de sanctimonialibus, quas secum ducit, curam et vigilantiam habeat, ut nulla eis detur peccandi licentia sive occasio. Sed et cum pergit, in monasterio talem in vice sua constituere debet, quae de sanctimonialium animabus curam et vigilantiam gerat. Habeat etiam abbatissa studium in aedificando ea, quae ad sanctimonialium necessitatem pertinent, et in restaurando. Sanctimoniales vero in monasterio constitutae habeant studium in legendo et in cantando, in psalmorum caelebratione sive oratione. Et horas canonicas, matutinam videlicet, primam, tertiam, sextam, nonam, vespertinam, conpletorium pariter celebrent; et omnes, excepta quam infirmitas tenet, in dormitorio dormiant, et omnibus diebus ad conlationem veniant. Et ut cetera servent, quae in regulis sanctimonialium continentur, et quae a sanctis patribus illis constituta sunt.

Appendix C

Jacques de Guise's Account of the Attempted Reform of Nivelles and Other Female Institutions in the Early Ninth Century

[Episcopus Cameracensis]... regulas atque constituciones factas in consilio Aquisgrani de monachis atque sanctimonialibus, presbyteris, clericis atque laicis episcopus Cameracensis, suam visitans parrochiam, collegiis, quibus congruebat, more debito exprimendo divulgavit. Walcandus etiam Leodiensis episcopus hoc idem faciendo venit Nivelle ad ecclesiam sancte Guertrudis et statuta consilii eis declaravit. Quibus perlectis et declaratis, episcopus inde ieiunus recedens dimisit eas in capitulo murmurantes, non valens eas quietare. Abhinc per totam diocesim dicta statuta declarans, tamdem reversus est ad propria.

The bishop of Cambrai, like his colleagues with whom he was in agreement, whilst he was visiting his parishes revealed in the customary way of doing so the rules and constitutions established at the council of Aachen on monks and women religious, priests, clerics, and laypeople. Similarly, Bishop Walcand of Liège went to Nivelles, to the monastery of Saint Gertrudis, to do the same and explain to them the council's statutes. Having read and explained them thoroughly, the fasting bishop withdrew as he realized he was unable to quiet the women, who were murmuring in the chapter. Eventually, having explained said statutes across his entire diocese, he returned to his residence.

Latin text taken from De Guise's *Annales Hannoniae*, ed. Sackur, 162–63.

Abbatissa Nivellensis cernens sui conventus distemperanciam, misit in Montibus, in Melbodio et alibi in locis quam pluribus ad temptandum, si Cameracensis episcopus onera tam gravia ex parte consilii eis imposuisset, et receperunt, quod sic. Que adinvicem conglobate miserunt Coloniam et repererunt ecclesias plures sanctimonialium cum ipsis concordantes, nolentes videlicet dictis statutis obedire. Conglobate tamdem adinvicem et consulte, de statutis non curantes, a gravaminibus illatis et inferendis et de iugo eis imposito ad futurum consilium ad papam Paschalem appellaverunt. Inter autem cetera statuta, que sanctimoniales tangebant, erat statutum, quod omnes sanctimoniales sub imperio ac Francorum regno degentes regulam beati Benedicti profiterentur, vivendo in obedientia atque castitate.

The abbess of Nivelles, noticing the discontent of her convent, enquired in Mons, Maubeuge, and many other places to see if the bishop of Cambrai had imposed on them similarly heavy burdens on behalf of the council, and if they had accepted them. Together they enquired in Cologne, finding many convents of women religious who were in agreement with them, and were not willing to obey said statutes. Having gathered, and having consulted each other, not caring for the statutes they appealed to Pope Paschalis for future counsel over the maltreatment they had been subjected to, and the yoke that had been imposed on them. Among the statutes that concerned women religious was one saying that all women religious living in the empire and kingdom of the Franks were to profess to the blessed Benedict's Rule, and live in obedience and chastity.

Cum audisset imperator, quod ille sanctimoniales a sacro consilio appellassent, misit ad Pascalem papam, quatinus acta sacri consilii confirmaret, quod et fecit. Audiens postmodum papa, quod ad ipsum appellassent, scripsit episcopo Leodiensi Walcando, quatinus ex parte summi pontificis eas induceret, ut saltim, si regulam beati Benedicti nollent profiteri, votum castitatis emitterent. Que concordi assensu petierunt consilium sex mensium, et tunc bene consulte responderent in Nivella. Emensis igitur sex mensibus omnibus abbatissis appellacioni adherentibus in Nivella congregatis, dominus Walcandus cum reverentia protulit eis verbum Dei.

When the emperor heard that these women religious appealed against the holy council, he called upon Pope Paschalis so that he would confirm its statutes, which he duly did. Afterwards, the pope learned that they had appealed to him, and wrote to Bishop Walcand of Liège so that he would instruct them on behalf of the highest pontiff that they would at least profess chastity, if they refused to vow to the Rule of the blessed Benedict. In harmonious agreement the women requested a council, to be held in six months' time at Nivelles, indicating that they would have sufficiently deliberated by that time to respond. Following those six months, all the abbesses belonging to the region gathered in Nivelles, and Lord Walcand reverently instructed them in the word of God.

Sermone finito, duce Lovaniensi, comite Montensi Albone multisque nobilibus personis presentibus, unanimiter concordi assensu omnium ecclesiarum appellacioni adherencium una voce responderunt: "Primo protestamur coram Deo et cunctis audientibus, quod regulam beati Benedicti nunquam profitebimur. Secundo castitatem tenere proponimus, sed sub volo obligari nullo modo faciemus. Tertio obedienciam abbatissis nostris et vite honestatem vovere parate sumus. Quarto, si ista responsio non sufficit, parate sumus nostram prosequi appellationem."

When his sermon was finished, in the presence of the duke of Louvain, Count Albo of Mons, and many noblemen and other people, all of the women belonging to all monasteries that belonged to this ecclesiastical region, having reached unanimity through harmonious agreement, responded in one voice: "First, we protest with God and all of those listening, that we have never vowed to the Rule of the blessed Benedict. Second, we promise to remain chaste, but we will not let ourselves be forced to accept the veil. Third, we are prepared to vow ourselves to obedience to our abbesses and an honest life. Fourth, if this response is not enough, we are prepared to lodge further appeals."

Walcandus hec audiens induxit principes illuc assistentes, sub quibus habebant possessiones atque morabantur, quatinus inducerent eis, ex quo de patrimoniis Crucifixi vivebant, quod obedienciam debebant suis episcopis et imperatori et per consequens consilio Aquensi et quam maxime summo pontifici, qui consilium approbaverat. Doda abbatissa Montensis minus digeste respondit, ceteris obmutescentibus. Que responsio principibus atque domno Walcando displicuit. Finaliter omnes sine conclusione discesserunt. Domnus Walcandus cuncta sub sigillo summo pontifici atque Ludovico imperatori rescripsit.

Upon hearing this, Walcand exhorted the lords present there, under whose lordship the sisters had properties and existed generally, that they would remind the women religious, who lived from the patrimonies of the Crucifix, that they were obliged to be obedient to their bishops and emperor and, as a result of this also to the council of Aachen, and most of all to the highest pontiff, who had approved of the council. While the rest remained silent, Abbess Doda of Mons responded with little restraint. This answer displeased the rulers and Lord Walcand. Eventually, they all went away without reaching any agreement. Lord Walcand recorded everything in writing under the seal of the highest pontiff and Emperor Louis.

Qui tamdem videntes mulierum obstinatos animos et pertinaciter velle quod inceperant prosequi, scientes etiam, quod coacta servicia Deo non placent, sed displicent, ut sine aliquali regula non remanerent, composuerunt formulam vite honeste brevem sine quocumque voto, nisi sicut ceteri christiani, cum paucis statutis et dictis mulieribus transmiserunt, addendo, quod de cetero religiose seculares et non sanctimoniales appellarentur. Et ad earum perpetuam punicionem pluribus ecclesiis earundem abbatissas deposuit, loco quarum principes seculares abbates plures stabilivit.

When the lords and rulers noticed the obstinate minds of the women, and that these were stubbornly intent on pursuing what they had begun—knowing that forced service displeases God, but refusing to accept that they would remain without any rule—the lords and rulers drafted a short instruction for an honest life without any vows, except for that of any Christian, and sent it to the women with a few statutes and sayings, adding that henceforth they would be called secular religious, not nuns. And as a token of their eternal punishment, Walcand deposed the abbesses of many monasteries, and installed in their place many noblemen as secular abbots.

Appendix D

The Compilation on the *Roll of Maubeuge*, c. Early Eleventh Century

Transcribed from Mons, Archives du Royaume, Coll. Archives locales, P 1755v. The present transcription, which is intended as a placeholder version for a future critical edition, silently corrects all obvious transcription errors and omits the first of the glossary fragments.

1. *Institutio sanctimonialium Aquisgranensis* (816), canon 28 (*Concilia aevi Karolini*, ed. Werminghoff, 1/1:455–56), with an added passage (in italics) concerning Maubeuge.

<28> UT HOSPITALE PAUPERUM EXTRA MONASTERIUM SIT PUELLARUM. XXVIII. Quia sanctarum scripturarum auctoritatibus liquido demonstratur quod hospitalitas modis omnibus sit diligenda, et res ecclesiae oblationes sint fidelium, praetia peccatorum patrimonia pauperum, quamquam ad portam monasterii locus talis sit rite habendus, in quo adventantes quique suscipiantur. Oportet tamen ut extra, iuxta ecclesiam scilicet, in qua presbiteri cum ministris suis divinum explent officium, sit hospitale pauperum, cui etiam praesit talis qui et avaritiam oderit et hospitalitatem diligat. *De villis unde sorores in Melbodio*

monasterio vivere debent unusquisque presbiter in sua parochia de laborato decimam partem accipiat. De novem partem et de censu et exceptis decimis quae de aecclesiae villis ibidem conferuntur de rebus aecclesiae, prout facultas subpetit, eidem deputentur hospitali unde pauperes ibidem recreentur et foveantur. Sed et de omnibus[1] quae a fidelibus sanctimonialibus deferuntur, decimae dentur ad eorundem sustentationem pauperum. His nanque, cui hospitale committitur nequaquam res pauperum in suos unus retorquaeat, ne cum Iuda loculus Domini furante sententiam dampnationis excipiat. Sit etiam intra monasterium receptaculum ubi viduae et pauperculae tantummodo recipiantur et alantur, et si non possint alio, saltim quadragesimae tempore sanctimoniales Domini adimplentes praeceptum earum lavent pedes iuxta illud: "Si ego Dominus et magister vester lavi vobis pedes, quanto magis vos debetis alter alterius lavare pedes?"

2. Hildemar of Corbie, *Commentary on Saint Benedict's Rule*, extracts from the prologue (edited in *Expositio Regulae*, ed. Mittermüller, p. 66). Omitted passages are given between angle brackets.

< A schola enim derivatur scholasticus; nam quia sit scholasticus vel discolus, docet Beda in epistolam beati Petri apostoli, ubi ipse apostolus dicit: > "Non tantum bonis et modestis, sed etiam discolis." < Ait enim: discolis, > indisciplinatis dicit nomine ducto a Grece eloquio, quia Grece scola vocatur locus, in quo adolescentes litteralibus studiis operam dare, et ad audiendis magistros vacare solent, unde scola vacatio interpretatur. Denique in psalmo ubi canimus: "Vacate, videte, quoniam ego sum Dominus" pro eo quod nos dicimus vacate, in Grece habetur scolasate.[2] Scolastici < Grece > sunt eruditi, discoli indocti et agrestes; sed utrisque vult obedire subditos < explicans apertius, quomodo nos supra omni humanae creaturae jusserit, esse subjectos. >

3. Fragment of an unidentified glossary (*Abtet vos* to *Affuit*).

(not edited)

4. Decrees of the council of Chalon-sur-Saône (813), canons 18, 54, and 59 (*Concilia aevi Karolini*, ed. Werminghoff, 1/1:277, 284, 285).

< 18 > Quaesti sunt preterea quidam fratres, quod essent aliqui episcopi et abbates, qui decimas non sinerent dare ad ecclesias, ubi illi coloni missas audiunt. Proinde decrevit sacer iste conventus, ut episcopi et abbates de agris et vineis, quae ad suum vel fratrum stipendium habent, decimas ad ecclesias suas deferri faciant; familiae vero ibi dent decimas suas, ubi infantes eorum baptizantur, et ubi per totum anni circulum missas audiunt.

< 54 > Abbatissae diligenter habeat curam de congregatione sibi commissa et provideat, ut in lectione et in officio et in psalmorum modulatione ipsae sanctae < . . . >[3] strenue sint et in omnibus operibus bonis illa eis ducatum praebeat utpote pro animabus earum rationem in conspectu Domini redditura et stipendia sanctimonialibus prebeat necessaria, ne forte pro indigentiam cibi aut potus peccare compellantur.

< 59 > Sancti< . . . >[4] in monasterio constitutae habeant studium in legendo et in cantando, in psalmorum celebratione et oratione et horas canonicas, matutinam videlicet, primam, tertiam, sextam, nonam, vespertinam, completoriam celebrent et omnes, excepta quam infirmitas tenet, in dormitorio dormiant et omnibus diebus ad collationem veniant.

5. Decrees of the council of Worms (868), canons 8 and 9 (*Die Konzilien der Karolingischen Teilreiche (860–874)*, ed. Hartmann, 266–67).

< 8 > In quota generatione sibi fideles iungantur. In copulatione fidelium generationum numerum non diffinimus, sed id statuimus, ut nulli liceat christiano de propria consanguinitate sive cognatione uxorem accipere, usque dum generatio recordatur, cognoscitur, aut memoria retinetur.

< 9 > De feminis sacro velamine consecratis. Femine scilicet quae sacro sunt consecratae velamine si fuerint, quod nolumus, fornicatae, velamen deponere non presumant; sed paenitentiae iugo submisse summopere decertare festinent, ut ad indulgentiae et remissionis valeant gratiam pervenire.

6. Unidentified inserted fragment.

... cum offerendis uniuscuiusque monasterii et tertia parte sepulture exstraneorum.

7. "Penitential glosses" (set of interlinear glosses to what appears to be an early redaction of the *Paenitentiale mixtum Pseudo-Bedae-Egberti*).

Glose penitentialis

Appendix D, Table 1

	Monumentis memoriis, historiis	
	Plurimis, multis, nonnullis	Excerpsimus, collegimus
Censoris, iudicis	Debiles, infirmi	Alicubi, ubicumque
Potius, maius	Pusillanimes, parvo anima	Eucharistiam sacrificium, bonam gratiam
Co(m)patiens, condolens	Perpetrata, acta, facta	Rixam, contentiam
Solertus, studiose	Ignovi, perdonavi	Iubente, imperante
Sexum, naturam conditionem	Memor, consuetudinem	Pro modulo, pro mensura
Curiose, intente	Errata, peccata	Scandalizat, offendit
Discernat, intendat, separat	Explicavi, nuntiavi	Laesus, offensus
In examine, in iudicio	Vacans, otiosus	Difficultate, tardidate
Discrete, mensurate	Constuprata, violata, fornicata	Compulsus, invitus
Casu, eventu	Addatus, adiungatus	Pro noxa, pro culpa
Sponte, voluntarie	Modum, mensuram	Favet, consentit
Diversitas, varietas	Poene, prope	Reticuerit, tacebit, silebit
Tractant, considerant	Perpessat, sustinuit	Contigit, evenit
Vehuntur, portantur	Vir, fortia	Praecipue, maxime
Inhiantes, desiderantes	Patitur, sustinetur	Universa, omnia
Alligabunt, colligabunt	Culmen, altitudo vel ingenia	Discretum, diffinitum
Quamdiu, quam longe	Flagitiis, peccatis	Urguente, compellente
Distingue, separa	Diutius, longius	Sordida, inmunda
Hebes, insipiens	Sordidantes, polluentes	Ingluvies, mundantia
Novens, sapiens	Nitens, temptans, querens	Sacrilegium, cultura idolorum vel sacrarum rerum furtum
	Parentes, pater et mater	Rapina, furtum per vim factum
	Facinora, delicta	Praelato, praeposito
	Simpliciter, puriter	

Appendix D, Table 2

Ignorans, nesciens vel insciens	Coactus, constrictus	Libet, placet	Matrimonio, coniugio	
Interimit, occidit	Obscuratus, tenebratus	Fortuitu, subito	Machina, ingenium	Incestum, incastum id est suas betdi peccator[1]
apellice id est meretrice				

1. *betdi* is old High German for "bed." The entire final part of this passage is difficult to reconstruct, but if the reading of *betdi* is correct, the exemplar of this glossary probably originated in an institution situated in the eastern parts of the (former) Carolingian Empire.

8. *Paenitentiale mixtum Pseudo-Bedae-Egberti*, canons 38, 41, 42, 47 and 46 (different from the common tradition edited in Schmitz, *Die Bussbücher* 2:696, 698, 700, and closer (but not identical, and possibly anterior) to the one found in Cologne, Erzbischöfliche Diözesan- und Dombibliothek, 118, p. 95–96, 98–99, 152–53).

XXXVIII. De eo qui peccatum fratris silebit. Qui reticuerit peccatum fratris quod est ad mortem, neque eum corripuerit iuxta <regulam> evangelicam, primum inter te et ipsum solum, deinde alios adhibeatur, deinde ad ecclesiam culpam illius si necesse fuerit referens, quanto tempore consentit, tanta peniteat.

XLI. De pretio redemptionis. Si quis forte non potuerit ieiunare et habuerit unde dare ad redimendum, si dives fuerit, pro VII. ebdomadibus det solidos XX. Si autem non habuerit tantum unde dare possit, det solidos X. Si autem multum pauper fuerit, det solidos III. Neminem vero conturbet quia iussemus dare solidos XX. aut minus, quia si dives fuerit, facilius est illi dare solidos XX. quam pauperi solidos III. Sed adtendat unusquisque cui dare debeat si pro redemptione captivorum sive super sancto altari pauperibus christianis erogandum.

XLII. De pretio unius mensis. Pro uno mense, quod in pane et aqua penitere debet, psalmos debet cantare mille et ducenta genuflexu vel sine genuflexu psalmos DCLXXX. Et postea omnes dies reficiat ad sextam nisi quartam et sextam feriam ieiunet usque ad horam nonam de carne et vino abstineat, et postquam psallit alium cibum sumat. Pro ebdomada CCC psalmos genua flectendo in ecclesia aut in uno loco per ordinem psallat. Qui vero psalmos non novit et ieiunare non potest, pro uno anno quod ieiunare debet in pane et aqua donet in elemosina solidos XXVI. Et in unaquaque ebdomada unum diem ieiunet usque ad nonam et alium ad vesperam et in III quadragesimas quantum sumit penset et medietatem tribuet in elemosyna sua. In secundo anno remissio erit penitentie.

< XLVII > De praecipuis festivitatibus. Istas praecipuas festivitates in anno totus populus sabbatizare debebit, id est Natalem Domini, Octabas Domini, Teophaniam, Purificationem Sanctae Mariae, Pascha Domini, Ascensionem Domini, Pentecosten, in natale sancti Iohannis, in natale sancti Petri < et Pauli>, in assumptione sanctae Mariae, in missa sancti Michahelis, in natale sancti Martini, in natale sancti Andreae. De natale Domini usque in epiphania et illos praedictos dies qui supra scribuntur in paenitentia non computentur.

< XLVI > Hieronimus. CXXti missae speciales cum tribus psalteriis et CCCtas palmatas excusant C. solidos auri cocti in elemosyna.

9. Passage concerning the temptations of the devil (different from the version edited in *Theologia*, ed. Amort, 3:561, but similar to that in Cologne, Erzbischöfliche Diözesan- und Dombibliothek, 118, p. 104, where it features at the end of a sermon *De penitentia* attributed to Augustine or, more commonly, Cesarius of Arles; *Sermones*, ed. Morin, sermon 63).

Tres suggestiones diabulus in mentem hominis mittit. Primum suggerit hominem ut non suam faciat confessionem, quia iuvenis < est >. Secundo dicit: "Quia alii gravius peccaverunt quam tu et diu vixerunt." Tertio: "Tu pecca quia magna est clementia et misericordia Dei indulget tibi peccata tua." Et per hanc securitatem ducit eum in infernum.

10. Instructions for prayers and chants during the liturgical week.

Pronuntationes orationum et laudium dicende in tota ebdomada. Die Dominici. In primo nocte: *Exurge Domine Deus exaltetur manu tua ne obliviscaris pauperum in finem.* In secundo nocte: *Mirifica misericordias tuas Domine qui salvos facis sperantes in te.* In tertia: *Misericordia tua Domine subsequetur nos omnibus diebus vite nostrae.* In matutina: *Admirabile est nomen tuum Domine in universa terra et elevata est magnificentia tua super celos.* Aliud: *Excelsus super omnes gentes Dominus.*

11. John Cassian, *Conferences*, extract/paraphrase of chapter 14:8 (ed. Pichery, *Jean Cassien*, 190–91).

Hierusalem secundum historiam civitas est Iudaeorum, secundum allegoriam ecclesia Christi, secundum tropologiam anima iusti viri, secundum anagogen caeleste regnum.

12. Inscription of a crucifix.

In cruce Domini Hebraeicae *Ysamalchus rex Iudaeorum,* G<rece> *basilion ton martyrion,* <Latine> *Ihesus Nazarenus rex Iudaeorum.*

13. Decrees of the council of Chalon-sur-Saône (813), canon 40 (*Concilia aevi Karolini*, ed. Werminghoff, 1/1:285) with an added passage (in italics) concerning prebends (first part, continues in number 15).

Non debere presbiteros amplius in monasterio puellarum immorari nisi donec missarum sollempnia celebrent aut aliquid ibi de Dei servitio et suo ministerio expleant; deinde egredierunt presbiteri de monasterio. *Talem prebendam accipiant iubente domno Karolo Magni imperatore et consentiente abbatisse loci illius* . . .

14. Inscription of a chalice.

Hunc fecit calicem Domino cumdere[5] < . . . >[6] in honore sanctae Aldegundis virginis. Qui hunc de Melbodio abstulerit anathema sit.

15. Passage concerning prebends (second part of number 13).

. . . *talem una ex sororibus habet; talem accipiat unusquisque presbiter omni tempore in ebdomada sua.*

<16. Lost page>

Appendix E

Letter by Abbess Thiathildis of Remiremont to Emperor Louis the Pious, c. 820s–840

Domino Ludwico divina ordinante providentia imperatori semper augusto, Theuthildis ancilla vestra omnesque ipsi in Deo subiecte cenobii Sancti Romarici sorores perpetuam orant gloriam.

Imperialis sollicitudo devotionis ac profunde discrecio gubernationis cum equa erga omnes lance pensetur cunctumque pacatissime regnum moderetur, sic ardua queque dispensat, ut tamen humillima eius censura iudicii non careant. Quod in nobis ancillulis vestris conpertum tenemus, quibus prae ceteris latissimos viscerum vestrorum sinus blanditer apertos conspicimus priscamque, nullis operum nostrorum praecedentibus meritis, misericordiam culminis vestri inlibatissime erga nos, famulas vestras, vigere ab initio probamus eademque semper sese robustius profusuram non diffidimus. Qua de re maximas graciarum actiones rependere vestre clementine sumopere cupimus, set pondere immensa regie dignitatis benignitatis presse, quam libet aliquid huiusmodi cogitare vel tenuiter queamus, nulla procul dubio racione, ut competit, effari valemus; set quidem saltim, si non, ut dignum est, tamen vel iubilantes aliquid innuimus. Scire igitur obtamus vestram inianter excellentiam, quod, quasi reconpensantes ineffabilibus clementie vestre muneribus, huius volvente anni circulo praesentique hoc in tempore pro vestra incolomitate

---

Based on the edition of the *Indicularius Thiathildis*, ed. Parisse, 154.

dignissimeque regine ac dulcissime diu servande regle prolis cecinimus psalteria mille, missas DCCC cum oblationibus ac letaniis creberrimis: quatenus dominus Iesus interiores exterioresque hostium catervas conterat sub pedibus vestris necnon et prospero hic cursu succiduisque temporibus regni, quod geritis, diademate mitissime coronando ad nostram omnium pacem brachio potencie corroboret et in futuro inter choros sanctorum constituendo eterne corona retribu[tionis] vos letabundae super ethera beatificet. Amen.

To Lord Louis, the always august emperor by ordination of divine providence, Thiathildis, your handmaiden, and all the sisters of the convent of Saint Romaric who are subjected to her in the Lord, pray for your eternal glory.

Since the solicitude of your imperial devotion and the measure of your eminent government are weighed with equal scales for all and govern the entire kingdom in the most peaceful way, so the examination of your judgment resolves all major difficulties without neglecting the less significant ones. We take it as assured as far as we, your little handmaidens, are concerned, to whom we see you opening with particular favor the innermost charity of your heart, we who from the beginning and without any justification from the merits of our efforts, have noted that the utmost compassion of your eminence operates unreservedly in favor of us, your servants; and we are confident that it will extend itself even more profusely. For that reason we deeply wish to return your clemency the grandest actions of grace: but overwhelmed by the immense weight of the generosity of your royal dignity, even if we are able to develop some thoughts in that sense, we are without a doubt unable to give it appropriate expression. But if our words lack dignity, at least they will have been said jubilantly. We therefore ardently wish your excellence to know that, as a way of compensating the unspeakable gifts of your clemency, we chant all through the year and even at this moment, for your sake, that of the very honorable queen and the very amiable royal descendants, of which we wish the lengthy well-being, a thousand psalters, eight hundred masses with offerings and very frequent litanies, so that Lord Jesus will trample under your feet the troops of your enemies, both within and without, and that, from now on during the prosperous current and coming time of the reign that you exercise, crowning you very generously with the diadem to bring us all peace, he would strengthen you with the arm of his might, and also, that in the future, placing you in the choir of the saints, he will offer you as a reward in heaven the crown of eternal beatitude. Amen.

Appendix F

John of Gorze's Encounter with Geisa, c. 920s–930s

Interea Iohannes et Mettis monasterio sancti Petri, ubi et domum vicinam habebat, sub occasione aecclesiae quam tenebat quae cum villa propria eidem monasterio subiacet, ebdomadarius sacri altaris ascitus. Post aliquod quam ibi idem offitium ceperat, tempus tali ordine salutis ei occasio divinitus providetur: In collegio puellarum eiusdem loci, quod nunc feliciter Domino miserante procedit, erat quedam moribus et conversatione remotior a ceteris, annis admodum puellaribus, nomine Geisa, quam amita eidem religiosa secretiori apud se custodia educebat; hec Fredeburg dicebatur. Ea ita que Geisa cum ad artiora se cotidie sancte conversationis extenderet, inter cetera sancti propositi ornamenta etiam sub omni veste cilicii usum addiderat. Iohannes eius vestimenti adhuc vix aut omnino ignarus, dum quadam die—quonam incertum loco—cum ea familiaribus, ut cum ceteris adsolebat, sermonibus quedam insereret, a pectore puellae intra interulam, quae fuerat subtilior, umbram cilicii ad carnem latentis sub dubio visu prospexit. Manu protinus ad explorandum quid esset iniecta, ubi rem asperior tactus edocuit, stupore vehementi et toto corpore tremore exhorruit. Quid deinde hic habitus praetenderet, percuntatus: verecundior illa et rubore vultu

---

Latin text taken from John of Saint-Arnoul, *Vita Johannis*, ed. Jacobsen, 192–98.

185

aspersa, postquam aliquandiu obticuerat, "Nescis," inquid, "nos non isti seculo vivere aut deservire debere? Hec, ad que plerosque deditos video, vana prorsus et animarum perditionem esse perpendo. Longe alius mihi animus ab his: proprii tantum periculi solicitam cogit existere." Plura in hunc modum sancti desiderii verba cum replicasset, Iohannes ab imo pectoris in alta excitatus suspiria "Ve," inquid, "misero mihi et ignavissimo, qui tamdiu moras non modo steriliter, sed etiam perdite vivendo protraxi! Scilicet me virum hunc fragiliorem sexum virtute preire oportuit, nam summo probro et contumelia non solum non consequor iam ambulantem, sed nec—deses et totus herens terre—ullo motu progredior aut conitor."

In those days, John was attached as *hebdomadarius* to the holy altar of the monastery of Saint-Pierre in Metz, where he also had a house, because the church he held and the village he came from belonged to this monastery. Having exercised his charge for a certain period of time, he was granted a miraculous opportunity for his salvation: this is how it happened. Among the female community of this monastery, which today prospers happily thanks to God's mercy, there was one named Geisa, still a young girl, whose habits and behavior set her apart from the others. Her aunt, a religious named Fredeburga, educated her while keeping her discretely by her side. This Geisa each day turned stricter the observance to which she submitted herself: in addition to other elements of her holy vocation, she had taken to wearing a hair shirt under her clothes. Knowing nothing of her dress, conversing with her in a familiar manner somewhere (in the monastery), as he did customarily with the others, John vaguely noticed on the bosom of this girl the hair shirt shining through the very fine shirt she was wearing. He extended his hand to see what it was, and when the coarseness of touch had taught him what it was, he was gripped by a vehement stupor, and shook from horror with his entire body. As he was perplexed about the meaning of this practice, the young girl, with great reluctance and while blushing, after a moment of silence said to him, "Are you not aware that we should not live for this world, or submit to its service? All the things I see so many people devoted to, to me mean vanity and loss of souls. As for me, for a long time another intention has compelled me to renounce these things, concerned as I am by my own peril." After she had recounted the reasons for her holy desire, John sighed from the bottom of his heart and said, "Woe me, miserable and incapable (man), for having lost so much time, not only by living in a sterile manner, but even by causing my own loss. So it has proven necessary for me to be outdone in courage, I a man, by the weaker sex. To my great shame and humiliation, not only was I incapable of reaching her heights, but unable to bring myself to move, I even fail to step forward or even make any effort."

His igitur acrius stimulatus et supra quam alias antehac cuiusquam exemplo virtutis accensus de perfectioris vitae institutione fixa mente deliberat.

Studium itaque lectionis divinae cum eisdem ancillis Dei summa vi statim arripuit, et primum sacrae bibliotecae historiam Veteris ac Novi testamenti percurrens ex integro, deinde quecumque in divinis officiis certis temporibus in aecclesia frequentantur: lectionis libri, qui Comitis dicitur, orationes et si qua sunt sacramentarii in usus diversos. Regulas supputationum temporalium, quae coram antedicto Bernero diacono prius ex multa parte relegerat, memoriae vicaciter ut nemo superius commendavit. Precepta canonicae institutionis, hoc est decreta conciliorum, iudicia penitentum, ordinem actionum ecclesiasticarum, ad hoc et secularium edicta legum ad unum usque ut ita dicam verbum corde recondita mire continuit. Omeliarum, sermonum ac diversorum tractatuum in lectionibus epistolarum vel euangeliorum, sed et gesta sanctorum si qua sunt memorabilium, tantam concepit notitiam, ut quociens postmodum ei oportunitas forte accessisset loquendi, acsi prae oculis liber adesset, a prima usque in extremam sententiam ex ordine tamquam visa persequens vestigia verbis communibus universa revolveret. Cantibus ecclesiasticis sub idem temporis insudare nec erubuit nec desperavit. Et licet nonnulli ut alieniori aetate deludi tacite riderent ingenium, pertinacia boni desiderii quamvis duro eluctato labore prorsus evicit.

Thus highly stimulated and inflamed more vividly (by this example) than by any other display of virtue, he began reflecting with determination on how to lead a more perfect life. Without delay and with the utmost vigor he threw himself, joined in this by the women servants of God, into divine reading. First, he ran through the entire holy Bible—the Old and the New Testament—then the rites practiced in the church at different moments of the office, the lections of the book called Comes,[1] the prayers, and all that is in the sacramentary for different purposes, and the rules of the computus, all things that he had previously read in large part with Deacon Bernier. All of this he committed to his memory with unrivaled intelligence. The precepts of the institution of the canons, that is to say the decrees of the councils, the penitentials, the order of the ecclesiastical offices, the edicts of ecclesiastical and secular laws, all of this he admirably memorized, almost word for word, so to speak. He acquired such knowledge of the homilies, sermons, and commentaries on the lections of the epistles or gospels, but also of the memorable deeds of the saints, that, each time he had the opportunity to discuss them, he could retrieve anything as if the book was before his eyes, and recited everything from one end to the other, from the first sentence to the last. He also felt no shame or discouragement at laboring over the ecclesiastical chants. Even though many would have mocked him for it behind his back, thinking that he wasted his time in an education that was not suitable for his age, the tenacity of his good intentions completely triumphed, despite the effort it had cost him.

APPENDIX F

Hec ei interim sanctorum negociorum ocia cum predictis ancillis Dei fuerunt. Ex cuius etiam collegii multitudine plerasque ab infimis delectationibus ad caelestium desideriorum flammas igne divini eloquii permutavit . . .

Such were his activities and saintly occupations while he was in the company of the aforementioned servants of God. Among their numerous community, thanks to the fire of his divine eloquence, he brought many from the basest pleasures to the flames of celestial desires . . .

Appendix G

Extract on Women Religious from the Protocol of the Synod of Rome (1059)

Siquidem a tempore apostolorum usque praefatum imperatorem Ludouuivcum nulli professioni sanctimonialium virginum vel viduarum constat istud fuisse ab aliquo sanctorum patrum concessum vel permissum, Domino nostro Jesu Christo praemonstrante et per gloriosum apostolum suum Paulum, qualiter virgines vel viduae debeant, decernente, "Si qua fidelis," inquit, "habet viduas, subministret illis, ut non gravetur aecclesia, ut his, quae verae viduae sunt, sufficiat." Porro, "Mulier innupta et virgo cogitat, quae Domini sunt, ut sit sancta corpore et spiritu." In quibus apostoli verbis aperte monstratur stipendia ecclesiastica his solummodo virginibus vel viduis deberi, quae facultates proprias aut non habuerunt aut reliquerunt. Cuius ergo auctoritatis erit regula illa, quae contra doctrinam apostolicam et orthodoxorum patrum traditionem sanctimonialibus in congregatione commanentibus sic concedit ecclesiastica stipendia et beneficia, ut retineant vel acquirant propria.

For, it is a fact that, since the time of the apostles until the aforementioned emperor Louis, no profession of women religious—virgins or widows—was allowed or permitted by any of the holy fathers, [except that which was] announced by our Lord Jesus Christ and indicated by his glorious apostle Paul, [when he wrote] on how

---

Latin text taken from *Die Konzilien Deutschlands und Reichsitaliens, 1023–1059*, ed. Jasper, 396–98.

virgins and widows should behave, where he says, "If any of the faithful have widows, let him minister to them, and let not the Church be charged: that there may be sufficient for them that are widows indeed." And further, "the unmarried woman and the virgin thinketh on the things of the Lord, that she may be holy both in body and in spirit." Through these words of the apostle it is clearly shown that ecclesiastical stipends are only due to virgins and widows if they do not dispose of or leave behind means of their own. On which authority will this rule be valid, that it concedes, against the apostolic doctrine of tradition of the orthodox fathers, ecclesiastical stipends and benefices to women religious who live in a congregation, for them to keep or acquire their own?

Et certe huiusmodi sanctimonialium institutionem usque nunc tota Asia, Africa simul et Europa, excepto unum minimo angulo Germaniae, nec scivit nec recepit. Quam quotquot receperunt, a tempore praefati Ludouuvici recepisse comprobantur. Unde constat ante illum sanctimoniales ubivis terrarum habuisse quam sequerentur regulam a sanctis patribus sibi conscriptam velut in Latina lingue a beato patre Benedicto, aliquibus dictionibus a virili sexu ad femineum translatis. Quam utique in sui regni provinciis inventam nec Ludowicus mutare quilibet ratione debuit aut potuit since auctoritate et consensu sanctae Romanae et apostolicae sedis, quia, quamvis imperator et devotus, tamen erat laicus. Sed nec episcoporum quisquam, quia non est illorum novam in ecclesias solo suo magisterio vel testatur discretione praecipuam, sermone luculentam. A cuius tramite in tantum aberravit compilator ille, ut videatur Sarabaitis spetialem regulam, quam usque as illud tempus nullo scripto, sed moribus tantum et factis noverant, promulgasse, ne timeant aut erubescant deinceps prave conversari, quibus proposita est velut regularis auctoritas transgrediendi.

Certainly, such an institution for women religious remains unknown and unreceived in all of Asia, Africa, and also Europe, except for a small corner of Germany. Those who did receive it, have been shown to have done so in the time of the foresaid Louis. So it is certain that before him, women religious in the entire world could be found who followed the rule prescribed to them by the holy fathers or in Latin by the blessed father Benedict, with some sayings changed from the male gender to the female one. On no grounds did Louis have the duty or right to change this rule, found in the provinces of his kingdom, without the authority and the consent of the holy Roman and apostolic see, for, although an emperor and a devoted man, he was still only a layman. But it was also not the duty or right of any bishop, for it is not their right to introduce anything new in their churches based only on their teaching, unless it was demonstrated to be significant based on judgment, or outstanding through speech. The compiler [of that rule] deviated so much from this path, that it seemed that he promulgated a rule made specifically for Sarabaites, which until then was known not *in writing but through their customs and deeds, with the result that those, to whom it was proposed as if it had the authority of a rule, would no longer hold fear or be ashamed about their depraved conversation.*

Post haec, dum consideraretur capitulum illud, quo uni personae IIIos librae panis et sex potus conceduntur, sacer conventus episcoporum exclamavit, hanc sententiam procul a canonica institutine removendam, quae non ad christianam temperantiam, sed ad Ciclopum, ut dicitur, sine aliqua Dei hominumque reverentia invitaret crapulam, et quod illa expensa magis videretur constituta maritis quam canonicis, matronis quam sanctimonialibus, scilicet ut habeant, unde sibi concilient greges leonum, scortorum vel agapetarum seu aliarum pestium ad integritatis vel castitatis pericumum seu ad alterius nequitiae viscarium. Tunc tamen aliqui fuere, qui assererent capitulum illud a clericis Remensibus insertum praesumptione, quod verisimile arbitratur, quo Gallos edacitate notatos a Sulpicio Severo et multis aliis recordatur. Pari modo etiam capitula illa, quae condedunt cum stipendiis ecclesiasticis.

Following this, when the members of the synod considered the chapter [of Louis's rule] that one person should be given three pounds of bread and six drinks, the holy gathering of bishops exclaimed that this decree was to be removed from the canonical institution, for it invited not to Christian temperance, but to a cyclopic (so to speak) stupor devoid of reverence for God or man, and that the expense seemed to suit more that of husbands than canons, or matrons than nuns, with the result that they would run—for this is how herds of pimps, lovers, light women, or other pests fraternize—a risk to their integrity or chastity, or some other harm through temptations. Some then speculated that this chapter had been inserted presumptuously by clerics from Reims, which was deemed accurate, for it was through Sulpicius Severus and many others that it was remembered that the Gauls were particularly noted for their audacity. Similarly [they condemned] those chapters that allowed for ecclesiastical benefices.

Appendix H

The Eviction of the Religious of Pfalzel as Recounted in the *Gesta Treverorum*, 1016

Est in suburbio Treverensi oppidum quoddam, quod vocatur Aula Palacii, ubi ex institucione unius filiarum Dagoberti regis preciosae virginis Athalae inibi quiescentis congregatio erat puellarum canonicam vitam profitentium. Accidit itaque, ut episcopus uni earum commissuram pallii mitteret, ut ipse ei exinde caligas, quibus, cum ad missarum sollempnia celebranda procederet, indueretur, aptaret. Quas illa suscipiens, et inpudicitiae suae participem fieri concupiscens, arte sua nescio qua venifica infecit, sutas remisit. Quibus mox episcopus indutis, mirum dictu, non visum est ei ultra id debere sospite vita procedere, nisi ad praesens haberet rem cum muliere. Attonitus de tam subitamentis mutacione tamque inopinata carnis titillacione, quippe qui disposuerat carnalibus desideriis non consentire, cum festinacione exuit, ac uni ut ita dicam de principibus sacerdotum, qui forte illic aderat, indutum dedit; qui mox ut induit, et ipse festinanter exuit, secum mirans, nichil tamen dicens. Tunc reliqui qui astabant, quid id miraculi esset admirati, unus post unum easdem caligas secreto capientes induerunt, et similia passi sunt; nullus tamen quid pateretur audebat pro pudore fateri. Novissime ventum est ad urbis praefectum; qui ut ab episcopo iussus induit, furore

---

Latin text taken from *Gesta Treverorum*, ed. Waitz, 176.

incredibili infremuit, et se incantatum esse proclamavit, sciscitantique quis iniquitatis huius auctor exstiterit, episcopus aperuit. Tunc omnes in unum sententias suas proferentes dicebant, maximum hoc esse dedecus ecclesiae, quod qui canonica vel etiam ecclesiastica censerentur professione tali polleret iniquitate; eam quidem quae rem hanc fecisset ab ordine sanctimoniae proici, dignum esse, ceteras vero ibi manentium, ne ab eis quodammodo tam infame procederet, mutatis vestibus ac pro albis nigris indutis, artiori vitae debere operam dare; quod si perpeti noluissent, melius esse, ut locus ille careret inhabitacione, quam ibi tales degerent personae, quae huiusmodi nequiciam gestarent sub religionis specie. Et ita factum est. Illa eiecta est; sed et ceterae nolentes nec habitum nec conversationem mutare, similiter sunt eiectae, et aliae in monasterium puellarum quod Horreum dicitur, aliae autem ad alia sui habitus migraverunt loca, vacavitque locus a aliquamdiu a divinis laudibus.

In the suburb of Trier there is a town called Aula Palacii, where there existed a congregation of women observing the canonical life; this had been founded by the previous virgin Athala (who also rests there), one of King Dagobert's daughters. One day, the bishop sent one of them a band from his pallium, so that she would make slippers out of it, for him to put on when walking to celebrate solemn masses. Having received this, and desirous to make him part of her impudence, she applied her venomous magic (of what nature it was I do not know), and returned the sewn goods. Soon, the bishop put them on—oh wonder—and it appeared to him that his life would not continue in health, unless he presently had intercourse with a woman. Struck like thunder by such a sudden transformation and an unexpected titillation of the flesh— for he had vowed not to allow carnal desire—he quickly removed them, and gave them to one of the leaders, so to speak, of the priests, who happened to be there by chance, and told him to put them on; when the priest obliged, he quickly removed the slippers, and although he felt amazement, said nothing. Then the others who were present at this event, wondering at its miraculous nature, one after one furtively took and put on the slippers, and experienced the same ordeal; but none who did so dared to admit it out of shame. Eventually, the prefect of the city came: when he put them on at the bishop's order, he trembled from an incredible fury, and declared that he was enchanted; and when he enquired who was the author of this crime, the bishop revealed it. Then, all expressed their sentence unanimously, that they were of the opinion that it was a great dishonor to the Church that the canonical or ecclesiastical profession should excel in such sinfulness; that she who did these things would be removed from the order of religious women; and that it would be appropriate that the others who were staying there, in order to avoid that such infamy would somehow come from them, having changed their clothing and put on black shirts, would devote themselves to a stricter life. Should they refuse to do so, it would be better that this place were not to be inhabited, for places like these should lack people, when crimes of this nature were done there under the pretence of religion. And so it was done. She was ejected; others, who refused to change their observance and their mode of life were similarly ejected; others were sent to the female monastery called Horreum, and others still moved to other places where their observance was practiced. And so this place did not see any divine service for a while.

Appendix I

The *Life* of Ansoaldis, Abbess of Maubeuge (d. 1050)

Haec igitur puella adhuc parvula in monasterio ancillarum Dei a genitoribus constituta, in puellaribus annis ostendit, qualis futura esset accessu temporis. Nam ut assolet illa aetas, numquam puellarum lascivias aut negligentias secuta, numquam ineptiis et ludis earum fuit delectata, sed tantum lectioni et meditationi animum servire cogens, cum ceterae concurrebant ad publicum, illa ibat ad monasterium, cum aliae streperent, psallerent, et puellariter choreis se exercerent, illa orationi procumbebat. Ubi vero maturior aetas successit, brevi ceteras supergressa, aliis bene vivendi exemplar enituit, aliis vitae merito terrori fuit; quotidianis enim afflictionibus corporis libidinem punivit, omnes animi passiones repugnando superavit. Vigilabat enim interdum totis noctibus, nonnumquam vero orando diem continuabat nocti;[1] cum vero necessitas somnum imperabat, aut pavimentum cubile habebat aut stando, raro autem sedendo, paullulum dormitabat. Cibus ei panis cum sale frequentior, potus erat aqua, raro legumina vel poma vel herbarum radices admittebat. Nam vino, sicera, carnibus, ovis et piscibus ac cibis lautioribus interdixerat penitus. Mansuetudine, patientia, humilitate, clementia et caritate adornata, virgineae castitati luxuriam subduxit; custos oris sui ad silentium, numquam sciens vel volens locuta est mendacium; semper cauta,

---

Latin text taken from *Vita Theoderici abbatis Andaginensis*, ed. Wattenbach, 40.

diligens et provida, numquam, si potuit, nisi sapientibus et castis sermonibus os aperuit. Quamvis saepe lacessita, numquam irata,[2] numquam visa est vel leviter, nisi pro causa Dei, commota; contentiones et rixas et feminarum certamina omnino a se fecit aliena et extranea. Balnea et lavationes contempsit, docens nullum extrinsecus posse pollui, nisi quem intrinsecus sordidat delectatio peccati. Turbarum strepitum et conventum ad se pro sui merito adventantium semper refugit, linguas detrahentium et favores se laudantium aequaliter habuit. His et ceteris cum gratia Dei redundaret virtutibus, multas in Malbodiensi monasterio ad similem virtutem excitavit, multas post lapsum ad poenitentiam revocavit. Et annuente Gerardo episcopo Cameracensi et Rainero comite Montensi, ordinem religionis monasticae, quae paene adnihilata erat, in eodem monasterio correxit et in melius reparavit. Sed quia castigat Dominus quos diligit, et flagellat quos recipit, ante septem dormitionis suae annos cancri ulcere percussa, nec bonae conversationis propositum usu et virtutum consuetudine exercitatum minuit, nec flagellis umquam murmuravit, immo quia Dei visitatione digna est habita, semper gratias egit; postremo felici excessu beata decore virgineae castitatis laeta migravit ad Dominum, receptura longi laboris praemium.

After her parents put [Ansoaldis], still a small girl, in the monastery of handmaidens of God, she revealed in her childhood years that into which she would later develop. She never took delight, as is customary at that age, in girls' lasciviousness and negligence, or in their ineptitudes and games, but exerted herself to serve her spirit through reading and meditation; so that, when the others ran to the public area, she retreated into the monastery; when others made noise, psalmodized, and in a girly way did their choir practices, she prostrated herself in prayer. When she came to a more mature age, she quickly surpassed the others, and shone to some like an exemplar of good living, and to others was a source of fear because of the reward they would reap of their own lives. She suppressed her bodily desire through daily chastisings, and surpassed all by her rejection of the passions of the soul. In the meantime, she held vigils all night, and often continued in the night the day's prayers; when she was overwhelmed by sleep, she took the paving stones as her bed, or slept standing, seldom sitting, and then very little. She very often ate only bread with salt, and drank water, and seldom allowed herself vegetables, fruit, or the roots of herbs. She completely abstained from wine, beer, meat, fowl, and fish, and luxurious foodstuffs. Adorned by softness, patience, humility, clemency, and love, she suppressed luxuriousness with chastity; she was a guard to her mouth, making it stay silent, and it never willingly or knowingly lied. Always cautious, diligent, and foreseeing, she never, if possible, opened her mouth unless to speak wise and chaste words. Although often troubled, she was never seen to be brought to anger or joy, except because of God; conflicts, disputes and the battles of women she made completely alien to herself. She spurned baths and ablutions, arguing that no one could be polluted on the outside, unless that person soiled themselves on the inside with pleasure through (committing) sin. The noise of the crowds and the gathering of people that came to her because of her merits she always fled, and she did equally with the tongues of detractors and those who praised her to obtain favors from her. With the grace of God she shone in these and other virtues, and incited many in the monastery of Maubeuge to the same virtue, and called back to penance many who had fallen. And with the consent of Bishop Gerard of Cambrai and Count Renier of Mons, she corrected in this monastery the order of monastic religion, which had almost completely been destroyed, and repaired it to a better state. But since God chastises those whom He loves, and flagellates those whom He receives, she was struck, seven years before her death, by a cancerous growth. Even then, she did not fall short of her goal of conversing well and exercising herself in the custom of virtue; and never complained about her afflictions, on the contrary always expressed her gratitude for having been considered worthy of being visited by God. Eventually, she rejoicingly traveled to the Lord, through a fortunate death adorned by virginal chastity, to receive the reward for her lengthy labors.

Appendix J

Letter by Pope Paschalis II to Abbess Ogiva of Messines (1107)

P<aschalis> episcopus, servus servorum Dei, dilecte filie sue O<giva>, Mecenensi abbatisse, salutem et apostolicam benedictionem. Meminisse debuisses filia, quomodo ecclesiam beneficiis patrum tuorum fundatum rogatu R<oberti> a<mici> nostri et uxoris sue, sororis tue, ea tibi ratione commissimus, ut in eadem videlicet ecclesia Deo aduivante per te monastica cresceret et vigeret religio. Sed quia in his hactenus te minus sollicitam fuisse cognovimus, quatinus id corrigere studeas paterno commonemus. Volumus ergo et Dei nostri auctoritate precipimus, ut sanctimoniales a clericis separes ita scilicet, ut seorsum clerici in alia ecclesia, seorsum sanctimoniales divina peragant; in ministerio tantum altaris presbiterum, diaconum, subdiaconum habeant. Precipimus etiam ut tam laici quam clerici ab ingressu claustri arceantur exceptis religiosis et boni testimonii viris, qui pro verbo salutis administrando aderint. Mandamus nichilominus, ut sanctimonialibus amodo necessaria provideas, ut proprietatibus deinceps careant. Clericis etiam ecclesia eiusdem, ut huic considerationi et mandato nostro obedient, predicta auctoritate precipimus. Data in concilio Trecensi.

Bishop Paschalis, servant of the servants of God, to his beloved daughter Ogiva, abbess of Messines, greetings and apostolic benediction. You need to remember,

---

Latin text taken from *Wolfenbüttler Fragmente*, ed. Sdralek, 112–13.

daughter, how we entrusted (at the request of our friends Robert and his wife, your sister) to you this monastery that was founded through the benefices of your relatives on condition that, God aiding, in there the monastic religion would grow and flourish through your assistance. But since we have learned that so far you have been less than industrious in this regard, we send you this fatherly admonishment to apply yourself to correcting this error. We therefore want and ordain by virtue of our authority through God, that you shall separate the women religious from the clerics, so that the clerics celebrate divine office in a separate church, and the women religious in another, but assisted for the celebration of the eucharist by a priest, a deacon, and a subdeacon. We also ordain that laymen and clerics should be prohibited from entering the cloister, except for men that are religious men and of good reputation and go there to carry out pastoral duties. We also mandate that you should provide the religious with the necessary things, so that they will henceforth have no possessions of their own. And by the aforementioned authority we also dictate that the clerics of this monastery obey this consideration and mandate of ours. Given at the council of Troyes.

Notes

Introduction

1. The evidence for Ruothildis's life is reviewed in Heyen, *Untersuchungen*, 18–19.

2. According to Franz-Josef Heyen, Ruothildis was educated at the monastery of Essen (ibid., 19), where several mid-tenth-century abbesses were also commemorated via inscribed tombstones; Bodarwé, *Sanctimoniales litteratae*, 36, 228–29. The same was true of Ruothildis's distant predecessor at Pfalzel, Warendrudis (d. around 850); see chap. 2, at n. 35.

3. *Die Lateinischen Dichter*, ed. Strecker and Fickermann, 314: "Sponsa rede(m)ptoris iacet hic tumulata Ruothildis / Sursum glorifica tripudians anima / Dum viguit mundo, nituit castissima virgo / Abbatissa chori candida virginei / Mansit sub sacro speciosa can(on)ica velo / Sed tamen in vita vera fuit monacha / Ipsa kalendis septenis defuncta Decembris / Ad sponsum rediit quem pie promeruit." A slightly different transcription may be found in the early eleventh-century *Libellus de rebus Trevirensibus*, ed. Waitz, 106.

4. These commentaries include those of Wengler, *Kurzer Rückblick*, 8; Cüppers, *Pfalzel*, 85–86; Heyen, *Pfalzel*, 42–43; and Parisse, "Der Anteil," 92. Only Parisse, *Les religieuses bénédictines*, 210–11, hints at the "ambiguous" meaning of the inscription.

5. See the discussion in chap. 5, at nn. 107–15.

6. Heyen, *Untersuchungen*, 20–26; also chap. 5, at nn. 116–20. The fate of Ruothildis's tombstone in the aftermath of Pfalzel's suppression as a female monastery is unknown: but it is unlikely that the local clerics would have long tolerated this visual reminder of the abbey's female past, since it so vocally expressed a view of religious identity that went counter to clerical discourse. In 1479, the stone was discovered below ground level, probably in the monastery's ambulatory. It was soon reburied. In 1772, it literally surfaced again when preparations were made for Dean Udalrich Milz's burial and was subsequently attached to the wall joining the cloister to the abbatial church; Heyen, *Pfalzel*, 31, 42–43. By that time, it had likely lost any meaning but that of monumental reminder of Pfalzel's ill-understood, now-innocuous female past.

7. The thesis outlined in this and the following two paragraphs was first developed in full in Karl Heinrich Schäfer's 1907 monograph *Die Kanonissenstifter*. Although criticized early on by Karl Levison in a review published in *Westdeutsche Zeitschrift für Geschichte und Kunst*, it shaped the standard narrative of female monasticism's development during much of the twentieth century: De Moreau, *Histoire*, 3:358–60; Hauck, *Kirchengeschichte*, 4:422–23; Schmitz, *Histoire*, 7:61–62; Despy, "Note sur deux actes," 428–29; Hilpisch, *Geschichte*, 26–27; Kottje, "Claustra," 143–44; Parisse, "Der Anteil," 94–95; and the references in the next three notes.

8. Philibert Schmitz described the situation as one of "complete decadence"; Schmitz, *Histoire,* 7:70. Also the comments in Hauck, *Kirchengeschichte,* 4:422–23 and Smith, *Ordering,* 142–43.

9. Wemple, *Women,* 172.

10. Ibid., 168–74, 187–88; Schulenburg, "Strict Active Enclosure"; and McNamara, *Sisters,* 148–75.

11. On the observance and spirituality of pre-800 female monasticism, Diem, *Das monastische Experiment;* also Diem, "Rewriting Benedict"; "Das Ende"; "The Gender"; "Inventing"; also Lifshitz, *Religious Women.* On institutional aspects, Felten, "Frauenklöster im Frankenreich" and Helvétius, "L'organisation."

12. On various aspects of reform in the next century-and-a-half, see among many others Felten, "Frauenklöster und Stifte"; Küsters, *Formen;* Hotchin, "Female Religious Life"; Beach, *Women; Manuscripts,* ed. Beach; Berman, *Women;* Lutter, *Geschlecht;* Griffiths, *The Garden;* Bodarwé, "Immer Ärger"; Griffiths, "The Cross"; Felten, "Waren die Zisterzienser"; Röckelein, "Die Auswirkung"; Röckelein, "Frauen"; Griffiths, "Women"; and *Partners in Spirit,* ed. Griffiths and Hotchin.

13. Hilpisch, *Geschichte,* 33–34. This narrative remains implicit in many studies of the eleventh- and twelfth-century reform of female monastic life.

14. Yorke, "Sisters," 95.

15. McNamara, *Sisters,* 220–22; Andermann, "Die unsittlichen und disziplinlosen Kanonissen"; Crusius, "Sanctimoniales"; and Bodarwé, "Immer Ärger." On the reformers' view of gender generally, McLaughlin, *Sex.*

16. Vanderputten, *Monastic Reform.*

17. Felten, *Äbte;* also refer to Boshof, "Kloster," 200; Verdon, "Notes," 335; and Parisse, "Noblesse," 174.

18. Refer to the discussion in chap. 3, n. 3, and onward.

19. Wemple, *Women* and Schulenburg, "Strict Active Enclosure."

20. Janet Nelson has warned against hasty conclusions about the catastrophic oppression of women religious in this period; Nelson, "Women," 57–58.

21. Van Osselaer and Buerman, "Feminization Thesis"; also *Beyond the Feminization Thesis,* ed. Pasture, Art, and Buerman.

22. McNamara, *Sisters,* 149.

23. Despy, "Les chapitres," 176; Helvétius, *Du monastère double;* Andermann, "Die unsittlichen und disziplinlosen Kanonissen," 39–40; Hirschmann, "Secundum regulam vivere"; Bodarwé, "Immer Ärger"; and Bodarwé, "Eine Männerregel," 238.

24. Schilp, *Norm* and Gaillard, *D'une réforme,* 130–32.

25. Bodarwé, "Eine Männerregel"; also Bodarwé, "Ein Spinnennetz," 28.

26. Bodarwé, "Eine Männerregel." Scholarship on this subject would benefit from a comprehensive study of female monastic ideals along the lines of Lynda Coon's *Dark Age Bodies.* In the mean time, refer to Corbet, *Les saints;* Helvétius, "Les modèles"; Schulenburg, *Forgetful;* Zola, "Radbertus's Monastic Voice"; Elliot, *The Bride;* and Matis, "The Seclusion."

27. For an overview, see the maps and appendix A. Not considered are the settlements in the lower Rhine valley, principally because their development warrants investigation in connection with those of Westphalia and Saxony; Hirschmann, "Secundum regulam vivere," 102–7; Engels, *Klöster;* and Felten, "Frauenklöster im Frankenreich."

28. Parisse, "Die Frauenstifte"; Parisse, "Les monastères de femmes"; Althoff, "Ottonische Frauengemeinschaften"; Ehlers, "Der helfende Herrscher"; Gerchow, "Sächsische Frauenstifte"; *Gandersheim*, ed. Hoernes and Bodarwé; Bodarwé, *Sanctimoniales litteratae*; Ehlers, "Franken"; Röckelein, "Bairische, sächsische und mainfränkische Klostergründungen im Vergleich"; and Moddelmog, "Stiftung."

29. Compare with, for other regions, Verdon, "Recherches (Nord)"; Verdon, "Recherches (Sud)"; and Skinner, "Benedictine Life" (Western Francia); Parisse, "Le monachisme féminin en Alsace" (Alsace) and Venarde, *Women's Monasticism* (Western Francia and England); Yorke, *Nunneries* and Foot, *Veiled Women* (England); and Wemple, "Female Monasticism" and La Rocca, "Monachesimo femminile" (Italy).

30. On Lotharingia's political and cultural identity, Bauer, *Lotharingien*; MacLean, "Shadow Kingdom"; and Schneider and Martine, "La production."

31. Scholarship on Lower and Upper Lotharingian female monasticism rarely intersects. For the former, see in first place Despy, "Les chapitres"; Nazet, "Crises"; Dierkens, *Abbayes*; Helvétius, "Du monastère double"; and Helvétius, *Abbayes*. For the latter, Parisse, "Der Anteil"; Semmler, "Das Erbe"; Boshof, *Kloster*; and Bönnen, Haverkamp, and Hirschmann, "Religiöse Frauengemeinschaften"; Gaillard, *D'une réforme*; Parisse, "Les religieuses bénédictines"; and Röckelein, "Frauen," 279–82.

32. According to Niklas Luhmann's theory of functional differentiation, a need for creativity and flexibility arises in contexts where normative definitions of social organization no longer provide an adequate answer to society's diversifying needs—a situation particularly applicable to female monasticism in the period under review; Luhmann, "Differentiation."

33. Parisse, *La noblesse*, 184.

34. Helvétius, "L'organisation," 168, with reference to Semmler, "Le monachisme occidental."

35. On intersectionality, a concept that "broadly encompass(es) the idea that differing forms of oppression can intersect and work together within society," and on the opportunity that currently presents itself for scholars to "explore overlapping identities that can result in a hierarchized and highly confining social structure," Weikert and Woodacre, *Gender*, 3–4; also refer to McCall, "The Complexity." For examples of the growing interest of gender scholars in this approach, *Nuns*, ed. Werner; *Religious Women*, ed. Raughter.

36. Compare with Watt, *Medieval Women's Writing*.

37. Wemple, *Women*; McNamara, *Sisters*; and Scheck, *Reform*.

38. Diem, "The Gender," 433.

1. Setting the Boundaries for Legitimate Experimentation

1. *Die Konzilien Deutschlands und Reichsitaliens 1023–1059*, ed. Jasper, 394–98, with the passage discussed here at 397–98. The Latin text and a translation are in app. G of this book.

2. Refer to the literature discussed in the introduction.

3. Wemple, *Women* and Schulenburg, "Strict Active Enclosure."

4. Felten, "Auf dem Weg"; Schilp, *Norm*, 11–39; and Bodarwé, "Eine Männerregel," 239.

5. Semmler, "Monachus"; Kramer, "Expectations"; also the literature cited in the next note.

6. Geuenich, "Anmerkungen"; Geuenich, "Gebetsgedenken"; De Jong, "Carolingian Monasticism"; Kettemann, "Subsidia"; and Raaijmakers, *The Making*, 126–27.

7. Clausen, *The Reform*.

8. Diem, "The Carolingians"; also Van der Meer, "The *Glosae*."

9. For instance, in Semmler, "Le monachisme," 84–85.

10. Felten, "Auf dem Weg," 74–87.

11. *Capitularia regum Francorum*, ed. Boretius, 1:35, c. 11.

12. Rudge, "Texts," 175–77, 216–17.

13. *Concilia aevi Karolini*, ed. Werminghoff, 2/1:171, c. 47.

14. *Capitularia regum Francorum*, ed. Boretius, 1:103, c. 34: "Ut abbatissae canonicae et sanctimoniales canonice secundum canones vivant, et claustra earum ordinabiliter composita sint" and c. 35: "Ut abbatissae regulares et sanctimoniales in monachico proposito existentes regulam intelligant et regulariter vivant, et claustra earum rationabiliter disposita sint." Also refer to Charlemagne's *Capitulare missorum* of 802; ibid., 95, c. 18.

15. *Concilia aevi Karolini*, ed. Werminghoff, 2/1:264, c. 13.

16. The decrees of the 813 councils of Arles and Tours do not distinguish between different communities of women religious, but merely refer to *monasteria puellarum* (monasteries of women); *Concilia aevi Karolini*, ed. Werminghoff, 2/1:251, c. 8; ibid., 290, c. 31. The contemporary Reims council makes no clear distinction either, referring to women religious as *puellae* and *sanctimoniales*; ibid., 256, c. 33.

17. Ibid., 421–56. Schmitz criticizes Werminghoff's hypercritical editorial technique; "Aachen 816," 552.

18. Regarding the contents of the *Institutio*, Werminghoff, "Die Beschlüsse"; De Clercq, *La législation*, 6–17; Van Waesberghe, *De Akense regels*; Schilp, *Norm*, 59–99; and Gaillard, *D'une réforme*, 123–41.

19. *Capitularia regum Francorum*, ed. Boretius, 1:276, c. 3: "Quia vero canonica professio a multis partim ignorantia partim desidia dehonestabatur, operae pretium duximus, Deo annuente, apud sacrum conventum ut ex dictis sanctorum patrum, velut ex diversis pratis quosdam vernantes flosculos carpendo, in unam regulam canonicorum et canonicarum congerere et canonicis vel sanctimonialibus servandam contradere, ut per eam canonicus ordo absque ambiguitate possit servari. Et quoniam illam sacer conventus ita etiam laudibus extulit, ut usque ad unum iota observandam percenseret, statuimus ut ab omnibus in eadem professiono degentibus indubitanter teneatur et modis omnibus sive a canonicis sive a sanctimonialibus canonice degentibus deinceps observetur."

20. Schäfer, *Die Kanonissenstifter*; also Crusius, "Sanctimoniales."

21. Despy, "Note sur le sens" and McNamara, *Sisters*, 169.

22. Karl Leyser writes that women's monasteries "shifted the burden of safeguarding and maintaining (the women) within their own caste into another sphere"; *Rule*, 64.

23. Unfortunately, a surviving report by one of the attendees of the Aachen council only references the discussions regarding male observance; *Statuta Murbacensia*, ed. Semmler, 437–45.

24. *Vita Odiliae abbatissae Hohenburgensis*, ed. Levison, 46: "iste, ut scitis, locus valde incompetens et laboriosus est regulari vitae, adeo ut nec aqua nisi cum magno labore hic adipisci possit"; also refer to the comments in Parisse, "Le 'monachisme,'" 228–30.

25. Jacques de Guise, *Annales Hannoniae*, ed. Sackur, 162–63; also app. C in this book. For scholarly interpretations of this passage, Hoebanx, *L'abbaye*, 171–79; Schulenburg, *Forgetful*, 112–15; and the literature referenced in Bodarwé, "Eine Männerregel," 257.

26. Semmler, "Corvey," 300. Compare with the remarks in Kottje, "Einheit."

27. Scholars have identified citations of, among others, Jerome, Cyprian, Pseudo-Athanasius, and Cesarius of Arles; Van Waesberghe, *De Akense regels*, 306–32; Schilp, *Norm;* and Schmitz, "Zu den Quellen."

28. Bodarwé, "Eine Männerregel," 238 onward.

29. *Concilia aevi Karolini*, ed. Werminghoff, 2/1:284–85, c. 52–65; for the text of these decrees, refer to app. B in this book. On the council, Schilp, *Norm*, 53–58.

30. Van Waesberghe, *De Akense regels*, 373; Wemple, *Women*, 168; Crusius, "Sanctimoniales," 15.

31. Smith, *Ordering*, 141. On liturgical service in Merovingian convents, Muschiol, *Famula Dei* and Muschiol, "Psallere"; on intercessory prayer in the ninth century, Choy, *Intercessory Prayer*.

32. Refer to the comments by Thomas Schilp in *Krone und Schleier*, ed. Frings and Gerchow, 188. As late as 1960, the German scholar Josef Semmler hoped to establish consolidated lists of Benedictine nunneries and *Damesstifte* on Eastern Frankish territory; Semmler, "Reichsidee," 51.

33. See the discussion in chap. 2. For Lotharingia, no ninth-century foundations of Benedictine houses are documented, except maybe Juvigny-les-Dames, which was dedicated at some point to Saint Scholastica, Saint Benedict's sister; Benoît, "Notes," 45 and Vestier, "Juvigny-sur-Loison," 158.

34. Diem, "The Gender," 433; also consider the comments in Dey, "Bringing Chaos."

35. *Annales Laurissenses minores*, ed. Pertz, 122; commentary in Schilp, "Die Wirkung," 163–64.

36. Fried, "Ludwig."

37. Raaijmakers, *The Making*, 127.

38. Fried, "Ludwig," esp. 241–50.

39. In northern Francia, the early medieval tide of aristocratic foundations was already abating in the eighth century, presumably because of the growing role of the Mass in lay spirituality and the declining freedoms of aristocratic women to found and endow new religious houses. Additionally, royal and episcopal agents were already taking over control of many monastic institutions; Gaillard, "Les fondations," 7–9.

40. Schilp, *Norm*, 176–85; also Garver, *Women*, 73–74. It would, however, be wrong to see communities of so-called canonesses from the ninth, tenth, and early eleventh centuries as reserves of an aristocratic elite (*Damesstifte*); Fink, "Standesverhältnisse"; Felten, "Auf dem Weg"; and Felten, "Wie adelig waren Kanonissenstifte."

41. Yorke suggests that women's monasteries in this period should not be thought of as the female institutional equivalent of male ones, because the religious in these houses remained to a significant extent the legal responsibility of their male kinsmen and because their situation generally remained closely tied up with relatives' proprietary interests; Yorke, "Sisters," 110–11.

42. Heuclin, *Hommes de Dieu*, 313–16.

43. Schilp, *Norm*, 144–45; Gaillard, "Moines," 242–43; and Gaillard, *D'une réforme*, 131–32. Compare with the remarks in Schuler, "'Regula.'"

44. Raaijmakers, *The Making*, 127–28.

45. Angenendt, *Kloster*, 22–24; McNamara, *Sisters*, 152–53; also further in this chapter, nn. 68–70.

46. Bodarwé, "Immer Ärger," 79.

47. Felten, "Auf dem Weg," 72 and Althoff, "Zum Verhältnis," 131–32, 144.

48. Levison, review in *Westdeutsche Zeitschrift*; also Parisse, "Les religieuses dans le nord de l'Allemagne," 132; Geuenich, "Die Frauengemeinschaft," 59; Andermann, "Die unsittlichen Kanonissen," 41; Felten, "Auf dem Weg," esp. 72–92; Röckelein, "Hiérarchie," 215; and Bodarwé, "Eine Männerregel," 238–39. "Abbess" (*abbatissa*) continued to be used for all female monastic superiors (Lifshitz, "Is Mother Superior," 128) and presumably even for people like Ada, the sister of Cluny's founder William of Aquitaine, who apparently lived on the future location of the abbey as a "household ascetic" (Magnani, "Cluny").

49. Munich, Bayerische Staatsbibliothek, Clm 14431, f. 7v: "Regula et modus vivendi sanctimonialium que vocantur canonicae." This manuscript, which was originally owned by the monks of Sankt Emmeram in Regensburg, also contains Cyprian's *De habitu virginum* and various other texts relevant to the life of women religious; Rudge, "Texts," 240, 245–46.

50. Chap. 6, at nn. 21–22. A similar transition took place around the same time in Anglo-Saxon England; Foot, *Veiled Women*, 1:96–104.

51. Parisse, "Les monastères," 150–51, also the discussion in chap. 5.

52. See the introduction, n. 3.

53. Early medieval ordination rituals for women religious consisted of a blessing, followed by the candidate's adoption of a habit and, occasionally, a veil. In the case of communities relying in some form or other on Saint Benedict's *Rule*, it also included a pronunciation of vows: Muschiol, *Famula Dei*, 263–95; Metz, *La consécration*, esp. 155–62; Gussone, "Die Jungfrauenweihe," 28–29; and Bugyis, "The Development."

54. Cambrai, Médiathèque, 164: Deshusses, *Le sacramentaire Grégorien*, nos. 214–16, pp. 341–42. Comments in Metz, *La consécration*, 155–57.

55. Orchard, "The Ninth- and Tenth-Century Additions."

56. Respectively, Paris, BNF, Lat. 12048 (*Liber sacramentorum Gellonensis*, ed. Dumas and Deshusses, 1:399–401) and Berlin, Deutsche Staatsbibliothek, Lat. fol. 105 (*Liber sacramentorum*, ed. Heiming, 193–94, 197–200).

57. Of note are an 820s–830s manuscript from Cambrai or Liège (Padua, Biblioteca Capitolare, D 47; *Die älteste erreichbare Gestalt*, ed. Mohlberg and Baumstark, with commentary in Deshusses, *Le sacramentaire Grégorien*, no. 57, pp. 419–20 and Metz, *La consécration*, 155–57, 174–75); one made for Bishop Drogo of Metz (826–55) (Paris, BNF, Lat. 9428; *Le sacramentaire*, ed. Pelt, 50, with commentary in Leroquais, *Les sacramentaires*, vol. 1, no. 6, pp. 16–18 and Unterkircher, *Zur Ikonographie*, 66); and two further ones from Cambrai in the second half of the ninth century (Cambrai, Médiathèque, 162–63; Deshusses, *Le sacramentaire Grégorien*, 35, and Paris, BNF, Lat. 2291; Leroquais, *Les sacramentaires* vol. 1, no. 19, pp. 56–58).

58. New York, Metropolitan Museum, 2015.560, f. 198v-9v; the ritual is edited and discussed in Vanderputten and West, "Inscribing Property," 307–11, 320–21.

59. On the *Romano-Germanic pontifical*, see most recently Parkes, *The Making*.

60. *Le pontifical Romano-Germanique*, ed. Vogel and Elze, 1:38–46, 48–62, 67–69, 76–82 (on the differences between the ordination ritual for abbesses and that for abbots, particularly the fact that abbesses are not given the *baculum* [pastoral staff], Lifshitz, "Is Mother Superior," 129). The script for the ordination of Benedictine nuns could, of course, be retrieved from Saint Benedict's *Rule*; Hilpisch, "Die Entwicklung," 29.

61. The *Liber memorialis* of Santa Giulia in Brescia contains a ritual for the veiling of female religious that appears to date from c. 900. Subsequent additions, while tweaking the actual veiling part of the ritual and its underlying ideology, do not identify more precisely the status or observance of women religious; *Der Memorial- und Liturgiecodex*, ed. Geuenich and Ludwig, 49–52, 199–201, 226.

62. Paris, BNF, Lat. 12052; *The Sacramentary*, ed. Orchard, with commentary in Leroquais, *Les sacramentaires*, vol. 1, no. 31, pp. 79–81.

63. Paris, BNF, Lat. 13313; discussion in Avril, Rabel, and Delaunay, *Manuscrits enluminés*, vol. 1, no. 62, pp. 77–78 and West, "Group Formation," 172.

64. A mid-eleventh-century pontifical from Cambrai, now Cologne, Erzbischöfliche Diözesan- und Dombibliothek, 141, contains rituals for the ordination of abbesses and the consecration of, respectively, virgins, virgins who will not be serving under an abbess, and widows (*Les ordines Romani*, ed. Andrieu, 1:112). A pontifical given by Bishop Bruno of Toul to Archpriest Hugh de Salins (1031–66) of Besançon does not contain any relevant rites; London, British Library, Ms. Add. 15222 (Ibid., 1:142–44).

65. Schulenburg, "Strict Active Enclosure."

66. Ibid., esp. 56–57; Muschiol, "Von Benedikt"; Ellger, "Das 'Raumkonzept'"; and Hartmann, *Die Synoden*, 424–27. On enclosure generally, Huyghe, *La clôture*; Leclercq, "Théorie"; Schulenburg, "Strict Active Enclosure," 56–57; Smith, *Ordering*, 155–82; Lutter, "Klausur"; Roitner, "Sorores," esp. 110–20; Röckelein, "Inklusion"; and Vanderputten, "Une espace."

67. *Concilia aevi Karolini*, ed. Werminghoff, 2/1:451–52, c. 19–20 and 455, c. 27.

68. Wemple, "Female Monasticism," 294–95; Wemple, *Women*, 168–69; and McNamara, *Sisters*, 152–53.

69. Respectively, *Die Admonitio Generalis*, ed. Mordek, Zechiel-Eckes, and Glatthaar, 192, c. 17 and *Concilia aevi Karolini*, ed. Werminghoff, 2/2:638–39, c. 39–46.

70. *Die Konzilien der Karolingischen Teilreiche, 843–859*, ed. Hartmann, 41, c. 7: "Si quae sanctimoniales causa religionis, ut eis falso videtur, vel virilem habitum sumunt vel crines attondent, quia ignorantia magis quam studio eas errare putamus, admonendas castigandasque decernimus. . . ." While the council's instructions may or may not refer to actual such practices in ninth-century female houses, they do repeat commentaries against such practices in earlier times; Schulenburg, *Forgetful*, 155–66 and Wade, "Gertrude's Tonsure."

71. Wemple, *Women*, 169.

72. *Concilia aevi Karolini*, ed. Werminghoff, 2/2:637–38, c. 41–43. Charlemagne's *Admonitio Generalis* had previously instructed bishops and abbots that abbesses were prohibited from blessing men by imposing hands and signing the cross, and from veiling virgins with a sacerdotal blessing; *Die Admonitio Generalis*, ed. Mordek, Zechiel-Eckes, and Glatthaar, 228, c. 74.

73. Schulenburg, *Forgetful*, 107–18; Wemple, "Female Monasticism," 302; Joye, *La femme*; and Stone, "The Invention."

74. Wemple, "Female Monasticism," 302; also generally Le Jan, *Famille*.

75. Wemple, *Women*, 167.

76. This partially explains why Carolingian lawmakers remained ambivalent about enclosure with respect to abbesses; Schilp, *Norm*, 52–58. On the *servitium regis* and military service, Hörger, "Die Reichsrechtliche Stellung" and Felten, *Äbte*.

77. MacLean, "Queenship," 7–12. Contemporary rituals for the consecration of queens use a vocabulary similar to that used for the ordination of abbesses; Nelson, "Early Medieval Rites," 309–10.

78. Stone, "The Invention."

79. MacLean, "Queenship," 12–13.

80. Rabin, "Courtly Habits," 294; also Martindale, "Immena," esp. 35.

81. Several examples of such interventions are documented for Archbishop Hincmar of Reims; Flodoard, *Historia Remensis ecclesiae*, ed. Stratmann, 347–50.

82. *Concilia aevi Karolini*, ed. Werminghoff, 2/2:713–14, c. 15: "Modus autem erga ipsarum congregationum disciplinam hic esse debet, id est ut canonici secundum id, quod continetur in libro, qui de eorum vita collectus est, religiose conversentur; monachi vero secundum traditam a beato Benedicto regulam unanimiter, quantumcumque posse est, cuiusque relegionis regularem vitam in omnibus sectentur. Sanctimoniales denique secundum id, quod earundem sexus fragilitati congruit, relegioni cum omni diligentia subdantur."

83. Ibid., 2/2:713, resp. c. 12 ("Illud namque necessarium visum est de monasteriis puellarum, quae in quibusdam locis lupanaria potius videntur esse quam monasteria propter neglegentiam stipendiorum aut certe insollerciam prelatarum. Unde postulandum est, ut relegiosi viri ad hoc dirigantur, ut talia inquirant et secundum relegionem Deo placabilem emendare studeant, sicuti superius de clericis decrevimus") and c. 15. Likewise, the 845–46 council of Meaux-Paris was not concerned with defining the obligations of women religious, but was instead keen to establish guidelines for how clerics should act when veiled women were accused of improper conduct; *Capitularia regum Francorum*, ed. Boretius and Krause, 2:415, c. 70.

84. *Die Konzilien der Karolingischen Teilreiche, 843–859*, ed. Hartmann, 169–70, c. 16; see app. B. This decree is largely based on the acts of the council of Chalon-sur-Saône of 813; *Concilia aevi Karolini*, ed. Werminghoff, 2/1:284–85, c. 57–59. Likewise, the 836 council of Aachen includes two brief instructions for female leaders (*praelatae*) of women's monasteries: to set a good example to their subjects and provide them with all necessities in food and clothing, and to see that there are no secluded areas in the monastery where the religious can dwell unsupervised; *Concilia aevi Karolini*, ed. Werminghoff, 2/2:713, c. 13–14.

85. *Capitularia regum Francorum*, ed. Boretius and Krause, 2:267, c. 1.

86. *Die Konzilien der Karolingischen Teilreiche, 875–911*, ed. Hartmann, Schröder, and Schmitz, 514.

87. *Die Urkunden der Deutschen Könige und Kaiser*. Vol. 1, *Die Urkunden Konrad I. Heinrich I. und Otto I.*, no. 206, pp. 284–85; also the commentary in Parisse, "Der Anteil," 92.

88. *Die Urkunden der Deutschen Könige und Kaiser*. Vol. 3, *Die Urkunden Heinrichs II. und Arduins*, ed. H. Bresslau, no. 44, pp. 52–53; also the commentary in Andermann, "Die unsittlichen Kanonissen," 40.

89. Bodarwé, "Eine Männerregel," 238.

90. *Die Konzilien Deutschlands und Reichsitaliens, 1023–1059*, ed. Jasper, 394–98; also app. G in this book.

91. Hauck, *Kirchengeschichte*, 4:423.

92. The book collection of the Metz sisters of Saint-Pierre-aux-Nonnains is referred to in the 980s *Life* of John of Gorze (John of Saint-Arnoul, *Vita Johannis*, ed. Jacobsen, 192–98); that of the sisters of Essen in Saxony was reconstructed via the preserved manuscripts of that institution (Bodarwé, *Sanctimoniales litteratae*, 232–302, 335–55. Also Scheck, "Reading Women"; Stofferahn, "Changing Views," esp. 79–82; and Stofferahn, "A Schoolgirl," esp. 28); and the Maubeuge collection—or at least a collection the local religious and their male associates had access to—can be partially reconstructed through study of the *Roll of Maubeuge*, discussed further in this chapter.

93. Munich, Bayerische Staatsbibliothek, Clm 28118; a facsimile is available as *Der Codex Regularum*, ed. Engelbert.

94. On reworkings of Saint Benedict's *Rule* for use by women prior, during, and beyond this period, Diem, *Rewriting Benedict*; Bodarwé, "Eine Männerregel," 259–64; and De Seilhac, "L'utilisation."

95. Bamberg, Staatsbibliothek, Ms. Lit. 142 and Berlin, Deutsche Staatsbibliothek, Theol. Lat. Qu. 199. From Obermünster, the other female community in Regensburg, we have a lightly redacted copy of the *Rule* from the early ninth century; Regensburg, Bischöfliche Zentralbibliothek, Fragment I.1.5, no. 6 (commentary in *Krone und Schleier*, ed. Frings and Gerchow, 188 and Bodarwé, "Eine Männerregel," 264–65).

96. On context, see Cohen, *The Uta Codex*, 17–22.

97. Morin, "Problèmes," 9–10; Cesarius of Arles, *Regula ad virgines*, ed. de Vogüé and Courreau, 1:129–34; Rudge, "Texts," 133–35. Lifshitz argues that many of the redactions were meant to "increase the power of the abbess"; "Is Mother Superior," 138. The interventions in Saint Benedict's text are light; Lifshitz, "Is Mother Superior," 138 and Bodarwé, "Eine Männerregel," 265–67.

98. Rudge, "Texts," 246–47. The nearby house of Sankt Emmeran in the ninth century owned the aforementioned Munich, Bayerische Staatsbiblilothek, Clm 14431, which besides the *Institutio* also contains Cyprian's *De habitu virginum*; *Krone und Schleier*, ed. Frings and Gerchow, 188.

99. Jayatilaka, "The Old English Benedictine Rule," 166 and Bodarwé, "Ein Männerregel," 260–62.

100. *Libellus a regula sancti Benedicti subtractus*, ed. Linage Conde; discussion in Bishko, "Salvus," 568–78.

101. The two texts, entitled *Item ex regula cuiusdam* and *Quid debent fratres vel sorores in monasterio serbare*, are edited in Pérez de Urbel, *Los monjes*, 2:609–11; refer to the discussion in *Libellus a regula sancti Benedicti subtractus*, ed. Linage Conde, 58–60, 113, 123–26 and Linage Conde, "En torno," 68.

102. *Libellus a regula sancti Benedicti subtractus*, ed. Linage Conde, 138–41.

103. For the pre-800 period, see, for instance, the late seventh- or early eighth-century *Regula sanctimonialium*, a fragment of a rule for women that marries a fragment from Cesarius of Arles's *Rule* for women with chap. 39 of Saint Benedict's *Rule* and excerpts taken from several of Saint Jerome's writings; see the independent editions of De Bruyne, "Un feuillet"; Masai, "Fragment"; and the subsequent corrections

in Masai, "Deux éditions." De Vogüé tentatively situates the text in Northern France (De Vogüé, *Histoire*, 12:312), while Gneuss and Lapidge state that the contemporary manuscript was probably made in England (Gneuss and Lapidge, *Anglo-Saxon Manuscripts*, 578). Dierkens speculates that the original manuscript (one leaf of which survives in a manuscript from the abbey of Saint-Jacques in Liège) may have been owned by the women at Aldeneik; "Les origines," 428.

104. Rabin, "Courtly Habits," 293. Certainly it is true, as Anthony Musson argues, that normative texts like rules and conciliar decrees had a potential role in "shaping people's values, beliefs, and aspirations and [were] also a passive agent providing a reserve of knowledge, memory and reflective thought"; Musson, *Medieval Law*, 1–2, quoted in Rabin, "Courtly Habits," 292.

105. See n. 92.

106. Mons, Archives du Royaume, Coll. Archives locales, P 1755. On the *Roll*, Daris, "Vie de S. Aldegonde," 40–47; Bonenfant, "Note," 225; Helvétius, *Abbayes*, 162; specifically on the compilation at the end, Vanderputten, "Debating Reform." Refer to chap. 6 of this book for further discussion of the *Roll*'s contents and the possible circumstances of its composition.

107. The most recent datable fragment in the compilation is from the Pseudo-Egbert penitential, drafted no later than the 870s or 880s (Haggenmüller, *Die Überlieferung*, 246–73; Meens, *Het tripartite boeteboek*, 58–59; and Körntgen, *Studien*, 234–43): but the palaeography and several internal indications in other parts of the *Roll* suggest a dating of the whole in the early eleventh century; Vanderputten, "Debating Reform."

108. Of nine known copies, four are from the ninth century, with three dating from shortly after 816; Schilp, *Norm*, 100–13; Schmitz, "Aachen 816," 500 onward. In contrast, the *Institutio canonicorum* survives in no fewer than seventy-three manuscripts; Schmitz, "Aachen 816," 497–99.

109. On Hildemar, De Jong, "Growing Up"; also Coon, *Dark Age Bodies*.

110. On the use and production of glossaries in the ninth century as a didactic tool for the study of Benedictine normative tradition, Van der Meer, "The *Glosae*." On glossaries as "treasuries of knowledge," McKitterick, "Glossaries," 73–74.

111. See the edition of the compilation in app. D.

112. On oral aspects of the study of monastic legislation in the ninth century, Masser, *Die lateinische und althochdeutsche Glossierungen*, 23–24, with reference to Ochsenbein, *Die St. Galler Klosterschule*, 98.

113. Goldsmith, *Uncreative Writing*; also Watt, *Medieval Women's Writing*.

114. On these concepts, Van Heijst and Derks, *Vrouwen*, esp. 25–32; Green, *Educating*; and Mangion, *Contested Identities*, 213–14, 225–28.

115. Würzburg, Universitätsbibliothek, M.p.th.q. 25, an 820s copy of the *Institutio sanctimonialium* that was presumably made for a female institution of the Würzburg area, has significantly rearranged passages dealing with women's active enclosure. According to Felice Lifshitz, this was a measure by the local women to mitigate the new legislation's oppressive impact; *Religious Women*, 12–13. For a different view on provenance and on the reason for the rearranged sections, Schilp, *Norm*, 104.

116. Schilp, *Norm*, 97–98. Regarding hospitality in the *Institutio*, ibid., 86–90, 90, 127.

117. On penance in monastic practice, Hamilton, *The Practice*, 81–94.

118. Stofferahn, "Changing Views," esp. 79–82 and Stofferahn, "A Schoolgirl," esp. 28.

119. On the 868 council, De Clercq, *La législation,* 2:269–74 and Hartmann, *Das Konzil.*

120. Cologne, Erzbischöfliche Diözesan- und Dombibliothek, 118. A facsimile and description may be found at Codices Electronici Ecclesiae Coloniensis (CEEC), accessed 2 January 2017, http://www.ceec.uni-koeln.de; also see the commentary in Haggenmüller, *Die Überlieferung,* 67–68.

121. Hartmann, *Kirche,* 81, 140, 328.

122. Compare with the evidence discussed in Van Rhijn, "The Local Church."

123. Smith, *Ordering,* 43–75; Parisse, "Les religieuses dans le nord de l'Allemagne," 132; Bodarwé, *Sanctimoniales litteratae,* 76–86; and Van Winter, "The Education."

124. Possibly toward the late tenth century, the *Mixed Pseudo-Bede-Egbert Penitential* became part of the collection of the sisters of Essen; Düsseldorf, Universitäts- und Landesbibliothek, B113 (comments in Haggenmüller, *Die Überlieferung,* 59–60 and Bodarwé, *Sanctimoniales litteratae,* 387–88). Bodarwé notes that the manuscript contains but one indication of study: a small cross in the margin of canon 38, entitled *De eo qui fratris peccatum silebit*; Bodarwé, *Sanctimoniales litteratae,* 267–68. But this also happens to be one of the passages reproduced on the *Roll,* indicating that it held special meaning for at least two communities.

125. Bugyis, "The Practice," esp. 48–63; on monks as providers of pastoral care, Hamilton, *The Practice,* 95–98.

2. Holy Vessels, Brides of Christ: Ambiguous Ninth-Century Realities

1. The German historian Albert Hauck concluded that, from that time onward, (non-Benedictine) women's houses became "little other than institutions providing care for the daughters of wealthy families.... No wonder, that consciousness of the obligation to respect the observance of a monastery was anything but secure"; Hauck, *Kirchengeschichte,* 4:422–23. In contrast, Jo Ann McNamara saw the religious rather as victims of these processes, stating there was little women religious could do to resist the subsequent "virtual collapse of secular and ecclesiastical hierarchies responsible for reform" and the resulting "thievery of reputation as well as property"; McNamara, *Sisters,* 171–72, 174.

2. The most recent discussion of these events may be found in Gaillard, *D'une réforme,* 172–84 and Helvétius and Gaillard, "Production." The bibliography up to 1991 is reviewed in Schmid, "Auf dem Weg."

3. The *Notitia de servitio monasteriorum,* a list of royal institutions from 819, does not contain a reference to Remiremont: but then only two female communities are mentioned in it; Wagner, "Zur *Notitia.*"

4. On the topography of the Saint-Mont, Kraemer, "Le Saint-Mont" and Kraemer, *Aux origines*. Presumably, Bishop Frothar of Toul would have been involved in these changes, spurred into action perhaps by a letter similar to one he received from Archbishop Hetti of Trier. This letter concerned the application of the reform decrees in communities of canons, particularly those decrees relating to the promotion of the "rule of religious life" and to the maintenance of buildings destined for the canons' exercise of duties; Frothar of Toul, *Letters,* ed. Hampe, no. 3, p. 278.

5. Gaillard, *D'une réforme,* 171–87.

6. *Liber memorialis*, ed. Hlawitschka, Schmid, and Tellenbach, f. 46v.

7. Helvétius and Gaillard, "Production," 392–93.

8. Gaillard, *D'une réforme*, 179–80; for royal visits between 821–64, ibid., 248.

9. Butz and Zettler, "Two Early Necrologies," 198, 220–34.

10. Ibid., 204.

11. *Liber memorialis*, ed. Hlawitschka, Schmid, and Tellenbach, f. 35r-v.

12. In the 840s–850s, a new necrology was made, additioning the older lists with the names of individuals who had died since the transition to the *Rule*; Butz and Zettler, "Two Early Necrologies."

13. Zettler, "Fraternitas."

14. Gaillard, *D'une réforme*, 279–80; for the case of Säckingen, Geuenich, "Die Frauengemeinschaft."

15. Geuenich, "Gebetsgedenken." For a comparative outlook on such practices involving the female community of Santa Giulia in Brescia, Ludwig, *Transalpine Beziehungen*.

16. *Liber memorialis*, ed. Hlawitschka, Schmid, and Tellenbach, f. 35r: "Nomina abbatissarum, que in isto loco fuerunt antequam suscepta esset regula sancti Benedicti"; and f. 46v: "sic coniunxsimus ad istam ordinem." Also f. 1v.

17. The magnificent *Theutberga Gospels*, a Metz or Toul product of the 830s, may have ended up in Remiremont thanks to these privileged connections; see *The Beck Collection*, 18–29; Tampière, "L'évangéliaire"; esp. Vanderputten and West, "Inscribing Property," 311–13.

18. *Indicularius Thiathildis*, ed. Parisse, 154–63.

19. Zürich, *Zentralbibliothek*, Rh. 131, f. 29v–35v; discussed in Mohlberg, *Katalog*, 1:223–24; and *Indicularius Thiathildis*, ed. Parisse, 151–52. Another suspected remnant of the abbey's library is Epinal, BM, 118, which holds a copy of Gregory the Great's *Dialogues*, as well as *Lives* of (among others) Saints Eufrosina and Eufrasia and the recluse Saint Pelagia; *Catalogue général*, 3: no. 14, pp. 402–3 and Gasse-Grandjean, "La naissance," 98. On Saint Pelagia's cult and literature in the Middle Ages, *Pélagie la pénitente*, ed. Petitmengin, Cazacu, and Dolbeau.

20. The ninth-century parts of the *Liber memorialis* include references to female provosts (*prepositae*) assisting the abbess with the worldly and spiritual government of the monastery; Parisse, "Les notices," 223.

21. At Gandersheim in Saxony, a late ninth-century author used the hagiographical genre to transmit Abbess Hathumoda's leadership principles; Corbet, *Les saints*, 45 and Schilp, "Die Vita." On the profiles and conduct of Frankish abbesses generally, Skinner, "French Abbesses."

22. Constable, *Letters*, 11; also Köhn, "Dimensionen," 319–26. On abbesses as figures of public authority, Jarrett, "Power," 251.

23. This classic expression also turns up in one of Louis's capitularies from 826–827; *Capitularia regum Francorum*, ed. Boretius, 1:313, c. 10.

24. *Indicularius Thiathildis*, ed. Parisse, 154; also app. E in this book.

25. *Indicularius Thiathildis*, ed. Parisse, 154.

26. Ibid., 156, 158.

27. Ibid., 158, 160.

28. Ibid., 162; Parisse indicates that the community in question might be that of Sainte-Croix in Poitiers or Säckingen; ibid., 153. On a comparative note, the female

abbeys of Maubeuge and Sainte-Waudru in Mons are mentioned in the 833 will of Ansegis, abbot of Fontenelle, Luxeuil, and Saint-Germer; *Gesta sanctorum patrum Fontanellensis coenobii,* ed. Lohier and Laporte, 110–17. According to Helvétius, the Mons community at least would have been associated with Ansegis's other monasteries through a prayer fraternity; Helvétius, *Abbayes,* 155; Laporte, "Une variété." Also, for a discussion of prayer fraternities between female religious communities in tenth- and eleventh-century Saxony, Bodarwé, "Ein Spinnennetz," 40–43.

29. Constable, "The 'Liber Memorialis,'" 277; on the *laus perennis,* Muschiol, *Famula Dei,* 129–32.

30. On "double monasteries," Parisse, "Recherches"; and Parisse, "La tradition," 122. I remain doubtful about the utility of the term to describe the institutional arrangements as they are documented for female monasteries in Lotharingia; also refer to the critical notes in Prinz, *Frühes Mönchtum,* 638–63; Haarländer, "Doppelklöster"; and Helvétius, "Du monastère double," 36. Not all institutions, especially the smaller ones, had an in-house group of clerics; Bodarwé, *Sanctimoniales litteratae,* 92.

31. Schmid, "Auf dem Weg," 91–93 and Gaillard, *D'une réforme,* 181.

32. Jakobi, "Der *Liber Memorialis,*" 110; Butz, "Herrschergedanken," 321; and Wilsdorf, "Remiremont." A charter by Louis the Pious for Bonmoutier references a certain Doddo as abbot; *Die Urkunden Ludwigs des Frommen,* ed. Kölzer, 1: no. 84, pp. 206–7, at p. 207. While Kölzer considers the charter text authentic, Gaillard finds it suspect; "Aux origines," 33–34.

33. Butz and Zettler, "Two Early Necrologies," 202–4. According to Eduard Hlawitschka's estimate, ideally the female community would have comprised seven groups of twelve individuals, a number that enabled it to perform the *laus perennis;* Hlawitschka, "Beobachtungen." Compare these numbers with the situation at Saint-Pierre d'Avenay in Reims, which in the third quarter of the ninth century numbered twenty clerics and forty women religious; Flodoard, *Historia Remensis ecclesiae,* ed. Stratmann, 350. A commemorative list of names from Saint-Etienne in Strasbourg from c. 845 mentions four priests for a female population of approximately thirty individuals; Geuenich, *Richkart,* 98–100. Normative indications are rare: in an 822–24 capitulary for Sainte-Croix of Poitiers, King Pippin of Aquitaine ordained that the number of clerics there was not to exceed thirty; *Capitularia regum Francorum,* ed. Boretius, 1:302, c. 7. On the diverse functions of male clerics in female communities in late medieval Essen, Schilp, "Sorores."

34. In his capitulary for Sainte-Croix of Poitiers, Pippin indicated that "(the clerics) must be in all things honestly and perfectly obedient and subjected to the said congregation" ("Ut . . . clerici . . . per omnia ad dictam congregationem sanctae crucis honeste et perfecte obedientes sint atque subiecti"); *Capitularia regum Francorum,* ed. Boretius, 1:302, c. 7.

35. On the commemorative service of women religious, Althoff, "Gandersheim." At Pfalzel near Trier, the epitaph of Abbess Warendrudis (d. around 850) emphasized the importance of her familial connections, and of catering for the commemorative needs of the lay and ecclesiastical elites: "Hic Warentrudis nimium veneranda quiescit / abbatissa animam sed paradisus habet / Hetti pontificis fuerat soror amita magni / Tietgaudi domini magnificique patris / cuius germanus vir clarus in omnibus extat / nomine Grimaldus ore et honore potens / quique iubent titulum scribi pro munere

amici / illius ut nomen tempora multa habeant" (*Die christlichen Inschriften*, ed. Kraus, 2:202; her sister Hulindis's epitaph may be found ibid.).

36. Gilchrist, *Gender*, 191.

37. Jones, "Monastic Identity," 15; also Diem, *Das monastische Experiment*, 323–28.

38. On Carolingian monastic space, Lauwers, "'Circuitus,'" with additional material in Collins, *The Carolingian Debate*; on the architecture and space of female convents specifically, Jäggi and Lobbedey, "Kirche." For the example of the supposedly "Benedictine" layout of Herford abbey, Wemhoff, *Das Damenstift*, 1:24–26.

39. Refer to the discussions in Bodarwé, "Kirchenfamilien"; Ellger, "Das '"Raumkonzept'"; Jäggi and Lobbedey, "Kirche"; Blennemann, "Raumkonzept"; and Vanderputten, "Un espace sacré." In a general sense, also Iogna-Prat, *La Maison-Dieu*.

40. John of Saint-Arnoul, *Vita, translationes et miracula sanctae Glodesindis*, ed. *AASS Julii* 6:207–8, 215–16 and *Gesta episcoporum Mettensium*, ed. Waitz, 541. Also refer to Blennemann, *Die Metzer Benediktinerinnen*, 62–63.

41. Boshof, "Kloster," 203 and Bodarwé, "Eine Männerregel," 246.

42. Blennemann, *Die Metzer Benediktinerinnen*, 63–64.

43. Drogo's handling of the remains of Saint Glossinde may have been documented in a now-lost narrative; Blennemann, "Die Darstellung," 161, 166. For the possible existence of a miracle collection and a Merovingian *Life* dedicated to Saint Glossinde, ibid., 161–62. On relic shrines in female convents generally, Smith, "The Problem," 31–32.

44. John of Saint-Arnoul, *Vita, translationes et miracula sanctae Glodesindis*, ed. *AASS Julii* 6:208–9; discussion in Goullet, "Les saints du diocèse de Metz," 283–87 and Philippart and Wagner, "Hagiographie," 623–64. Shortly after 983, Bishop Adalbero II of Metz offered to send his colleague Hildeward of Halberstadt relics of Saint Stephen and Saint Glossinde as protection against the Slavic invaders; Blennemann, "Die Darstellung," 174.

45. Bodarwé, "Eine Männerregel," 247 and Blennemann, "Raumkonzept," 323.

46. Blennemann, "Raumkonzept," 324.

47. Compare with Muschiol, "Das 'gebrechliche Geschlecht,'" esp. 26–27.

48. Helvétius, *Abbayes*, 159–60. The sisters up to that point had probably attended office in a nearby church dedicated to Saint Peter; ibid., 164.

49. *De beata Ava virginis*, ed. *AASS Aprilis* 3:628; also Gerzaguet, *L'abbaye de Denain*, 38–49.

50. Chantinne and Mignot, "La collégiale," 515–18. This structure was replaced by a major basilica in 1046; see chap. 5, at n. 88.

51. Mertens, "Recherches," 93–111; also the comments in Smith, "L'accès," 92–94. On "families of churches" around female monasteries, Bodarwé, "Kirchenfamilien," 116–18; and Ellger, "Das 'Raumkonzept,'" 130–31.

52. *Vita Harlindis et Relindis*, ed. *AASS Martii* 3:386–91. Recent excavations showed that the church consisted of a single nave and was of modest proportions; communicated by Maaseik's town archaeologist Anja Neskens.

53. Dierkens, "L'abbaye d'Aldeneik pendant le haut moyen âge," 1:135–42 and Dierkens, "Les origines," 391. Heymans dates the elevation to 856–62; "Een vita," 123–24.

54. Heymans, "The Convent," 13–15.

55. Louis, "'Sorores'"; Louis and Blondiaux, "L'abbaye"; and Louis, "Espaces," 457–63. For Hamage's history in earlier centuries, Taylor, *Epic Lives*, 241–46.

56. Taylor, *Epic Lives*, 246.

57. Louis, "Espaces," 443–46, 453.

58. Refer to the comments on textual production by and for women in Watt, introduction to *Medieval Women's Writing*.

59. *Vita, translationes et miracula sanctae Glodesindis*, ed. *AASS Julii* 6:209 (first version) and 223 (second); also the commentary in Blennemann, "Raumkonzept," 325. On the involvement of religious in sacramental activities in the tenth century, McNamara, *Sisters*, 208; also the discussion in chap. 3, at nn. 97–107.

60. *Vita sanctae Aldegundis secunda*, ed. *AASS Januarii* 2:1035: "memoria et vita sanctorum Patrum non mediocriter cordi sunt adhibenda: ubi certamen martyrum, constantia sacerdotum, fides confessorum, continentia viduarum, et caelibatus depingitur virginum."

61. Ibid., 1036.

62. Ibid., 1036–38, 1040.

63. For the concept in the *Institutio*, Van Waesberghe, *De Akense regels*, 374–76; in Merovingian and Carolingian hagiography, Réal, *Vies de saints*, 184–98 and Heene, *The Legacy*, 128–34; in earlier traditions, Cooper, "The Bride." In the 820s and again in the 850s, Paschasius Radbertus wrote three treatises for the nuns of Sainte-Croix in Poitiers, focusing on bridal imagery and referencing the religious there as secluded brides of Christ; Härdelin, "An Epithalamium"; Zola, "Radbertus's Monastic Voice," 79–91; and Matis, "The Seclusion."

64. *Vita sanctae Aldegundis secunda*, ed. *AASS Januarii* 2:1040: "Estque ipse locus grege puellarum farcitus, aliorumque Deo servientium numerositate repletus; ubi frequens curatio infirmorum, illuminatio caecorum, saltatio claudorum, restauratio debilium membrorum, et remissio fidelium deprecantium pro peccatis suis, per intercessionem beatissimae excellentissimae virginis. . . ."

65. *Vita sanctae Aldegundis prima*, ed. Ghesquière, 4:323.

66. *Vita sanctae Aldegundis secunda*, ed. *AASS Januarii* 2:1039.

67. It may be significant that the new text omits a passage from the eighth-century version of the *Life* referencing several of the sisters' liturgical practices. Mentioned in that earlier text are the singing of psalms and of hymns as part of the liturgy of the hours and the commemoration of the dead; compare with the discussion in Muschiol, *Famula Dei*, 91, 125–26, 187–88.

68. Regarding the *cura monialium* in later centuries, Hotchin, "Female Religious Life"; Griffiths, *The Garden*, esp. 24–48; Griffiths, "The Cross"; Mews, "Negotiating"; and various papers in *Partners*, ed. Griffiths and Hotchin. In 972–74, a synod of abbots called together by Archbishop Adalbero of Reims warned that monks and possibly also clerics should not have close relationships with male or female companions (*compater* and *commater*), for this inevitably made them sexually active beings, and their female companions no better than women "who consent to obscenity" (Quid in hoc nomine a secularibus perpenditur, nisi turpitudini consentanea?); Richer of Saint-Remi, *Historiae*, ed. Hoffmann, 188.

69. Smith, "The Problem," 35.

70. On the difficulties of finding out to what extent male authors intervened in the cultic and personal memories of women, Koziol, "Flothilde's Visions," 168, and the bibliography cited there.

71. *Vita sanctae Waldetrudis*, ed. Daris, 218–32; commentary in De Vriendt, "Le dossier," 12, 23–24. According to Helvétius, the text is from the very end of the ninth century; Helvétius, *Abbayes*, 320–22.

72. The *Vita Aldegundis secunda* merely alludes to Aldegondis's and her sister's poverty; ed. *AASS Januarii* 2:1039; also Helvétius, *Abbayes*, 157–58.

73. As Bodarwé has shown for Saxony, female saints were the subject of different interpretations depending on context and audience; Bodarwé, "Roman Martyrs."

74. For instance, Georges Despy saw in a passage of the *Life* of Saint Waldetrudis—where the author indicates that all the religious who joined the saint were "noble" (*nobiliores genere feminae*)—a reference to the Maubeuge community's focus on recruiting wealthy, aristocratic women as part of a strategy to remain economically self-sufficient; "Les chapitres," 176. However, there is no guarantee that Waldetrudis's persona as it is represented in the *Life* was intended as an exemplar of the social profile of the local religious c. 900. Refer also to the literature cited in chap. 1, n. 40.

75. *Vita Harlindis et Relindis*, ed. *AASS Martii* 3:386–91.

76. Ibid., 388: "easque regularibus institutionibus, quibus erant catechizatae, pleniter instruebant, ac postmodum regularia vota adimplere fecerant, et erant illis secundum regulam omnia communia."

77. Ibid., 389.

78. Ibid.

79. Ibid., 388.

80. On this risk, Schilp, "Die Vita," esp. 6–7.

81. Chap. 1, at n. 49.

82. Dierkens, "L'abbaye d'Aldeneik pendant le haut moyen âge," 1:7–25, 142–43.

83. Ibid., 1:62–66. Einhard's passing mention in the *Translatio sancti Marcellini et Petri* (c. 828–30/4) of a *monasterium sanctimonialium* does not shed any light on the local religious' observance at this time; Einhard, *Translatio sancti Marcellini et Petri*, ed. Waitz, 262.

84. *Vita Harlindis et Relindis*, ed. *AASS Martii* 3:386.

85. Ibid., 388, 389.

86. On the risk of reading hagiographic texts as models or recommendations for "ordinary" members of monastic communities, Helvétius, "Les modèles."

87. Maaseik, Treasury of the church of Saint Catherine; Derolez, "The Manuscript."

88. Collery, "Tissus"; Dierkens, "Evangéliaires"; and Budny and Tweddle, "The Maaseik Embroideries."

89. Bodarwé, "Frauenleben"; also Garver, *Women*, 224–68; Garver, "Girlindis"; Garver, "Textiles"; and chap. 5, at nn. 39, 119, in this book.

90. Bodarwé, "Eine Männerregel."

91. On the hagiography in honor of these saints, Goullet, "Les saints du diocèse de Toul," 51–69.

92. Rome, Bibliotheca Angelica, 10; also Gaillard, *D'une réforme*, 41–54; Butz and Zettler, "Two Early Necrologies," 200–201; and Butz, "Die Sorge." Rosamund McKit-

terick recognizes female scribes in this manuscript (*Women*), a view that is rejected in Schmid, "Auf dem Weg," 68.

93. Butz and Zettler, "Two Early Necrologies," 198, 220–34.

94. Nine out of ten notices are formulaic texts recording the donation of serfs; the remainder concern properties and rents; Parisse, "Les notices," 218.

95. Constable, "The 'Liber Memorialis,'" 263. Various authors have noted the impractical lay out of the *Liber memorialis*, arguing the existence of another necrology; Butz and Zettler, "Two Early Necrologies," 209 and Dierkens and Margue, "Memoria," 878.

96. Gaillard, *D'une réforme*, 49–54. Jakobi dismisses Gaillard's redating of the *Liber memorialis* as implausible; Jakobi, "Der *Liber Memorialis*," 105–6.

97. Hlawitschka, *Studien*, 37. Charles the Bald later married Adalhard's niece Ermentrudis; Gilsdorf, *The Favor*, 97.

98. Heidecker, *The Divorce*. Lothar's concubine Waldrada (d. after 869) was buried at the monastery; Blennemann, *Die Metzer Benediktinerinnen*, 66. Lothar and Waldrada also feature in a notice that has been associated with a putative royal meeting at Remiremont in 861, just before the *Liber memorialis* was assembled; *Liber memorialis*, ed. Hlawitschka, Schmid, and Tellenbach, f. 43r, with comments in Constable, "The 'Liber memorialis,'" 267.

99. Hlawitschka, *Studien*, 37; Jakobi, "Diptychen"; Schmid, "Ein karolingischer Königseintrag"; Gaillard, *D'une réforme*, 51–52, 227; and Butz, "Herrschergedanken," 319.

100. Gaillard, *D'une réforme*, 180.

101. Bernhardt, *Itinerant Kingship*, 75–84. We have no way of measuring the impact of these assignments on monastic economies; but several of the royal female monasteries owned estates that were decidedly small compared to their male neighbors. Those of Sainte-Waudru in Mons (4,000 hectares), Marchiennes (4,200), and Maubeuge (5,000), Denain (2,376), Hamage (2,200), and Hasnon (1,600) were no match for the male monastery of Saint-Amand (12,000), but came fairly close to minor male houses like Crespin (4,500), Hautmont (4,300), and Maroilles (5,500); Gerzaguet, *L'abbaye*, 89–90.

102. *Liber memorialis*, ed. Hlawitschka, Schmid, and Tellenbach, f. 52v.

103. Bodarwé, "Eine Männerregel," 244.

104. Voigt, *Die karolingische Klosterpolitik*.

105. The treaty of Meersen is preserved in the *Annales Bertiniani*, ed. Waitz, 109–13. Charles's institutions are Aldeneik, Andenne, Antoing, Condé-sur-Escaut, Denain, Maubeuge, Meerbeke, and Nivelles; those of Louis are Bonmoutier, Herbitzheim, Hohenbourg, Oeren, Remiremont, Saint-Pierre-aux-Nonnains in Metz, and Susteren. According to McNamara, the text of the Meersen treaty reflects the "damage" done by rulers to female monasticism; McNamara, *Sisters*, 154.

106. For the leadership of Lotharingian female monasteries, see app. A.

107. Helvétius, "L'abbatiat laïque," 293. Much the same thing happened at Santa Giulia in Brescia, an institution that was given to Lothar I's wife Ermengardis and their daughter Gisela; Andenna, "Le monache," 24.

108. On Ermentrudis I and Richildis, Hyam, "Ermentrude" and Helvétius, "L'abbatiat laïque," 292.

109. Helvétius, "L'abbatiat laïque," 293.

110. *Recueil des actes de Charles II le Chauve*, ed. Giry, Tessier, and Prou, no. 435, pp. 471–75, at 472–73.

111. Choux, "Décadence," 205. Theutberga also owned Saint-Pierre d'Avenay, in Champagne.

112. Waldrada also owned the monasteries of Lure and Zürich; Hartmann, "Concubina," 554 and Esmyol, *Geliebte*, 159–66.

113. Hartmann, "Concubina," esp. 549–50; Gaillard, "Du pouvoir," 312, esp. n. 52; also Wood, *The Proprietary Church*, 316–17. See, for instance, the discussion of arguments pro and contra for seeing Richildis as lay abbess of Nivelles in Helvétius, "L'abbatiat laïque," 292–93, n. 28.

114. Andenna, "San Salvatore," 231.

115. Mentioned in John of Saint-Arnoul's late tenth-century *Vita, translationes et miracula sanctae Glodesindis*, ed. *AASS Julii* 6:220; also Blennemann, *Die Metzer Benediktinerinnen*, 65–66.

116. On Charles's diplomatic output and his aristocratic policy, Koziol, *The Politics*, 187–211.

117. *Recueil des actes de Charles II le Chauve*, ed. Giry, Tessier, and Prou, no. 435, pp. 472–33.

118. Ibid., no. 436, pp. 475–77.

119. Ibid., no. 433, pp. 466–68.

120. Edited in Gerzaguet, *L'abbaye*, 149.

121. Lesne, *L'origine*; Choux, "Décadence," 209–11; Bernhardt, *Itinerant Kingship*, 85–110; and Gaillard, *D'une réforme*, 111–18.

122. *Recueil des actes de Charles II le Chauve*, ed. Giry, Tessier, and Prou, no. 435, pp. 471–75.

123. Ibid., no. 436, pp. 475–77; also Gerzaguet, *L'abbaye*, 149.

124. *Recueil des actes de Charles II le Chauve*, ed. Giry, Tessier, and Prou, no. 433, pp. 466–68; also Hoebanx, *L'abbaye*, 107 and Delattre, "L'hôpital," 54. On monastic hospices and hospitals in earlier centuries, Dey, *Diaconiae*.

125. *Annales Bertiniani*, ed. Waitz, 134. Gaëlle Calvet-Marcadé argues that these measures likely derived from the Carolingian reformers' intention, stated long before the 870s, to structurally reorganize monastic properties and award each *ordo* involved in monastic houses a set part of its income; Calvet-Marcadé, "L'abbé spoliateur," 318–20.

126. Helvétius, "L'abbatiat laïque," 297–98; also Nelson, *Charles*, 61–62. Ultimately, though, (lay) abbots and abbesses stayed in control of the management of the entire monastic estate, even following the creation of *mensae*; Calvet-Marcadé, "L'abbé spoliateur," 324–26.

127. Daris, "Vie," 42–44; also Helvétius, *Abbayes*, 161–68.

128. Daris, "Vie," 43: "ut neque aliquis neque ex abbatissis et rectricibus eiusdem monasterii ulla aliquo in tempore quippiam inmutare et convellere, atque a presenti ordinatione, quam pro amore Christi feci, alienare praesumat, sed ita omni tempore inviolatam permaneat."

129. Helvétius, *Abbayes*, 164–65: also the references in n. 113 of this chapter.

130. Dierkens, "L'abbaye d'Aldeneik pendant le haut moyen âge," 1:161–62.

131. Felten, *Äbte* and Helvétius, "L'abbatiat laïque," esp. 285–86.

132. *Die Urkunden der Deutschen Karolinger*. Vol. 1, *Die Urkunden Ludwigs des Deutschen, Karlmanns und Ludwigs des Jüngeren*, ed. Kehr, no. 168, pp. 234–37; also Blennemann,

Die Metzer Benediktinerinnen, 66 and Blennemann, "Eine Bildurkunde," 172, 182 (which notifies the reader that the charter was interpolated in the later 1130s).

133. Blennemann, *Die Metzer Benediktinerinnen*, 65.

134. Fray, "Le temporel," 105: this would explain the monastery's absence in the Treaty of Meersen.

135. Calvet-Marcadé, "L'abbé spoliateur," 324–26. A case study from the second half of the 820s of a conflict over the resources pertaining to the *mensa conventualis* between the abbot of Moyenmoutier and his monks may be found in three letters by Bishop Frothar of Toul; *Letters*, ed. Hampe, nos. 21–23, pp. 290–92.

136. In the early tenth century, King Charles III the Simple of Western Francia (898–922) and Lotharingia (911–23) issued several charters that likewise condemned the lay abbacy, as part of a move to reassert the royal status of Carolingian monasteries and reclaim control over the awarding of their benefices and offices to lay associates; Koziol, *The Politics*, 504–24.

137. On virile female saints, Smith, "The Problem," 19–20. No doubt, women religious were keenly aware that the royal documentation, contrary to local discourse, almost never mentioned their patron saints. See chap. 3, n. 59.

3. Transitions, Continuities, and the Struggle for Monastic Lordship

1. For instance, in Parisse, "L'abbaye de Gorze," 58–62 and Skinner, "Benedictine Life," 87.

2. Smith, *Ordering*, 142–43.

3. The best introduction remains Parisot, *Le royaume*, 336 onward.

4. D'Haenens, *Les invasions*, 45–61. Norman incursions before the 880s are discussed ibid., 43–45; on resistance to these and later attacks, ibid., 97–124. For the archdiocese of Trier, Choux, "Décadence," 208–9.

5. Choux, "Décadence," 209; Hlawitschka, "Herzog," 426; Kellner, *Die Ungarneinfälle*, 28–30; and, for a gripping testimony of the episode at Remiremont, further, at nn. 18–19. In 922, the women religious at Gerresheim in the Lower Rhine valley were forced to flee their institution in the face of new attacks, seeking refuge in Cologne (Engels, *Klöster*, 29); in 926, Verdun was sacked and burned (Kellner, *Die Ungarneinfälle*, 23–24); and in the same year, a recluse near Sankt Gallen was killed by the Hungarians (Ekkehard of Sankt Gallen, *Vita Wiboradae*, ed. Berschin, 89); finally, in 937, religious institutions in the dioceses of Soissons and Reims were attacked (Huysmans, "Peace," 312–14).

6. *Sacrorum collectio*, ed. Mansi, 18: col. 77–78: "videmus in nobis completum esse quod per prophetam Dominus dicit, "Terram vestram in conspectu vestro alieni devorant, et erit in vastitate hostili." Ergo qualiter a Northmannis haec omnia in nobis completa sint, nemo dubitat: quomodo etiam a perversis Christianis undique atteramur, omnes in commune sentimus, sicut scriptum est: "Populum tuum, Domine, humiliaverunt, et haereditatem tuam venaverunt." Quaerenda est igitur pietas Christi, qua pagani arceantur, et statuenda est lex Dei, qua crudelissimi nostrae gentis homines a vastatione pauperum repellantur." On the synod, De Clercq, *La législation* 2:337–38. A similar discourse is articulated in the acts of the 881 council of Fismes (*Die Konzilien der Karolingischen Teilreiche, 875–911*, ed. Hartmann, Schröder, and

Schmitz, 181–82, c. 4); the 888 council of Mainz (ibid., 257–58, c. 6, 263, c. 25); and famously also the 909 council of Trosly (ibid., 497–562; also Héfèle and Leclercq, *Histoire*, 4/2:722–25 and Pontal, *Les conciles*, 49–52).

7. *Sacrorum collectio*, ed. Mansi, 18: col. 80, c. 9: "Duae sanctimoniales propter suum facinus de monasterio sancti Petri sine velamine erant eiectae: sed iuxta canones sancta constituit synodus, ut velamina illis redderentur, et intra monasterium in ergastulo ponerentur, parvo pane, et aqua brevi, cum abundantia divini verbi, usque ad satisfactionem fruerentur."

8. The 817 Aachen council had decreed that monasteries should lock up their fugitive or violent monks in a separate room; on these and other provisions, Ohm, "Der Begriff" and Lusset, "Entre les murs," 155. Very similar decrees are known from the Worms synod of 868 (*Die Konzilien der Karolingischen Teilreiche, 860–874*, ed. Hartmann, 267, c. 9) and that of Tribur of 895 (*Capitularia regum Francorum*, ed. Boretius and Krause, 2:228, c. 26). Decisions regarding individual women religious are rarely documented in ninth-century conciliar decrees. The closest match is the case, treated at the 874 council of Douzy, of a woman religious who had broken her vow of chastity; *Capitularia regum Francorum*, ed. Boretius and Krause, 2:587–96.

9. The 909 council of Trosly had faith in the ability of monastic and clerical leaders to see to it that "monks and women religious . . . live, according to their profession, in a sober, pious, and simple manner, and implore (God) for the king's welfare, the peace of the kingdom, and the tranquility of the Church" (Monachi vero vel sanctimoniales iuxta suam professionem sobrie et pie ac simpliciter vivant et pro regum salute ac regni pace et ecclesiae tranquillitate supplicent; *Die Konzilien der Karolingischen Teilreiche, 875–911*, ed. Hartmann, Schröder, and Schmitz, 514). By no means does this passage or the remainder of the Trosly canon on monks and nuns suggest a "vast programme of reform," as argued in Dumas, "L'église," 12–13.

10. Schulenburg, "Women's Monastic Communities," 276.

11. Recent studies have noted the indications of continuity in Anglo-Saxon female monasticism; Yorke, "Sisters"; Yorke, *Nunneries*; and Foot, *Veiled Women*, 1:71–84.

12. D'Haenens, *Les invasions*, 13–14, 18–20.

13. Ibid., 160–62.

14. Ibid., 20–33, 212–308.

15. Zimmer, "Das Kloster," 49–50. According to one tradition, the female monastery of Sankt Symphorian in Trier also went under because of Norman attacks; but as Frank Hirschmann indicates, it is not even certain that this seventh-century foundation had made it beyond the late eighth century; Hirschmann, "Secundum regulam vivere," 102–3.

16. Zimmer, "Das Kloster," 53.

17. Hucbald, *Vita sanctae Rictrudis Marchianensis*, ed. *AASS Maii* 3:81: "haec quae referebant, eadem olim tradita litteris fuerint; sed infestatione Northmannicae depopulationis deperierint."

18. *Translationes et miracula sanctorum Romarici, Amati et Adelphii*, ed. *AASS Septembris* 3:835: "Irruentibus Hungaris, crudeli atque effera gente, ac Lotharingiam saeva populatione pervagantibus, necesse habuerunt sacrae virgines in suum castellum confugere, ut se ac suorum sanctorum reliquias in tuto collocarent. Nonnullae etiam e Romaricensium coetu moniales, in aquas a barbaris demersae, sanctorum patrono-

rum ope incolumes emerserunt: mirumque illud fuit, cum hostium equi collotenus aquis obvolverentur; tamen aquas easdem sacris reliquiis famulanti turbae vix usque ad genua pertinuisse." Also Hlawitschka, "Herzog," 426.

19. *Translations et miracula sanctorum Romarici, Amati et Adelphii*, ed. *AASS Septembris* 3:385: "Per eos tumultus, cum omnia, quaecumque in conditis erant, vitae subsidia, depraedationi patuissent; in res ad tuendam vitam Romaricensi familiae necessarias, sacrarum lecticarum aurum omne atque argentum impendi debuit. Interim, quanti servos suos in caelis aestimaret, crebris miraculis bonitas divina testata est: quibus permoti pii complures ac religiosi viri, sacras easdem thecas suis impensis reparare, pristinoque ornatui restituere aggressi sunt."

20. Regarding references to abductions and destruction by "Huns" and "pagans" from later decades, chap. 4, at n. 116.

21. D'Haenens, *Les invasions*, 152–57.

22. Regino of Prüm, *Chronica*, ed. Kurze, 151.

23. Hucbald, *Vita sanctae Rictrudis Marchianensis*, ed. *AASS Maii* 3:81: "haec quae referebant, eadem olim tradita litteris fuerint; sed infestatione Northmannicae depopulationis deperierint" and "nulla certa relationis de his scripta videram vel audieram."

24. In 879, the monks of Lobbes, Saint-Amand, and Saint-Vaast in Arras evacuated their monastery, taking with them relics of their patron saints, books, archival material, and other treasures. Those of Saint-Vaast did so again in 881; D'Haenens, *Les invasions*, 127–43.

25. Ibid., 194–95. In the early twelfth century, a local commentator would reprise these arguments about Norman devastations to claim a number of the abbey's supposedly lost estates; *L'histoire-polyptyque*, ed. Delmaire, 74–75.

26. *Translationes et miracula sanctorum Romarici, Amati et Adelphii*, ed. *AASS Septembris* 3:835–37.

27. Ibid., 837: "qua necessitate compulsae tam abbatissa quam omnis congregatio, consilio inito, contra morem loci elegerunt ex sanctimonialibus timentibus Deum, et miserunt illas ad principem Richardum supplicantes, ut res ablatas restitui iuberet. . . . Quo responso accepto, famulae Dei introgressae vineam vindemiare iusserunt, et in cellario iuxta ecclesiam collocaverunt. Quo audito, perfidus Walo indignatione commotus misit unum de militibus suis. . . . Qui veniens cum comminatione illud recipere gestiens, una ex famulabus Dei calceamentum beati Romarici manu tenens simul cum clavi, et fiducialiter contra illum erigens dixit, 'Accipe clavem hanc, quam requiris, ad cumulum damnationis tuae.'"

28. See nn. 107–15 in these endnotes.

29. *Gesta episcoporum Cameracensium*, ed. Bethmann, 459; also Mériaux, *Gallia irradiata*, 315.

30. Respectively, Ploegaerts, "Le monastère," 273–74; Dierkens, *Abbayes*, 67. It was possibly at Moustier-sur-Sambre that the monks of Deurne, fleeing the Norman attack on their region in 836–37, deposited the relics of Saint Fredegand; Despy, "Moustier-sur-Sambre," 155–59; D'Haenens, *Les invasions*, 323–24; and Dierkens, *Abbayes*, 67.

31. *Gesta episcoporum Cameracensium*, ed. Bethmann, 464; also Mériaux, *Gallia irradiata*, 265.

32. Hugh of Lobbes, *Vita sanctae Berlendis*, ed. *AASS Februarii* 1:381; also Van De Perre, "De Vita." A 966 charter states Nivelles's ownership of the *villa* of Meerbeke,

and a royal letter from 1059 says that it was a benefice of the abbess; Van Droogenbroeck, "Hugo," 660–62. Van De Perre's article debunks older claims about the existence of a female monastery in Moorsel; Van De Perre, "De Vita," 29–31.

33. *Gesta episcoporum Cameracensium*, ed. Bethmann, 460–61. Dewez claims, on what basis is unclear, that a Norman raid in 880 destroyed Hasnon; Dewez, *Histoire*, 55.

34. On these traditions, Despy, "Moustier-sur-Sambre," 149 and Dierkens, *Abbayes*, 68. Possibly Ermengardis is the same as Ermesindis, wife of Count Albert of Namur, who in 1020 donated the estate of Gerpinnes to the religious at Moustier-sur-Sambre; Dierkens, *Abbayes*, 68–69.

35. Dierkens, "L'abbaye d'Aldeneik pendant le haut moyen âge," 1:157–59; some of Dierkens's observations are summarized in his paper "L'abbaye d'Aldeneik au IXe siècle."

36. Gerzaguet, *L'abbaye*, 53.

37. Van der Eycken and Van der Eycken, "*Wachten op de prins*," 34; and Leclère, "L'abbaye d'Andenne," 119–20. I was unable to consult Plenevaux's thesis on Munsterbilzen; Plenevaux, "L'abbaye."

38. *Die Urkunden der Deutschen Karolinger*. Vol. 3, *Die Urkunden Arnolfs*, ed. Kehr, no. 85, pp. 126–27: "quandam abbatiam in Masalante consistentem, quae vulgari vocabulo Suestra nuncupatur, ubi sanctae moniales faeminae divinum subministrant officium." Also further, at nn. 53–54 in this chapter, for a discussion of this transfer.

39. Helvétius, *Abbayes*, 235–44; also Bertrand, "La vie," 39.

40. Nazet, "Crises," 466.

41. Compare, for Anglo-Saxon England, with Crick, "The Wealth," 159–60.

42. One possible example for Upper Lotharingia of a substitution of male clerics for female religious is Bonmoutier, which according to interpolated or forged charter evidence ceased housing women before 912; see charters by Charles the Fat from 884 (*Die Urkunden der Deutschen Karolinger*. Vol. 2, *Die Urkunden Karls III*, ed. Kehr, no. 96, pp. 156–57, which does not indicate if the *monasteriolum* housed female or male religious) and Charles the Simple from 912 (*Recueil des actes de Charles III le Simple*, ed. Lauer, no. 70, pp. 157–59, which mentions canons and monks). Michèle Gaillard suggests that both documents are unreliable indicators of Bonmoutier's status c. 900; Gaillard, "Aux origines," 35.

43. *Recueil des actes de Charles II le Chauve*, ed. Giry, Tessier, and Prou, no. 435, pp. 471–75.

44. A summary of Etienne Louis's findings is in Taylor, *Epic Lives*, 248–49. I remain skeptical of Louis's and Anna Lisa Taylor's assumption that the Normans destroyed Hamage; ibid., 247.

45. Recent excavations have shown that considerable efforts were made at some point in the later ninth century to surround the monastic compound of Hamage with a palisade for defensive purposes; Louis, "Espaces," 463–71. Potentially relevant to Marchiennes's situation in these years is the acquisition, perhaps early on in the tenth century, of an evangeliary of Breton origin; Douai, Bibliothèque Marceline Desbordes-Valmore, 13. According to Louis Lemoine, there might be a connection with the Landevennec community's seeking refuge around 913 from the Normans at Boulogne-sur-Mer; Lemoine, "Contribution," 267.

46. Helvétius, "L'abbatiat laïque," 294; also Dierkens, *Abbayes*, 328–29, n. 7.

47. Folcuin, *Gesta abbatum Lobbiensium*, ed. Pertz, 61: "monasterium Anthonium dictum, tunc puellarum, nunc canonicorum"; also Dierkens, *Abbayes*, 328–29, n. 7. Jean-Pierre Devroey indicates that Antoing remained temporarily functional as a separate institution; *Le polyptyque*, ed. Devroey, XC. By 960–65, at the time of the installation of the regular abbacy at Lobbes, it may have been integrated into Lobbes's *mensa*; ibid., XCII.

48. Wemple, *Women*, 167.

49. Crick, "The Wealth," 160.

50. Helvétius, "L'abbatiat laïque," 289–90. Compare with the comments on the dissolution, c. 900, of female monasteries in Anglo-Saxon England in Yorke, "Sisters," 104–6.

51. *Capitularia regum Francorum*, ed. Boretius and Krause, 2:228, c. 26: "Numerum etiam canonicorum et monachorum sive sanctimonialium uniuscuiusque loci describant . . . ubi minor numerus fuerit, nostra auctoritate addamus."

52. Refer to Martindale, "Immena," 38–40.

53. *Die Urkunden der Deutschen Karolinger.* Vol. 3, *Die Urkunden Arnolfs*, ed. Kehr, no. 85, pp. 126–27; also the discussion in Habets, "Bijdragen," 459–61.

54. *Die Urkunden der Deutschen Karolinger.* Vol. 4, *Die Urkunden Zwentibolds und Ludwigs des Kindes,* ed. Schieffer, no. 2, pp. 18–20.

55. Bauer, *Lotharingien*, 615, n. 33.

56. Margue, "Nous ne sommes ni de l'une, ni de l'autre," 422–23 and Gaillard, "Du pouvoir," 309. Martina Hartmann has little confidence in Aegidius's account; Hartmann, "Lotharingien," 138.

57. *Die Urkunden der Deutschen Karolinger.* Vol. 4, *Die Urkunden Zwentibolds und Ludwigs des Kindes,* ed. Schieffer, no. 16, pp. 45–47. On Gisela's precise status there, Gaillard, "Du pouvoir," 312, n. 52.

58. Hoebanx, *L'abbaye*, 103, 107–8. A charter issued in 906 by King Louis the Child mentions a trade between Bishop Stephen of Liège and Liutard, a vassal of Gisela; *Die Urkunden der Deutschen Karolinger.* Vol. 4, *Die Urkunden Zwentibolds und Ludwigs des Kindes,* ed. Schieffer, no. 50, pp. 174–75.

59. *Die Urkunden der Deutschen Karolinger.* Vol. 4, *Die Urkunden Zwentibolds und Ludwigs des Kindes,* ed. Schieffer, no. 16, p. 46: "nos dilectissime neptis nostre interventu Gissele quasdam res Nyuialensis abbaciae sibi concesse unanimitati fratrum seu sororum inibi commoranti et sanctissime Gerethrudis virginis, cuius veneranda membra in ipso memorato Nyuialensi monasterio condita sunt, condignis laudibus incessabiliter excubanti in proprios usus delegavimus." The hagiography of Saint Gertrudis of Nivelles was one of very few traditions regarding the patronesses of female houses in Lotharingia to be known beyond the local level; Smith, "The Problem," 13.

60. *Die Urkunden der Deutschen Könige und Kaiser.* Vol. 2, bk. 1, *Die Urkunden Otto des II,* no. 21, pp. 28–30.

61. Blennemann, *Die Metzer Benediktinerinnen*, 68.

62. Regino of Prüm, *Chronica*, ed. Kurze, 144; for a slightly different account of the same episode, *Libellus de rebus Trevirensibus*, ed. Waitz, 104. Refer also to the commentary in Hartmann, "Lotharingien," 132–33.

63. *Die Urkunden der Deutschen Karolinger.* Vol. 4, *Die Urkunden Zwentibolds und Ludwigs des Kindes,* ed. Schieffer, no. 57, pp. 183–85: "quandoquidem mansit semper fidelis." Also Levy, *Geschichte*, 6–7 and Parisse, "Les religieuses bénédictines," 204.

64. Charter by Henry the Fowler from 916; *Oorkondenboek*, ed. Koch, 1: no. 26, pp. 40–43. Potentially revealing of the Prüm leadership's intentions with Susteren is that the latter is not identified as a female monastery, but instead the more neutral term *abbatia* is used.

65. In 949, Otto I confirmed Prüm's ownership of Susteren; *Die Urkunden der Deutschen Könige und Kaiser.* Vol. 1, *Die Urkunden Konrad I. Heinrich I. und Otto I.*, no. 111, pp. 194–95. Also Habets, "Bijdragen," 466–68.

66. Regino of Prüm, *Chronica*, ed. Kurze, 151.

67. Parisse, "L'abbaye de Gorze," 52–58.

68. *Libellus de rebus Trevirensibus*, ed. Waitz, 106; also the discussions in Heyen, *Untersuchungen*, 15 and Heyen, "Pfalzel," 590.

69. Metz, Archives Départementales de la Moselle, H 3959; partially edited in Blennemann, *Die Metzer Benediktinerinnen*, 69, n. 226. This document is the oldest charter included in the local cartulary; *Le cartulaire*, ed. Bernhaupt.

70. Blennemann, *Die Metzer Benediktinerinnen*, 68–69.

71. Helvétius, *Abbayes*, 248–52.

72. Ibid., 235–44.

73. Giselbert's life and career are detailed in Barth, *Der Herzog*, 39–104.

74. Meyer, "Ein übersehenes Diplom," 120–21; *Die Urkunden der Deutschen Könige und Kaiser.* Vol. 1, *Die Urkunden Konrad I. Heinrich I. und Otto I*, no. 466, p. 638; also Dierkens, "L'abbaye d'Aldeneik pendant le haut moyen âge," 1:161–64.

75. Hlawitschka, "Herzog"; Parisse, "Les notices," 229. Our understanding of Giselbert's actions is severely compromised by the *damnatio memoria* that befell him following his defeat against Otto I in 939. In any case, his memory at Remiremont remained highly positive; Margue, "Nous ne sommes ni de l'une, ni de l'autre," 423.

76. For demonstration of the fact that in "the vocabulary, shape and structure of politics there were many continuities"; MacLean, *Kingship*, quote from 233.

77. *Libellus de rebus Trevirensibus*, ed. Waitz, 106; also Heyen, *Untersuchungen*, 15 and Heyen, "Pfalzel," 590.

78. On the membership of Saint-Pierre-aux-Nonnains in 918, see chap. 4, at n. 10, and app. A; for Giselbert's restitutions to Remiremont and Aldeneik, see nn. 108–15.

79. Helvétius, *Abbayes*, 248–52. For a comparative outlook on Northern Italy, where we can see a similar shift in political control over female monasteries, Andenna, "Le monache," 28–30.

80. Hlawitschka, *Studien*, 39–41.

81. *Liber memorialis*, ed. Hlawitschka, Schmid, and Tellenbach, f. 52v.

82. As Eva-Maria Butz's analysis has shown, the early tenth-century entries in the *Liber Memorialis* reveal a shift from commemorating Carolingian royalty to acknowledging, through liturgical remembrance, the interventions of numerous members of the regional elite; Butz, "Herrschergedenken," 321–26. Also Gaillard, *D'une réforme*, 387–88.

83. Hlawitschka, "Herzog," 425–26.

84. The thirteenth-century necrology of Munsterbilzen (Brussels, Bibliothèque des Bollandistes, 437) mentions a translation of relics of Saint Amor from Maastricht to the abbey that may have taken place around this time. The ceremony was, again according to the same source, commissioned by a Count Clodulph and his wife Hilda.

The former was also buried at Munsterbilzen, as was a Count Berenger and his wife Bertha; *Nécrologe de l'abbaye de Munsterbilzen*, ed. J. Weale, de Borman, and Bormans, 32, 52, 58; also the discussion in Van der Eycken and Van der Eycken, "Wachten op de prins," 29–31.

85. *Vita, translationes et miracula sanctae Glodesindis*, ed. *AASS Julii* 6:206–10. The narrative indicates that men seeking the saint's intervention were allowed access to the abbatial church, but not to the actual site of the saint's grave; ibid., 207, 209. On sacred space at Sainte-Glossinde, Blennemann, "Die Darstellung," 166–67; also the discussion in chap. 2 of this work.

86. *Vita sanctae Madelbertae*, ed. Bertrand, 55–71. Helvétius dates the text to the tenth century, whereas Paul Bertrand proposes a dating of after 870 (Bertrand, "Réformes," 70) or early in the tenth century (Bertrand, "La vie," 44).

87. Bertrand, "Réformes," 71. Michel Parisse notes that the tenth-century notices in Remiremont's *Liber memorialis* and in the late ninth-century evangeliary now known as Epinal, BM 105, are inconsistent as regards orthography. Yet he also notes that the Latin of the texts is excellent, which suggests that these inconsistencies cannot be regarded as indications of a decline in education or discipline; Parisse, "Les notices," 220–21.

88. Bertrand, "La vie," 39.

89. *Inventio et miracula Gisleni Hanoniensis*, ed. Ghesquière, 386–87; also Helvétius, *Abbayes*, 247. Compare with other cases discussed in Geary, *Furta sacra*; and (for thefts of relics by women religious specifically) Schulenburg, *Forgetful*, 89–90.

90. Ugé, *Creating*, 98–110.

91. Hucbald of Saint-Amand, *Vita sanctae Rictrudis Marchianensis*, ed. *AASS Maii* 3:81.

92. Ibid., 87. For a radically different interpretation, Elliot, *The Bride*, 103–5.

93. *Vita sanctae Madelbertae*, ed. Bertrand, 60: "in orationibus assidua, in vigiliis prompta, in elemosinis larga, mirae caritatis pietatis humilitatisque ornata Christi de lampade . . . pauper effecta est"; also Bertrand, "La vie," 44–45, 72. The *Life* of Madelberta also bears traces of Gregory the Great's *Dialogues*, a staple of monastic reading in this period.

94. *Vita, translationes et miracula sanctae Glodesindis*, ed. *AASS Julii* 6:204. See, however, Michel Parisse's doubts on whether use of the words *regula* and *regulariter* in contemporary documents necessarily denotes a Benedictine inspiration; Parisse, "Les religieuses dans le nord de l'Allemagne," 133.

95. Hucbald, *Vita sanctae Rictrudis Marchianensis*, ed. *AASS Maii* 3:88. See chap. 2, n. 137.

96. The *Life* emphasizes the role of male counselors as spiritual guides; the noble ancestry of the abbey's leadership; and the need to distinguish oneself as a woman religious by rejecting secular clothing and taking the veil and suppressing libidinous thoughts through prayer, vigils and fasting; Hucbald of Saint-Amand, *Vita sanctae Rictrudis Marchianensis*, ed. *AASS Maii* 3:84–85.

97. *Liber memorialis*, ed. Hlawitschka, Schmid, and Tellenbach, f. 32v.

98. Hlawitschka, *Studien*, 39–41. Others have related the division of monastic incomes into different *mensae* to the subsequent emergence of individual prebends; for instance, Despy, "Note sur deux actes," 428.

99. Jakobi, "Der *Liber Memorialis*," 108 and McNamara, *Sisters*, 183. On Boso, see also Parisse, "L'abbaye de Gorze," 56–58.

100. Parisse, "Les notices," 221–22.

101. New York, Metropolitan Museum, 2015.560, f. 198v–99v; the ordination ritual is edited and discussed in Vanderputten and West, "Inscribing Property," 320–21. René Metz points out that earlier such orders occasionally use the term *diacona* to reference abbesses; Metz, *La consécration*, 156, at n. 70.

102. Chap. 2, at n. 48.

103. *Translationes et miracula sanctorum Romarici, Amati et Adelphii*, ed. *AASS Septembris* 3:835: "una quaepiam, cum ante altaris gradus substitisset, tres manus perspexit, quae super ipsas beatorum confessorum lipsanothecas exporrectae, viam indicarent." A mid-eleventh-century tradition indicates that the monks of Saint-Vanne in Verdun had a female servant named Eugenia to whom they assigned unspecified duties in the vicinity of the altars of their abbatial church; Bertarius, *Gesta episcoporum Virdunensium*, ed. Waitz, 46; also Hirschmann, *Verdun*, 1:258.

104. Bugyis, "The Practice," esp. 48–63. On monks as providers of pastoral care, Hamilton, *The Practice*, 95–98.

105. *El archivo*, ed. Udina Martorell, 43: "orator et pretor et sponsa Christi . . . ante faciem Domini"; also the discussion in Jarrett, "Power," 235–36.

106. Schaefer, *Women*, 288–99, 220–24.

107. Ekkehard of Sankt Gallen, *Vita sancta Wiboradae*, ed. Berschin, 64–65; discussion of this passage in Stocker, "Die Opfergeräte."

108. *Liber memorialis*, ed. Hlawitschka, Schmid, and Tellenbach, f. 6r: "Dumnus Gislibertus dux, qui pro re[me]dium anime sue et seniori sui dumni Henrici et uxori sue et infantibus suis omnes heclesias sancti Petri nobis restituit. Dumnus Gislibertus dux cum om[n]ibus fidelibus suis. Dumna Girberga. Ainricus, Haduidis. Gottefridus comes cum infantibus et omnibus fidelibus suis. Ermentridis comitissa. Arnulfus comes cum omnibus suis. Rodbertus. Dumnus Adhelbero cum omnibus suis. Dumnus Gauzlinus ep(iscopus). Dumnus Ruodbertus archiep(iscopus))."

109. Hlawitschka, "Herzog," esp. 434.

110. Helvétius, *Abbayes*, 235–43; Hlawitschka, "Herzog"; and Parisse, "Noblesse," 185–86.

111. Semmler, "Das Erbe," 38 and Hlawitschka, "Herzog," 441–48. Eduard Hlawitschka speculates (without much foundation it seems) that Abbess Berta (attested in the 940s–950s) may have come under the influence of the "Gorze reform"; Hlawitschka, *Studien*, 43.

112. Jakobi, "Der *Liber Memorialis*," 108.

113. See Chap. 4, at nn. 106–15.

114. Margue, "Autorité," 1:60–67; Dierkens and Margue, "Memoria," 876–77; West, "Group Formation," 169–70; and MacLean, *Ottonian Queenship*, 62–63.

115. Barth, *Der Herzog*, 66–69.

116. Vanderputten, *Monastic Reform*, 31–49.

117. Meyer, "Ein übersehenes Diplom," 120–21.

118. *Die Urkunden der Deutschen Könige und Kaiser*. Vol. 1, *Die Urkunden Konrad I. Heinrich I. und Otto I*, no. 466, p. 638; also Dierkens, "L'abbaye d'Aldeneik pendant le haut moyen âge," 1:161–64.

4. Reforms, Semi-Reforms, and the Silencing of Women Religious in the Tenth Century

1. Boshof, "Kloster"; Semmler, "Das Erbe"; Parisse, "Noblesse"; Parisse, "L'abbaye de Gorze"; Parisse, "Restaurer"; and Nightingale, *Monasteries*. On the suspected involvement of women religious in the so-called Gorze reform movement, Parisse, "Der Anteil"; Röckelein, "Frauen"; also chap. 3, n. 111.

2. Quoted from Skinner, "Benedictine Life," 87.

3. Nightingale, *Monasteries*.

4. Both the increased involvement of bishops in female communities and the growing number of Benedictine communities are phenomena that would become equally apparent in Saxony, albeit roughly half a century after they became prominent in Lotharingia; Parisse, "Les monastères," 149.

5. Compare with the commentary in Koziol, "Flothilde's Visions," esp. 169, 182. Also the discussion in Magnani, "Cluny."

6. John of Saint-Arnoul, *Vita Johannis*, ed. Jacobsen, 192–98; also app. F in this book.

7. On John's previous education, Wagner, "La vie" and Parisse, "Restaurer," 61.

8. John of Saint-Arnoul, *Vita Johannis*, ed. Jacobsen, 192.

9. John of Saint-Arnoul, *Vita, translationes et miracula sanctae Glodesindis*, ed. *AASS Julii* 6:210–23.

10. Ricuin's 918 charter is signed by twenty-four men (including a provost named Hugo) and twenty-six women, presumably members of the community; Metz, Archives Départementales de la Moselle, H 3959. Because Fredeburga is not mentioned as abbess, Parisse speculates that she was merely overseeing, not leading, the monastic community; "Parisse Der Anteil," 84–85.

11. Signori, "Anchorites," 48–52. According to Wiborada's biographer—a contemporary of John of Saint-Arnoul—she too had worn a hair shirt under her ordinary clothes, and following her death, she had been found to have worn a penitential chain around her waist; Ekkehard of Sankt Gallen, *Vita Wiboradae*, ed. Berschin, 89. In the *Life* of John of Gorze, John of Saint-Arnoul also references Einold, abbot of Gorze, and John himself as assiduous wearers of the hairshirt; *Vita Johannis*, ed. Jacobsen, 220, 293.

12. Koziol, "Flothilde's Visions." Flodoard of Reims also dedicated a poem to Saint Pelagia, a former actress turned urban recluse; Rothschild and Strubel, "Sainte Pélagie." The abbey of Remiremont may have owned a copy of a *Life* of this saint; see chap. 2, n. 19.

13. Refer to the discussion of Ansoaldis of Maubeuge's behavior in chap. 6, at nn. 8–13; more generally to Vanderputten, "Reformatorische lichamelijkheid."

14. John of Saint-Arnoul, *Vita, translationes et miracula sanctae Glodesindis*, ed. *AASS Julii* 6:222.

15. Widric, *Vita Gerardi episcopi Tullensis*, ed. Waitz, 494. According to Augustin Calmet, a female monastery dedicated to Saint Geneviève existed in the town of Toul before 900: but it was dissolved before the tenure of Bishop Berthold of Toul (995–1018), who reconstructed the former abbatial church as a parish church; Calmet, *Histoire de la Lorraine* 1:1027–28 (also the commentary in Parisse, *Noblesse*, 430 and Fray, *Villes*, 194). However, Sainte-Geneviève's status as a female institution at any time in this period is

obscured by a lack of reliable sources; Gaillard in *D'une réforme* does not mention its existence.

16. Refer to the discussion of the early eleventh-century reform of Pfalzel in chap. 5, at nn. 115–120.

17. John of Saint-Arnoul, *Vita Johannis*, ed. Jacobsen, 228.

18. Ibid., 270.

19. The only contemporary discussion on how to organize eremitical life, Grimlaicus's ninth- or tenth-century *Regula solitarium*, is addressed exclusively to male users; Frank, "Grimlaicus." There does seem to be some overlap between Grimlaicus's views and those found in Ekkehard of Sankt Gallen's early 970s *Life* of Wiborada of Sankt Gallen (*Vita Wiboradae*, ed. Berschin), particularly when the two authors compare the recluse to Mary (as an exemplar of a contemplative existence) and Martha (as another one, of an active life). Long held to be a late tenth-century treatise, Adalgerus's *Admonition to the (woman) recluse Nonsuinda*—which discusses the key virtues for eremitical life—appears to date from the seventh century (*Admonitio ad Nonsuindam reclusam*, ed. Anspach; see Jestice, *Wayward Monks*, 93). However, the fact that it was copied in the ninth and tenth centuries does suggest renewed interest in women's asceticism at that time; Robles Carcedo, "Anotaciones." Two copies of this text bring us close to the context of the Lotharingian communities studied in this book: one is Berlin, Deutsche Staatsbibliothek, Phillips 1723 (late tenth or early eleventh century, from the library of the male house of Saint-Vincent in Metz; Rose, *Verzeichnis*, 47–50) and Verdun, BM 30 (early eleventh century, from another male house, that of Saint-Vanne in Verdun; http://www1.arkhenum.fr/bm_verdun_ms/_app/index.php, consulted 2 May 2017).

20. Bautier, *Les origines*, 20–22.

21. See chap. 5, at nn. 44, 57–58.

22. O'Brien O'Keeffe, *Stealing*, 240–41: "Such women lived lives of religion, individually or in small communities, taking vows of some sort and dressing distinctively, but without supervision of an abbess or the liturgical structure of a convent. These women were primarily widows, although some virgins were included in their numbers. Such vowesses could live lives of relative ease on their own estates or lives of prayer and fasting." In addition to the references cited there, see also Foot, "Unveiling."

23. John of Saint-Arnoul, *Vita Johannis*, ed. Jacobsen, 248: "Sanctimonialium habitacula, quod ea, etsi non re, fama tamen obscurari quam aegre ferebat, omni sinistrae suspitionis morsu eripuit et ad idem quo monachos institutum et in nullo dispares observationes pro sexus virtute coercuit."

24. One of John's associates, the Scottish immigrant Caddroë, in the 940s gave spiritual counsel at least once to a community of women religious at Bucilly, a small monastic settlement in today's Aisne region of northern France, some forty kilometres south of Maubeuge; *Vita Caddroe abbatis Walciodorensis*, ed. Colgan, 498. Josef Semmler speculates that these women, like Caddroë himself, were recent migrants from the British Isles (Semmler, "Iren," 946); but according to Ortwin Huysmans, they might as well have come from the nearby female house of Origny, which may have been dissolved around this time (Huysmans, "Tutor," 157). On the role of Insular migrants in Lotharingian monasticism generally, Vanderputten, "Reconsidering Religious Migration."

25. *Passio Maxellendis prima*, ed. *AASS Belgii* 3:580–87; also Helvétius, "La *Passio*," 169, 178–79. Saint Maxellendis's cult turned up as early as the 940s in the documentation of the Ottonian monastery of Essen; Bertrand and Mériaux, "Cambrai-Magdebourg," 6.

26. Helvétius, "La *Passio*," 176–77.

27. *Passio Maxellendis prima*, ed. Ghesquière, *AASS Belgii* 3:580–87; also Helvétius, "La *Passio*," 176.

28. *Passio Maxellendis prima*, ed. Ghesquière *AASS Belgii* 3:586: "constituit ordinem ministrorum ex utroque sexu, clericos scilicet ac foeminas Deo devotas, quatenus deinceps omni tempore, prout dignum erat, debitum inibi expleretur officium."

29. Helvétius, "La *Passio*," 178. Anne-Marie Helvétius suspects the bishop of Cambrai and his clergy were involved in creating the text, but does not speculate on a possible connection with the Cambrai episcopate's foundation of the female monastery of Honnecourt, also in Cambrai. According to the late eleventh-century *Life of Lietphard*, Bishop Fulbert (d. 956) established a Benedictine nunnery there, and arranged for the women (*sanctimoniales*) to be served by a small group of canons; *Vita Lietphardi*, ed. *AASS Februarii* 1:496. By the early eleventh century the women were gone, and the sanctuary, now a benefice of "armed men" (*viri militares*), was served only by a few canons; *Gesta episcoporum Cameracensium*, ed. Bethmann, 458 (also Mériaux, "Fulbert," 537 and Mériaux, *Gallia Irradiata*, 285–86). Alternative, apparently spurious accounts of the abbey's tenth-century history are detailed in Bulteau, "Etude," 5–6.

30. Helvétius, "La *Passio*," 180–81.

31. Semmler, "Das Erbe," 35; Parisse, "Der Anteil," 85–86; Parisse, "Les religieuses bénédictines," 204–5; Erkens, "Gorze"; Nightingale, *Monasteries*, 116–9; and Parisse, "Un évêque."

32. Oschema, "Zur Gründung," 188–90, at 188: "Deo preordinante, invenimus quasdam sanctimoniales, velut oves errantes sed tamen aeternae vitae pascua querentes, Dei dilectione ferventes et ad serviendum illi locum remotum desiderantes, quarum miseratione permoti, consultu predicti abbatis ceterorumque Deum timentium nostrorumque fidelium, iam dictam cellulam eis ad habitandum delegavimus, praeficientes illis unam earum, Rothildim scilicet, abbatissam, quae illarum regeret vitam."

33. Bautier, *Les origines*, 16. Parisse speaks of "an informal group of women religious"; Parisse, "Un évêque," 72–73.

34. Bautier, *Les origines*, no. 3, pp. 67–68.

35. Ibid., 20–22. Charters documenting her transactions are edited ibid., no. 5, pp. 70–72, no. 8, pp. 77–78; and in Oschema, "Zur Gründung," 188–90.

36. John of Saint-Arnoul, *Vita Johannis*, ed. Jacobsen, 270; also the discussion above, at n. 18.

37. Below, at nn. 50–52.

38. Nightingale, *Monasteries*, 150.

39. Parisse, "Les religieuses bénédictines," 205.

40. Otto's 960 charter for Bouxières emphasizes the sisters' adherence to a regular life (*sub regularibus institutis*) and the efforts and exhortations of the bishop to that effect (*conatu et exortatione . . . episcopi*); *Die Urkunden der Deutschen Könige und Kaiser*. Vol. 1, *Die Urkunden Konrad I. Heinrich I. und Otto I*, no. 211, pp. 291–92.

41. The *Deeds of the Bishops of Toul* from the second half of the eleventh century state that Gozelin created the monastery "from the foundations" (*a fundamentis*) and adds an entirely fictional account of how Gozelin's brother Hadrad had discovered the abandoned sanctuary while hunting a wild boar; *Gesta episcoporum Tullensium*, ed. Waitz, 639–40.

42. Choux, "Décadence," 217. On Gozelin of Langres, Hlawitschka, *Die Anfänge*, 30–42.

43. Sproemberg, "Die lothringische Politik," esp. 111–52.

44. Parisse, "Les religieuses bénédictines," 205.

45. The three men had appeared in this order of significance in a 916 charter by Charles the Simple; Schneider and Martine, "La production." Kunigunde belonged to the Ardenne family, members of which later came to control much of Lotharingia's higher politics; Margue, "Face à l'évêque."

46. Parisse, *La noblesse*, 1:21.

47. Nightingale, *Monasteries*, 72–74.

48. Ibid., 156.

49. Ibid., 114–66, esp. 154–55. According to one hypothesis, Rothildis may have been a granddaughter via her mother of Charles the Bald and Empress Richildis, and a daughter of Count Hugo of Bourges and his wife Rothildis, herself abbess of Chelles; Bautier, *Les origines*, 18–19. Her high noble descent is mentioned in a charter of Emperor Otto I from 965; *Die Urkunden der Deutschen Könige und Kaiser*. Vol. 1, *Die Urkunden Konrad I. Heinrich I. und Otto I.*, no. 31, p. 105–8.

50. Rothildis is mentioned in Bouxières's charters from October 937: Bautier, *Les origines*, no. 7, pp. 76–77; no. 8, pp. 77–78 (where she is referenced as *omni veneratione nominanda*); and no. 9, pp. 79–80 (likely a forged document).

51. Bautier, *Les origines*, no. 33, p. 111.

52. Ibid., no. 25, 31–32.

53. Ibid., no. 15, p. 88 (where he is referred to as *Christi domini humilis famulus*, or "humble servant of Lord Christ") and no. 16, p. 89 (before 4 June 960, where he is mentioned as abbot). Also Nightingale, *Monasteries*, 150–51.

54. Oschema, "Zur Gründung," 189. Also compare with nearly identical demands he made to the monks of Saint-Evre; Nightingale, *Monasteries*, 135–6.

55. Odelric's lay abbacy did not infringe on the community's right of free election; ibid. In 960, Otto I confirmed Bouxières's foundation and privileges and the free election of their abbesses; Bautier, *Les origines*, no. 25, pp. 95–98 and no. 31, pp. 105–8.

56. Hlawitschka, "Zur Lebensgeschichte"; Semmler, "Das Erbe," 38–39; Parisse, "Der Anteil," 86; and Bautier, *Les origines*, 24. Several of Odelric's relatives had been involved in the 931–36 charter by Duke Giselbert for Remiremont.

57. Hlawitschka, "Zur Lebensgeschichte," 15, notes how Count Arnulf of Chaumontois had been present at Giselbert's 930s restitution act for Remiremont.

58. Ibid., 14–15.

59. Bautier, *Les origines*, 30.

60. Ibid., no. 15, pp. 87–89, at 88: "ubi non pauca ancillarum eius multitudo consistit."

61. Ibid., no. 33, pp. 111–13, at 112: "in quo utique loco sacrarum virginum erga divinum cultum infatigabilis desudat sollicitudo."

NOTES TO PAGES 100–103   231

62. Boshof, "Untersuchungen"; also *L'avouerie en Lotharingie,* particularly Genicot, "Sur le vocabulaire," 25 and 29; and Parisse, "Noblesse," 190. Regarding Frederic's position at Saint-Pierre-aux-Nonnains, Blennemann, *Die Metzer Benediktinerinnen,* 87. Frederic also held the abbeys of Saint-Mihiel, Juvigny, Moyenmoutier, and Saint-Dié and was lay advocate of Gorze and Saint-Mihiel; Parisse, "Les possessions," 246–47. On the role of Lotharingian dukes as advocates, Werner, "Der Herzog," 410–15.

63. On Gerard of Toul, Parisse, "Un prélat" and Nightingale, "Bishop."

64. Widric, *Vita Gerardi episcopi Tullensis,* ed. Waitz, 494.

65. Bautier, *Les origines,* 41–44.

66. Ibid., no. 38, pp. 119–20: "hanc cartae notitiam fieri decrevi et anulo regis cuiuscumque Deus regno preesse elegerit."

67. Sproemberg, "Die lothringische Politik," 152–65.

68. Bautier, *Les origines,* no. 26, pp. 98–101.

69. Ibid., no. 27, pp. 101–2.

70. Ibid., no. 32, pp. 109–10. On Ermenaidis, Nightingale, *Monasteries,* 162.

71. Nightingale, *Monasteries,* 164–66.

72. Bautier, *Les origines,* 46–47, with Conrad's charter edited as no. 40, pp. 122–23, and that of Berthold as no. 39, pp. 120–22.

73. *Die Urkunde Ludwigs,* ed. Wolfram, no. F, pp. 17–20. Particularly the list of properties, with the exception of the estate of Hastière, is an interpolation (Parisse, "Der Anteil," 85; Blennemann, *Die Metzer Benediktinerinnen,* 76; and Blennemann, "Eine Bildurkunde," 172, 182). For a completely opposite view, which considers the list of properties more or less the only authentic part of the document, Fray, "Le temporel," 105, n. 15.

74. *Die Urkunde Ludwigs,* ed. Wolfram, no. F, p. 17: "Hoc erat necesse, ad restauracionem reducere cupientes normam sancti Benedicti, ut fuit olim inibi statuimus ac neptem nostram Himiltrudem sanctimonialibus, que in hac vita Deo degerent, preficimus." John of Saint-Arnoul recounts Himiltrudis's appointment as follows: "Unde et hoc idem beatae virginis collegium, praefecta ibi Domna Himmiltrude, sanguine, et quod majus est, spiritu sibi propinqua, ad monasticam institutionem coegit. De cuius sancti pontificis dignis Deo operibus proprium est merito quod desideretur opus nec hujus articuli brevitate tantam concludi fas fuerit majestatem"; John of Saint-Arnoul, *Vita, translationes et miracula sanctae Glodesindis,* ed. AASS Julii 6:224.

75. On Otto's use of charters as indicators of social positioning, Keller, "Otto"; also Blennemann, *Die Metzer Benediktinerinnen,* 83 and 86. On his involvement in the Benedictine reform of monastic communities to expand his direct influence in the westernmost regions of his empire, Martine, "Les mouvements."

76. The interpolated parts concern only the description of the abbey's estates; Blennemann, *Die Metzer Benediktinerinnen,* 79.

77. *Die Urkunden der Deutschen Könige und Kaiser.* Vol. 1, *Die Urkunden Konrad I. Heinrich I. und Otto I,* no. 210, p. 290: "nostrae corroborationis auctoritate sanctimonialibus iam dicti monasterii secundum sancti patris Benedicti instituta sub regula vel abbatissa liceret militare." And "ut predictae monachae sine gravi labore domino possint militare pro nobisque atque successoribus nostris alacrius intercedere." In 977, Otto II confirmed his father's privilege; *Die Urkunden der Deutschen Könige und Kaiser.* Vol. 2, bk. 1, *Die Urkunden Otto des II.,* no. 159, p. 179.

78. John of Saint-Arnoul, *Vita, translationes et miracula sanctae Glodesindis*, ed. *AASS Julii* 6:224: "Hic monasteria, quaecumque per amplitudinem suae erant providentiae, retro a multis iam annis interius et exterius spiritalibus et corporalibus opibus nimium lapsa, studio praeter cetera egregie animum recuperare induxit. Et primum quidem eius operum spiritualium Gorzia monasterium fuit, ubi magnarum virtutum viro domino Eginoldo promoto, et brevi copiosa religiosorum turba eo confluente, et in beatitudinem pauperum spiritu sub regula beati Benedicti conspirante, ad eius exemplar reliqua extra vel infra virorum ac feminarum, si qua etiam sub nomine canonicorum erant, composuit monasteria." Also the slightly different account in the eleventh-century *Fundatio Sancti Petri*; Paris, BNF, Nouvelles Acquisitions Françaises 6700, f. 91–92, edited in Blennemann, *Die Metzer Benediktinerinnen*, 290.

79. Otto's 960 privilege hints at change prior to the reform; *Die Urkunden der Deutschen Könige und Kaiser*. Vol. 1, *Die Urkunden Konrad I. Heinrich I. und Otto I*, no. 210, p. 290: "tam ea quae ante observationem regule quam nostris temporibus, ut pretaxavimus, iterum inchoare coeperunt."

80. Martine, "Les mouvements."

81. *Die Urkunde Ludwigs*, ed. Wolfram, no. F, pp. 17–20; also Dierkens, *Abbayes*, 149–55; Nightingale, *Monasteries*, 75–76; and Blennemann, *Die Metzer Benediktinerinnen*, 78–79.

82. In 969, Hastière was again reclaimed by Liège parties and attached as a (presumably male) priory to the monastery of Waulsort; Dierkens, *Abbayes*, 149.

83. Adalbero acted no differently from his nephew, Thierry I, in using female institutions as political commodities. Thierry, duke of Upper Lotharingia, later on captured Juvigny, Queen Richildis's foundation. His claim on that institution likely derived from the inheritance of his wife, also named Richildis and possibly the queen's distant relative. The fact that Juvigny represented this claimed association to the Carolingian dynasty presumably made it a significant acquisition for Adalbero's relatives; *Chronique*, ed. Bur, 128.

84. Parisse, "Généalogie," 22.

85. Blennemann, *Die Metzer Benediktinerinnen*, 87.

86. Ricuin's relations with Adalbero's predecessor Wigeric (917–27) undoubtedly had been cool, as the two men had been on opposite sides in the struggle for control over Lotharingian politics. And as we saw earlier, Adalbero's father and relatives had also been direct opponents of Ricuin's; Blennemann, *Die Metzer Benediktinerinnen*, 74–75. Possibly adding to Adalbero's resentment of Ricuin was Wigeric's putative kinship to Wigeric, father of Adalbero I; Gaillard, *D'une réforme*, 432 and Nightingale, *Monasteries*, 74–75.

87. Barth, *Der Herzog*, 130–67.

88. Martine, "Les mouvements."

89. Nightingale, *Monasteries*, 71–72 and 77–86. Relations between Bishop Gozelin of Toul and the abbey of Saint-Evre were likewise tense; ibid., 135–36.

90. *Die Urkunden der Deutschen Könige und Kaiser*. Vol. 1, *Die Urkunden Konrad I. Heinrich I. und Otto I*, no. 466, p. 638: "sanctis monialibus in illo digne ac devote Domino famulantibus."

91. Ibid., no. 154, pp. 235–36: "quoddam monasterium Eiche vocatum"; also Dierkens, "L'abbaye d'Aldeneik pendant le haut moyen âge," 166–68.

NOTES TO PAGES 106–107   233

92. Oeren's status is referred to in Otto I's charter of that year; *Die Urkunden der Deutschen Könige und Kaiser.* Vol. 1, *Die Urkunden Konrad I. Heinrich I. und Otto I*, no. 168, pp. 249–50. For Oeren's transferral to the archbishopric of Trier, see Otto's charter from 966; ibid., no. 322, pp. 436–37.

93. *Die Urkunden der Deutschen Könige und Kaiser.* Vol. 1, *Die Urkunden Konrad I. Heinrich I. und Otto I*, no. 168, pp. 249–50; also Zimmer, *Das Kloster*, 57–58.

94. John of Saint-Arnoul, *Vita, translationes et miracula sanctae Glodesindis*, ed. *AASS Julii* 6:224: "matrem praedictam loci ipsius reparandi, quia vetustas et brevitas monere videbatur, cupido cepit immodica. Id per se, quoniam non nisi sacro corpore interim submoto fieri poterat, non praesumens, quid animo conceperat, episcopo intimat. Ille de fabrica, ut fieret, gratum omnino habens, suamque benigne pollicitus operam, de sublevatione sacri corporis diu cunctabundus, tandem Domini super hoc voluntatem ut exquireret, imperavit: communicato deinde negotio patribus tunc venerandis Einoldo ... et Ansteo aeque viro religioso, e proximo sancti Arnulphi collegio, ipsisque animos eidem sancto pontifici vel abbatissae magis addentibus, in communi decretum est, ut fieret ... ad arcam virginis aperiendam pontifex venerandus, cumque eo patres monasteriorum simul et ceteri ex clero religiosi, digne Deo sanctaeque virgini submissi, reverenter accedunt. Moxque sacrosanctos artus, loculo tunc pro tempore praeparato exceptos, in proximam quamdam domum interim conservandos transponunt." On this new version of the *Life*, Blennemann, *Die Metzer Benediktinerinnen*, 27–30 and Goullet, "Les saints du diocèse de Metz," 288–95.

95. Blennemann, *Die Metzer Benediktinerinnen*, 78; also (for the abbatial church) Voltz, "Historique."

96. John of Saint-Arnoul, *Vita, translationes et miracula sanctae Glodesindis*, ed. *AASS Julii* 6:221–24. The author mentions that the saint's relics were kept inside a small, house-like structure (*domuncula*) inside the abbatial church; this is reminiscent of the structure of the same name in which the remains of Irish Saint Furseus were presented for veneration at Péronne; Crook, *The Architectural Setting*, 72, 274.

97. The text of the charter states that it was drafted specifically at the abbess's request ("signum dominae Hermentrudis abbatissae quae hanc cartam fieri rogavit"); Müsebeck, "Die Benediktinerabtei," no. 4, pp. 228–29. Probably she was the sister of Bishop Thierry II of Metz (1006–47); Parisse, "Généalogie," 28. At the time of the charter's creation, the monks of Saint-Arnoul were facing difficulties warding off the bishop's encroachments on their properties; Müller, *Am Schnittpunkt*, 237–38. This may or may not explain the abbess's prominence in this document.

98. *Vita Caddroe abbatis Walciodorensis*, ed. Colgan, 500: "his praeterea mater, nomine Helvidis, omni actu et conversatione ab ipsis incunabulis paene incomparabilis."

99. *Die Urkunden der Deutschen Könige und Kaiser.* Vol. 2, bk. 2, *Die Urkunden Otto des III*, no. 117, pp. 528–29. Hadewidis's background is unknown, but in later centuries, she was locally remembered as the monastery's first abbess; Paris, BNF, Lat. 10028, f. 99 (on this necrology, Blennemann, "Le nécrologe"). This peculiar tradition recalls the situation at Niedermünster in Regensburg, where the systematic recording of necrological notices in support of the sisters' commemorative prayer began in 991, shortly after the appointment of reformist Abbess Uta (990–1025); Bodarwé, "Eine Männerregel," 256.

100. Hirschmann, *Verdun* 1:257–58, n. 1220; with reference to the edited document in "Chartes," ed. Schaeffer, no. 24, p. 156.

101. Fößel, in "Ottonische Äbtissinnen," warns against overestimating the political influence of high-ranking abbesses.

102. Nightingale, *Monasteries*, 76 and Blennemann, *Die Metzer Benediktinerinnen*, 77.

103. Hoebanx, *L'abbaye*, 111–12.

104. *Die Urkunden der Deutschen Könige und Kaiser*. Vol. 1, *Die Urkunden Konrad I. Heinrich I. und Otto I*, no. 318, pp. 432–33 (Otto I, interpolated charter from 966); *Die Urkunden der Deutschen Könige und Kaiser*. Vol. 2, bk 1, *Die Urkunden Otto des II*, no. 21, p. 28–30 (Otto II, 972); and ibid., no. 222, pp. 251–52 (Otto II, 980). On the Ottonians' support of female institutions in Saxony, Ehlers, "Der helfende Herrscher."

105. Hoebanx, *L'abbaye*, 117.

106. Epinal, BM, 105, edited in Hlawitschka, *Studien*, 130–43; also refer to the notes in *Chartes de l'abbaye*, ed. Bridot, 53–54.

107. Parisse, "Les notices," 213, 220–21. On attempts to reorganize the information entered in the *Liber memorialis*, for instance, by grouping related notices, and also evidence of a growing division of labor in written practices and estate management; ibid., 214, 223–27 and Dierkens and Margue, *Memoria*, 878.

108. Compare with the sacramentary of Essen from around 900, which also includes memorial notices; Huth, "Die Düsseldorfer Sakramentarhandschrift"; Niederkorn-Bruck, "Verschriftlichung"; and Schilp, "Überlegungen."

109. *Liber memorialis*, ed. Hlawitschka, Schmid, and Tellenbach, f. 65r–71v. Giles Constable notes that the list covers the abbey's rents and fifty-two extra grants; Constable, "The 'Liber Memorialis,'" 263.

110. Hlawitschka, "Herzog," 450; Perrin, *Recherches*, 147–69. There are some references in Remiremont's 980s–990s notices of significant land clearance in the wooded area around the monastic site; Constable, "The 'Liber Memorialis,'" 276.

111. Jacques-Henri Perrin speculates that the list focuses on the incomes of the office of the *secreta*, the sister responsible for the maintainance of the altars, candles, and the abbey's treasury; Perrin, *Recherches*, 147–69 (on the office of the *secreta*, see Gasse-Grandjean, *Les livres*, 86–88). In contrast, Michel Parisse claims that the *censier* indicates the creation of two separate *mensae*, one for the abbess and one for the community; Parisse, "Les notices," 220–23.

112. Vanderputten and West, "Inscribing Property." Hans-Werner Goetz however calls for caution when speculating on the structure and exploitation of female monastic properties and incomes for this poorly documented age; Goetz, "Besitz," 129–32.

113. Parisse, "Les notices," 232. Compare with the remarks on the government of Abbess Emma of Sant Joan de les Abadesses in Jarrett, "Power," esp. 242–43.

114. Parisse, "Les notices," 230. Notable from Odelric's time in office is a trade of properties with his other institution of Bouxières; Bautier, *Les origines*, no. 32, pp. 109–11.

115. Eduard Hlawitschka observes a shift toward a more noble background for community members (with sisters referred to as *dominae*); Hlawitschka, *Studien*, 44–54 (see, however, the notes in Parisse, "Les notices," 222). But according to Friedrich Oediger, the religious at that time were in fact Benedictine nuns, since members of the community were recruited, between 953 and 965, to staff the newly reformed

nunnery of Sankt Maria im Kapitol, in Cologne; Oediger, "St. Maria," 77–79. Against this, Hlawitschka convincingly argues that the status of the Cologne religious is unclear, and that the reform there was in fact a new foundation; Hlawitschka, "Zu den klösterlichen Anfängen."

116. Respectively, *Liber memorialis*, ed. Hlawitschka, Schmid, and Tellenbach, f. 57v ("Nomina defunctorum pro fide Christi a paganis occisorum") and f. 32v ("Rotbertus et Dodana pro remedio animarum nostrarum . . . nostram sancto Petro dedimus unam feminam cum infantibus suis pietatis et dulcedinis causa, quam Huni predaverunt et postea (redi)derunt"; also a similar notice, which mentions her name as Ermentrudis and states that she and her children were due a yearly rent, on f. 33v); and Hlawitschka, *Studien*, 142 ("Memoria misericordiae post occisorum a paganis homines de potestate quae dicitur Lietzeis, servitium integrum reverti praecipimus ad medietatem ex omni potestate de sortibus indominicatis").

5. New Beginnings

1. The absence of evidence of intellectual activity in Lotharingian Benedictine houses of the later tenth and early eleventh centuries reminds us of Salvus of Albelda's 950s–960s adaptation of Saint Benedict's *Rule* for use by women religious, which omits any of Saint Benedict's instructions in chap. 54 on studies; Bishko, "Salvus," 573; and Bodarwé, "Eine Männerregel," 263.

2. Translated quote from Le Jan, "De la France," 183.

3. Parisse, "Les religieuses dans le nord de l'Allemagne," 126–27; also the updated notes in Röckelein, "Bairische, sächsische und mainfränkische Klostergründungen."

4. Refer to the comments for Alsace in Parisse, "Le 'monachisme,'" 230–31.

5. See chap. 4, at n. 15.

6. Parisse, "Les religieuses bénédictines," 205–6.

7. Nancy, Archives Départementales de Meurthe-et-Moselle H 2427: "monasterium meum quod construximus in honore sanctae Mariae necnon omnium sanctorum ubi [sanctimoniales sub regula in habitu] conversandum misimus." The part that refers to the *Rule* may be an interpolation; Jean, *Une intéressante donation*.

8. Hlawitschka, *Die Anfänge*, esp. 57.

9. Bautier, *Les origines*, no. 28, p. 103.

10. *Liber memorialis*, ed. Hlawitschka, Schmid, and Tellenbach, f. 46r; also Nightingale, *Monasteries*, 159–60.

11. Aristocratic foundations of female monasteries near strategic sites or in other locations that were central or emblematic to a family's lordship and property holdings were not unusual; Röckelein, "Bairische, sächsische und mainfränkische Klostergründungen," 54–55.

12. Leyser, *Rule*, 70–71.

13. *Vita Leonis IX*, ed. Krause, Jasper, and Lukas, 90.

14. An interpolated version of Leo's bull is in Calmet, *Histoire de la Lorraine 2: Preuves*, cclxxxvii–ix. On Leo's involvement with Hesse, Legl, *Studien*, 210–13; Seibert, *Abtserhebungen*, 251; Iogna-Prat, "Léon IX," 379.

15. Oberste, "Papst Leo IX," 429.

16. *Les bulles*, ed. Choux, no. 4, pp. 15–17. On Bleurville and the privilege, Parisse, "Les règlements," no. 7, pp. 161, 169; Parisse, "Der Anteil," 90; and Legl, *Studien*, 211–12. On the eleventh-century remains of the abbatial church and the church's tenth-century crypt, Fahrenheim, "Une construction."

17. *Les bulles*, ed Choux, no. 4, p. 15. According to a forgery of a 1052 charter by Bishop Udo of Toul, Leo refused to name Count Frederic, son-in-law of Count Rainard of Toul, as advocate because of unspecified misconduct by Frederic's wife Gertrudis. Leo subsequently asked the bishop of Toul to award the advocacy to Frederic based on his ownership of the title by hereditary right; ed. Calmet, *Histoire de la Lorraine 2: Preuves*, cclxxiv–vi (also "Les actes," ed. Schuellen, 172; and Bönnen, *Die Bischofsstadt*, 58). Eleventh-century religious from Remiremont also became abbesses at Lunéville; on the former institution's observance, see the discussion in chap. 4, nn. 106–15, of this work.

18. On Leo's monastic policy generally, Bloch, "Die Klosterpolitik"; and Oberste, "Papst Leo IX," 431–33.

19. *Oorkondenboek*, ed Koch, 1: no. 61, pp. 111–16; also Blok, "De stichtingsbrief"; and Kersken, *Zwischen Glaube und Welt*, 29–30.

20. Bijsterveld, "De oorsprong," 211 and Kersken, *Zwischen Glaube und Welt*, 25. On the founding couple, see most recently Kersken, *Zwischen Glaube und Welt*, 30–48. According to an alternative hypothesis, the wife of Ansfrid's uncle (also Ansfrid) was the founder; Jongbloed, "Listige Immo," 36–37.

21. Kersken, *Zwischen Glaube und Welt*, 58–64.

22. Ibid., 69–72.

23. Thietmar of Merseburg, *Chronicon*, ed. Hotzmann, 171–72; also the discussion in Kersken, *Zwischen Glaube und Welt*, 48–57.

24. Wolters, *Notice*, 5–7.

25. Dierkens, "Les Ansfrid," 69.

26. Kersken, *Zwischen Glaube und Welt*, resp. 132 and 107–11.

27. Ibid., 76–78.

28. Ibid., 74.

29. Ibid., 75–76.

30. *Die Urkunden der Deutschen Könige und Kaiser.* Vol. 3, *Die Urkunden Heinrichs II. und Arduins*, ed. H. Bresslau, no. 140, pp. 166–77. See Kersken, *Zwischen Glaube und Welt*, 78–93; also Linssen, *Een bijdrage*, 4; and generally, Kupper, *Notger*, 86.

31. On the abbesses, Van der Eycken and Van der Eycken, "Wachten," 35; on the coinage, *Munt in Limburg*, 99; Steinbach, *Das Geld*, 113; and Ilisch, "Die Münzprägung," 335–36. No legal documentation from this period survives: a notice purporting to be from 1040 is a forgery from the 1160s; Hansay, *Une prétendue charte*.

32. Dupont, "Les domaines" and Parisse, "Généalogie," 30.

33. Herman and Gerard of Lunéville's interpolated charter is in Calmet, *Histoire de la Lorraine 2: Preuves*, cclxxvi–vii. Lunéville's actual founder was their father, Count Folmar, a vassal of the bishop; Gérard and Gérard, "Lunéville," 204–8.

34. Oda was included in Sankt Gallen's memorial books on the basis of her aristocratic descent, not the fact that she had been abbess of Remiremont; Hlawitschka, *Äbtissinnenreihe*, 68–74 and Parisse, "Généalogie," 34. Before her appointment, Geoffrey, episcopal count of Metz, was installed as the abbey's advocate; Gérard and

Gérard, "Lunéville," 206. Compare with Parisse's comments on the quasihereditary nature of abbatial office in many proprietary monasteries in Saxony; Parisse, "Les religieuses dans le nord de l'Allemagne," 129.

35. *Die Urkunden der Deutschen Könige und Kaiser.* Vol. 3, *Die Urkunden Heinrichs II. und Arduins,* ed. H. Bresslau, no. 140, p. 167.

36. Ibid., pp. 166–67. On market privileges issued by the Ottonian rulers, Irsigler, "Markt- und Messeprivilegien."

37. Steinbach, *Das Geld,* 116–19, 238; Kersken, *Zwischen Glaube und Welt,* 93–100.

38. See n. 66 in this chapter; also McNamara, *Sisters,* 186. Such observations may be relevant to the case of other modestly endowed Benedictine nunneries. It is, after all, unknown if the principle of individual poverty was actually enforced in these communities.

39. According to the revised redaction of Rainer of Ghent, *Inventio et miracula Gisleni Hanoniensis,* ed. Poncelet, 287; also Kersken, *Zwischen Glaube und Welt,* 102–3. The mostly rural *gynaecea* were often supervized by aristocratic women; Garver, "Learned Women," 129; esp. Garver, *Women,* 260–61.

40. Bertarius, *Gesta episcoporum Virdinensium (continuatio),* ed. Waitz, 47 and Hugh of Flavigny, *Chronicon,* ed. Pertz, 391–92; also Hirschmann, *Verdun* 1:238–61; and Guild, Héber-Suffrin, and Wagner, "Saint-Maur." Of the abbatial church, only the early eleventh-century crypt survives; compare with the Essen crypt as described in Lange, "Die Krypta."

41. Crick, "The Wealth," 158.

42. Onulph and Everhelm, *Vita Popponis,* ed. Wattenbach, 299–300.

43. Bertarius, *Gesta episcoporum Virdunensium,* ed. Waitz, 48: "Erat namque tunc temporis quaedam religiosa femina in reclusione vitam solitariam ducens apud aecclesiam beatae Mariae, die et nocte orationibus et ieiuniis et vigiliis studiose insistens. Huic nocte ipsa, qua consilium migrandi fuerat, divinitus imperatum est, ut ab ergastulo illo, quo se per plures annos obstruserat, egrederetur, et abbati nuntiaret, quatinus praedictos viros, quod solum restabat, monachili professione sine mora deviniret, ne eos aecclesia funditus amitteret. Quae iussis obtemperans, omni mirante populo egreditur a cellula et visa vel audita abbati nuntiat." Also Hirschmann, *Verdun* 1:257–61 and Guild, Héber-Suffrin, and Wagner, "Saint-Maur," 351. On two recluses in mid-tenth-century Verdun, see chap. 4, at n. 18, in this book.

44. *Actes,* ed. Evrard, no. 27, pp. 65–68, at p. 67: "Ad hospites curtem recipiendos decimas indominicatas, scilicet de Pontepetrino, de Sampiniaco . . . quae medietates girovagis per civitatem mulieribus quae Deo sarratae *(sic)* dicebantur, satis inhonestae et inutiliter hactenus sunt collatae." The use of the word *gyrovagae* is a reference to Saint Benedict's *Rule,* 1:10–11, where he condemns a type of monk named *gyrovagi,* "who spend their whole lives tramping from province to province . . . they indulge in their own wills and succumb to the allurements of gluttony"; Benedict of Nursia, *Regula monachorum,* ed. De Vogüé and Neufville, 1:438 and 440.

45. In tenth-century Milan, only men were allowed to found hospices. Still, it was a local community of nuns that subsequently took over the yearly poor feast; Balzaretti, "Women," 549. There is evidence from early twelfth-century Reims that women worked at the hospital owned by the regular canons there; Hirschmann, *Verdun* 1:260.

46. Vanderputten, *Imagining,* 73–103.

47. Guild, Héber-Suffrin, and Wagner, "Saint-Maur," 350. In a passage that defies belief, Hugh of Flavigny tells us that Abbot Richard of Saint-Vanne was involved in appointing the first abbess, Eva of Saint-Maur, who then traveled to Cluny to seek advice on how to organize her institution; Hugh of Flavigny, *Chronicon*, ed. Pertz, 391. The nunnery's foundation may have taken place around the same time as the writing of a *Life* of Saint Maur; Hugh of Flavigny, *Chronicon*, ed. Pertz, 353.

48. *Actes*, ed. Evrard, no. 55, pp. 112–14, at 113. Thierry's charter confirms the sisters' right to appoint the clerics serving the altars on the monastery's properties. For Pope Leo's 1049 bull, Calmet, *Histoire de la Lorraine*, 2: *Preuves*, cclxx–ii.

49. Hirschmann, *Verdun* 1:240 and Guild, Héber-Suffrin, and Wagner, "Saint-Maur," 350–51.

50. Hirschmann, *Verdun* 1:242 and Guild, Héber-Suffrin, and Wagner, "Saint-Maur," 351.

51. Hirschmann, *Verdun* 1:261–66.

52. John's bull, which confirms the abbey's rights and grants free election of the abbess (albeit with the consent of the bishop), indicates that Haimo "adorned the small troop of women religious with the rule for monastic life" (quodque antecessor eius episcopus Haimo pro tempore et pro posse construxit sancti monialiumque turmula viteque monastice regula decoravit); *Papsturkunden*, ed. Meinert, no. 5, pp. 179–81. Pope Leo IX in 1049 reprised John's bull: this document, which appears to be interpolated, is edited in Calmet, *Histoire de la Lorraine*, 2: *Preuves*, cclxxx–ii. A 1041 charter by Henry III confirms the original donation and the abbey's properties: but this is available only as a very deficient transcription of an interpolated original; Von Mitis, "Archivreise," 199; also Hirschmann, *Verdun* 1:242.

53. Hirschmann, *Verdun*, 2:512.

54. Folz, "Adalbéron II."

55. His predecessor Thierry I (965–84) preferred patronizing existing institutions. All we have from him is a forged charter for Sainte-Glossinde, purporting to be from 974 and confirming Adalbero I's 945 charter for the abbey (edited in *Die Urkunde*, ed. Wolfram, no. C, pp. 12–14. Also Blennemann, "Eine Bildurkunde," 172, 182), and indications that he was involved in the government of Remiremont (Folz, "Un évêque," 146). On Thierry's eleventh-century *Life*, Philippart and Wagner, "Hagiographie," 647–49.

56. Parisse, "Der Anteil," 87. An early eleventh-century list of members of Saint-Pierre-aux-Nonnains holds thirty-three names; Wiegand, "Ein Nonnen-Verzeichnis," 269; Matzel, "Die Namenliste," 241–43; Blennemann, *Die Metzer Benediktinerinnen*, 199, at n. 208; also App. A.

57. Blennemann, *Die Metzer Benediktinerinnen*, 88–93.

58. Constantin of Saint-Symphorien, *Vita Adalberonis II Mettensis episcopi*, ed. Pertz, 662: "Xenodochium quidam locellus infra urbem Mettensem habebatur antiquissimus, pauperculus, vilissimus, preter id quod beatae Mariae semper virginis nomini erat dicatus; quem amore Christi et matris Christi Domini, in quem aedificiorum splendorem reerexit, quantis divitiarum opibus aggregatas ibidem ancillas Dei ad laudes perpetuo Creatori omnium caelebrandas ditaverit, res acta inditio est."

59. On the *Life* of Saint Terentius and the fact that it insists (like the contemporary *Life* of Saint Goëry) on early medieval bishops' ownership of properties in the Massif Central region, Goullet, "Les saints du diocèse de Metz," 207–12.

60. Constantin of Saint-Symphorien, *Vita Adalberonis II Mettensis episcopi*, ed. Pertz, 662.
61. *Die Urkunden der Deutschen Könige und Kaiser.* Vol. 3, *Die Urkunden Heinrichs II. und Arduins*, ed. Bresslau, no. 104, pp. 129–30; also Parisse, "Les religieuses bénédictines," 206.
62. Constantin of Saint-Symphorien, *Vita Adalberonis II Mettensis episcopi*, ed. Pertz, 662; also Philippart and Wagner, "Hagiographie," 641–42.
63. Parisse, "Der Anteil," 88 and Houot, "Fondation," 6.
64. Sigebert of Gembloux, *Vita Deoderici*, ed. Pertz, 470; also De Morembert, *Epinal*, 605; Houot, "Fondation," 8; and Parisse, "Thierry," 102. On Thierry's relic collections, Wagner, "Collection," esp. 336–37.
65. Parisse, "Der Anteil," 88; compare, for the Empire, with Röckelein, "Bairische, sächsische und mainfränkische Klostergründungen," 52 and 54–55.
66. Parisse, "Thierri," 102. In later decades, sisters from Remiremont and Epinal owned prebends from each other's institutions; Parisse, "Les religieuses de Lorraine," 218. Regarding prebends at Bouxières, Lepage, *L'abbaye*, 139.
67. *Die Urkunden der Deutschen Könige und Kaiser.* Vol. 3, *Die Urkunden Heinrichs II. und Arduins*, ed. Bresslau, no. 58, pp. 69–73. All versions of this charter are suspect; Houot, "Fondation," 5 and Bourgeois, "Un diplôme suspect."
68. On the cult of Saint Goëry, Goullet, "Les saints du diocèse de Metz," 234–41 and Philippart and Wagner, "Hagiographie," 624–27. Perhaps around this time the abbey acquired the famous, ninth-century *Purple evangeliary* (Epinal, BM, 265).
69. Tronquart, "L'église," 136, 137, and 139.
70. Hirschmann, *Stadtplanung*.
71. In 1050, Pope Leo concluded the lengthy process of establishing the abbey as a major religious institution and a hallmark of episcopal presence in the region by dedicating the fortress-like abbatial church and granting a privilege, the contents of which are reprised in a charter by Bishop Pibo of Toul from 1090; Choux, *Recherches*, no. 47, p. 213 and Iogna-Prat, "Léon IX," 381.
72. Tronquart, "L'église."
73. Compare with similar findings for South-West Germany in Auge, "'Aemulatio.'"
74. Regarding Berthold, see North and Cutler, "The Bishop."
75. Parisse, "Une abbaye," 104–6. The only available version of the *Life* of Saint Menna is a seventeenth-century reworking of an earlier text; *Vita sanctae Mennae*, ed. *AASS Octobris* 2:150–57. Once made pope, Leo ratified the monastery's rights and properties; Calmet, *Histoire de la Lorraine*, 2: *Preuves*, ccxc-ii, at ccxc, with discussion in Parisse, "Une abbaye," 107–9. Poussay is mentioned in Leo's biography; *Vita Leonis IX*, ed. Krause, Jasper, and Lukas, 138.
76. Parisse, "Une abbaye," 106. Leo possibly gave the religious the lavish *Evangeliary of Poussay*, made in the 980s at Reichenau; Paris, BNF, Lat. 10514.
77. Leyser, *Rule*, 71.
78. See chap. 4, at nn. 103–5.
79. *Die Urkunden der Deutschen Könige und Kaiser.* Vol. 2, bk. 1, *Die Urkunden Otto des II*, no. 179, p. 204.
80. *Die Urkunden der Deutschen Könige und Kaiser.* Vol. 2, bk. 2, *Die Urkunden Otto des III*, no. 91, p. 501.

81. In the first half of the eleventh century, the community also erected a collegial church to replace the Carolingian basilica; Hoebanx, *L'abbaye*, 137–43.

82. For analogies with Saxony, Parisse, "Les monastères," 149.

83. *Chartes inédites*, ed. Wauters, no. 4, pp. 444–45; discussion in Hoebanx, *L'abbaye*, 128–29, n. 4. A likely forged charter from 1003, in which a woman named Gisla gives herself and her offspring to the abbey, mentions an Alhedis as abbess, and the counts of Louvain as advocates; *Opera historica et diplomatica*, ed. Miraeus and Foppens, 1:348; also Hoebanx, *L'abbaye*, 155–56, n. 8. Another private charter purporting to be from 1005 is mentioned in Tarlier and Wauters, *La Belgique* 1:26.

84. Hoebanx, *L'abbaye*, 118–19.

85. Delanne, *Histoire*, 225 onward. Generally on the conflict involving Nivelles in the early eleventh century, Laret-Kayser, "La fonction," 136.

86. *Die Urkunden der Deutschen Könige und Kaiser*. Vol. 5, *Die Urkunden Heinrichs III*, ed. Bresslau and Kehr, no. 52, pp. 66–68. The 1041 charter, which covers the same ground, mentions Nivelles as the "town where the presence of the virgin (Gertrudis) is celebrated" (*burgus in quo veneratur virginis presentia*); ibid., no. 80, pp. 104–5. The current version was interpolated in the twelfth or thirteenth centuries; Hoebanx, *L'abbaye*, 160.

87. Hoebanx, *L'abbaye*, 156–62.

88. Sigebert of Gembloux, *Chronica*, ed. Bethmann, 358.

89. *Die Urkunden der Deutschen Könige und Kaiser*. Vol. 5, *Die Urkunden Heinrichs III*, no. 52, pp. 67–68; also ibid., no. 80, p. 105. A charter of Henry IV from 1059 is a forgery; *Die Urkunden der Deutschen Könige und Kaiser*. Vol. 6, *Die Urkunden Heinrichs IV*, ed. von Gladiss and Gawlik, 1: no. 49, pp. 62–65. On the partially unedited papal bulls of 1047 and 1049, Hoebanx, *L'abbaye*, 161.

90. Compare with Parisse, "Les monastères," 149–50.

91. Boshof, "Untersuchungen," 82–83; Parisse, "Les notices," 230; and Seibert, *Abtserhebungen*, 251. Gerard was related to the Matfrid clan, which formerly controlled several monastic institutions in the region. We can only wonder if the Matfridis and Berta referenced in a late tenth-, early eleventh-century list of religious at Saint-Pierre-aux-Nonnains were relatives of his; see Matzel, "Die Namenliste," 243; app. A in this book.

92. Parisse, "Les notices," 231 and Boshof, "Untersuchungen," 87.

93. Hlawitschka, *Studien*, no. 3, p. 144.

94. Parisse, "Les notices," 230–31.

95. A forgery from around 1100 replaced Leo's original, which may have been lost in a fire that ravaged the monastery in 1057; *Chartes de l'abbaye*, ed. Bridot, no. 19, pp. 59–63. Local *hebdomadarius* Humbert of Silva Candida would later become one of the masterminds behind the Church reform under Popes Leo IX and Gregory VII; Bautz, "Humbert."

96. *Translationes et miracula sanctorum Romarici, Amati et Adelphii*, ed. *AASS Septembris* 3:829–37; the protocol of the translation is edited in *Chartes de l'abbaye*, ed. Bridot, no. 18, pp. 58–59. On the mid-eleventh-century hagiography of saints venerated at Remiremont, Goullet, "Les saints du diocèse de Toul," 59–61 and Philippart and Wagner, "Hagiographie," 671–73.

97. Iogna-Prat, "Léon IX," 381 and Goullet, "Les saints du diocèse de Toul," 59–61.

98. *Vita secunda sancti Romarici*, ed. Serarius, 109–10, 113–14, and 120–24.

99. *Chartes de l'abbaye*, ed. Bridot, nos. 2–3, pp. 32–41 (where a dating in the late eleventh century is given for the first piece).

100. Ibid., no. 26, pp. 71–75.

101. Neiske, "Réforme"; Andermann, "Die unsittlichen Kanonissen"; and Felten, *Frauen*.

102. Chap. 1, at n. 1.

103. Heyen, *Untersuchungen*, 19–20. In a lost charter from 988–93, Egbert donated a village and several other properties; *Libellus de rebus Trevirensibus*, ed. Waitz, 106. On Egbert's tenure generally, *Egbert*, ed. Weiner, Heyen, and Ronig.

104. Heyen, "Pfalzel," 594–95; also Cüppers, "Pfalzel," 30–33.

105. *Urkundenbuch*, ed. Beyer, 1: no. 260, pp. 317–18; the original of her charter is preserved as Koblenz, Laudeshauptarchiv, Abt. 157, no. 2. The *Libellus de rebus Trevirensibus*, ed. Waitz, 106, includes a reference to a now-lost document recording her 988 donation of a village named *Emendadesdorf*. Ruothildis's ownership of substantial properties was nothing out of the ordinary, as can be shown via the example of other abbesses from contemporary Saxony and Catalonia; Parisse, "Les religieuses dans le nord de l'Allemagne," 136 and Jarrett, "Power," 251.

106. Refer to the discussion in chap. 6. Also compare with the remarks on the (self-) representation of Ottonian abbesses in Worm, "'You Shall all Live Together,'" 38–55.

107. *Die Urkunden der Deutschen Könige und Kaiser. Vol. 1, Die Urkunden Konrad I. Heinrich I. und Otto I*, no. 168, pp. 249–50.

108. Ibid., no. 322, pp. 436–37; also Zimmer, "Das Kloster," 54–8.

109. Knichel, *Trier*, 941.

110. Zimmer, "Das Kloster," 13–14; also Dopsch, "Trierer Urkundenfälschungen," 317 onward. The 902 forgery awards the nunnery peace and *ban* on its properties; *Die Urkunden der Deutschen Karolinger. Vol. 4, Die Urkunden Zwentibolds und Ludwigs des Kindes*, ed. Schieffer, no. 80, pp. 218–21.

111. *Die Urkunden der Deutschen Könige und Kaiser. Vol. 2, bk. 1, Die Urkunden Otto des II*, no. 55, pp. 65–66; *Die Urkunden der Deutschen Könige und Kaiser. Vol. 2, bk. 2, Die Urkunden Otto des III*, no. 367, p. 796; and ibid., no. 368, pp. 796–97. Discussion in Zimmer, "Das Kloster," 58–61.

112. Knichel, "Trier," 941.

113. Zimmer, "Das Kloster," 61; on Oeren's mint, Steinbach, *Das Geld*, 93.

114. Bertha of Vilich, *Vita Adelheidis abbatissae Vilicensis*, ed. Holder-Egger, 757–58. Kersken argues that the reference in that text to the "regular institution of Saint Jerome" (*regularem institutionem sancti Iheronimi*) might be read as a reference to the *Institutio sanctimonialium*; Kersken, *Zwischen Glaube und Welt*, 110.

115. Heyen, *Untersuchungen*, 24 and Heyen, "Pfalzel," 591. On the background of this conflict, Twellenkamp, "Das Haus," 479–84 and Parisse, "Généalogie," 27.

116. Heyen, *Untersuchungen*, 72. The creation of the *Libellus* coincided with a campaign of hagiographic writing at Sankt Paulin; Krönert, *L'exaltation*, 216–40.

117. Heyen, *Untersuchungen*, 20. The original recension of the *Gesta Treverorum*, ed. Waitz, 172, states that Poppo gave away some of the abbey's benefices, whereas subsequent recensions B and C indicate that Poppo supported all his monasteries except Sankt Paulin and Pfalzel; *Gesta Treverorum*, ed. Waitz, 173.

118. The *Libellus de rebus Trevirensibus*, which dates from the first years of the eleventh century, gives a transcription of Ruothildis's epitaph. It changes the reference to the abbess as a "most chaste virgin" (*castissima virgo*) into one where she is described as a "most notable virgin" (*clarissima virgo*). It is unclear if this change was intentional, or simply a scribal error; *Die lateinischen Dichter*, ed. Strecker and Fickermann, 314, compared to the new text as edited in *Libellus de rebus Trevirensibus*, ed. Waitz, 106.

119. On the production of textiles by women religious, Griffiths, "Like the Sister" and Miller, *Clothing the Clergy*, 141–76. Also see chap. 2, n. 89.

120. *Gesta Treverorum*, ed. Waitz, 176. See app. H in this book for the complete passage and a translation.

121. *Gesta episcoporum Cameracensium*, ed. Bethmann, 461: "Seculo autem semper, ut diximus, in deterius viciato, ipsarum etiam puellarum ordo viciari et depravari coeperat; iamque magis ac magis depravatus mos in degeneri posteritate usque in presens duraverat. Nuper vero iamdictus abbas Leduwinus, Gerardo episcopo et marchione Balduino satagentibus, feminas turpiter viventes mundato loco exturbavit, ac monachos qui melius et religiosius Deo et prelibatae virgini, quae ibidem quiescit, deserviant, constituit."

122. Ibid.: "consilio domni Gerardi episcopi et Leduwini abbatis, moderno tempore Balduinus comes ad pristinum statum restituit, ibique monialibus regulariter institutis, abbatissam nomine Ermentrudem praefecit." Also Gerzaguet, *L'abbaye*, 57–58.

123. *L'histoire-polyptyque*, ed. Delmaire, p. 84, n. 47; also the discussion in Vanderputten, "Fulcard's Pigsty."

124. *Recueil des actes de Lothaire et de Louis V, rois de France (954–987)*, ed. Halphen and Lot, no. 39, pp. 93–94. The reverse of the charter contains a forgery in which Judith accepts the restitution. This document is partially edited in Le Glay, "Mémoire," 129–30; also refer to Finot, "Liste," 152–53.

125. Lot, *Les derniers Carolingiens*, 83–89. On Lothar's 960s interventions in Ghent, Vanderputten, *Monastic Reform*, 59.

126. Louis, "Espaces," 458.

127. *Vita sanctae Eusebiae*, ed. *AASS Martii* 2:447–50; also Brasme, Brousselle, Caillet, Chaffenet, Detant, Gaillard, Krönert, and Mériaux, "La Vie," 385–89. The *Vita metrica Eusebiae* is preserved in Douai, Bibliothèque Marceline Desbordes-Valmore, 849; discussion in Taylor, *Epic Lives* and Snijders, "Textual Diversity."

128. *Vita sanctae Rictrudis metrica*, ed. Silagi and Bischoff.

129. Taylor, *Epic Lives*, 253–82, esp. 270. An eleventh-century copy of Gregory the Great's *Dialogues* provides evidence of efforts to build or maintain a library at Hamage; Douai, Bibliothèque Marceline Desbordes-Valmore, 312.

130. A 1309 relic label commemorating this event is edited in L'Hermitte, *Histoire*, 600–602; also Louis, "Les plus anciennes authentiques." Hucbald's 907 *Life* of Saint Rictrudis mentions that Mauront is buried at the monastery; Hucbald of Saint-Amand, *Vita sanctae Rictrudis Marchianensis*, ed. *AASS Maii* 3:88.

131. *Lectiones in commemoratione et transitu Sancti Ionati confessoris qui celebratur kalendis Augusti*, ed. *AASS Augusti* 1:74.

132. Andreas of Marchiennes, *De vita et miraculis sanctae Rictrudis libri tres*, ed. *AASS Maii* 3:106: "Reliquae vero sancti Mauronti . . . nescio seu permittente seu volente Deo, furtim sublatae, Duacum translatae sunt."

133. *Lectiones in commemoratione et transitu Sancti Ionati confessoris qui celebratur kalendis Augusti*, ed. *AASS Augusti* 1:74. The narrative admittedly does state that Judith was assisted by servants and associates of the Cambrai episcopate: "abbatissa Judith a sede Cameracensi ministros et fideles suo pontifici accersens viros, ad corpus sancti Jonati summovendum debitam curam impendit." She also entrusted male clerics with the task to wrap the bones and ashes of the saint in silk garnments: "cuius ossa et cineres clericorum manibus in sericis indumentis excipi fecit."

134. Helvétius, "La *Passio*," 174–75, 180. On the influence of Sulpicius Severus's *Life of Saint Martin* on the hagiographies of Carolingian female saints, Smith, "The Problem," 13.

135. Mériaux, *Gallia irradiata*, 264–65.

136. *Die Urkunden der Merowinger*, ed. Kölzer, 1: no. 100, pp. 255–57. The hagiographer Fulbert used this document while compiling the *Life* of Bishop Autbert of Cambrai from around 1015; Helvétius, *Abbayes*, 251 and Joye and Bertrand, "Les 'testaments,'" 304.

137. *Die Urkunden der Merowinger*, ed. Kölzer, 1: no. 100, p. 256; also Helvétius, *Abbayes*, 161–62, 250–52 and Helvétius and Nazet, "Nouvelles considérations," 193–94. It is easy to read too much into the primary evidence. At an undetermined date in the early to mid-eleventh century, ten prebends of Sainte-Waudru in Mons were reserved for male recipients, presumably canons of the chapter of Saint-Pierre who were charged with the management of the monastery's properties and income; Helvétius, *Abbayes*, 246. While this measure might be interpreted as yet another encroachment on the rights of women religious, it may just as well have been a measure to consolidate ongoing procedures for estate management.

138. *Gesta episcoporum Cameracensium*, ed. Bethmann, 461. On Gerard's attitudes to reform, Vanderputten, *Monastic Reform*, 93 onward.

139. *Die Urkunden der Deutschen Könige und Kaiser.* Vol. 1, *Die Urkunden Konrad I. Heinrich I. und Otto I*, no. 154, pp. 235–36. Dierkens in contrast speculates that the move was intended to reverse the abbey's secularization; Dierkens "L'abbaye d'Aldeneik pendant le haut moyen âge," 166–68.

140. Dierkens, *Abbayes*, 149–55 and Blennemann, *Die Metzer Benediktinerinnen*, 76–77.

141. Stoepker, "Archeologisch Onderzoek."

142. For Susteren, Hopp, *Die ehemalige Frauenstiftskirche*; for Thorn, Van Cauteren, *De abdijkerk*, 8–11 and Kersken, *Zwischen Glaube und Welt*, 90, n. 146.

143. Respectively, Maaseik, Treasury of Saint-Catherine's church, *Codex Eyckensis II* and Brussels, KBR, 9219 (on the latter manuscript, Van Den Gheyn, *Catalogue* 1: no. 464, pp. 290–91). On the Aldeneik religious' new acquisition, Dierkens, "L'abbaye d'Aldeneik pendant le haut moyen âge," 90–91; Dierkens, "Les origines," 410; Hendrickx and Sangers, *De kerkschat*, 36; and *1000 jaar kerkelijke kunst*, no. 5. In the tenth century, the abbey of Gandersheim also acquired an evangeliary, made around 860 at Metz; Beuckers, "Das älteste Gandersheimer Schätzverzeichnis," 122.

6. Monastic Ambiguities in the New Millennium

1. Hugh of Lobbes, *Vita sanctae Berlendis*, ed. *AASS Februarii* 1:380: "Nihil unquam neque hyemis, neque aestatis tempore, praeter cilicium, quo super nudum corpus ute-

batur, mattulamque, atque lapidem capiti suppositum, sibi substerni patiebatur. Vigiliis et orationibus assiduis, ieiuniisque continuis corpus macerabat. Bis tantum in hebdomada, praeter diem Dominicum apostolicasque solemnitates, reficiebat. Carnem a die consecrationis suae non comedebat, piscem aut cibum alium praeter panem et aquam, nisi in praeclaris solemnitatibus, non attingebat."

2. Epinal, BM, 146; *Catalogue*, 429.

3. Epinal, BM, 147; the contents include a *Life* of Saint Leodegarius, a *Passion* of Saints Crispin and Crispinian, a *Passion* of Saint Margareta; *Lives* of Saints Augustine, Brendan, Symeon of Trier, Giles, Mansuetus of Milan, Mary the Egyptian, and Avra; and *Passions* of Saints Satyrus and Saturninus, Revocatus, Felicitas, and others; *Catalogue*, 425–27. The attribution to the collection of Remiremont is also found in Paulmier-Foucart and Wagner, "Lire," 15, with reference to Gasse-Grandjean, *Les livres*, 182.

4. On the *Life* of Symeon, Heikkilä, *Vita*; on its relation to spiritual ideals in the circle of Eberwin of Tholey and Richard of Saint-Vanne, Vanderputten, *Imagining*, 63–65.

5. Of Ruothildis, the *Libellus de rebus Trevirensibus*, ed. Waitz, 106, claims that she was educated at the monastery of *Esnede*, which some historians have identified as the Ottonian monastery of Essen. Thanks to the preservation of an extraordinary collection of mostly tenth-century manuscripts, the contents of Essen's library are fairly well known, and the reading culture at the monastery has been established as extremely diverse; Bodarwé, *Sanctimoniales litteratae*.

6. *Vita Theoderici abbatis Andaginensis*, ed. Wattenbach, 40.

7. On Thierry's training at Maubeuge, van 't Spijker, "Een jeugd;" on the education of boys in Ottonian nunneries, Van Winter, "The Education," 91–92. Evidence of educational practices in Lotharingian female convents is rare. For the example of Maubeuge in the ninth century, see chap. 2, at n. 67; for the abbey of Saint-Pierre-aux-Nonnains in the 920s or 930s, see app. F. The eleventh-century *Roll* of Maubeuge reveals that members of that institution had access to a range of texts that were commonly used for didactical purposes, such as Hildemar's commentary on the *Rule,* and a glossary on the *Rule*. Also on the *Roll* is a fragment of a glossary (on the *Pseudo-Bede-Egbert-Penitential*) that appears to contain a word in the vernacular, also educational use; see app. D in this book. The abbey of Munsterbilzen in the fifteenth century owned a now-lost tenth-century psalter with interlinear glosses made presumably on an original from the Trier region but adapted to reflect the local dialect. Where or when exactly this version was made is unclear; De Grauwe, *De Wachtendonkse psalmen*. On vernacular glosses in the manuscripts from tenth-century Ottonian nunneries, Bodarwé, *Sanctimoniales litteratae*, 254 and Tiefenbach, "Frühmittelalterliche Volkssprache."

8. *Vita Theoderici abbatis Andaginensis*, ed. Wattenbach, 40–41, at 40: "non incongruum videtur de eius virtutibus et vita ad laudem Christi nominis interserere pauca." For the text and a translation, see app. I.

9. The late eleventh and early twelfth centuries were a period in which many monastic commentators called for moderation in ascetic conduct; Constable, "Moderation."

10. Corbet, *Les saints Ottoniens*, 111–19, 262–63 and Schulenburg, *Forgetful*, 118–25.

11. Regarding the author's borrowing from the *Life* of Saint Martin, Manitius, *Geschichte*, 3:556. In describing Ansoaldis's younger years and her rejection of childish behavior and in outlining her moderation and virtues, the text strikingly resembles

the ninth-century *Life* of Abbess Hathumoda of Gandersheim (d. 874); Paxton, *Anchoress*, 60–61. Also note the similarities between the description of Ansoaldis's behavior and that of Saint Berlendis of Nivelles; see the discussion at n. 1.

12. The biographies of Liutbirg and Wiborada are edited, respectively, as *Vita Liutbirgae*, ed. Menzel and Ekkehard, *Vita sanctae Wiboradae*, ed. Berschin (also the discussion in Signori, "Anchorites," 48–52); for Geisa, see chap. 4, at nn. 7–8; for Adelheid, see Bertha of Vilich, *Vita Adelheidis abbatissae Vilicensis*, ed. Holder-Egger.

13. Koziol, "Flothilde's Visions," 178, with reference to Bynum, *Holy Feast*. In the decades around the year 1000, female monastic groups were also actively promoting asceticism to prominent aristocratic women. Two (late tenth- and early eleventh-century) *Lives* of Mathilde (d. 968), wife of King Henry the Fowler, borrow from Venantius Fortunatus's sixth-century *Life* of Saint Radegundis of Poitiers to highlight the queen's devotion to Christ and her preferring to spend the night in prayer rather than in her husband's bed, as well as her many acts of charity; Gilsdorf, *Queenship*, esp. 37–43. See also the discussion of the *Passion of Maxellendis* in chap. 4, at nn. 25–30.

14. Liétard, *Les chanoinesses*, 38.

15. Theys, *Le bienheureux Thierry*, 5–6 and Warichez, *L'abbaye*, 122, 178.

16. Vanderputten, *Imagining*, 121.

17. *Vita sanctae Aldegundis quinta*, ed. *AASS Januarii* 2:1040–52. The *Deeds of the Bishops of Cambrai*, written in 1024/5, do not mention the 'reform' at Maubeuge. This makes acceptable a dating for Gerard and Renier's intervention at Maubeuge of shortly after 1025; Helvétius, *Abbayes*, 288.

18. *Vita sanctae Aldegundis quinta*, ed. *AASS Januarii* 2:1044.

19. Mons, Archives du Royaume, Coll. Archives locales, P 1755; refer also to the discussion of this document in chap. 1. The *Roll* currently consists of four leaves and contains traces on the bottom suggesting that at least one extra leaf is missing.

20. Chap. 1, nn. 95–99.

21. "Vie de S. Aldegonde," ed. Daris, 40: "Cancri morbum in dextera mamilla percepit gaudensque ob martyrum palmam dilexit, neptasque suas venerabiles Aldedrudem ac Madelbertam canonicae tradidit vitae." The passage in the *Vita Madelbertae* has "monasticae tradidit vitae"; Bertrand, *Réformes ecclésiastiques*, 72–73.

22. *Concilia aevi Karolini*, ed. Werminghoff, 2/1:284, c. 54. The *Roll*'s version of the text may be found in app. D, no. 4.

23. For instance in Helvétius, *Abbayes*, 253.

24. "Vie de S. Aldegonde," ed. Daris, 49–51.

25. Ibid., 37–41.

26. According to Sylvie Joye and Paul Bertrand the *Testament* may also date from around the *Roll*'s creation; "Les 'testaments,'" 302–3.

27. Helvétius, *Abbayes*, 330–31, with reference to passages edited in "Vie de S. Aldegonde," ed. Daris, 39 and 40. The author likely also relied on the first *Testament* of Saint Aldegondis and on Childeric's confirmation.

28. "Vie de S. Aldegonde," ed. Daris, 44–45.

29. *Vita sanctae Aldegundis quarta*, ed. *Catalogus codicum* 2:133–35. The edition is incomplete, and the only known copy is a fourteenth-century manuscript known as Brussels, KBR, 7808, pp. 444–45; also the discussion in Helvétius, *Abbayes*, 253–54, 334–35.

30. Helvétius, *Abbayes*, 253–54, 308–9 and Bertrand, *Réformes ecclésiastiques*, 74. On the putative existence of a female community at Cousolre and the reference in the text to twelve women religious installed there by the abbey's founder, Helvétius, *Abbayes*, 254, n. 47. One of several known versions of the *Vita secunda Aldegundis*—one that so far has not been edited—refers to Cousolre as Saint Aldegondis's place of burial. According to Helvétius, the *Vita tertia* relied on this specific version (oral communication to the author, January 2014).

31. Brussels, KBR, 7808, p. 445: "O dilectissimi fratres in Christo credentes, venire vos oportet ad sepulchrum eius, genua flectentes, cum lacrimis eam deprecantes, ut intercedere dignetur pro vobis." Regarding Taylor's interpretation of the evidence for Hamage, see chap. 5, at nn. 126–28.

32. *Die Urkunden der Merowinger*, ed. Kölzer, 1: no. 100, pp. 255–56. Kölzer posits that the forged charter of King Childeric was added only in the late eleventh or early twelfth century.

33. App. D, nos. 1 and 4. Also refer to Bishop Thierry of Verdun's charter for the religious of Saint-Maur, discussed in chap. 5, n. 48.

34. Thierry of Saint-Hubert [?], *Vita sanctae Aldegundis quinta*, ed. *AASS Januarii* 2:1040–52; also Helvétius, *Abbayes*, 340–42.

35. There are references to the subsequent foundation at Cousolre of a priory, but this seems to have been dissolved fairly rapidly; Helvétius, *Abbayes*, 254.

36. Joye and Bertrand, "Les 'testaments,'" 303.

37. Ejection of unwilling religious was a common practice around this time: besides the aforementioned examples of Pfalzel and Marchiennes, there is evidence of another such intervention at late tenth- or early eleventh-century Niedermünster in Regensburg, where Abbess Uta introduced a Benedictine (but not necessarily unambiguous) regime; Bodarwé, "Eine Männerregel," 256.

38. The contemporary Niedermünster codex, which contains a copy of Saint Benedict's *Rule* and a benedictinized version of Cesarius of Arles's *Rule* for women (discussed in chap. 1, n. 95–99), in the early eleventh century was removed to the male monastery of Sankt Michael in Bamberg, and its version of the former text again adapted for use by monks. According to Gude Suckale-Redlefsen, this may have been because the religious at Niedermünster had rejected the strict Benedictine regime proposed by their institution's leadership; *Krone und Schleier*, ed. Frings and Gerchow, 186. But in a scenario that seems just as likely, the transfer may have been part of clerical efforts to suppress the women's ambiguous observance. A handbook for use in chapter meetings (Berlin, Deutsche Staatsbibliothek, Theol. Lat. Qu. 199) reveals the benedictinization of the community after Abbess Uta's death in 1025; *Krone und Schleier*, ed. Frings and Gerchow, 187.

39. See chap. 5, at nn. 78–79 and 87–90.

40. *Recueil des actes de Lothaire et de Louis V, rois de France (954–987)*, ed. Halphen and Lot, no. 39, pp. 93–94. The document restitutes a number of properties not to the religious generally—as was customary in earlier such charters for female houses—but explicitly to "Abbess Judith and the aforementioned sisters and brothers of this monastery" (*tam abbatissa Judith quam predictae sorores necnon fratres ipsius monasterii*).

41. Late-tenth-century Ottonian charters for Saint-Pierre-aux-Nonnains in Metz reveal the same ambition; chap. 4, at n. 77.

42. *Die Urkunden der Deutschen Könige und Kaiser.* Vol. 5, *Die Urkunden Heinrichs III,* ed. Bresslau and Kehr, no. 52, p. 67: "Niuialensis ergo abbacia vel ecclesia quantis fluctuacionibus sit quassata, quantis calamitatibus attrita. . . . Tanta utique premebantur oppressione, ut ad ipsum claustrum usque comitis extenderetur beneficium, nec erat sacratissime virgini Gertrudi ibidem quiescenti aliquis debite reverencie locus, quamvis ipsum locum propriis excoluerit manibus."

43. In the 950s–980s, Sainte-Glossinde likewise revived the cult of its patron saint; chap. 4, at n. 94.

44. *Die Urkunden der Deutschen Könige und Kaiser.* Vol. 5, *Die Urkunden Heinrichs III,* ed. Bresslau and Kehr, no. 80, p. 105.

45. *Chartes inédites,* ed. Wauters, no. 4, p. 445: "iram Dei omnipotentis et sancte Gertrudis incurrat."

46. *Recueil des actes de Lothaire et de Louis V, rois de France (954–987),* ed. Halphen and Lot, no. 39, p. 94: "iram Dei omnipotentis et beatae Rectrudis sanctorumque omnium incurrat."

47. On this phenomenon generally, Kersken, *Zwischen Glaube und Welt,* 50–51.

48. Dupont, "Les domaines" and Parisse, "Généalogie," 30.

49. Chap. 3, at n. 55.

50. Lepage, *L'abbaye,* 9, n 1. On "gendered" modes of archival preservation and on the possibility that some original charters were preserved as if they were secondary relics, Bodarwé, "Gender."

51. Lepage, *L'abbaye,* 90–112 and Barrucand, "Le trésor." Gozelin's evangeliary, now in the treasury of Nancy Cathedral, has been dated to the ninth century, and likely originated in Tours; Barrucand, "Le trésor," 100 and Rand, *A Survey,* 1:137. Compared to the relic treasures of major Ottonian institutions such as Essen and Gandersheim, the Bouxières and Vergaville ones were modest; compare with Röckelein, "Gandersheimer Reliquienschätze" and Beuckers, "Das älteste Gandersheimer Schatzverzeichnis."

52. Lepage, *L'abbaye,* 15 and 84.

53. Jean, *Une intéressante donation,* 7. On Eva's role at Bouxières, see chap. 4, at nn. 41 and 59.

54. Kerskens, *Zwischen Glaube und Welt,* 48–57.

55. Helvétius, *Abbayes,* 340.

56. Revised redaction of Rainer of Ghent, *Inventio et miracula Gisleni Hanoniensis,* ed. Poncelet, 287; also El Kholi, *Lektüre,* 267–68. Thorn was one of several institutional recipients of a copy of Saint Gislen's *Life*; Snijders, "Handschriftelijke productie," 18–20. For their part, the monks of Saint-Ghislain acquired *Lives* of Maubeuge's Saints Waldetrudis, Aldetrudis, and Madelberta; Mons, Bibliothèque Universitaire de Mons-Hainaut, 845. A similar transaction or a prayer association (which may also have been established between Thorn and Saint-Ghislain on this occasion) presumably explains why an early eleventh-century list of religious of Saint-Pierre-aux-Nonnains in Metz ended up in a miscellaneous hagiographical manuscript from another, unidentified Metz institution; Blennemann, *Die Metzer Benediktinerinnen,* 199.

57. Revised redaction of Rainer of Ghent, *Inventio et miracula Gisleni Hanoniensis,* 287–88.

58. *Chartes inédites,* ed. Wauters, no. 4, pp. 444–45: "quo eius beneficia creberimis miraculorum celebritatibus exuberant."

59. Olbert of Gembloux, *Historia sancte Veroni confessoris Lembecensis*, ed. Holder-Egger, 752.

60. Steinbach, *Das Geld*, 111–13, 233–34. Toward the end of the century, reworked versions of Gertrudis's hagiography were published: *Vita tertia Gertrudis Nivialensis*, ed. Ryckel, 35–101 and *Vita tripartita Gertrudis Nivialensis*, ed. Ryckel, 103–93. On the mediocre quality of the edition of these texts, Van Der Essen, "Etude," 1–13; Hoebanx, *L'abbaye*, 40–44 and Holvoet, "Sainte Gertrude."

61. Hugh of Lobbes, *Vita sanctae Berlendis*, ed. *AASS Februarii* 1:378–81; also Van De Perre, "De *Vita*" and Van Droogenbroeck, "Hugo."

62. For the calendar, see Brussels, KBR, 2031–2; for Giselbert's chants, see Renier of Saint-Laurent, *De ineptiis*, ed. Arndt, 598. A *Life* of Saint Begga was written only in the late eleventh century: *Vita sanctae Beggae*, ed. Ghesquière. On all of these documents, Leclère, "L'abbaye."

63. Olbert of Gembloux, *Historia sancte Veroni confessoris Lembecensis*, ed. Holder-Egger and Olbert of Gembloux, *Vita secunda Waldetrudis*, ed. *AASS Aprilis* 1:837–42.

64. Sigebert of Gembloux, *Gesta abbatum Gemblacensium*, ed. Pertz, 245; also Helvétius, *Abbayes*, 245 and De Vriendt, Le dossier," 24–32.

65. De Brueker, "Suaire/Lijkwade." According to the late twelfth-century chronicler Gislebert of Mons, Count Renier of Mons in the early eleventh century considered abolishing the community of Sainte-Waudru in Mons, perhaps to give more prominence to the local male chapter of Saint-Germain or to the religious of Maubeuge. In the end, so Gislebert tells us, the Mons community was allowed to continue, without adopting the *Rule*; Gislebert of Mons, *Chronicon Hannoniae*, ed. Vanderkindere, 32–33, cited in Helvétius, *Abbayes*, 242–44.

66. Chap. 5, at n. 96. The mid-eleventh-century *Life* of Saint Romaric of Remiremont introduces a new element in local hagiographical memory by stating that the saint had established a large male community there; *Vita secunda sancti Romarici*, ed. Serarius, 109. Roughly from the same period is a new, presumably less controversial *Life* of Saint Adelphius; *Vita secunda sancti Adelphii*, ed. *AASS Septembris* 3:818–20.

67. *Lectiones in commemoratione et transitu Sancti Ionati confessoris qui celebratur kalendis Augusti*, partially edited in *AASS Augusti* 1:74–75, with additional material in *Catalogus codicum hagiographicorum* 2:273–75. Jonat's attraction with the lay public appears to have been limited, for once the religious were replaced by monks in the 1020s, not he, but Rictrudis and Mauront would be promoted as the monastery's two principal saints; Vanderputten, *Monastic Reform*, 140–41; also Vanderputten, "Universal Historiography."

68. For instance, Heriger of Lobbes, *Vita, translationes, miracula Landoaldi, Landradae et sociorum*, ed. Holder-Egger (with additions in Kupper, "Les voies"); also Thierry of Saint-Trond, *Vita Landradae Belisiensis*, ed. Surius.

69. The 2010 excavation report is at https://oar.onroerenderfgoed.be/publicaties/STUA/13/STUA013-001.pdf, accessed 6 March 2015.

70. Steinbach, *Das Geld*, 113–14, 135 and Ilisch, "Die Münzprägung," 335. The clearest reproduction of the iconography of this coin is in De Coster, "Trouvaille," plate XXI, no. 22.

71. Egebert, *Vita Sancti Amoris*, ed. *AASS Octobris* 4:343–47; also Coens, "Sur le prologue," 344–45. At Moustier-Sur-Sambre, the principal local cult was that of Saint

Fredegand of Deurne, to whom a hagiographic narrative was dedicated in the late eleventh century; from the early twelfth century, it was probably complemented with the cult of Saint Rolendis of Gerpinnes; Despy, "Moustier-sur-Sambre," 159 and further, n. 92 in these endnotes.

72. Leyser, *Rule*, 70–71; also Le Jan, "De la France," 183. In the 1130s, local scribes interpolated the tenth-century charters of Bishops Adalbero I and Thierry I of Metz for Sainte-Glossinde to include a list of twenty-four prebends for the sisters; chap. 4, n. 73, and chap. 5, n. 55.

73. On the changing role of clerics in female houses during the later Middle Ages, Schilp, "Sorores."

74. See chap. 5, n. 121.

75. Gerzaguet, *L'abbaye*, 89 and 93.

76. *Miracula sanctae Ragenfredis*, ed. *AASS Octobris* 4: 318–21; also Gerzaguet, *L'abbaye*, 60–63.

77. Huyghebaert, "Abbaye," 217; Huyghebaert, "Abbesse Frisilde" and Huyghebaert, "Adela"; also Vanderputten, "Female Monasticism," 369–72.

78. See n. 76. An undated office in honor of Ragenfredis's mother Regina is edited as *Vita beatae Reginae*, ed. *AASS Julii* 1:268–71.

79. Gerzaguet, *L'abbaye*, 145–49; on the many forgeries made at Messines during the third quarter of the eleventh century, De Simpel, "Une officine."

80. Gerzaguet, *L'abbaye*, 59.

81. A few examples: Sainte-Glossinde in Metz (Blennemann, *Die Metzer Benediktinerinnen*, 95–105; also n. 72 in this chapter's endnotes); Remiremont (chap. 5, at nn. 95–100); and Munsterbilzen (also chap. 5, n. 32).

82. Gerzaguet, "La fondation." On Etrun's situation in the late eleventh and early twelfth centuries, Vanderputten, "Female Monasticism," 373–75.

83. In 1117, religious from Etrun would be recruited to populate the new monastery of Guînes, a foundation of Count Manasses of Guînes. They were also involved in the 1126 foundation of the nunnery of Ghislengien, by prominent noblewoman Ida of Chièvres; Vanderputten, "Female Monasticism," 375.

84. Edited in Gerzaguet, *L'abbaye*, no. 10, pp. 157–58: "sicut relatione quorundam audivimus, ita laxis habenis post vestra desideria curritis, ut vestri voti memoria videatur a vobis penitus excidisse, et videamini retrorsum abire, cum ad anteriora deberetis totis viribus anhelare. Sane caritatis igniculus qui fomes et nutrimentum honestatis esse dignoscitur, peccatis exigentibus, adeo in vobis refriguit quod monasterium vestrum tam in spiritualibus quam etiam in temporalibus est plurimum imminutum. Nos igitur . . . venerabili fratri nostro Godescalco Attrebatensi episcopo . . . dedimus in mandatis, ut gratam Deo religionem in vobis studeat reformare, et monasterium vestrum ad frugem melioris vitae reducere."

85. Ibid., 80.

86. For Denain, ibid., 82. This attitude on the part of post-1050 observers may also lie behind claims that the religious of Bouxières became canonesses in the eleventh century; Lepage, *L'abbaye*, 36–37.

87. *Wolfenbüttler Fragmente*, ed. Sdralek, 112–13; see app. J in this book.

88. Vanderputten, "Female Monasticism," 379–80.

89. Chap. 5, n. 66. A tenth-century charter from Saint-Evre may indicate that one of the religious at Bouxières also retained some private property after entering the monastic state; Hirschmann, *Verdun*, 1: 257–58, at n. 1220.

90. See nn. 63–64 in this chapter's endnotes.

91. Dierkens, *Abbayes*, 68–69.

92. In later centuries, Saint Rolendis became the subject of a regional cult, bringing pilgrims to visit her grave in the late eleventh-century crypt. The only known hagiography dedicated to this saint dates from the late thirteenth century; *Vita seu legenda sanctae Rolendis Garpiniensis*, ed. Coens, 336–47 (on this text, Dierkens, "Le culte").

93. Dierkens, "Le culte," 34–38, which revises earlier datings by Mertens in "L'église," 204–10.

94. Edited in Koninckx, "De abdij," 109–10: "quando placuerit ipsi abbatisse, seu viventi seu obeunte ea, onmis census horum prediorum, redigatur in cotidianam prebendam Deo servientium sororum. Cetera verso que ad placitum pertinent in servicium dispensetur succedentium abbatissarum. De censu vero usque ad XXX sororibus eque dividatur vestitura et victus." For a considerable period of time, certainly into the thirteenth century, the terminology in primary sources to denote the observance of certain communities remained vague; for instance, Gerzaguet, *L'abbaye* and Van der Eycken and Van der Eycken, *"Wachten,"* 40–41.

95. Tanner, *Families*, 140–42.

96. Marcigny, the first female daughter house of Cluny, was founded around 1050; on its model of religious life for women, see Wischermann, *Marcigny-Sur-Loire*; Andenna, *Sanctimoniales*; and Roitner, "Sorores."

97. For instance, *Partners*, ed. Griffiths and Hotchin; Lester, *Creating*; Gill, "Scandala"; and French, "Religion."

98. Brussels, Bibliothèque des Bollandistes, 299, f. 71r; fascimile in Van der Eycken and Van der Eycken, *"Wachten,"* 38. *Tesi* is edited in *Corpus*, ed. Gysseling, ser. 2, 1:131–33; also refer to the discussion in Goossens, "Tesi" and Goossens, "Over Tesi."

Appendix A: The Leadership and Members of Female Religious Communities in Lotharingia, 816–1059

1. *Vita Harlindis et Relindis*, ed. *AASS Martii* 3:390.

2. Einhard, *Translatio sancti Marcellini et Petri*, ed. Waitz, 262.

3. Bull by Pope Leo IX, 1050; *Les bulles*, ed. Choux, no. 4, p. 16.

4. Ibid., 15.

5. Charter by Louis the Pious, 816; *Die Urkunden Ludwigs des Frommen*, ed. Kölzer, 1: no. 84, p. 207. Doddo's status is discussed in Gaillard, "Aux origines," 33; Gaillard, *D'une réforme*, 181–82, 261.

6. Charters by the priest Osteus, 937 (Bautier, *Les origines*, no. 7, p. 76); Hersendis, 932/41 (ibid., no. 8, p. 78); Lotha/Jorsa, 965/77 (ibid., no. 34, p. 114).

7. Charter by Otto II, 977; ibid., no. 37, p. 117.

8. Charters by Count Teutbert, 960/5 (ibid., no. 27, 101) and Otto I, 965 (ibid., no. 31, p. 107).

9. Charters by Otto I, 960 (ibid., no. 25, p. 96) and 965 (ibid., no. 31, p. 107).

10. Same as n. 9.

11. Charter by Ermenaidis, 966; ibid., no. 32, p. 109.

12. Ibid.

13. Charter by Aldrada for the abbey of Saint-Evre in Toul, before 973; "Chartes," ed. Schaeffer, no. 24, p. 156. According to Hirschmann, *Verdun* 1: 257–58, n. 1220, the *Helvidis sanctimonialis* named in that document likely was a member of the Bouxières community.

14. Charter by Odelric, before 960; Bautier, *Les origines*, no. 37, p. 117.

15. *Gesta episcoporum Cameracensium*, ed. Bethmann, 461.

16. *Miracula sanctae Ragenfredis*, ed. *AASS Octobris* 4:318–21.

17. *De beata Ava virginis*, ed. *AASS Aprilis* 3:628.

18. Emma is mentioned as an older religious serving under Fredesendis; *Miracula sanctae Ragenfredis*, ed. *AASS Octobris* 4:318–21.

19. Charter by Henry II, 1003 (interpolated, but Dietbuhrc is mentioned in two separate versions); *Die Urkunden der Deutschen Könige und Kaiser*. Vol. 3, *Die Urkunden Heinrichs II. und Arduins*, ed. Bresslau, no. 58, p. 72.

20. *Historia monasterii Hasnoniensis*, ed. Holder-Egger, 151; additionally, *Gallia Christiana* 3:400; Dewez, *Histoire*, 48.

21. Same as n. 20.

22. Same as n. 20.

23. Charter by Charles the Bald, 877; *Recueil des actes de Charles II le Chauve*, ed. Giry, Tessier, and Prou, no. 436, p. 475.

24. *Historia monasterii Hasnoniensis*, ed. Holder-Egger, 151; additionally, *Gallia Christiana* 3:400 and Dewez, *Histoire*, 47.

25. Same as n. 24.

26. Same as n. 24.

27. Same as n. 24.

28. Charter by Pope Leo IX, 1050; Calmet, *Histoire de la Lorraine*, 2: *Preuves*, cclxxxvii.

29. *Gallia Christiana* 13:616; also Vestier, "Juvigny-sur-Loison," 158.

30. Charter by Geoffrey and Herman of Lunéville, 1034; Calmet, *Histoire de la Lorraine*, 2: *Preuves*, cclxxvi.

31. Notice from c. 1160 included in Lunéville's twelfth-century cartulary-roll; Gérard and Gérard, "Lunéville," 208.

32. Gérard and Gérard, "Lunéville," 206.

33. Charter by Lothar of Western Francia, 976; *Recueil des actes de Lothaire et de Louis V, rois de France (954–987)*, ed. Halphen and Lot, no. 39, p. 94; and the *Lectiones in commemoratione et transitu Sancti Ionati confessoris qui celebratur kalendis Augusti*, partially edited in *AASS Augusti* 1:74.

34. *Inventio et miracula Gisleni Hanoniensis*, ed. Ghesquière, 386–87.

35. *Vita Theoderici abbatis Andaginensis*, ed. Wattenbach, 40.

36. John of Saint-Arnoul, *Vita Johannis*, ed. Jacobsen, 192, 228; also a charter (where she is not named as abbess) by Ricuin of Metz, 918 (Metz, Archives Départementales de la Moselle, H 3959).

37. Charters by Otto I, 960 (*Die Urkunden der Deutschen Könige und Kaiser*. Vol. 1, *Die Urkunden Konrad I. Heinrich I. und Otto I*, no. 210, p. 290) and Otto II, 977 (*Die Urkunden*

252 NOTES TO PAGES 162–163

der Deutschen Könige und Kaiser. Vol. 2, bk. 1, *Die Urkunden Otto des II,* no. 159, p. 179). Also *Vita Caddroe abbatis Walciodorensis* (ed. Colgan, 500) and the abbey's thirteenth-century necrology (Paris, BNF, Lat. 10028, f. 99r).

38. Charter by Otto III, 993; *Die Urkunden der Deutschen Könige und Kaiser.* Vol. 2, bk. 2, *Die Urkunden Otto des III,* no. 117, p. 522.

39. Early eleventh-century list of convent members; Rome, Bibliotheca Apostolica Vaticana, Reg. Lat. 566, f. 38r-v. None of the editions so far is entirely accurate, the best one being that of Matzel, "Die Namenliste," 242–43.

40. Charter by Ricuin of Metz, 918; Metz, Archives Départementales de la Moselle, H 3959.

41. John of Saint-Arnoul, *Vita Johannis,* ed. Parisse, 56.

42. Charter by Ricuin of Verdun, 918; Metz, Archives Départementales de la Moselle, H 3959.

43. John of Saint-Arnoul, *Vita Johannis,* ed. Jacobsen, 194, 228.

44. See n. 38.

45. Charter by Adalbero I of Metz, 945 (*Die Urkunde,* ed. Wolfram, no. F, p. 17); also John of Saint-Arnoul, *Vita, translationes et miracula sanctae Glodesindis* (ed. *AASS Julii* 6:224).

46. Charter by Thierry I of Metz, 974 (pseudo-original); Metz, Archives Départementales de la Moselle, H 4058/3.

47. Charter by Abbot Benedict of Saint-Arnoul in Metz and Abbess Hermentrudis of Sainte-Glossinde, 1012; Müsebeck, "Die Benediktinerabtei," no. 4, p. 228–29.

48. Jacques de Guise, *Annales Hannoniae,* ed. Sackur, 163.

49. Gislebert of Mons, *Chronica Hannoniae,* ed. Vanderkindere, 22.

50. Eighteenth-century list edited in Doppler, "Het adelijk stift," 164.

51. Ibid.

52. Ibid.

53. *Gallia Christiana* 3:577.

54. Ibid.

55. Charters by: Zwentibold, 896 (*Die Urkunden der Deutschen Karolinger.* Vol. 4, *Die Urkunden Zwentibolds und Ludwigs des Kindes,* ed. Schieffer, no. 11, p. 37); the same, 897 (ibid., no. 16, p. 46); Louis the Younger, 906 (ibid., no. 50, p. 175); the same, 907 (ibid., no. 55, p. 182); the same, 908 (ibid., no. 57, p. 184).

56. Hoebanx, *L'abbaye,* 112.

57. Ibid., 326.

58. Pseudo-authentic (?) charter by Gisla, 1003; *Opera historica et diplomatica,* ed. Miraeus and Foppens, 1:348.

59. Pseudo-authentic (?) charter by Count Arnulf, 1011; *Chartes inédites,* ed. Wauters, no. 4, p. 444–45.

60. *Gallia Christiana* 3:577.

61. Charter by Henry III, 1040; *Die Urkunden der Deutschen Könige und Kaiser.* Vol. 5, *Die Urkunden Heinrichs III,* ed. Bresslau and Kehr, no. 52, p. 67.

62. Charter by Gisla, 1003 (authentic?); *Opera historica et diplomatica,* ed. Miraeus and Foppens, 1:348.

63. Same as n. 62.

64. Pseudo-authentic (?) charter by Count Arnulf, 1011; *Chartes inédites*, ed. Wauters, no. 4, p. 444–45.

65. Charter by Henry II, 1018; *Die Urkunden der Deutschen Könige und Kaiser.* Vol. 3, *Die Urkunden Heinrichs II. und Arduins,* ed. Bresslau, no. 396, p. 508–9.

66. Knichel, "Trier," 957.

67. Epitaph, transcribed in *Libellus de rebus Trevirensibus*, ed. Waitz, 106 and *Die christlichen Inschriften,* ed. Kraus, 2:202.

68. *Libellus de rebus Trevirensibus,* ed. Waitz, 106.

69. Charter by Ruothildis and her brother, 989; *Urkundenbuch*, ed. Beyer, 1: no. 260, p. 317–18. Also an epitaph from the late tenth century, edited after the original inscription in *Die Lateinischen Dichter*, ed. Strecker and Fickermann, 314; an alternate transcription from c. 1000 is available in *Libellus de rebus Trevirensibus;* ed. Waitz, 106.

70. Epitaph, after modern transcriptions; *Die christlichen Inschriften,* ed. Kraus, 2:202.

71. Charter by Pope Leo IX, 1049; Calmet, *Histoire de la Lorraine,* 2: *Preuves,* ccxc.

72. The primary source record for Remiremont's female leadership is both extensive and challenging; this survey is based on the analysis of the primary evidence as presented in Hlawitschka, *Studien zur Äbtissinnenreihe,* with important corrections in Parisse, "Les notices"; Gaillard, *D'une réforme.*

73. Refer to the index of *Liber memorialis von Remiremont,* ed. Hlawitschka, Schmid, and Tellenbach.

74. Same as n. 73.

75. Same as n. 73.

76. Same as n. 73.

77. Post-1050 traditions excerpted in Habets, "Bijdragen," 463; Bauer, *Lotharingien,* 614–15.

78. Same as n. 77.

79. Eleventh-century commentators merely state that Benedicta was the eldest daughter of founding couple Ansfrid and Hereswint; Thietmar of Merseburg, *Chronicon,* ed. Holtzmann, 175; Alpertus of Metz, *De diversitate temporum,* ed. Van Rij, 34. But in the thirteenth century, Aegidius of Orval claimed that she was Thorn's first abbess; *Gesta episcoporum Leodiensium,* ed. Heller, 60. Discussion of these traditions may be found in Kersken, *Zwischen Glaube und Welt,* 132.

80. Hildewardis is first mentioned in an early eighteenth-century catalogue of abbesses. In it, she is listed as Thorn's first abbess; Kersken, *Zwischen Glaube und Welt,* 134.

81. Same as n. 80.

82. Revised redaction of Rainer of Ghent, *Inventio et miracula Gisleni Hanoniensis,* ed. Poncelet, 287.

83. Hildegardis is first mentioned in an early eighteenth-century catalogue; Kersken, *Zwischen Glaube und Welt,* 134. The *Gallia Christiana* (3:997) additionally lists three abbesses after Benedicta/Hildewardis that cannot be placed with certainty before 1059: these are Godeildis, Aleidis, and Elisabetha.

84. Calmet, *Histoire ecclésiastique,* 3:clix.

85. Same as n. 84.

86. Same as n. 84; also a letter by Bishop Thierry of Verdun from the late 1040s (*Actes,* ed. Evrard, no. 55, p. 113).

87. Hugh of Flavigny (*Chronicon*, ed. Pertz, 391) and the *Gallia Christiana* (13:1313, using the necrology of Saint-Vanne in Verdun) mention Ava/Eva as the first abbess, but Calmet, who relies on an unknown source, lists her as the fourth, after Alix (Calmet, *Histoire de la Lorraine*, 2: *Preuves*, clix). It is possible that Hugh's reference to Ava is a simple case of mistaken identity and that he meant to reference one of her three presumed predecessors.

88. Calmet, *Histoire ecclésiastique*, 3:clix. Berverga may simply be an alternative spelling for Girberga.

89. Same as n. 88; also refer to *Gallia Christiana* 13:1313–4.

90. *Gallia Christiana* 13:936; Calmet, *Histoire ecclésiastique*, 3:ccv. The *Gallia Christiana* and Calmet give the names of seventeen abbesses of Vergaville prior to 1280. It is unclear when any of these women ruled, and the relevance of the above three names to the period reviewed in this study is pure conjecture.

91. Same as n. 90.

92. Same as n. 90.

Appendix D: The Compilation on the *Roll of Maubeuge*, c. Early Eleventh Century

1. Written on an erased word, probably *oblationibus*, which is the standard reading of this decree.
2. Mittermüller gives σχολάζετε (scholazete).
3. Erased section, originally *moniales*.
4. Erased section, originally *-moniales*.
5. Probably for *condere*.
6. Erased donor's name, possibly Alpaidis.

Appendix F: John of Gorze's Encounter with Geisa, c. 920s–930s

1. Smaragdus of Saint-Mihiel's *Liber comitis*, so Matthew Ponesse explains, is "a compendium of biblical exegesis organized around the readings used in the liturgy"; alternatively, the title was also used to indicate a lectionary, evangeliary, or epistolary (Ponesse, "Standing," 71). A mid-ninth-century copy of Smaragdus's text was in the library of the religious at the monastery of Quedlinburg in Saxony; Bodarwé, *Sanctimoniales litteratae*, 426–27.

Appendix I: The *Life* of Ansoaldis, Abbess of Maubeuge (d. 1050)

1. Compare with Sulpicius Severus's *Dialogues* 3:14; ed. Halm, *Sulpicii Severi libri*, 212.
2. Compare with Sulpicius Severus's *Life* of Saint Martin, 27:1; ed. Fontaine, *Vie*, 314.

Bibliography

Unedited Primary Sources

1. Manuscripts

Bamberg, Staatsbibliothek
    Ms. Lit. 142 (monastic rulebook from Niedermünster in Regensburg)
Berlin, Deutsche Staatsbibliothek
    Lat. fol. 105 (pontifical from Sankt Maximin in Trier)
    Phill. 1723 (miscellaneous collection of treatises and excerpts on ascetic life from Saint-Vincent in Metz)
    Theol. Lat. Qu. 199 (chapter book from Niedermünster in Regensburg)
Brussels, Bibliothèque des Bollandistes
    299 (evangeliary from Munsterbilzen)
    437 (necrology of Munsterbilzen)
Brussels, Koninklijke Bibliotheek van België / Bibliothèque Royale de Belgique
    2031–2 (calendar of Saint-Laurent in Liège)
    7808 (legendary of Sainte-Waudru in Mons)
    9219 (evangeliary from Aachen cathedral [?])
    18018 (legendary of Lobbes)
Cambrai, Médiathèque
    162 and 163 (sacramentary of Cambrai)
    164 (sacramentary of Bishop Hildoard of Cambrai)
Cambridge, Corpus Christi College
    178 (St Benedict's *Rule*, adapted for use by women)
Cologne, Erzbischöfliche Diözesan- und Dombibliothek
    118 (collection of penitentials and legal excerpts)
    141 (pontifical of Cambrai)
Douai, Bibliothèque Marceline Desbordes-Valmore
    13 (Breton evangeliary from Marchiennes)
    312 (Gregory the Great's *Dialogues* from Hamage)
    849 (hagiographical manuscript of Marchiennes)
Düsseldorf, Universitäts- und Landesbibliothek
    B113 (penitential handbook from Essen)
Epinal, Bibliothèque Municipale
    105 (evangeliary from Remiremont)
    118 (legendary from Remiremont [?])
    146 (florilegium from Remiremont [?])

BIBLIOGRAPHY

    147 (legendary/florilegium from Remiremont [?])
    265 (*Purple evangeliary of Epinal*)
London, British Library
    Ms. Add. 15222 (pontifical of Besançon)
Maaseik, Treasury of Saint-Catherine's church
    Codex Eyckensis I (evangeliary from Aldeneik)
    Codex Eyckensis II (evangeliary from Aldeneik)
Mons, Archives du Royaume
    Coll. Archives locales, P 1755 (*Roll of Maubeuge*)
Mons, Bibliothèque Universitaire de Mons-Hainaut
    845 (legendary of Saint-Ghislain)
Munich, Bayerische Staatsbibliothek
    Clm 14431 (*Institutio sanctimonialium* from Sankt Emmeran in Regensburg)
    Clm 28118 (Benedict of Aniane's *Codex regularum*, from Sankt Maximin in Trier)
Nancy, Cathedral treasury
    Evangeliary of St Gozelin (from Bouxières)
New York, Metropolitan Museum
    2015.560 (*Gospels of Theutberga*, presumably from Remiremont)
Padua, Biblioteca Capitolare
    D 47 (sacramentary from Cambrai or Liège, later used at Verona)
Paris, Bibliothèque Nationale de France
    Lat. 2291 (sacramentary of Saint-Amand)
    Lat. 9428 (sacramentary of Bishop Drogo of Metz)
    Lat. 10028 (necrology of Saint-Pierre-aux-Nonnains in Metz)
    Lat. 10514 (evangeliary of Poussay)
    Lat. 12048 (sacramentary of Gellone, made for Bishop Ratholdus of Cambrai)
    Lat. 12052 (sacramentary of Bishop Ratholdus of Cambrai, used at Saint-Vaast)
    Lat. 13313 (benedictional/pontifical of Metz)
    Nouvelles Acquisitions Françaises 6700 (miscellaneous collection on Metz, incl. *Fundatio Sancti Petri*)
Regensburg, Bischöfliche Zentralbibliothek
    Fragment I.1.5, no. 6 (St. Benedict's *Rule* from Obermünster in Regensburg)
Rome, Bibliotheca Angelica
    10 (*Liber memorialis* of Remiremont)
Rome, Bibliotheca Apostolica Vaticana
    Reg. Lat. 566 (miscellaneous hagiographical manuscript, incl. early eleventh-century list of religious of Saint-Pierre-aux-Nonnains)
Verdun, Bibliothèque Municipale
    30 (florilegium from Saint-Vanne in Verdun)
Würzburg, Universitätsbibliothek
    M.p.th.q. 25 (incl. *Institutio sanctimonialium*)
Zürich, Zentralbibliothek
    Rh. 131 (miscellaneous letter collections, incl. *Indicularius Thiathildis*)

2. *Original Charter Material (Including Pseudo-originals)*
Epinal, Archives Départementales des Vosges

G 2661 (Henry II for Epinal, 1003; pseudo-original)
Hasselt, Rijksarchief
    Abdij van Munsterbilzen, Oorkonden, 1 (Regenza for Munsterbilzen, 1040; pseudo-original)
Koblenz, Landeshauptarchiv
    Abt. 157, no. 2 (Abbess Ruothildis and her brother for Pfalzel, 989)
    Best. 1A, Urkunden, Urkunde 18 (Otto I for Oeren, 966)
    Best. 201, no. 3 (Otto I for Oeren, 953)
Lille, Archives Départementales du Nord
    10 H 60/40 Musée 29 recto (Lothar of Western Francia for Marchiennes, 976)
    10 H 60/40 Musée 29 verso (Abbess Judith for Marchiennes, c. 976; pseudo-original)
    J 423 Musée 358 (Charles the Bald for Marchiennes, 877; pseudo-original)
Maastricht, Regionaal Historisch Centrum Limburg (formerly Rijksarchief in Limburg)
    Archief Abdij Thorn, Bestand Inventaris Habets, I, no. 4 (Henry II for Thorn, 1007)
Metz, Archives Départementales de la Moselle
    H 3904/2 (Otto II for Saint-Pierre-aux-Nonnains, 977)
    H 3904/23 (Otto III for Saint-Pierre-aux-Nonnains, 993)
    H 3959 (Count Ricuin of Verdun for Saint-Pierre-aux-Nonnains, 918; pseudo-original [?])
    H 4058/1 (Louis the German for Sainte-Glossinde, 875; pseudo-original)
    H 4058/2 (Bishop Adalbero I of Metz for Sainte-Glossinde, 945; pseudo-original)
    H 4058/3 (Bishop Thierry I of Metz for Sainte-Glossinde, 974; pseudo-original)
Nancy, Archives Départementales de Meurthe-et-Moselle
    1 J 173 (Ermenaidis for Bouxières, 966)
    2 F 1/3 (Pope Leo IX for Bleurville, 1050)
    H 1503 (Counts Geoffrey and Herman for Lunéville, 1034)
    H 3000 (Alda for Bouxières, c. 978)
    H 3000 (réserve) (Otto I for Bouxières, 942)
    H 3011 (Bishop Gozelin of Toul for Bouxières, 941)
    H 3011 (réserve) (Hersendis for Bouxières, 932/41)
Nancy, Bibliothèque Municipale
    Collection Pfister, no. 1 (Abbot Odelric for Bouxières, 959/60)
Paris, Bibliothèque Nationale de France
    Lat. 9307 (Henry III for Oeren, 1051)
    Nouvelles Acquisitions Latines 2547/6 (protocol of translation of relics at Remiremont, 1049)
Trier, Stadtarchiv
    Urk D4 (Otto II for Oeren, 973)
    Urk Q57 (Otto III for Oeren, 1000)
    Urk Q58 (Otto III for Oeren, 1000)
Vienna, Österreichische Nationalbibliothek
    Cod. Ser. nov. 12672 (Bishop Gozelin of Toul for Bouxières, 938)
Wolfenbüttel, Niedersächsisches Landesarchiv, Standort Wolfenbüttel
    Bestand 6, Urk no. 11 (Otto II for Theophanu, 972)

Edited Primary Sources

"Les actes des évêques de Toul des origines à 1069." Edited by André Schuellen. Unpublished master's thesis, University of Nancy II, 1985.

"Actes des princes lorrains, 2ème série: Princes ecclésiastiques. Vol. 3, Les évêques de Verdun; A - Des origines à 1107." Edited by Jean-Pol Evrard. Unpublished master's thesis, University of Nancy II, 1977.

Adalgerus/Adalherus. *Admonitio ad Nonsuindam reclusam.* Edited by August E. Anspach. *S. Isidori Hispalensis Episcopi Commonitiuncula ad Sororem.* Escorial: Typis Augustinianis Monasterii Escurialensis, 1935.

Die Admonitio Generalis Karls des Grossen. Edited and translated by Hubert Mordek, Klaus Zechiel-Eckes, and Michael Glatthaar. *MGH Fontes iuris Germanici antiqui in usum scholarum separatim editi* 16. Hanover: Hahnsche Buchhandlung, 2012.

Aegidius of Orval. *Gesta episcoporum Leodiensium.* Edited by Johannes Heller. *MGH SS* 25:14–129. Hanover: Hahnsche Buchhandlung, 1880.

Alpertus of Metz. *De diversitate temporum. Libri II.* Edited by Hans van Rij (in collaboration with Anna S. Abulafia). *De diversitate temporum et Fragmentum de Deoderico primo episcopo Mettensi / Gebeurtenissen van deze tijd: Een fragment over bisschop Diederik I van Metz; De mirakelen van de heilige Walburg in Tiel,* 2–105. Amsterdam: Verloren, 1980.

Die älteste erreichbare Gestalt des Liber sacramentorum anni circuli der Römischen Kirche (Cod. Pad. D47, fol. 11r–100r). Edited by Leo K. Mohlberg and Anton Baumstark. Münster: Verlag der Aschendorffschen Buchhandlung, 1927.

Andreas of Marchiennes. *De vita et miraculis sanctae Rictrudis libri tres.* Edited in *AASS Maii* 3:89–118. Antwerp: Michael Cnobarus, 1680.

Annales Bertiniani. Edited by Georg Waitz. *MGH SS Rerum Germanicarum in usum scholarum ex monumentis Germaniae historicis recusi* 5. Hanover: Hahnsche Buchhandlung, 1883.

Annales Laurissenses minores. Edited by Georg H. Pertz. *MGH SS* 1:112–23. Hanover: Hahnsche Buchhandlung, 1826.

El Archivo Condal de Barcelona en los Siglos IX–X: Estudio crítico de sus fondos. Edited by F. Udina Martorell. Madrid: Consejo Superior de Investigaciones Científicas, 1951.

De beata Ava virginis. Edited in *AASS Aprilis* 3:628. Antwerp: Michael Cnobarus, 1675.

Benedict of Nursia. *Regula monachorum.* Edited by Adalbert De Vogüé and Jean Neufville. *La règle de Saint Benoît.* 7 vols. *Sources Chrétiennes* 181–86. Paris: Les Editions du Cerf, 1971–77.

Bertarius. *Gesta episcoporum Virdinensium.* Edited by Georg Waitz. *MGH SS* 4:45–51. Hanover: Hahnsche Buchhandlung, 1841.

Bertha of Vilich. *Vita Adelheidis abbatissae Vilicensis.* Edited by Oswald Holder-Egger. *MGH SS* 15/2:755–63. Hanover: Hahnsche Buchhandlung, 1888.

Les bulles de Léon IX pour l'église de Toul. Edited by Jacques Choux. In *Lotharingia.* Vol. 2, *Archives lorraines d'archéologie, d'art et d'histoire.* Edited by Hubert Collin, 5–19. Nancy: Soc. Thierry Alix, 1990.

Capitularia regum Francorum. Edited by Alfred Boretius and Victor Krause. 2 vols. *MGH Legum* 2. Hanover: Hahnsche Buchhandlung, 1883–97.

"Le cartulaire de Saint Pierre aux Nonnains." Edited by J. Bernhaupt. Unpublished Diplôme d'études supérieures, University of Nancy, 1954.
Cesarius of Arles. *Regula ad virgines*. Edited by Adalbert de Vogüé and Joël Courreau. *Césaire d'Arles. Oeuvres monastiques*. Vol. 1, *Oeuvres pour les moniales: Introduction, texte critique, traduction et notes*. Sources Chrétiennes 345. Paris: Les Editions du Cerf, 1988.
———. *Sermones*. Edited by Germain Morin. CCSL 103. Turnhout: Brepols, 1953.
Chartes de l'abbaye de Remiremont des origines à 1231. Edited by Jean Bridot. 2nd ed. Turnhout: Brepols, 1997.
"Chartes de l'abbaye Saint-Epvre de Toul des origines à 1228." Edited by Michèle Schaeffer. Unpublished master's thesis, Université de Nancy II, 1984.
Chartes inédites concernant le chapitre de Nivelles. Edited by A. Wauters. *Revue d'histoire et d'archéologie* 3 (1862): 368–73, 444–45.
Chartes originales antérieures à 1121 conservées en France. Edited by Cédric Giraud, Jean-Baptiste Renault, and Benoît-Michel Tock. Accessed 8 April 2015. http://www.cn-telma.fr/originaux/index.
Die christlichen Inschriften der Rheinlande von der Mitte des achten bis zur Mitte des dreizehnten Jahrhunderts. Edited by Frans Xaver Kraus. 2 vols. Freiburg i. B.: Akademische Verlagsbuchhandlung von J. C. B. Mohr, 1890–94.
Chronique ou livre de fondation du monastère de Mouzon: Chronicon Mosomense seu Liber fundationis monasterii sanctae Mariae O.S.B. apud Mosomum in dioecesi Remensi. Edited by Michel Bur. Paris: Editions du Centre National de la Recherche scientifique, 1989.
Der Codex Regularum des Benedikt von Aniane: Faksimile der Handschrift Clm 28118 der Bayerischen Staatsbibliothek München. Edited by Pius Engelbert. St. Ottilien: EOS Verlag, 2016.
Concilia aevi Karolini. Edited by Albert Werminghoff. 2 vols. Hanover: Hahnsche Buchhandlung, 1906–8.
Constantin of Saint-Symphorien. *Vita Adalberonis II Mettensis episcopi*. Edited by Georg H. Pertz. MGH SS 4:659–72. Hanover: Hahnsche Buchhandlung, 1841.
Corpus van Middelnederlandse teksten (tot en met het jaar 1300). Edited by Maurits Gysseling. 15 vols. The Hague: Nijhoff, 1980.
Egebert. *Vita sancti Amoris*. Edited in *AASS Octobris* 4:343–7. Brussels: Typis Regis, 1780.

 Additional material in Maurice Coens. "Sur le prologue original de la Vie de S. Amour patron de Munsterbilzen." *Analecta Bollandiana* 84 (1966): 344–45.

Einhard. *Translatio sancti Marcellini et Petri*. Edited by Georg Waitz. MGH SS 15/1:238–61. Hanover: Hahnsche Buchhandlung, 1887.
Ekkehard of Sankt Gallen. *Vita sanctae Wiboradae*. Edited by Walter Berschin. *Vitae sanctae Wiboradae: Die ältesten Lebensbeschreibungen der hl. Wiborada*, 32–107. St. Gall: Historischer Verein des Kantons St. Gallen, 1983.
Flodoard. *Historia Remensis ecclesiae*. Edited by Martina Stratmann. MGH SS 36. Hanover: Hahnsche Buchhandlung, 1998.
Folcuin. *Gesta abbatum Lobbiensium*. Edited by Georg H. Pertz. MGH SS 4:54–74. Hanover: Hahnsche Buchhandlung, 1841.

260   BIBLIOGRAPHY

Frothar of Toul. *Letters*. Edited by Karl Hampe. *MGH Epistolarum* 5. *Karolini Aevi* 3:275–98. Berlin: Apud Weidmannos, 1889.

Fundatio Sancti Petri. Edited by Gordon Blennemann. *Die Metzer Benediktinerinnen im Mittelalter: Studien zu den Handlungsspielräumen geistlicher Frauen*, 281–91. Husum: Matthiesen Verlag, 2011.

Gesta episcoporum Cameracensium. Edited by Ludwig Bethmann. *MGH SS* 7:402–87. Hanover: Hahnsche Buchhandlung, 1846.

Gesta episcoporum Mettensium. Edited by Georg Waitz. *MGH SS* 10:531–44. Hanover: Hahnsche Buchhandlung, 1852.

Gesta episcoporum Tullensium. Edited by Georg Waitz. *MGH SS* 8:631–48. Hanover: Hahnsche Buchhandlung, 1848.

Gesta episcoporum Virdunensium (continuatio). Edited by Georg Waitz. *MGH SS* 4:45–51. Hanover: Hahnsche Buchhandlung, 1841.

Gesta sanctorum patrum Fontanellensis coenobii. Edited by Fernand Lohier and Jean Laporte. Rouen: A. Lestringant, 1936.

Gesta Treverorum. Edited by Georg Waitz. *MGH SS* 8:111–260. Hanover: Hahnsche Buchhandlung, 1848.

Gislebert of Mons. *Chronica Hannoniae*. Edited by Léon Vanderkindere. *La chronique de Gislebert de Mons*. Brussels: Kiessling, 1904.

Heriger of Lobbes. *Vita, translationes, miracula Landoaldi, Landradae et sociorum*. Edited by Oswald Holder-Egger. *MGH SS* 15/2:601–7. Hanover: Hahnsche Buchhandlung, 1887.

Additional material in *Analecta Bollandiana* 4 (1885): 192–94 and Jean-Louis Kupper. "Les voies de la création hagiographique: Lettre d'envoi par l'évêque Notger de Liège de la *Vita sancti Landoaldi*, 19 juin 980." In *Autour de Gerbert d'Aurillac, le pape de l'an mil: Matériaux pour l'histoire, publiés par l'Ecole des chartes*, edited by Olivier Guyotjeannin and Emmanuel Poulle, 301–5. Paris: Ecole des chartes, 1996.

Hildemar of Corbie. *Expositio Regulae*. Edited by Ruppert Mittermüller. Regensburg: Pustet, 1880.

L'histoire-polyptyque de l'abbaye de Marchiennes (1116–1121): Etude critique et édition. Edited by Bernard Delmaire. Louvain-la-Neuve: Centre belge d'histoire rurale, 1985.

Historia monasterii Hasnoniensis. Edited by Oswald Holder-Egger. *MGH SS* 14:149–58. Hanover: Hahnsche Buchhandlung, 1883.

Hucbald of Saint-Amand. *Vita sanctae Rictrudis Marchianensis*. Edited in *AASS Maii* 3:81–9. Antwerp: Michael Cnobarus, 1680.

Hugh of Flavigny. *Chronicon*. Edited by Georg H. Pertz. *MGH SS* 8:288–502. Hanover: Hahnsche Buchhandlung, 1848.

Hugh of Lobbes. *Vita sanctae Berlendis*. Edited in *AASS Februarii* 1:378–81. Antwerp: Johannes Meursius, 1658.

Inventio et miracula Gisleni Hanoniensis. Edited by Joseph Ghesquière. *Acta sanctorum Belgii selecta* 4:385–89. Brussels: Matthaeus Lemaire, 1787.

Jacques de Guise. *Annales Hannoniae*. Edited by Ernst Sackur. *MGH SS* 30/1:44–334. Hanover: Hahnsche Buchhandlung, 1896.

John Cassian. *Collationes*. Edited by E. Pichery. *Jean Cassien, Conférences*. 3 vols. Sources Chrétiennes 42, 54, 64. Paris: Le Cerf, 1955–59.

John of Saint-Arnoul. *Vita Johannis Gorziensis*. Edited and translated by Peter C. Jacobsen. MGH Scriptores rerum Germanicarum in usum scholarum separatim editi 81. Wiesbaden: Harrasowitz Verlag, 2016.

——. *Vita, translationes et miracula sanctae Glodesindis*. Edited in *AASS Julii* 6:210–24. Antwerp: Jacobus du Moulin, 1729.

Die Konzilien der Karolingischen Teilreiche, 843–859. Edited by Wilfried Hartmann. MGH Concilia 3, Concilia aevi Karolini. Hanover: Hahnsche Buchhandlung, 1984.

Die Konzilien der Karolingischen Teilreiche, 860–874. Edited by Wilfried Hartmann. MGH Concilia 4, Concilia aevi Karolini. Hanover: Hahnsche Buchhandlung, 1998.

Die Konzilien der Karolingischen Teilreiche, 875–911. Edited by Wilfried Hartmann, Isolde Schröder, and Gerhard Schmitz. MGH Concilia 5, Concilia aevi Karolini. Hanover: Hahnsche Buchhandlung, 2012.

Die Konzilien Deutschlands und Reichsitaliens, 1023–1059. Edited by Detlev Jasper. MGH Concilia 8, Concilia aevi Saxonici et Salici. Hanover: Hahnsche Buchhandlung, 2010.

Die Lateinischen Dichter des Deutschen Mittelalters. Vol. 5, *Die Ottonenzeit*. Edited by Karl Strecker and Norbert Fickermann. Leipzig: Karl W. Hiersemann, 1937.

Lectiones in commemoratione et transitu Sancti Ionati confessoris qui celebratur kalendis Augusti. Edited in *AASS Augusti* 1:73–75. Antwerp: Jacobus Antonius Van Gherwen, 1733.

Additional material in *Catalogus codicum hagiographicorum Bibliothecae regiae Bruxellensis I: Codices latini membranei* 2:273–75. Brussels: Polleunis, Ceuterick et Lefébure, 1889.

Libellus a regula sancti Benedicti subtractus. Edited by Antonio Linage Conde. *Una regla monastica riojana femenina del siglo X: El "Libellus a regula sancti Benedicti subtractus."* Salamanca: Universidad de Salamanca, 1973.

Libellus de rebus Trevirensibus. Edited by Georg Waitz. MGH SS 14:99–106. Hanover: Hahnsche Buchhandlung, 1883.

Liber memorialis von Remiremont. Edited by Eduard Hlawitschka, Karl Schmid, and Gerd Tellenbach. 2 vols. MGH Libri Memoriales 1. Dublin: Weidmann, 1970.

Liber sacramentorum Augustodunensis. Edited by O. Heiming. CCSL 159b. Turnhout: Brepols Publishers, 1984.

Liber sacramentorum Gellonensis. Edited by Auguste Dumas and Jean Deshusses. 2 vols. CCSL 159, 159a. Turnhout: Brepols, 1981.

Der Memorial- und Liturgiecodex von San Salvatore / Santa Giulia in Brescia. Edited by Dieter Geuenich and Uwe Ludwig. MGH Libri Memoriales et necrologia, Nova Series 4. Hanover: Hahnsche Buchhandlung, 2000.

Miracula sanctae Ragenfredis. Edited in *AASS Octobris* 4:295–334. Brussels: Typis Regiis, 1780.

Nécrologe de l'abbaye de Munsterbilzen. Edited by J. Weale, C. de Borman, and S. Bormans. *Bulletin de l'Institut Archéologique Liégeois* 12 (1874): 27–60.

Olbert of Gembloux. *Historia sancte Veroni confessoris Lembecensis inventionis miraculorum et translationis*. Edited by Oswald Holder-Egger. MGH SS 15/2:750–3. Hanover: Hahnsche Buchhandlung, 1887.

——. *Vita secunda Waldetrudis*. Edited in *AASS Aprilis* 1:837–42. Antwerp: Michael Cnobarus, 1675.

Onulph and Everhelm. *Vita Popponis*. Edited by Wilhelm Wattenbach. *MGH SS* 11:291–316. Hanover: Hahnsche Buchhandlung, 1854.

Oorkondenboek van Holland en Zeeland tot 1299. Vol. 1, *Eind van de 7e eeuw tot 1222*. Edited by A. C. F. Koch. The Hague: Martinus Nijhoff, 1970.

Opera diplomatica et historica. Edited by Aubertus Miraeus and Franciscus Foppens. 2nd ed., 2 vols. Louvain: Aegidius Denique, 1723.

Les ordines Romani du Haut moyen âge. Edited by Michel Andrieu. 6 vols. Louvain: Spicilegium sacrum lovaniense, 1961–85.

Paenitentiale mixtum Pseudo-Bedae-Egberti. Edited by Hermann J. Schmitz. *Die Bussbücher und das kanonische Bussverfahren nach handschriftlichen Quellen dargestellt* 2:675–701. Düsseldorf: L. Schwann, 1888.

Papsturkunden in Frankreich. Neue Folge. Vol. 1, *Champagne und Lothringen*. Edited by Hermann Meinert. Berlin: Weidmannsche Buchhandlung, 1932.

Passio Maxellendis prima. Edited by Joseph Ghesquière. *Acta sanctorum Belgii selecta* 3:580–87. Brussels: Matthaeus Lemaire, 1785.

Passio Maxellendis secunda. Edited by Joseph Ghesquière. *Acta sanctorum Belgii selecta* 3:588–89. Brussels: Matthaeus Lemaire, 1785.

Le polyptyque et les listes de biens de l'abbaye Saint-Pierre de Lobbes (IXe–XIe siècles). Edition critique. Edited by Jean-Pierre Devroey. Brussels: Palais des Académies, 1986.

Le pontifical Romano-Germanique du dixième siècle. Edited by Cyrille Vogel and Reinhard Elze. 2 vols. Vatican City: Bibliotheca Apostolica Vaticana, 1963.

Rainer of Ghent. *Inventio et miracula Gisleni Hanoniensis*. Edited by Poncelet. *Analecta Bollandiana* 5 (1886): 239–88.

Recueil des actes de Charles II le Chauve, roi de France. Edited by Arthur Giry, Georges Tessier, and Maurice Prou. 3 vols. Paris: Imprimerie Nationale, 1943–55.

Recueil des actes de Charles III le Simple, roi de France (893–923). Edited by Philippe Lauer. 2 vols. Paris: Imprimerie Nationale, 1940–49.

Recueil des actes de Lothaire et de Louis V, rois de France (954–987). Edited by Louis Halphen and Ferdinand Lot. Paris: Imprimerie Nationale, 1908.

Regino of Prüm. *Chronica*. Edited by Friedrich Kurze. *MGH SS rerum Germanicarum in usum scholarum separatim editi* 50. Hanover: Hahnsche Buchhandlung, 1890.

Renier of Saint-Laurent. *De ineptiis cuiusdam idiotae libellus*. Edited by Wilhelm Arndt. *MGH SS* 20:593–603. Hanover: Hahnsche Buchhandlung, 1868.

Richer of Saint-Remi. *Historiae*. Edited by Hartmut Hoffmann. *MGH SS* 38. Hanover: Hahnsche Buchhandlung, 2000.

Le sacramentaire de Drogon. Edited by Jean-Baptiste Pelt. Metz: Imprimerie du Journal Le Lorrain, 1936.

The Sacramentary of Ratoldus (Paris, Bibliothèque nationale de France, lat. 12052). Edited by Nicholas Orchard. London: Henry Bradshaw Society, 2005.

Sacrorum conciliorum nova et amplissima collectio. Edited by Dominicus Mansi. 31 vols. Florence and Venice: Antonius Zatta, 1759–98.

Sigebert of Gembloux. *Chronica*. Edited by Ludwig C. Bethmann. *MGH SS* 6:300–74. Hanover: Hahnsche Buchhandlung, 1844.

———. *Gesta abbatum Gemblacensium*. Edited by Georg H. Pertz. *MGH SS* 8:523–57. Hanover: Hahnsche Buchhandlung, 1848.

———.*Vita Deoderici*. Edited by Georg H. Pertz. *MGH SS* 4:462–83. Hanover: Hahnsche Buchhandlung, 1841.

Statuta Murbacensia. Edited by Josef Semmler. *Corpus consuetudinum monasticarum* 1:437–50. Siegburg: Schmidt, 1963.

Sulpicius Severus. *Dialogi*. Edited by Carolus Halm. *Sulpicii Severi libri qui supersunt*, 152–216. Vienna: C. Geboldi filius, 1886.

———. *Vita Martini*. Edited by Jacques Fontaine. *Vie de Saint Martin*. 3 vols. Sources Chrétiennes 133–35. Paris: Les Editions du Cerf, 1967–69.

Theologia eclectica, moralis et scholastica. Edited by Eusebius Amort. 4 vols. Vienna: Martin Veith, 1752.

Thiathildis of Remiremont. *Indicularius Thiathildis*. Edited and translated by Michel Parisse. *La correspondance d'un évêque carolingien: Frothaire de Toul (ca. 813–847) avec les lettres de Theuthilde, abbesse de Remiremont*, 154–63. Paris: Publications de la Sorbonne, 1998.

Previously edited by Karl Zeumer. *MGH Formulae Merowingici et Karolingici Aevi*, 525–28. Hanover: Hahnsche Buchhandlung, 1886.

Thierry of Saint-Hubert [?]. *Vita sanctae Aldegundis quinta*. Edited in *AASS Januarii* 2:1040–52. Antwerp: Johannes Meursius, 1643.

Thierry of Saint-Trond. *Vita Landradae Belisiensis*. Edited by Laurentius Surius. *De probatis sanctorum historiis* 4:135–41. Cologne: Geruinus et haeredes Quentelii, 1573.

Thietmar of Merseburg. *Chronicon*. Edited by Robert Holtzmann. *Die Chronik des Bischofs Thietmar von Merseburg und ihre Korveier Überarbeitung*. Scriptores rerum Germanicarum, Nova series 9. Berlin: Weidmannsche Buchhandlung, 1935.

Translationes et miracula sanctorum Romarici, Amati et Adelphii. Edited in *AASS Septembris* 3:829–37. Antwerp: Bernardus Albertus Vander Plassche, 1750.

Die Urkunde Ludwigs des Deutschen für das Glossindenkloster. Edited by Georg Wolfram. *Mitteilungen des Instituts für Österreichische Geschichtsforschung* 11 (1890): 1–27.

Die Urkunden der Deutschen Karolinger. Vol. 1, *Die Urkunden Ludwigs des Deutschen, Karlmanns und Ludwigs des Jüngeren*. Edited by P. Kehr. *MGH Diplomata regum Germaniae ex stirpe Karolinorum*. Berlin: Weidmannsche Buchhandlung, 1934.

Die Urkunden der Deutschen Karolinger. Vol. 2, *Die Urkunden Karls III*. Edited by P. Kehr. *MGH Diplomata Regum Germaniae ex stirpe Karolinorum*. Berlin: Weidmannsche Buchhandlung, 1937.

Die Urkunden der Deutschen Karolinger. Vol. 3, *Die Urkunden Arnolfs*. Edited by P. Kehr. *MGH Diplomata regum Germaniae ex stirpe Karolinorum*. Berlin: Weidmannsche Buchhandlung, 1940.

Die Urkunden der Deutschen Karolinger. Vol. 4, *Die Urkunden Zwentibolds und Ludwigs des Kindes*. Edited by Theodor Schieffer. *MGH Diplomata regum Germaniae ex stirpe Karolinorum*. Berlin: Weidmannsche Verlagsbuchhandlung, 1960.

Die Urkunden der Deutschen Könige und Kaiser. Vol. 1, *Die Urkunden Konrad I. Heinrich I. und Otto I*. *MGH Diplomata regum et imperatorum Germaniae*. Hanover: Hahnsche Buchhandlung, 1879–84.

BIBLIOGRAPHY

Die Urkunden der Deutschen Könige und Kaiser. Vol. 2, bk. 1, *Die Urkunden Otto des II.* MGH Diplomata regum et imperatorum Germaniae. Hanover: Hahnsche Buchhandlung, 1888.

Die Urkunden der Deutschen Könige und Kaiser. Vol. 2, bk. 2, *Die Urkunden Otto des III.* MGH Diplomata regum et imperatorum Germaniae. Hanover: Hahnsche Buchhandlung, 1893.

Die Urkunden der Deutschen Könige und Kaiser. Vol. 3, *Die Urkunden Heinrichs II. und Arduins.* Edited by H. Bresslau. MGH Diplomata regum et imperatorum Germaniae. Hanover: Hahnsche Buchhandlung, 1900–1903.

Die Urkunden der Deutschen Könige und Kaiser. Vol. 5, *Die Urkunden Heinrichs III.* Edited by H. Bresslau and P. Kehr. MGH Diplomata regum et imperatorum Germaniae. Berlin: Weidmannsche Verlagsbuchhandlung, 1931.

Die Urkunden der Deutschen Könige und Kaiser. Vol. 6, *Die Urkunden Heinrichs IV.* Edited by D. Von Gladis and A. Gawlik. MGH Diplomata regum et imperatorum Germaniae. Berlin: Weidmannsche Verlagsbuchhandlung / Weimar: Verlag Hermann Böhlaus Nachfolger / Hanover: Hahnsche Buchhandlung, 1941–78.

Die Urkunden der Karolinger. Vol. 3, *Die Urkunden Lothars I. und Lothars II.* Edited by Theodor Schieffer. MGH Diplomata Karolinorum. Berlin: Weidmannsche Buchhandlung, 1966.

Die Urkunden der Merowinger. Edited by Theo Kölzer. 2 vols. MGH Diplomata regum Francorum e stirpe Merovingica. Hanover: Hahnsche Buchhandlung, 2001.

Die Urkunden Ludwigs des Frommen. Edited by Theo Kölzer and others. 3 vols. MGH Diplomata Karolinorum 2. Wiesbaden: Harrassowitz Verlag, 2016.

Urkundenbuch zur Geschichte der jetzt die Preussischen Regierungsbezirke Coblenz und Trier bildenden mittelrheinischen Territorien. Edited by Heinrich Beyer. Vol. 1. Koblenz: J. Hölscher, 1860.

"Vie de S. Aldegonde; Charte de dotation de l'abbaye de Maubeuge; Revenus de ses terres." Edited by Jacques Daris. *Analectes pour servir à l'histoire ecclésiastique de la Belgique* 2:36–47. Louvain: Ch. Peeters, 1865.

Vita beatae Reginae. Edited in *AASS Julii* 1:268–71. Antwerp: Jacobus du Moulin, 1719.

Vita Caddroe abbatis Walciodorensis. Edited by John Colgan. *Acta Sanctorum veteris et maioris Scotiae seu Hiberniae sanctorum Insulae* 1:494–507. Louvain: Everard De Witte, 1645.

Vita Harlindis et Relindis. Edited in *AASS Martii* 3:386–91. Antwerp: Jacobus Meursius, 1668.

Vita Leonis IX. Edited and translated by Michel Parisse and Monique Goullet. *La vie du pape Léon IX (Brunon, évêque de Toul).* Paris: Les Belles Lettres, 1997.

Also edited by Hans Georg Krause, Detlev Jasper, and Veronika Lukas. *Die Touler Vita Leos IX.* MGH SS rerum Germanicarum in usum scholarum separatim editi 70. Hanover: Hahnsche Buchhandlung, 2007.

Vita Lietphardi. Edited in *AASS Februarii* 1:495–97. Antwerp: Jacobus Meursius, 1658.

Vita Liutbirgae. Edited by Ottokar Menzel. *Das Leben der Liutbirg: Eine Quelle zur Geschichte der Sachsen in karolingischer Zeit.* Leipzig: Karl W. Hiersemann, 1937.

Vita Odiliae abbatissae Hohenburgensis. Edited by W. Levison. MGH SS Rerum Merovingicarum 6:24–50. Hanover and Leipzig: Hahn, 1913.

Vita sanctae Aldegundis prima. Edited by Joseph Ghesquière. *Acta sanctorum Belgii selecta* 4:315–26. Brussels: Matthaeus Lemaire, 1787.
Vita sanctae Aldegundis secunda. Edited in *AASS Januarii* 2:1035–40. Antwerp: Johannes Meursius, 1643.
Vita sanctae Aldegundis tertia. Edited by Jacques Daris. "Vie de S. Aldegonde; Charte de dotation de l'abbaye de Maubeuge; Revenus de ses terres." *Analectes pour servir à l'histoire ecclésiastique de la Belgique* 2:37–41. Louvain: Archives du Bureau, 1865.
Vita sanctae Aldegundis quarta. Edited in *Catalogus codicum hagiographicorum Bibliothecae regiae Bruxellensis I: Codices latini membranei* 2:133–35. Brussels: Polleunis, Ceuterick et Lefébure, 1889.
Vita sanctae Aldetrudis. Edited in *AASS Februarii* 3:510–1. Antwerp: Johannes Meursius, 1658.

Additional material in *Catalogus codicum hagiographicorum Bibliothecae regiae Bruxellensis I: Codices latini membranei* 2:379–81. Brussels: Polleunis, Ceuterick et Lefébure, 1889.

Vita sanctae Beggae. Edited by Joseph Ghesquière. *Acta sanctorum Belgii selecta* 5:111–24. Brussels: Veuve Franciscus Pion, 1789.
Vita sanctae Eusebiae. Edited in *AASS Martii* 2:447–50. Antwerp: Jacobus Meursius, 1668.
Vita sanctae Madelbertae. Edited and translated by Paul Bertrand. "La Vie de Ste Madelberte de Maubeuge. Edition du texte (BHL 5129) et traduction française." *Analecta Bollandiana* 115 (1997): 39–76, at 55–71.
Vita sanctae Mennae. Edited in *AASS Octobris* 2:150–57. Antwerp: Petrus Johannes van der Plassche, 1768.
Vita sanctae Rictrudis metrica. Edited by Gabriel Silagi and Bernhard Bischoff. *Die Lateinischen Dichter des Deutschen Mittelalters*. Vol. 5, *Die Ottonenzeit 3*. MGH Poetae 5/3: 566–96. s.l.: Monumenta Germaniae Historica, 1979.
Vita sanctae Waldetrudis. Edited by Jacques Daris. "La vie de sainte Waudru, patronne de la ville de Mons, d'après un manuscrit du XIe siècle." *Analectes pour servir à l'histoire ecclésiastique de la Belgique* 4:218–31. Louvain: Ch. Peeters and H. Goemaere, 1867.
Vita secunda sancti Adelphii. Edited in *AASS Septembris* 3:818–20. Antwerp: Bernardus Albertus Vander Plassche, 1750.
Vita secunda sancti Romarici. Edited by Nicolaus Serarius. *Comitum par genere, potentie, opibus, heroicaque virtute inclytum B. Godefridus, Vuestphalus, S. Romaricus, Austrasius e manuscriptis libris, cum notatiunculis*, 97–144. Mainz: Balthasar Lippius, 1605.
Vita seu legenda sanctae Rolendis Garpiniensis. Edited by Maurice Coens. "La Vita Rolendis dans sa recension gerpinoise." *Analecta Bollandiana* 78 (1960): 328–55, at 336–47.
Vita tertia Gertrudis Nivialensis. Edited by Geldolph a Ryckel. *Historia S. Gertrudis principis virginis primae Nivellensis abbatissae*, 35–101. Brussels: Godefrid Schovart, 1637.
Vita, translationes et miracula sanctae Glodesindis. Edited in *AASS Julii* 6:203–10. Antwerp: Jacobus du Moulin, 1729.

Vita tripartita Gertrudis Nivialensis. Edited by Geldolph a Ryckel. *Historia S. Gertrudis principis virginis primae Nivellensis abbatissae,* 107–43, 35–77, 145–81. Brussels: Godefrid Schovart, 1637.

Vita Theoderici abbatis Andaginensis. Edited by Wilhelm Wattenbach. *MGH SS* 12:37–57. Hanover: Hahnsche Buchhandlung, 1866.

Widric. *Vita Gerardi episcopi Tullensis.* Edited by Georg Waitz. *MGH SS* 4:490–505. Hanover: Hahnsche Buchhandlung, 1841.

Wolfenbüttler Fragmente: Analekten zur Kirchengeschichte des Mittelalters aus Wolfenbüttler Handschriften. Edited by Maximilian Sdralek. Munster i. W.: H. Schöningh, 1891.

Secondary Literature

1000 jaar kerkelijke kunst in Limburg: Tentoonstelling uit het kunstpatrimonium van Belgisch- en Nederlands Limburg. Hasselt: St. Quintinus drukkerij, 1961.

Althoff, Gerd. "Gandersheim und Quedlinburg: Ottonische Frauenklöster als Herrschafts- und Überlieferungszentren." *Frühmittelalterliche Studien* 25 (1991): 123–44.

———. "Ottonische Frauengemeinschaften im Spannungsfeld von Kloster und Welt." In *Essen und die sächsischen Frauenstifte im Frühmittelalter,* edited by Jan Gerchow and Thomas Schilp, 29–44. Essen: Klartext Verlag, 2003.

———. "Zum Verhältnis von Norm und Realität in sächsischen Frauenklöstern der Ottonenzeit." *Frühmittelalterliche Studien* 40 (2006): 127–44.

Andenna, Giancarlo. "Le monache nella cultura e nella storia europea del primo medioevo." In *Arte, cultura e religione in Santa Giulia,* edited by Giancarlo Andenna, 17–34. Brescia: Grafo edizione, 2004.

———. *Sanctimoniales Cluniacenses: Studi sui monasteri femminili di Cluny e sulla loro legislazione in Lombardia (XI–XV secolo).* Münster: LIT Verlag, 2004.

———. "San Salvatore di Brescia e la scelta religiosa delle donne aristocratiche tra eta longobarda ed eta franca (VIII-IX secolo)." In *Female "vita religiosa" between Late Antiquity and the High Middle Ages,* edited by Gert Melville and Anne Müller, 209–33. Vienna: LIT Verlag, 2011.

Andermann, Ulrich. "Die unsittlichen und disziplinlosen Kanonissen: Ein Topos und seine Hintergründe, aufgezeigt an Beispielen sächsischer Frauenstifte (11.–13. Jahrhundert)." *Westfälische Zeitschrift* 146 (1996): 39–63.

Angenendt, Arnold. *Kloster und Stift: Das Motiv der kultischen Reinheit als Ferment ihrer Entwicklung.* Duisburg: Verein zur Erhaltung des Xantener Domes, 1992.

Auge, Oliver. "'Aemulatio' und Herrschaftssicherung durch sakrale Repräsentation: Zur Symbiose von Burg und Stift bis zur Salierzeit." In *Die Stiftskirche in Südwestdeutschland: Aufgaben und Perspektiven der Forschung. Erste wissenschaftliche Fachtagung zum Stiftskirchenproject des Instituts für Geschichtliche Landeskunde und historische Hilfswissenschaften der Universität Tübingen (17.–19. März 2000, Weingarten),* edited by Sönke Lorenz and Oliver Auge, 207–30. Leinfelden-Echterdingen: DRW Verlag, 2003.

L'avouerie en Lotharingie: Actes des 2es Journées Lotharingiennes, 22–23 oct. 1982. Luxembourg: Publications de la section historique de l'Institut Grand-Ducal de Luxembourg, 1984.

Avril, François, Claudia Rabel, and Isabelle Delaunay. *Manuscrits enluminés d'origine germanique*. 2 vols. Paris: Bibliothèque Nationale de France, 1995.
Balzaretti, Ross. "Women, Property and Urban Space in Tenth-Century Milan." *Gender and History* 23 (2011): 547–75.
Barrucand, Marianne. "Le trésor de saint Gauzelin à la cathédrale de Nancy." *Le Pays Lorrain* 63 (1982): 89–106.
Barth, Rüdiger E. *Der Herzog in Lotharingien im 10. Jahrhundert*. Sigmaringen: Jan Thorbecke Verlag, 1990.
Bauer, Thomas. *Lotharingien als historischer Raum: Raumbildung und Raumbewußtsein im Mittelalter*. Cologne: Böhlau Verlag, 1997.
Bautier, Robert-Henri. *Les origines de l'abbaye de Bouxières-aux-dames au diocèse de Toul: Reconstitution du chartrier et édition critique des chartes antérieures à 1200*. Nancy: Société d'Archéologie Lorraine, 1987.
Bautz, Friedrich W. "Humbert von Silva Candida." In *Biographisch-Bibliographisches Kirchenlexikon* 2:1164–5. Bautz: Hamm, 1990.
Beach, Alison I. *Women as Scribes: Book Production and Monastic Reform in Twelfth-Century Bavaria*. Oxford: Oxford University Press, 2003.
The Beck Collection of Illuminated Manuscripts. London: Sotheby's, 1997.
Benoît, Arthur. "Notes sur le Clermontois: L'abbaye royale de Juvigny-les-Dames." *Mémoires de la Société des Lettres, Sciences et Arts de Bar-le-Duc*, 3rd ser., 1 (1892): 45–84.
Berlière, Ursmer. "Monastère d'Andenne." In *Monasticon Belge* 1:61–3. Maredsous: Abbaye de Maredsous, 1890.
Berman, Constance H. *Women and Monasticism in Medieval Europe: Sisters and Patrons of the Cistercian Reform*. Kalamazoo, MI: Medieval Institute Publications, 2002.
Bernhardt, John W. *Itinerant Kingship & Royal Monasteries in Early Medieval Germany, c. 936–1075*. Cambridge: Cambridge University Press, 1993.
Bertrand, Paul. "Réformes ecclésiastiques, luttes d'influence et hagiographie à l'abbaye de Maubeuge, IXe-XIe s." In *Medieval Narrative Sources. A Gateway Into the Medieval Mind*, edited by Werner Verbeke, Ludo Milis, and Jean Goossens, 55–75. Louvain: Universitaire Pers, 2005.
Bertrand, Paul, and Charles Mériaux. "Cambrai-Magdebourg: Les reliques des saints et l'intégration de la Lotharingie dans le royaume de Germanie au milieu du Xe siècle." *Médiévales* 51 (2006): 85–96.
Beuckers, Klaus G. "Das älteste Gandersheimer Schatzverzeichnis und der Gandersheimer Kirchenschatz des 10./11. Jahrhunderts." In *Gandersheim und Essen: Vergleichende Untersuchungen zu sächsischen Frauenstiften*, edited by Martin Hoernes and Hedwig Röckelein, 97–131. Essen: Klartext Verlag, 2006.
Beyond the Feminization Thesis: Gender and Christianity in Modern Europe, edited by Patrick Pasture, Jan Art, and Thomas Buerman. Louvain: Leuven University Press, 2012.
Bijsterveld, Arnoud-Jan A. "De oorsprong van de oudste kapittels in het noorden van het bisdom Luik: Een voorlopige synthese." In *In de voetsporen van Jacob van Maerlant: Liber amicorum Raf de Keyzer; Verzameling opstellen over middeleeuwse geschiedenis en geschiedenisdidactiek*, edited by Raoul Bauer, 206–11. Louvain: Universitaire Pers Leuven, 2002.

Bishko, Charles J. "Salvus of Albelda and Frontier Monasticism in Tenth Century Navarre." *Speculum* 23 (1948): 559–90.

Blennemann, Gordon. "Eine Bildurkunde aus dem Benediktinerinnenkloster Sainte-Glossinde in Metz: Zugleich ein Beitrag zur mediävistischen Bild- und Objektwissenschaft." In *Konstanz und Wandel: Religiöse Lebensformen im europäischen Mittelalter*, edited by Gordon Blennemann, Christine Kleinjung, and Thomas Kohl, 169–98. Affalterbach: Didymos-Verlag, 2016.

———. "Die Darstellung und Deutung des räumlichen im hagiographischen Dossier der Hl. Glodesindis, Äbtissin in Metz (BHL 3562–3564)." In *Heilige - Liturgie - Raum*, edited by Dieter R. Bauer, Klaus Herbers, Hedwig Röckelein, and Felicitas Schmieder, 157–74. Stuttgart: Franz Steiner Verlag, 2010.

———. *Die Metzer Benediktinerinnen im Mittelalter: Studien zu den Handlungsspielräumen geistlicher Frauen.* Husum: Matthiesen Verlag, 2011.

———. "Le nécrologe du livre du chapitre de l'abbaye Saint-Pierre-aux-Nonnains de Metz (BNF lat. 10028)." Unpublished thesis, Ecole des Chartes, 2006.

———. "Raumkonzept und liturgische Nutzung: Eine Spurensuche zur Frühgeschichte der Metzer Frauenklöster Sainte-Glossinde und Saint-Pierre-aux-Nonnains." In *Frauen - Kloster - Kunst. Neue Forschungen zur Kulturgeschichte des Mittelalters: Beiträge zum Internationalen Kolloquium vom 13. bis 16. Mai 2005 anlässlich der Ausstellung "Krone und Schleier,"* edited by Jeffrey F. Hamburger and Carola Jäggi, 319–26. Turnhout: Brepols, 2007.

Bloch, Raissa. "Die Klosterpolitik Leos IX. in Deutschland, Burgund und Italien." *Archiv für Urkundenforschung* 11 (1930): 176–257.

Blok, P. J. "De stichtingsbrief van Thorn." *Nederlands Archievenblad* (1892): 29–36.

Bodarwé, Katrinette. "Frauenleben zwischen Klosterregeln und Luxus? Alltag in frühmittelalterlichen Frauenklöstern." In *Königin, Klosterfrau, Bäuerin: Frauen im Frühmittelalter 19.–22. Oktober 1995*, edited by Helga Brandt and Julia K. Koch, 117–43. Münster: Agenda-Verlag, 1996.

———. "Gender and the Archive: The Preservation of Charters in Early Medieval Communities." In *Saints, Scholars, and Politicians: Gender as a Tool in Medieval Studies. Festschrift in Honour of Anneke Mulder-Bakker on the Occasion of Her Sixty-Fifth Birthday*, edited by Mathilde Van Dijk and Renée Nip, 111–32. Turnhout: Brepols, 2005.

———. "Immer Ärger mit den Stiftsdamen: Reform in Regensburg." In *Nonnen, Kanonissen und Mystikerinnen: Religiöse Frauengemeinschaften in Süddeutschland. Beiträge zur interdisziplinären Tagung vom 21. bis 23. September 2005 in Frauenchiemsee*, edited by Eva Schlotheuber, 79–102. Göttingen: Vandenhoeck und Ruprecht, 2008.

———. "'Kirchenfamilien.' Kapellen und Kirchen in frühmittelalterlichen Frauengemeinschaften." In *Herrschaft, Liturgie und Raum: Studien zur mittelalterlichen Geschichte des Frauenstifts Essen*, edited by Katrinette Bodarwé and Thomas Schilp, 111–31. Essen: Klartext Verlag, 2002.

———. "Eine Männerregel für Frauen: Die Adaption der Benediktsregel im 9. und 10. Jahrhundert." In *Female "vita religiosa" between Late Antiquity and the High Middle Ages*, edited by Gert Melville and Anne Müller, 235–74. Vienna: LIT Verlag, 2011.

———. "Roman Martyrs and their Veneration in Ottonian Saxony: The Case of the Sanctimoniales of Essen." *Early Medieval Europe* 9 (2000): 345–65.

———. *Sanctimoniales litteratae: Schriftlichkeit und Bildung in den ottonischen Frauenkommunitäten Gandersheim, Essen und Quedlinburg*. Münster: Aschendorff Verlag, 2004.

———. "Ein Spinnennetz von Frauenklöstern: Kommunikation und Filiation zwischen sächsischen Frauenklöstern im Frühmittelalter." In *Lesen, Schreiben, Sticken und Erinnern: Beiträge zur Kultur- und Sozialgeschichte mittelalterlicher Frauenklöster*, edited by Gabriela Signori, 27–52. Bielefeld: Verlag für Regionalgeschichte, 2000.

Bonenfant, Paul. "Note critique sur le prétendu testament de sainte Aldegonde." *Bulletin de la Commission Royale d'Histoire* 98 (1934): 219–38.

Bönnen, Gerold. *Die Bischofsstadt Toul und ihr Umland während des hohen und späten Mittelalters*. Trier: Verlag Trierer Historische Forschungen, 1996.

Bönnen, Gerold, Alfred Haverkamp, and Frank G. Hirschmann. "Religiöse Frauengemeinschaften im räumlichen Gefüge der Trierer Kirchenprovinz während des hohen Mittelalters." In *Herrschaft, Kirche, Kultur: Beiträge zur Geschichte des Mittelalters; Festschrift für Friedrich Prinz zu seinem 65. Geburtstag*, edited by Stephanie Haarländer and Georg Jenal, 369–415. Stuttgart: Hiersemann, 1993.

Boshof, Egon. "Kloster und Bischof in Lotharingen." In *Monastische Reformen im 9. und 10. Jahrhundert*, edited by Raymund Kottje and Helmut Maurer, 197–245. Sigmaringen: Jan Thorbecke Verlag, 1989.

———. "Untersuchungen zur Kirchenvogtei in Lothringen im 10. und 11. Jahrhundert." *Zeitschrift der Savigny-Stiftung für Rechtsgeschichte: Kanonistische Abteilung* 65 (1979): 55–119.

Bourgeois, Alfred. "Un diplôme suspect de l'empereur Henri le Saint, à l'abbaye d'Epinal." *Bulletin historique et philologique du Comité des Travaux Historiques et Scientifiques* (1895): 383–88.

Brasme, Maryvonne, Isabelle Brousselle, François-Xavier Caillet, Paul Chaffenet, Boris Detant, Michèle Gaillard, Klaus Krönert, and Charles Mériaux. "La Vie de sainte Eusébie de Hamage (Nord)." *Revue du Nord* 97 (2015): 385–98.

Budny, Mildred, and Dominic Tweddle. "The Maaseik Embroideries." *Anglo-Saxon England* 13 (1984): 65–97.

Bugyis, Katie. "The Development of the Consecration Rite for Abbesses and Abbots in Central Medieval England." *Traditio* 71 (2016): 91–141.

———. "Ministers of Christ: Benedictine Women Religious in Central Medieval England." Unpublished PhD dissertation, University of Notre Dame, 2015.

———. "The Practice of Penance in Communities of Benedictine Women Religious in Central Medieval England." *Speculum* 92 (2017): 36–84.

Bulteau. "Etude historique et archéologique sur les abbayes de Honnecourt et de Vaucelles." *Bulletin de la Commission d'Histoire du Département du Nord* 16 (1883): 1–111.

Butz, Eva-Maria. "Herrschergedenken als Spiegel von Konsens und Kooperation: Zur politischen Einordnung von Herrschereinträgen in den frühmittelalterlichen *Libri memorialis*." In *Libri vitae. Gebetsgedenken in der Gesellschaft des Frühen*

Mittelalters, edited by Dieter Geuenich and Uwe Ludwig, 305–28. Cologne: Böhlau Verlag, 2015.

———. "Die Sorge um das rechte Gebetsgedenken: Liturgische Memoria und Schriftlichkeit im Nonnenkloster Remiremont im frühen Mittelalter." In *Glaube und Geschlecht: Fromme Frauen, spirituelle Erfahrungen, religiöse Traditionen*, edited by Ruth Albrecht, Annette Bühler-Dietrich, and Florentine Strzelczy, 153–73. Cologne: Böhlau, 2008.

Butz, Eva-Maria, and Alfons Zettler. "Two Early Necrologies: The Examples of Remiremont (c. 820) and Verona (c. 810)." In *Texte, liturgie et mémoire dans l'Eglise du Moyen Âge*, edited by Jean-Luc Dueffic, 197–242. Turnhout: Brepols, 2012.

Bynum, Caroline. *Holy Feast and Holy Fast: The Religious Significance of Food to Medieval Women*. Berkeley: University of California Press, 1987.

Calmet, Augustin. *Histoire ecclésiastique et civile de Lorraine*. 4 vols. Nancy: Jean-Baptiste Vusson, 1728.

———. *Histoire de la Lorraine*. 2nd ed., 7 vols. Nancy: A. Leseure, 1745–1757.

Calvet-Marcadé, Gaëlle. "L'abbé spoliateur de biens monastiques (Francie du Nord, IXe siècle)." In *Compétition et sacré au Haut moyen âge: Entre Médiation et Exclusion*, edited by Philippe Depreux, François Bougard, and Régine Le Jan, 313–27. Turnhout: Brepols, 2015.

Catalogue général des manuscrits des bibliothèques publiques des Départements. Vol. 3. Paris: Imprimerie Nationale, 1861.

Chantinne, Frédéric, and Philippe Mignot. "La collégiale Sainte-Gertrude de Nivelles: Réexamen du dossier archéologique." *Hortus artium medievalium* 20 (2014): 513–19.

Choux, Jacques. "Décadence et réforme monastique dans la province de Trêves, 855–959." In *Gérard de Brogne et son oeuvre réformatrice: Etudes publiées à l'occasion du millénaire de sa mort*. Special issue, *Revue bénédictine* 70 (1960): 204–23. Maredsous: Abbaye de Maredsous, 1960.

———. *Recherches sur le diocèse de Toul au temps de la réforme grégorienne. L'épiscopat de Pibon, évêque de Toul (1069–1107)*. Nancy: Société d'Archéologie Lorraine, 1952.

Choy, Renie S. *Intercessory Prayer and the Monastic Ideal in the Time of the Carolingian Reforms*. Oxford: Oxford University Press, 2016.

Clausen, M. A. *The Reform of the Frankish Church: Chrodegang of Metz and the Regula canonicorum in the Eighth Century*. Cambridge: Cambridge University Press, 2004.

Codex Eyckensis: An Insular Gospel Book from the Abbey of Aldeneik. Introduction by Christian Coppens, Albert Derolez, and Hubert Heymans. Maaseik: Maaseik Town Council, 1994.

Cohen, Adam S. *The Uta Codex: Art, Philosophy, and Reform in Eleventh-Century Germany*. University Park: Pennsylvania State University Press, 2000.

Collery, M. "Tissus et broderies attribuées aux saintes Harlinde et Relinde." *Bulletin de la Société Royale d'Archéologie de Bruxelles* (1951): 1–26.

Collins, Samuel W. *The Carolingian Debate over Sacred Space*. New York: Palgrave, 2012.

Constable, Giles. *Letters and Letter-collections*. Turnhout: Brepols, 1976.

———. "The 'Liber Memorialis' of Remiremont." *Speculum* 47 (1972): 261–67.

——. "Moderation and Restraint in Ascetic Practices in the Middle Ages." In *Culture and Spirituality in Medieval Europe*, art. 10:315–27. Aldershot: Variorum, 1996.

Coon, Lynda L. *Dark Age Bodies: Gender and Monastic Practice in the Early Medieval West*. Philadelphia: University of Pennsylvania Press, 2011.

Cooper, Kate. "The Bride of Christ, the 'Male Woman,' and the Female Reader in Late Antiquity." In *The Oxford Handbook of Women and Gender in Medieval Europe*, edited by Judith M. Bennett and Rutz Mazo Karras, 530–44. Oxford: Oxford University Press, 2013.

Corbet, Patrick. *Les saints ottoniens: Sainteté dynastique, sainteté royale et sainteté féminine autour de l'an Mil*. Sigmaringen: Jan Thorbecke Verlag, 1986.

Crick, Julia. "The Wealth, Patronage, and Connections of Women's Houses in Late Anglo-Saxon England." *Revue bénédictine* 109 (1999): 154–84.

Crook, John. *The Architectural Setting of the Cult of Saints in the Early Christian West c. 300–c. 1200*. Oxford: Oxford University Press, 2000.

Crusius, Irene. "Sanctimoniales quae se canonicas vocant: Das Kanonissenstift als Forschungsproblem." In *Studien zum Kanonissenstift*, edited by Irene Crusius, 9–38. Göttingen: Vandenhoeck und Ruprecht, 2001.

Cüppers, Heinz. "Pfalzel—Römischer Palast, Kloster und Stift, Burg und Stadt." In *Pfalzel: Geschichte und Gegenwart*, 13–117. Trier: Arbeitsgemeinschaft Pfalzeler Chronik, 1989.

Daris, Jacques. "Vie de S. Aldegonde; Charte de dotation de l'abbaye de Maubeuge; Revenus de ses terres." *Analectes pour servir à l'histoire ecclésiastique de la Belgique* 2:36–47. Louvain: Ch. Peeters, 1865.

De Brueker, M. "Suaire de Sainte Waudru, IXe–Xe siècle / Lijkwade van Sint-Waldetrudis, 9de–10de eeuw." *Bulletin. Institut royal du patrimoine artistique / Koninklijk Instituut voor het Kunstpatrimonium* 26 (1994–95): 234–35.

De Bruyne, Donatien. "Un feuillet oncial d'une règle de moniales." *Revue bénédictine* 35 (1923): 126–28.

De Clercq, Carlo. *La législation religieuse franque: Etude sur les actes de conciles et les capitulaires, les statuts diocésains et les règles monastiques*. Vol. 2, *De Louis le Pieux à la fin du Xe siècle (814–900)*. Antwerp: Centre de recherches historiques, 1958.

De Coster, L. "Trouvaille de monnaies du onzième siècle." *Revue de la Numismatique Belge*, 2nd ser., 6 (1856): 398–439.

De Grauwe, Luc. *De Wachtendonckse psalmen en glossen: Een lexicologisch-woordgeografische studie met proeve van kritische leestekst en glossaria*. 2 vols. Ghent: Secretariaat van de Koninklijke Academie voor Nederlandse Taal- en Letterkunde, 1979–82.

De Jong, Mayke. "Carolingian Monasticism: The Power of Prayer." In *The New Cambridge Medieval History*, edited by Rosamund McKitterick, 2:622–53. Cambridge: Cambridge University Press, 1995.

——. "Growing Up in a Carolingian Monastery: Magister Hildemar and His Oblates." *Journal of Medieval History* 9 (1983): 99–128.

Delanne, Blanche. *Histoire de la ville de Nivelles: Des origines au XIIIe siècle*. Nivelles: Havaux, 1944.

Delattre, Jean-Luc. "L'hôpital monastique de Nivelles des origines à 1136." *Het Belgisch ziekenhuis / L'hôpital Belge* 8, no. 48 (1964): 49–60.

De Moreau, Edouard. *Histoire de l'église en Belgique*. 6 vols. Brussels: L'édition universelle, 1940–48.

De Morembert, T. Epinal [S. Goery]. In *Dictionnaire d'histoire et de géographie ecclésiastiques* 15:605–7. Paris: Letouzey et Ané, 1963.

Derolez, Albert. "The Manuscript." In *Codex Eyckensis: An Insular Gospel Book from the Abbey of Aldeneik*. Introduction by Christian Coppens, Albert Derolez, and Hubert Heymans, 17–37. Maaseik: Maaseik Town Council, 1994.

De Seilhac, Lazare. "L'utilisation de la Règle de Saint Benoît dans les monastères féminins." In *Atti del 7° Congresso internazionale di studi sull'alto medioevo: Norcia, Subiaco, Cassino, Montecassino, 29 settembre–5 ottobre 1980*, 2:527–49. Spoleto: Centro italiano di studi sull'alto Medioevo, 1982.

Deshusses, Jean. *Le sacramentaire Grégorien: Ses principales formes d'après les plus anciens manuscrits*. Freiburg: Editions Universitaires Fribourg, 1971.

De Simpel, Francis. "L'abbaye de Messines, une officine de faussaires au XIe siècle." *Mémoires de la Société d'Histoire de Comines-Warneton et de la Région* 35 (2005): 19–30.

Despy, Georges. "Les chapitres de chanoinesses nobles en Belgique au moyen âge." *Annales du XXXVIe congrès de la fédération archéologique et historique de Belgique*, 169–79. Ghent: Maatschappij voor Geschiedenis en Oudheidkunde, 1956.

———. "Moustier-sur-Sambre, abbaye Mérovingienne." *Annales de la Société Archéologique de Namur* 45 (1949–50): 147–61.

———. "Note sur deux actes pontificaux inédits du XIIIe siècle concernant le statut des chanoinesses séculières." *Bulletin de la Commission Royale d'Histoire—Handelingen van de Koninklijke Commissie voor Geschiedenis* 115 (1950): 427–41.

———. "Note sur le sens de capitulum." *Archivum Latinitatis Medii Aevi* 20 (1950): 245–54.

De Vogüé, Adalbert. *Histoire littéraire du mouvement monastique dans l'Antiquité: Première partie: Le monachisme latin*. Vol. 12, *À l'aube du Moyen Âge (650–830)*. Paris: Les Editions du Cerf, 2008.

De Vriendt, François. "Le dossier hagiographique de Ste Waudru, abbesse de Mons (IXe–XIIe s.)." *Mémoires et publications de la Société des Sciences, des Arts et des Lettres du Hainaut* 98 (1996): 1–37.

Dewez, Jules. *Histoire de l'abbaye de Saint-Pierre d'Hasnon*. Lille: Imprimerie Salésienne, 1890.

Dey, Hendrik W. "Bringing Chaos Out of Order: New Approaches to the Study of Early Western Monasticism." In *Western Monasticism ante litteram: The Spaces of Monastic Observance in Late Antiquity and the Early Middle Ages*, edited by Hendrik Dey and Elisabeth Fentress, 19–40. Turnhout: Brepols, 2011.

———. "*Diaconiae, xenodochia, hospitalia* and Monasteries: 'Social Security' and the Meaning of Monasticism in Early Medieval Rome." *Early Medieval Europe* 16 (2008): 398–422.

D'Haenens, Albert. *Les invasions Normandes en Belgique au IXe siècle: Le phénomène et sa répercussion dans l'historiographie médiévale*. Louvain: Bureaux du Recueil and Publications Universitaires de Louvain, 1967.

Diem, Albrecht. "The Carolingians and the Regula Benedicti." In *Religious Franks: Religion and Power in the Frankish Kingdoms; Studies in Honour of Mayke de Jong*, edited by Dorine Van Espelo, 231–51. Manchester: Manchester University Press, 2016.

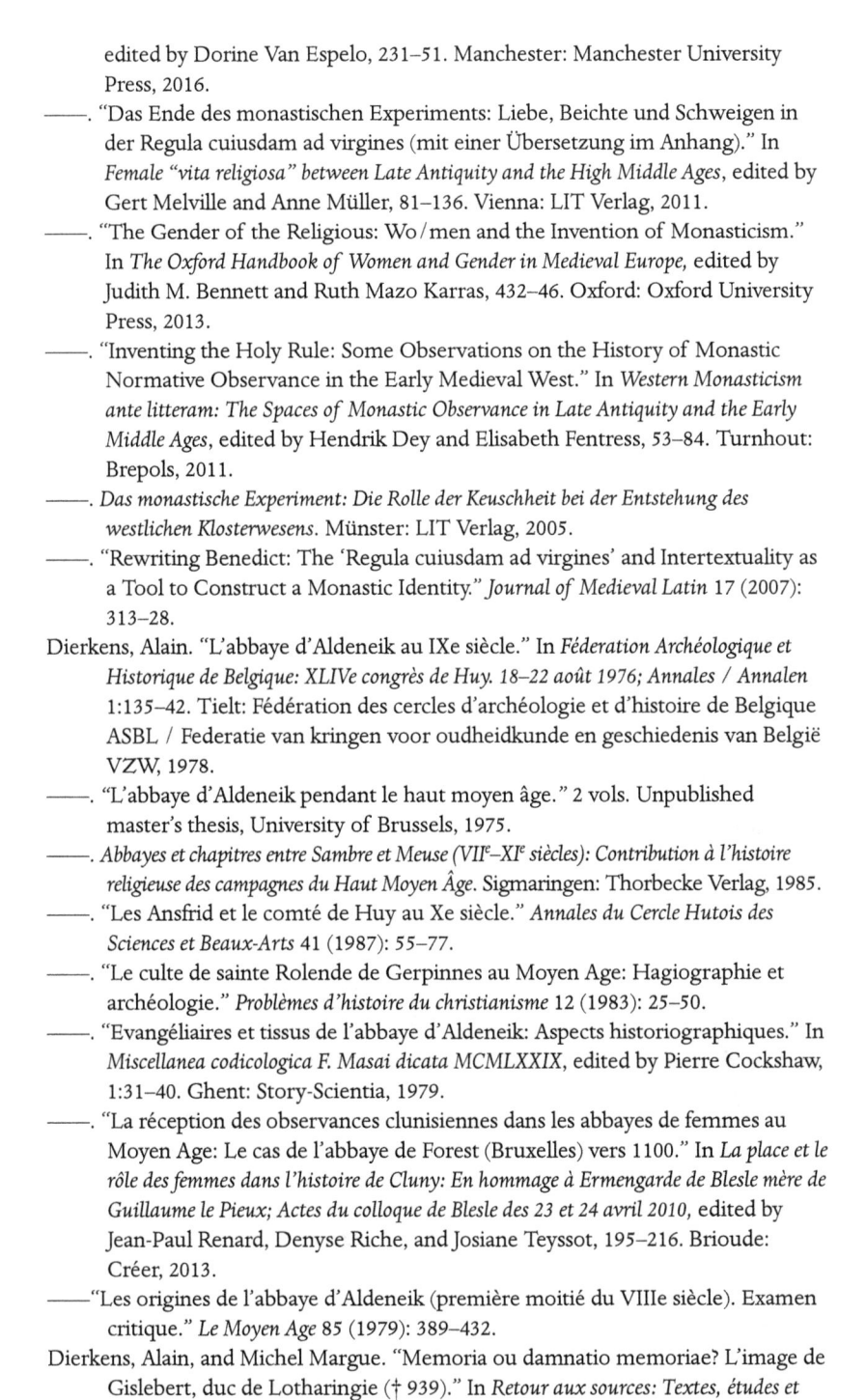

———. "Das Ende des monastischen Experiments: Liebe, Beichte und Schweigen in der Regula cuiusdam ad virgines (mit einer Übersetzung im Anhang)." In *Female "vita religiosa" between Late Antiquity and the High Middle Ages*, edited by Gert Melville and Anne Müller, 81–136. Vienna: LIT Verlag, 2011.

———. "The Gender of the Religious: Wo/men and the Invention of Monasticism." In *The Oxford Handbook of Women and Gender in Medieval Europe*, edited by Judith M. Bennett and Ruth Mazo Karras, 432–46. Oxford: Oxford University Press, 2013.

———. "Inventing the Holy Rule: Some Observations on the History of Monastic Normative Observance in the Early Medieval West." In *Western Monasticism ante litteram: The Spaces of Monastic Observance in Late Antiquity and the Early Middle Ages*, edited by Hendrik Dey and Elisabeth Fentress, 53–84. Turnhout: Brepols, 2011.

———. *Das monastische Experiment: Die Rolle der Keuschheit bei der Entstehung des westlichen Klosterwesens*. Münster: LIT Verlag, 2005.

———. "Rewriting Benedict: The 'Regula cuiusdam ad virgines' and Intertextuality as a Tool to Construct a Monastic Identity." *Journal of Medieval Latin* 17 (2007): 313–28.

Dierkens, Alain. "L'abbaye d'Aldeneik au IXe siècle." In *Fédération Archéologique et Historique de Belgique: XLIVe congrès de Huy. 18–22 août 1976; Annales / Annalen* 1:135–42. Tielt: Fédération des cercles d'archéologie et d'histoire de Belgique ASBL / Federatie van kringen voor oudheidkunde en geschiedenis van België VZW, 1978.

———. "L'abbaye d'Aldeneik pendant le haut moyen âge." 2 vols. Unpublished master's thesis, University of Brussels, 1975.

———. *Abbayes et chapitres entre Sambre et Meuse (VIIe–XIe siècles): Contribution à l'histoire religieuse des campagnes du Haut Moyen Âge*. Sigmaringen: Thorbecke Verlag, 1985.

———. "Les Ansfrid et le comté de Huy au Xe siècle." *Annales du Cercle Hutois des Sciences et Beaux-Arts* 41 (1987): 55–77.

———. "Le culte de sainte Rolende de Gerpinnes au Moyen Age: Hagiographie et archéologie." *Problèmes d'histoire du christianisme* 12 (1983): 25–50.

———. "Evangéliaires et tissus de l'abbaye d'Aldeneik: Aspects historiographiques." In *Miscellanea codicologica F. Masai dicata MCMLXXIX*, edited by Pierre Cockshaw, 1:31–40. Ghent: Story-Scientia, 1979.

———. "La réception des observances clunisiennes dans les abbayes de femmes au Moyen Age: Le cas de l'abbaye de Forest (Bruxelles) vers 1100." In *La place et le rôle des femmes dans l'histoire de Cluny: En hommage à Ermengarde de Blesle mère de Guillaume le Pieux; Actes du colloque de Blesle des 23 et 24 avril 2010*, edited by Jean-Paul Renard, Denyse Riche, and Josiane Teyssot, 195–216. Brioude: Créer, 2013.

———. "Les origines de l'abbaye d'Aldeneik (première moitié du VIIIe siècle). Examen critique." *Le Moyen Age* 85 (1979): 389–432.

Dierkens, Alain, and Michel Margue. "Memoria ou damnatio memoriae? L'image de Gislebert, duc de Lotharingie († 939)." In *Retour aux sources: Textes, études et documents d'histoire médiévale offerts à Michel Parisse*, edited by Sylvain Gouguenheim, 869–90. Paris: Editions A & J Picard, 2004.

Doppler, P. "Het adelijk stift van Munsterbilsen." *De Maasgouw* 9 (1887): 162–64.

Dopsch, Alfons. "Trierer Urkundenfälschungen." *Neues Archiv der Gesellschaft für ältere deutsche Geschichtskunde* 25 (1900): 317–44.

Dumas, Auguste. "L'église de Reims au temps des luttes entre Carolingiens et Robertiens (888–1027)." *Revue d'histoire de l'église de France* 30 (1944): 5–38.

Dupont, Christiane. "Les domaines des ducs en basse-Lotharingie au XIe siècle." In *La maison d'Ardenne Xe-XIe siècles: Actes des Journées Lotharingiennes 24–26 octobre 1980*, 241–57. Luxembourg: Publications de la section historique de l'Institut G.-D. de Luxembourg ci-devant "Société Archéologique du Grand-Duché", 1981.

Egbert Erzbischof von Trier 977–993. Gedenkschrift der Diözese Trier zum 1000. Todestag, 2 vols, edited by Andreas Weiner, Rita Heyen, and Franz J. Ronig. Trier: Selbstverlag des Rheinisches Landesmuseums, 1993.

Ehlers, Caspar. "Franken und Sachsen gründen Klöster: Beobachtungen zu Integrationsprozesses des 8.-10. Jahrhunderts am Beispiel von Essen, Gandersheim und Quedlinburg." In *Gandersheim und Essen: Vergleichende Untersuchungen zu sächsischen Frauenstiften*, edited by Martin Hoernes and Hedwig Röckelein, 11–31. Essen: Klartext Verlag, 2006.

——. "Der Helfende Herrscher: Immunität, Wahlrecht und Köngisschutz für sächsische Frauenstifte bis 1024." In *Essen und die sächsischen Frauenstifte im Frühmittelalter*, edited by Jan Gerchow and Thomas Schilp, 45–58. Essen: Klartext Verlag, 2003.

El Kholi, Susann. *Lektüre in Frauenkonventen des ostfränkisch-deutschen Reiches vom 8. Jahrhundert bis zur Mitte des 13. Jahrhunderts*. Würzburg: Königshause und Neumann, 1997.

Ellger, Otfried. "Das 'Raumkonzept' der Aachener *Institutio sanctimonialium* von 816 und die Topographie sächsischer Frauenstifte im früheren Mittelalter: Eine Problemübersicht." In *Essen und die sächsischen Frauenstifte im Frühmittelalter*, edited by Jan Gerchow and Thomas Schilp, 129–59. Essen: Klartext Verlag, 2003.

Elliot, Dyan. *The Bride of Christ Goes to Hell: Metaphor and Embodiment in the Lives of Pious Women, 200–1500*. Philadelphia: University of Pennsylvania Press, 2011.

Engels, Odilo. *Klöster und Stifte von der Merowingerzeit bis um 1200*. Bonn: Habelt-Verlag, 2006.

Erkens, Franz-Reiner. "Gorze und St-Evre. Anmerkungen zu den Anfängen der lothringischen Klosterreform des 10. Jahrhunderts." In *Lotharingia. Eine europäische Kernlandschaft um das Jahr 1000. Referate eines Kolloquiums vom 24. bis 26. Mai 1994 in Saarbrücken*, edited by Hans-Walter Herrmann and Reinhard Schneider, 121–41. Saarbrücken: SDV Saarbrücker Druckerei und Verlag, 1995.

Esmyol, Andrea. *Geliebte oder Ehefrau? Konkubinen im frühen Mittelalter*. Cologne: Böhlau, 2002.

Fahrenheim, Günther. "Une construction du premier art roman dans les Vosges: L'église du prieuré de Bleurville." *Le Pays Lorrain* 56 (1975): 3–25.

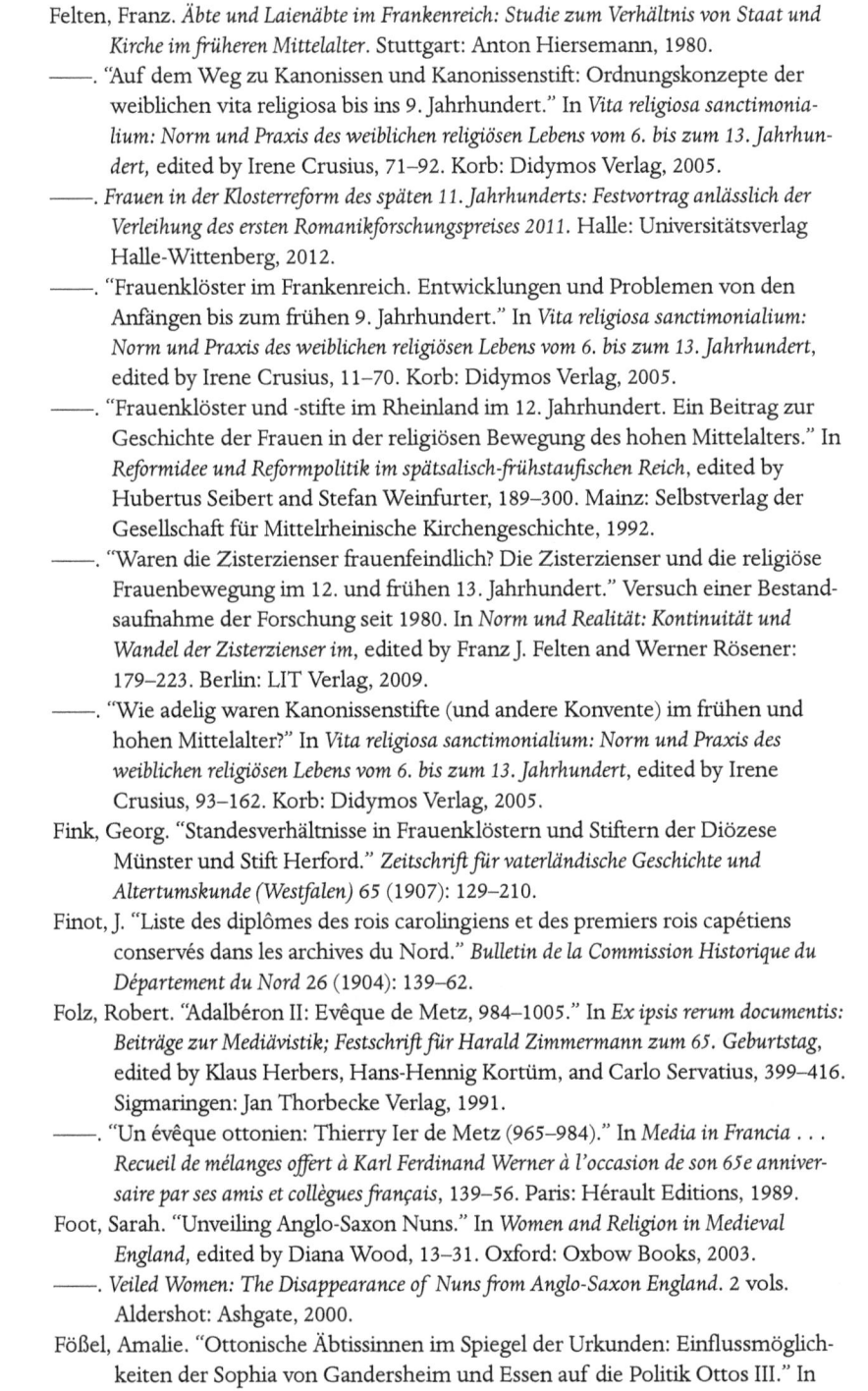

Felten, Franz. *Äbte und Laienäbte im Frankenreich: Studie zum Verhältnis von Staat und Kirche im früheren Mittelalter.* Stuttgart: Anton Hiersemann, 1980.

———. "Auf dem Weg zu Kanonissen und Kanonissenstift: Ordnungskonzepte der weiblichen vita religiosa bis ins 9. Jahrhundert." In *Vita religiosa sanctimonialium: Norm und Praxis des weiblichen religiösen Lebens vom 6. bis zum 13. Jahrhundert,* edited by Irene Crusius, 71–92. Korb: Didymos Verlag, 2005.

———. *Frauen in der Klosterreform des späten 11. Jahrhunderts: Festvortrag anlässlich der Verleihung des ersten Romanikforschungspreises 2011.* Halle: Universitätsverlag Halle-Wittenberg, 2012.

———. "Frauenklöster im Frankenreich. Entwicklungen und Problemen von den Anfängen bis zum frühen 9. Jahrhundert." In *Vita religiosa sanctimonialium: Norm und Praxis des weiblichen religiösen Lebens vom 6. bis zum 13. Jahrhundert,* edited by Irene Crusius, 11–70. Korb: Didymos Verlag, 2005.

———. "Frauenklöster und -stifte im Rheinland im 12. Jahrhundert. Ein Beitrag zur Geschichte der Frauen in der religiösen Bewegung des hohen Mittelalters." In *Reformidee und Reformpolitik im spätsalisch-frühstaufischen Reich,* edited by Hubertus Seibert and Stefan Weinfurter, 189–300. Mainz: Selbstverlag der Gesellschaft für Mittelrheinische Kirchengeschichte, 1992.

———. "Waren die Zisterzienser frauenfeindlich? Die Zisterzienser und die religiöse Frauenbewegung im 12. und frühen 13. Jahrhundert." Versuch einer Bestandsaufnahme der Forschung seit 1980. In *Norm und Realität: Kontinuität und Wandel der Zisterzienser im,* edited by Franz J. Felten and Werner Rösener: 179–223. Berlin: LIT Verlag, 2009.

———. "Wie adelig waren Kanonissenstifte (und andere Konvente) im frühen und hohen Mittelalter?" In *Vita religiosa sanctimonialium: Norm und Praxis des weiblichen religiösen Lebens vom 6. bis zum 13. Jahrhundert,* edited by Irene Crusius, 93–162. Korb: Didymos Verlag, 2005.

Fink, Georg. "Standesverhältnisse in Frauenklöstern und Stiftern der Diözese Münster und Stift Herford." *Zeitschrift für vaterländische Geschichte und Altertumskunde (Westfalen)* 65 (1907): 129–210.

Finot, J. "Liste des diplômes des rois carolingiens et des premiers rois capétiens conservés dans les archives du Nord." *Bulletin de la Commission Historique du Département du Nord* 26 (1904): 139–62.

Folz, Robert. "Adalbéron II: Evêque de Metz, 984–1005." In *Ex ipsis rerum documentis: Beiträge zur Mediävistik; Festschrift für Harald Zimmermann zum 65. Geburtstag,* edited by Klaus Herbers, Hans-Hennig Kortüm, and Carlo Servatius, 399–416. Sigmaringen: Jan Thorbecke Verlag, 1991.

———. "Un évêque ottonien: Thierry Ier de Metz (965–984)." In *Media in Francia . . . Recueil de mélanges offert à Karl Ferdinand Werner à l'occasion de son 65e anniversaire par ses amis et collègues français,* 139–56. Paris: Hérault Editions, 1989.

Foot, Sarah. "Unveiling Anglo-Saxon Nuns." In *Women and Religion in Medieval England,* edited by Diana Wood, 13–31. Oxford: Oxbow Books, 2003.

———. *Veiled Women: The Disappearance of Nuns from Anglo-Saxon England.* 2 vols. Aldershot: Ashgate, 2000.

Fößel, Amalie. "Ottonische Äbtissinnen im Spiegel der Urkunden: Einflussmöglichkeiten der Sophia von Gandersheim und Essen auf die Politik Ottos III." In

Frauen bauen Europa. Internationale Verflechtungen des Frauenstifts Essen, edited by Thomas Schilp, 89–106. Essen: Klartext Verlag, 2011.

Frank, Karl Suso. "Grimlaicus, 'Regula solitarium.'" In *Vita religiosa im Mittelalter: Festschrift für Kaspar Elm zum 70. Geburtstag*, edited by Franz J. Felten and Nikolas Jaspert, 21–35. Berlin: Duncker und Humblot, 1999.

Fray, Jean-Luc. *Villes et bourgs de Lorraine: réseaux urbains et centralité au Moyen âge*. Clermont-Ferrand: Presses Universitaires Blaise Pascal, 2006.

——. "Le temporel de l'abbaye Sainte-Glossinde de Metz (XIe–XIIIe siècles)." *Annuaire de la Société d'Histoire et d'Archéologie de la Lorraine* 80 (1980): 103–34.

French, Katherine L. "Religion and Popular Beliefs: Choices, Constraints, and Creativity for Christian Women." In *A Cultural History of Women in the Middle Ages*, edited by Kim M. Phillips, 59–83. London: Bloomsbury, 2013.

Fried, Johannes. "Ludwig, Papsttum und die fränkische Kirche." In *Charlemagne's Heir: New Perspectives on the Reign of Louis the Pious (814–840)*, edited by Peter Godman and Roger Collins, 231–73. Oxford: Oxford University Press, 1990.

Gaillard, Michèle. *D'une réforme à l'autre (816–934): Les communautés religieuses en Lorraine à l'époque Carolingienne*. Paris: Publications de la Sorbonne, 2006.

——. "Du pouvoir des femmes en Francia Media: Epouses et filles des souverains (ca. 850–ca. 950)." In *De la Mer du Nord à la Méditerranée. Francia Media, une région au coeur de l'Europe (c. 840–c. 1050): Actes du colloque international (Metz, Luxembourg, Trèves, 8–11 février 2006)*, edited by Michèle Gaillard, Michel Margue, Alain Dierkens, and Hérold Pettiau, 301–14. Luxemburg: CLUDEM, 2011.

——. "Les fondations d'abbayes féminines dans le Nord et l'Est de la Gaule à la fin du VIe siècle." *Revue d'histoire de l'église de France* 76 (1990): 6–20.

——. "Moines, chanoines et religieuses en Lorraine au IXe siècle." In *Frühformen von Stiftskirchen in Europa. Funktion und Wandel religiöser Frauengemeinschaften vom 6. bis zum Ende des 11. Jahrhunderts. Festgabe für Dieter Mertens zum 65. Geburtstag*, edited by Sönke Lorenz and Thomas Zotz, 231–49. Leinfelden-Echterdingen: DRW-Verlag, 2005.

——. "Aux origines de Saint-Sauveur: Le monastère de Bonmoutier du VIIe siècle au début du XIe siècle." In *L'abbaye Saint-Sauveur-en-Vosges, mille ans d'histoire: Actes du Colloque du Millénaire de Saint-Sauveur*, edited by Catherine Guyon and Cédric Andriot. *Annales de l'Est* (2010): 31–36.

Gallia christiana in provincias ecclesiasticas distributa, 16 vols. Various publishers: 1715–1865.

Gandersheim und Essen: Vergleichende Untersuchungen zu sächsischen Frauenstiften. Edited by Martin Hoernes and Hedwig Röckelein. Essen: Klartext, 2006.

Garver, Valerie L. "Learned Women? Liutberga and the Instruction of Carolingian Women." In *Lay Intellectuals in the Carolingian World*, edited by Patrick Wormald and Janet L. Nelson, 121–38. Cambridge: Cambridge University Press, 2007.

——. "Girlindis and Alpais: Telling the Lives of Two Textile Fabricators in the Carolingian Empire." In *Writing Medieval Women's Lives*, edited by Charlotte N. Goldy and Amy F. Livingstone, 155–72. New York: Palgrave Macmillan, 2012.

——. "Textiles as a Means of Female Religious Participation in the Carolingian World." In *Religious Participation in Ancient and Medieval Societies: Rituals, Interaction and Identity*, edited by Sari Katajala-Peltomaa and Ville Vuolanto, 133–44. Rome: Institutum Romanum Finlandiae, 2013.

——. *Women and Aristocratic Culture in the Carolingian World*. Ithaca, NY: Cornell University Press, 2009.

Gasse-Grandjean, Marie-José. *Les livres dans les abbayes vosgiennes du moyen âge*. Nancy: Presses Universitaires de Nancy, 1992.

——. "La naissance de la bibliothèque de Remiremont." *Annales de l'Est* 46 (1994): 83–102.

Geary, Patrick J. *Furta sacra: Theft of Relics in the Central Middle Ages*. Rev. ed. Princeton: Princeton University Press, 1990.

Genicot, Léopold. "Sur le vocabulaire et les modalités de l'avouerie dans la Belgique actuelle." In *L'avouerie en Lotharingie: Actes des 2es Journées Lotharingiennes, 22–23 oct. 1982*, 9–42. Luxembourg: Publications de la section historique de l'Institut Grand-Ducal de Luxembourg, 1984.

Gérard, Pierre, and Thérèse Gérard. "Lunéville des origines à l'aube du XIIIème siècle." *Annales de l'Est*, 5th ser., 22 (1970): 199–220.

Gerchow, Jan. "Sächsische Frauenstifte im Frühmittelalter." In *Essen und die sächsischen Frauenstifte im Frühmittelalter*, edited by Jan Gerchow and Thomas Schilp, 11–28. Essen: Klartext Verlag, 2003.

Gerzaguet, Jean-Pierre. *L'abbaye féminine de Denain des origines à la fin du XIIIe siècle*. Turnhout: Brepols, 2008.

——. "La fondation d'une communauté de moniales bénédictines à Etrun (diocèse d'Arras-Cambrai en 1088 (?))." In *Retour aux sources: Textes, études et documents d'histoire médiévale offerts à Michel Parisse*, edited by Sylvain Gouguenheim, 129–41. Paris: Editions A & J Picard, 2004.

Geuenich, Dieter. "Anmerkungen zur sogenannten 'anianischen Reform.'" In *Mönchtum, Kirche, Herrschaft 750–1000: Festschrift für Josef Semmler zum 65. Geburtstag*, edited by Dieter R. Bauer, Rudolf Hiestand, Brigitte Kasten, and Lorenz Sönke, 99–112. Sigmaringen: Thorbecke, 1998.

——. "Die Frauengemeinschaft des coenobium Sichingis im X. Jahrhunderts." In *Frühe Kultur in Säckingen: Zehn Studien zu Literatur, Kunst und Geschichte*, edited by Walter Berschin, 55–69. Sigmaringen: Thorbecke, 1990.

——. "Gebetsgedenken und anianische Reform: Beobachtungen zu den Verbrüderungsbeziehungen der Äbte im Reich Ludwigs des Frommen." In *Monastische Reformen im 9. und 10. Jahrhundert*, edited by Raymund Kottje and Helmut Maurer, 79–106. Sigmaringen: Jan Thorbecke Verlag, 1989.

——. "'Richkart, ancilla dei de caenobio Sancti Stephani': Zeugnisse zur Geschichte des Straßburger Frauenklosters St. Stephan in der Karolingerzeit." In *Festschrift für Eduard Hlawitschka zum 65. Geburtstag*, edited by Karl Schnitz and Roland Pauler, 97–110. Kallmünz: Lessleben, 1993.

Gilchrist, Roberta. *Gender and Material Culture: The Archaeology of Religious Women*. London: Routledge, 1994.

Gill, Katherine. "Scandala: Controversies concerning clausura and Women's Religious Communities in Late Medieval Italy." In *Christendom and Its*

Discontents: Exclusion, Persecution, and Rebellion, 1000–1500, edited by Scott L. Waugh and Peter D. Diehl, 177–203. Cambridge: Cambridge University Press, 1996.

Gilsdorf, Sean. *The Favor of Friends: Intercession and Aristocratic Politics in Carolingian and Ottonian Europe.* Leiden: Brill, 2014.

———. *Queenship and Sanctity: The Lives of Mathilda and the Epitaph of Adelheid.* Washington, DC: Catholic University of America Press, 2004.

Goetz, Hans-Werner. "Besitz und Grundherrschaft des Frauenstifts Essen im früheren Mittelalter." In *Frauen bauen Europa: Internationale Verflechtungen des Frauenstifts Essen,* edited by Thomas Schilp, 107–40. Essen: Klartext Verlag, 2011.

Goldsmith, Kenneth. *Uncreative Writing: Managing Language in the Digital Age.* New York: Columbia University Press, 2011.

Goossens, Jan. "Tesi samanunga was edele unde scona." In *Spel van Zinnen: Album A. van Loey,* edited by Ria Jansen-Sieben, Sera De Vriendt, Roland Willemyns, and A. Van Loey, 137–48. Brussels: Editions de l'université de Bruxelles, 1975.

———. "Over Tesi samanunga en zijn context." *Verslagen en mededelingen van de Koninklijke Academie voor Nederlandse taal- en letterkunde* (1999): 175–91.

Goullet, Monique. "Les saints du diocèse de Metz." In *Miracles, vies et réécritures dans l'Occident médiéval,* edited by Martin Heinzelmann and Monique Goullet, 149–317. Ostfildern: Jan Thorbecke Verlag, 2006.

———. "Les saints du diocèse de Toul." In *L'hagiographie du haut moyen âge en Gaule du Nord: Manuscrits, textes et centres de production,* edited by Martin Heinzelmann, 11–89. Stuttgart: Jan Thorbecke Verlag, 2001.

Gneuss, Helmut, and Michael Lapidge. *Anglo-Saxon Manuscripts: A Bibliographical Handlist of Manuscripts and Manuscript Fragments Written or Owned in England up to 1100.* Toronto: University of Toronto Press, 2014.

Green, Laura M. *Educating Women: Cultural Conflict and Victorian Literature.* Columbus: Ohio University Press, 2001.

Griffiths, Fiona J. "The Cross and the 'Cura monialium.' Robert of Arbrissel, John the Evangelist, and the Pastoral Care of Women in the Age of Reform." *Speculum* 83 (2008): 303–30.

———. *The Garden of Delights: Reform and Renaissance for Women in the Twelfth Century.* Philadelphia: University of Pennsylvania Press, 2007.

———. "'Like the Sister of Aaron': Medieval Religious Women as Makers and Donors of Liturgical Textiles." In *Female "vita religiosa" Between Late Antiquity and the High Middle Ages,* edited by Gert Melville and Anne Müller, 343–74. Vienna: LIT Verlag, 2011.

———. "Women and Reform in the Central Middle Ages." In *The Oxford Handbook of Women and Gender in Medieval Europe,* edited by Judith M. Bennett and Ruth Mazo Karras, 447–63. Oxford: Oxford University Press, 2013.

Guild, Rollins, François Heber-Suffrin, and Anne Wagner. "Saint-Maur dans l'organisation ecclésiale de Verdun: Un monastère de femmes et son pèlerinage." In *Espace ecclésial et liturgie au Moyen Âge,* edited by Anne Baud, 347–68. Lyon: Maison de l'Orient et de la Méditerranée Jean Pouilloux, 2010.

BIBLIOGRAPHY

Gussone, Nikolaus. "Die Jungfrauenweihe in ottonischer Zeit nach dem Ritus im "Pontificale Romano-Germanicum." In *Frauen - Kloster - Kunst: Neue Forschungen zur Kulturgeschichte des Mittelalters*, edited by Jeffrey F. Hamburger, 25–42. Turnhout: Brepols, 2007.

Haarländer, Stephanie. "Doppelklöster und ihre Forschungsgeschichte." In *Fromme Frauen - unbequeme Frauen? Weibliches Religiosentum im Mittelalter*, edited by Edeltraud Klueting, 27–44. Hildesheim: Olms, 2006.

Habets, Joseph. "Bijdragen tot de geschiedenis van de voormalige stad Susteren en van de adellijke vrouwenabdij Sint-Salvator aldaar." *Publications de la Société Historique et Archéologique dans le Limbourg* 6 (1869): 441–567.

Haggenmüller, Reinhold. *Die Überlieferung der Beda und Egbert zugeschriebenen Bußbücher*. Frankfurt am Main: Peter Lang, 1991.

Hamilton, Sarah. *The Practice of Penance, 900–1050*. Woodbridge: Boydell Press, 2001.

Hansay, A. *Une prétendue charte originale de l'année 1040 concernant l'abbaye de Munsterbilsen*. Hasselt: Imprimerie et Librairie Fr. Olyff, 1907.

Härdelin, Alf. "An Epithalamium for Nuns: Imagery and Spirituality in Paschasius Radbertus' 'Exposition of Psalm 44 (45).'" In *In Quest of the Kingdom: Ten Papers on Medieval Monastic Spirituality*, edited by Alf Härdelin, 79–107. Stockholm: Almquist and Wiksell International, 1991.

Hartmann, Martina. "Concubina vel regina? Zu einigen Ehefrauen und Konkubinen der karolingischen Könige." *Deutsches Archiv für Erforschung des Mittelalters* 63 (2007): 545–68.

———. "Lotharingien in Arnolfs Reich: Das Königtum Zwentibolds." In *Kaiser Arnolf: Das ostfränkische Reich am Ende des 9. Jahrhunderts*, edited by Franz Fuchs and Peter Schmid, 122–42. Munich: Verlag C. H. Beck, 2002.

Hartmann, Wilfried. *Kirche und Kirchenrecht um 900: Die Bedeutung der spätkarolingischen Zeit für Tradition und Innovation im kirchlichen Recht*. Hanover: Hahnsche Buchhandlung, 2008.

———. *Das Konzil von Worms 868: Überlieferung und Bedeutung*. Göttingen: Vandenhoeck und Ruprecht, 1977.

———. *Die Synoden der Karolingerzeit im Frankenreich und in Italien*. Paderborn: Ferdinand Schöningh, 1989.

Hauck, Albert. *Kirchengeschichte Deutschlands*. 8th ed., 6 vols. Berlin: Akademie-Verlag, 1954.

Heber-Suffrin, François. "Saint-Pierre-aux-Nonnains." In *Congrès archéologique de France: 149e session, 1991; Les Trois-Evêchés et l'ancien duché de Bar*, 495–515. Paris: Société Française d'Archéologie, 1995.

Heene, Katrien. *The Legacy of Paradise: Marriage, Motherhood and Woman in Carolingian Edifying Literature*. Frankfurt am Main: Peter Lang, 1997.

Héfèle, Karl Joseph, and Henri Leclercq. *Histoire des conciles d'après les documents originaux*. 11 vols. Paris: Letouzey, 1907–52.

Heidecker, Karl. *The Divorce of Lothar II: Christian Marriage and Political Power in the Carolingian World*. Ithaca, NY: Cornell University Press, 2010.

Heikkilä, Tuomas. *Vita S. Symeonis Treverensis: Ein hochmittelalterlicher Heiligenkult im Kontext*. Helsinki: Buchhandlung Tiedekirja, 2002.

Helvétius, Anne-Marie. "L'abbatiat laïque comme relais du pouvoir royal aux frontières du royaume: Le cas du nord de la Neustrie au IXe siècle." In *La royauté et les élites dans l'Europe Carolingienne (du début du IXe aux environs de 920)*, edited by Régine Le Jan, 285–99. Villeneuve d'Ascq: Université Charles de Gaulle–Lille 3, 1998.

——. *Abbayes, évêques et laïques: Une politique du pouvoir en Hainaut au moyen âge (VIIe–XIe siècle)*. Brussels: Crédit Communal, 1994.

——. "Les modèles de sainteté dans les monastères de l'espace Belge du VIIIe au Xe siècle." *Revue bénédictine* 103 (1993): 51–67.

——. "Du monastère double au chapitre noble: Moniales et chanoinesses en Basse-Lotharingie." In *Les chapitres de dames nobles entre France et empire: Actes du colloque d'avril 1996 organisé par la Société d'Histoire Locale de Remiremont*, 31–45. Paris: Editions Messene, 1998.

——. "L'organisation des monastères féminins à l'époque mérovingienne." In *Female "vita religiosa" between Late Antiquity and the High Middle Ages*, edited by Gert Melville and Anne Müller, 151–69. Vienna: LIT Verlag, 2011.

——. "La *Passio* de sainte Maxellende et la réforme d'une communauté féminine en Cambrésis." In *Normes et hagiographie dans l'Occident (VIe–XVIe siècle): Actes du colloque international de Lyon 4–6 octobre 2010*, edited by Marie-Céline Isaïa and Thomas Garnier, 167–81. Turnhout: Brepols, 2014.

Helvétius, Anne-Marie, and Michèle Gaillard. "Production de textes et réforme d'un monastère double: L'exemple de Remiremont du VIIe au IXe siècle." In *Frauen - Kloster - Kunst: Neue Forschungen zur Kulturgeschichte des Mittelalters*, edited by Jeffrey F. Hamburger, 383–94. Turnhout: Brepols, 2007.

Helvétius, Anne-Marie, and Jacques Nazet. "Nouvelles considérations sur les faux testaments de sainte Aldegonde de Maubeuge." In *Congrès de Namur: 18–21 VIII. 1988: Actes. XLIXe Congrès de la Fédération des cercles d'archéologie et d'histoire de Belgique et 3e Congrès de l'association des cercles francophones d'histoire et d'archéologie de Belgique*, 1:193–94. Namur: Société Archéologique de Namur, 1988.

Hendrickx, M., and W. Sangers. *De kerkschat van de Sint-Catharinakerk te Maaseik: Beschrijvende inventaris*. s.l.: Provincie Limburg, 1963.

[L'Hermitte, Martin]. *Histoire des saints de la province de Lille, Douay, Orchies: Avec la naissance, progrès, lustre de la religion catholique en ses chastellenies*. Douai: Imprimerie de Barthélémy Bardou, 1638.

Heuclin, Jean. *Hommes de Dieu et fonctionnaires du roi en Gaule du Nord du Ve au IXe siècle (438–817)*. Lille: Presses universitaires du Septentrion, 1998.

Heyen, Franz-Josef. "Pfalzel (Trier-Pfalzel)." In *Germania Benedictina*. Vol. 9, *Die Männer- und Frauenklöster der Benediktiner in Rheinland-Pfalz und Saarland*, edited by Friedhelm Jürgensmeier, 589–98. St. Ottilien: EOS Verlag, 1999.

——. *Untersuchungen zur Geschichte des Benediktinerinnenklosters Pfalzel bei Trier (ca. 700 bis 1016)*. Göttingen: Vandenhoeck und Ruprecht, 1966.

Heymans, Hubert. "The Convent of Eycke and Its Surroundings." In *Codex Eyckensis: An Insular Gospel Book from the Abbey of Aldeneik*. Introduction by Christian Coppens, Albert Derolez, and Hubert Heymans, 11–5. Maaseik: Maaseik Town Council, 1994.

——. "Een Vita roept vragen op. Bijdragen tot de kersteningsgeschiedenis rond het monasterium Eycke." *Limburg* 62 (1983): 123–34.

Hilpisch, Stephan. "Die Entwicklung des Profeßritus der Nonnen." *Studien und Mitteilungen aus dem Benediktiner- und Zisterzienserorden* 66 (1955): 28–34.
———. *Geschichte der Benediktinerinnen*. St. Ottilien: EOS Verlag, 1951.
Hirschmann, Frank G. "Secundum regulam vivere? Zur Instabilität -und Stabilitätmittelalterlicher Frauenklöster im Rheinland." *Rheinische Vierteljahrsblätter* 71 (2007): 101–31.
———. *Stadtplanung, Bauprojekte und Grossbaustellen im 10. und 11. Jahrhundert: Vergleichende Studien zu den Kathedralstädten westlich des Rheins*. Stuttgart: Hiersemann, 1998.
———. *Verdun im hohen Mittelalter: Eine lothringische Kathedralstadt und ihr Umland im Spiegel der geistlichen Institutionen*. 3 vols. Trier: Verlag Trierer Historische Forschungen, 1996.
Hlawitschka, Eduard. *Die Anfänge des Hauses Habsburg-Lothringen: Genealogische Untersuchungen zur Geschichte Lothringens und des Reiches im 9., 10. und 11. Jahrhundert*. Saarbrücken: Minerva-Verlag Thiennes und Nolte, 1969.
———. "Beobachtungen und Überlegungen zur Konventsstärke im Nonnenkloster Remiremont während des 7.– 9. Jahrhunderts." In *Secundum regulam vivere: Festschrift für P. Norbert Backmund O.Praem*, edited by Gert Melville, 31–40. Windberg: Poppe-Verlag, 1978.
———. "Herzog Giselbert von Lothringen und das Kloster Remiremont." *Zeitschrift für die Geschichte des Oberrheins* 108 (1960): 422–65.
———. "Zur Lebensgeschichte Erzbischof Odelrichs von Reims." *Zeitschrift für die Geschichte des Oberrheins* 109 (1961): 1–20.
———. *Studien zur Äbtissinnenreihe von Remiremont (7.–13. Jahrhundert)*. Saarbrücken: Institut für Landeskunde des Saarlandes, 1963.
———. "Zu den klösterlichen Anfängen in St. Maria im Kapitol zu Köln." *Rheinische Vierteljahrsblätter* 31 (1966–67): 1–16.
Hoebanx, J. J. *L'abbaye de Nivelles des origines au XIVe siècle*. Brussels: Palais des Académies / Paleis der Academiën, 1952.
Holvoet, Camille. "Sainte Gertrude de Nivelles: La Vita tripartita du XIe siècle et les techniques de réécriture." Unpublished master's thesis, University of Brussels, 2005–6.
Hopp, Cornelius. *Die ehemalige Frauenstiftskirche St. Salvator zu Susteren und ihre Stellung in der Architektur des 11. Jahrhunderts*. Berlin: LIT Verlag, 2015.
Hörger, Karl. "Die reichsrechtliche Stellung der Fürstäbtissinnen." *Archiv fur Urkundenforschung* 9 (1926): 195–270.
Hotchin, Julie. "Female Religious Life and the 'Cura monialium' in Hirsau Monasticism, 1080 to 1150." In *Listen Daughter: The Speculum Virginum and the Formation of Religious Women in the Middle Ages*, edited by Constant J. Mews, 59–84. New York: Basingstoke, 2001.
Houot, Bernard. "Fondation et origines de la ville d'Epinal." *Annales de la Société d'Emulation du Département des Vosges*, new ser., 1 (1983): 5–14.
Huth, Volkhard. "Die Düsseldorfer Sakramentarhandschrift D1 als Memorialzeugnis: Mit einer Wiedergabe der Namen und Namengruppen." *Frühmittelalterliche Studien* 20 (1986): 213–98.

Huyghe, Gérard. *La clôture des moniales des origines à la fin du XIIIme siècle: Etude historique et juridique*. Roubaix: Imprimerie J. Verschave-Hourquin, 1944.

Huyghebaert, Nicolas-Norbert. "Abbaye de Notre-Dame à Messines." In *Monasticon Belge*. Vol. 3, *Province de Flandre occidentale*, 1:211–38. Liège: Centre national de recherches d'histoire religieuse, 1960.

———. "L'abbesse Frisilde et les débuts de l'abbaye de Messines." *Revue d'histoire ecclésiastique* 50 (1955): 141–57.

———. "Adela van Frankrijk, gravin van Vlaanderen, stichteres van de abdij van Mesen (ca. 1017–1079)." *Iepers Kwartier* 15 (1979): 66–132.

Huysmans, Ortwin. "Peace and Purges: Episcopal Administration of Religious Communities and the Contested See of Reims (c. 931–53)." *Revue bénédictine* 126 (2016): 287–323.

———. "Tutor ac nutritor. Episcopal Agency, Lordship and the Administration of Religious Communities: Ecclesiastical Province of Rheims c. 888–1073." Unpublished doctoral dissertation, University of Louvain, 2016.

Hyam, Jane. "Ermentrude and Richildis." In *Charles the Bald: Court and Kingdom. Papers Based on a Colloquium Held in London in April 1979*, edited by Margaret T. Gibson and Janet Nelson, 153–68. Oxford: British Archaeological Reprints, 1981.

Ilisch, Peter. "Die Münzprägung im Herzogtum Niederlothringen II: Die Münzprägung im südwestlichen Niederlothringen und in Flandern im 10. und 11. Jahrhundert." *Jaarboek van het Koninklijk Nederlandsch Genootschap voor munt- en penningkunde* 100 (2014).

Iogna-Prat, Dominique. "Léon IX, pape et consécrateur." In *Léon IX et son temps: Actes du colloque international organisé par l'Institut d'Histoire Médiévale de l'Université Marc-Bloch, Strasbourg-Eguisheim, 20–22 juin 2002*, edited by Georges Bischoff and Benoît-Michel Tock, 355–83. Turnhout: Brepols, 2006.

———. *La Maison-Dieu: Une histoire monumentale de l'église au moyen âge v. 800–v. 1200*. Paris: Editions du Seuil, 2006.

Irsigler, Franz. "Markt- und Messeprivilegien auf Reichsgebiet im Mittelalter." In *Das Privileg im Europäischen Vergleich*, edited by Barbara Dölemeyer and Heinz Mohnhaupt, 2:189–214. Frankfurt a. M.: Klostermann, 1999.

Jäggi, Carola, and Uwe Lobbedey. "Kirche und Klausur: Zur Architektur Mittelalterlicher Frauenklöster." In *Krone und Schleier: Kunst aus mittelalterlichen Frauenklöstern*, edited by Jutta Frings, 88–103. Munich: Hirmer, 2005.

Jakobi, Franz-Josef. "Diptychen als frühe Form der Gedenk-Aufzeichnungen. Zum 'Herrscher-Diptychon' im Liber Memorialis von Remiremont." *Frühmittelalterliche Studien* 20 (1986): 186–212.

———. "Der *Liber Memorialis* von Remiremont." In *Libri vitae. Gebetsgedenken in der Gesellschaft des Frühen Mittelalters*, edited by Dieter Geuenich and Uwe Ludwig, 87–121. Cologne: Böhlau Verlag, 2015.

Jarrett, Jonathan. "Power over Past and Future: Abbess Emma and the Nunnery of Sant Joan de les Abadesses." *Early Medieval Europe* 12 (2003): 229–58.

Jayatilaka, Rohini. "The Old English Benedictine Rule: Writing for Women and Men." *Anglo-Saxon England* 32 (2003): 147–88.

Jean, L. *Une intéressante donation au Xe siècle: Charte de fondation de l'abbaye de Vergaville*. 2nd ed. Metz: Imprimerie Lorraine, 1896.

Jestice, Phyllis. *Wayward Monks and the Religious Revolution of the Eleventh Century.* Leiden: Brill, 1997.

Jones, Christopher A. "Monastic Identity and Sodomitic Danger in the Occupatio by Odo of Cluny." *Speculum* 82 (2007): 1–53.

Jongbloed, Hein H. "Listige Immo en Herswind: Een politieke wildebras in het Maasdal (938–960) en zijn in Thorn rustende dochter." *Jaarboek: Limburgs Geschied- en Oudheidkundig Genootschap* 145 (2009): 9–67.

Joye, Sylvie. *La femme ravie: Le mariage par rapt dans les sociétés occidentales du haut Moyen Âge.* Turnhout: Brepols, 2012.

Joye, Sylvie, and Paul Bertrand. "Les 'testaments des saints' en Chrétienté occidentale." In *Normes et hagiographie dans l'Occident (VIe–XVIe siècle): Actes du colloque international de Lyon 4–6 octobre 2010*, edited by Marie-Céline Isaïa and Thomas Garnier, 293–307. Turnhout: Brepols, 2014.

Keller, Hagen. "Otto der Große urkundet im Bodenseegebiet: Inszenierungen der 'Gegenwart des Herrschers' in einer vom König selten besuchten Landschaft." In *Mediaevalia Augiensia. Forschungen zur Geschichte des Mittelalters*, edited by Jürgen Petersohn, 205–45. Stuttgart: Jan Thorbecke Verlag, 2001.

Kellner, Maximilian G. *Die Ungarneinfälle im Bild der Quellen bis 1150: Von der "Gens detestanda" zur "Gens ad fidem Christi conversa."* Munich: Verlag Ungarisches Institut, 1997.

Kersken, Hartwig. *Zwischen Glaube und Welt: Studien zur Geschichte der religiösen Frauengemeinschaft Thorn von der Gründung bis zur Mitte des 14. Jahrhunderts.* Hilversum: Uitgeverij Verloren, 2016.

Kettemann, Walter. "Subsidia Anianensia: Überlieferungs- und textgeschichtliche Untersuchungen zur Geschichte Witiza-Benedikts, seines Klosters Aniane und zur sogenannten 'anianischen Reform.'" Unpublished PhD dissertation, University of Duisburg-Essen, 2008.

Knichel, Martina. "Trier (-Oeren), St. Irminen." In *Germania Benedictina*. Vol. 9, *Die Männer- und Frauenklöster der Benediktiner in Rheinland-Pfalz und Saarland*, edited by Friedhelm Jürgensmeier, 938–68. St. Ottilien: EOS Verlag, 1999.

Köhn, Rolf. "Dimensionen und Funktionen des Öffentlichen und Privaten in der mittelalterlichen Korrespondenz." In *Das Öffentliche und Private in der Vormoderne*, edited by Gert Melville and Peter Von Moos, 309–58. Cologne: Böhlau, 1998.

Koninckx, E. H. A. "De abdij van Munsterbilzen en haar heiligen." *Limburg* 29 (1950): 13–20, 29–32, 47–50, 88–94, 105–12, 127–34.

Körntgen, Ludger. *Studien zu den Quellen der frühmittelalterlichen Bußbücher.* Sigmaringen: Thorbecke Verlag, 1993.

Kottje, Raymund. "Claustra sine armario? Zum Unterschied von Kloster und Stift im Mittelalter." In *Consuetudines monasticae: Festgabe für Kassius Hallinger*, edited by Joachim F. Angerer and Josef Lenzenweger, 125–44. Rome: Pontificio Ateneo S. Anselmo, 1982.

——. "Einheit und Vielfalt des kirchlichen Lebens in der Karolingerzeit." *Zeitschrift für Kirchengeschichte* 76 (1965): 323–42.

Koziol, Geoffrey. "Flothilde's Visions and Flodoard's Histories: A Tenth-Century Mutation?" *Early Medieval Europe* 24 (2016): 160–84.

284 BIBLIOGRAPHY

——. *The Politics of Memory and Identity in Carolingian Royal Diplomas: The West Frankish Kingdom (840–987)*. Turnhout: Brepols, 2012.

Kraemer, Charles. *Aux origines de Remiremont: Le Saint-Mont. Guide historique et archéologique du Saint-Mont et de ses environs*. Epinal: Groupe de recherches archéologiques des Hautes-Vosges, 1991.

——. "Le Saint-Mont: Première implantation monastique de Lorraine." *Archéologie médiévale* 19 (1989): 57–79.

Kramer, Rutger. "Great Expectations: Imperial Ideologies and Ecclesiastical Reforms from Charlemagne to Louis the Pious (813–822)." Unpublished PhD dissertation, Free University of Berlin, 2014.

Krone und Schleier: Kunst aus mittelalterlichen Frauenklöstern, edited by Jutta Frings and Jan Gerchow. Bonn: Hirmer Verlag / Essen: Kunst- und Ausstellungshalle der Bundesrepublik Deutschland, and Ruhrlandmuseum, 2005.

Krönert, Klaus. *L'exaltation de Trèves: Ecriture hagiographique et passé historique de la métropole mosellane VIIIe–XIe siècle*. Sigmaringen: Jan Thorbecke Verlag, 2010.

Kupper, Jean-Louis. *Liège et l'église impériale 11e–12e siècles*. Paris: Société d'édition Les Belles lettres, 1981.

——. *Notger de Liège (972–1008)*. Brussels: Académie Royale de Belgique, 2015.

Küsters, Urban. "Formen und Modelle religiöser Frauengemeinschaften im Umkreis der Hirsauer Reform des 11. und 12. Jahrhunderts." In *Hirsau St. Peter und Paul 1091–1991*. Vol. 2, *Geschichte, Lebens- und Verfassungsformen eines Reformklosters*, edited by Klaus Schreiner, 195–220. Stuttgart: Kommissionsverlag and Konrad Theiss Verlag, 1991.

Lange, Klaus. "Die Krypta der Essener Stiftskirche: Heuristische Überlegungen zu ihrer architektonisch-liturgischen Konzeption." In *Essen und die sächsischen Frauenstifte im Frühmittelalter*, edited by Jan Gerchow and Thomas Schilp, 161–83. Essen: Klartext Verlag, 2003.

Laporte, Jean. "Une varieté de rouleaux des morts: Le testament de saint Ansegise." *Revue Mabillon* 42 (1952): 45–55.

Laret-Kayser, Arlette. "La fonction et les pouvoirs ducaux en Basse-Lotharingie au XIe siècle." In *La maison d'Ardenne Xe–XIe siècles: Actes des Journées Lotharingiennes 24–26 octobre 1980*, 133–52. Luxembourg: Publications de la section historique de l'Institut Grand-Ducal de Luxembourg, 1981.

La Rocca, Cristina. "Monachesimo femminile e poteri delle regine tra VIII e IX secolo." In *Il monachesimo italiano dall'età longobarda all'età ottoniana (secc. VIII–X)*, edited by Giovanni Spinelli, 119–43. Cesena: Centro Storico Benedettino Italiano, 2006.

Lauwers, Michel. "'Circuitus et figura': Exégèse, images et structuration des complexes monastiques dans l'Occident médiéval (IXe–XIIe siècle)." In *Monastères et espace social: Genèse et transformation d'un système de lieux dans l'Occident médiéval*, edited by Michel Lauwers, 43–109. Turnhout: Brepols, 2014.

Leclercq, Jean. "Théorie et pratique de la clôture au moyen-âge." In *Les religieuses dans le cloître et dans le monde, des origines à nos jours: Actes du Deuxième Colloque International du C.E.R.C.O.R., Poitiers, 29 septembre–2 octobre 1988*, 471–77. Poitiers: Publications de l'Université de Saint-Etienne, 1994.

Leclère, Sophie. "L'abbaye d'Andenne, VIIe–XIIIe siècle: De la fondation aristocratique par sainte Begge à la transformation en chapitre noble." 2 vols. Unpublished master's thesis, University of Brussels, 2011.
Legl, Frank. *Studien zur Geschichte der Grafen von Dagsburg-Egisheim*. Saarbrücken: Saarbrücker Druckerei und Verlag, 1998.
Le Glay. "Mémoire sur les archives de l'abbaye de Marchiennes." *Mémoires de la Société Impériale d'Agriculture, Sciences et Arts, séant à Douai, centrale du Département du Nord*, 2nd ser., 2 (1852–53): 127–94.
Le Jan, Régine. "De la France du Nord à l'Empire: Réflexions sur les structures de parenté au tournant de l'An Mil." In *Hommes et sociétés dans l'Europe de l'an mil: Actes du colloque de Conques, 19–21 mai 2000*, edited by Pierre Bonnassié and Pierre Toubert, 163–84. Toulouse: Presses universitaires du Mirail, 2004.
———. *Famille et pouvoir dans le monde franc (VIIe–Xe siècle): Essai d'anthropologie sociale*. Paris: Publications de la Sorbonne, 1995.
Lemoine, Louis. "Contribution à la reconstitution des scriptoria bretons du haut moyen âge." *Archivum Latinitatis Medii Aevi* 59 (2001): 261–68.
Lepage, Henri. *L'abbaye de Bouxières*. Nancy: Wiener, 1859.
Leroquais, Victor. *Les sacramentaires et les missels manuscrits des bibliothèques publiques de France*. 4 vols. Paris: Imprimerie Nationale, 1924.
Lesne, Emile. *L'origine des menses dans le temporel des églises et des monastères de France au IXe siècle*. Lille: R. Giard / Paris: H. Champion, 1910.
Lester, Anne E. *Creating Cistercian Nuns: The Women's Religious Movement and Its Reform in Thirteenth-Century Champagne*. Ithaca, NY: Cornell University Press, 2011.
Levison, Wilhelm. Review of Schäfer's *Die Kanonissenstifter*. *Westdeutsche Zeitschrift für Geschichte und Kunst* 27 (1909): 491–512.
Levy, Joseph. *Geschichte des Klosters, der Vogtei und Pfarrei Herbitzheim*. Strassburg: Buchdruckerei E. Bauer, 1892.
Leyser, Karl J. *Rule and Conflict in an Early Medieval Society: Ottonian Saxony*. London: Edward Arnold, 1979.
Liétard, C. *Les chanoinesses de Maubeuge (661–1790)*. Lille: E. Raoust-Leleu, 1933.
Lifshitz, Felice. "Is Mother Superior? Towards a History of Feminine Amtscharisma." In *Medieval Mothering*, edited by John C. Parsons and Bonnie Wheeler, 117–38. New York: Garland, 1996.
———. *Religious Women in Early Carolingian Francia: A Study of Manuscript Transmission and Monastic Culture*. New York: Fordham University Press, 2014.
Linage Conde, Antonio. "En torno a la benedictinización: La recepción de la regla de San Benito en el monacato de la Península Ibérica vista a través de Leyre y aledaños." *Príncipe de Viana* 46 (1985): 57–92.
Linssen, Joseph. *Een bijdrage voor de geschiedenis van de abdij Thorn*. Roermond: s.n., 1963.
Lot, Ferdinand. *Les derniers Carolingiens: Lothaire, Louis V, Charles de Lorraine, 954–991*. Paris: Emile Bouillon, 1891.
Louis, Etienne. "Espaces monastiques sacrés et profanes à Hamage (Nord), VIIe–IXe siecles." In *Monastères et espaces social: Genèse et transformation d'un système de*

lieux dans l'Occident médiéval, edited by Michel Lauwers, 435–72. Turnhout: Brepols, 2014.

———. "Les plus anciennes authentiques de reliques de la collégiale Saint-Amé de Douai." Unpublished typescript, 2016.

———. "'Sorores ac fratres in Hamatico degentes': Naissance, évolution et disparition d'une abbaye au Haut Moyen Âge; Hamage (France, Nord)." *De la Meuse à l'Ardenne* 29 (1999): 15–47.

Louis, Etienne, and Joël Blondiaux. "L'abbaye mérovingienne et carolingienne de Hamage (Nord): Vie, mort et sépulture dans une communauté monastique féminine." In *Inhumations de prestige ou prestige de l'inhumation? Expressions du pouvoir dans l'au-delà, IVe–XVe siècle*, edited by Armelle Alduc-Le Bagousse, 117–50. Caen: CRAHM, 2009.

Ludwig, Uwe. *Transalpine Beziehungen der Karolingerzeit im Spiegel der Memorialüberlieferung: Prosopographische und sozialgeschichtliche Studien unter besonderer Berücksichtigung des Liber vitae von San Salvatore in Brescia und des Evangeliars von Cividale*. Hanover: Hahnsche Buchhandlung, 1999.

Luhmann, Nicholas. "Differentiation of Society." *Canadian Journal of Sociology* 2 (1977): 29–53.

Lusset, Elisabeth. "Entre les murs: L'enfermement punitif des religieux criminels au sein du cloître (XIIe–XVe siècle)." In *Enfermements: Le cloître et la prison, VIe–XVIIIe siècle: Actes du colloque international organisé par le Centre d'études et de recherche en histoire culturelle*, edited by Isabelle Heullant-Donat, Julie Claustre, and Elisabeth Lusset, 153–68. Paris: Publications de la Sorbonne, 2011.

Lutter, Christina. *Geschlecht und Wissen, Norm und Praxis, Lesen und Schreiben: Monastische Reformgemeinschaften im 12. Jahrhundert*. Vienna: Oldenbourg, 2005.

———. "Klausur zwischen realen Begrenzungen und spirituellen Entwürfen: Handlungsspielräume und Identifikationsmodelle der Admonter Nonnen im 12. Jahrhundert." In *Virtuelle Räume: Raumwahrnehmung und Raumvorstellung im Mittelalter; Akten des 10. Symposiums des Mediävistenverbandes; Krems, 24.–26. März 2003*, edited by Elisabeth Vavra, 305–24. Berlin: Akademie Verlag, 2005.

Maclean, Simon. *Kingship and Politics in the Late Ninth Century: Charles the Fat and the End of the Carolingian Empire*. Cambridge: Cambridge University Press, 2003.

———. *Ottonian Queenship*. Oxford: Oxford University Press, 2017.

———. "Queenship, Nunneries and Royal Widowhood in Carolingian Europe." *Past and Present* 178 (2003): 3–38.

———. "Shadow Kingdom: Lotharingia and the Frankish World, c. 850–c. 1050." *History Compass* 11 (2013): 443–56.

Magnani, Eliana. "Cluny and Religious Women (9th-11th Centuries)." In *A Companion to the Abbey of Cluny in the Middle Ages*, edited by Scott Bruce and Steven Vanderputten. Leiden: Brill, forthcoming.

Mangion, Carmen M. *Contested Identities: Catholic Women Religious in Nineteenth-Century England and Wales*. Manchester: Manchester University Press, 2008.

Manitius, Max. *Geschichte der lateinischen Literatur des Mittelalters*. Vol. 3, *Vom Ausbruch des Kirchenstreites bis zum Ende des zwölften Jahrhunderts*. Munich: Beck, 1974.

Manuscripts and Monastic Culture: Reform and Renewal in Twelfth-Century Germany, edited by Alison Beach. Cambridge: Cambridge University Press, 2004.

Margue, Michel. "Autorité publique et conscience dynastique: Etudes sur les représentations du pouvoir entre Meuse et Moselle; Les origines du comté de Luxembourg (Xe–début XIIe s.)." 3 vols. Unpublished PhD dissertation, University of Brussels, 1998–99.

———. "Face à l'évêque, le comte: Politique ottonienne et pouvoir comtal en Lotharingie à l'époque de Notger." In *Évêque et prince: Notger et la Basse-Lotharingie aux alentours de l'an mil*, edited by Alexis Wilkin and Jean-Louis Kupper, 237–70. Liège: Presses Universitaires de Liège, 2013.

———. "'Nous ne sommes ni de l'une, ni de l'autre, mais les deux à la fois': Entre France et Germanie, les identités Lotharingiennes en question(s) (2e moitié du IXe–début du XIe siècle)." In *De la Mer du Nord à la Méditerranée: Francia Media, une région au coeur de l'Europe (c. 840–c. 1050). Actes du colloque international (Metz, Luxembourg, Trèves, 8–11 février 2006)*, edited by Michèle Gaillard, Michel Margue, Alain Dierkens, and Hérold Pettiau, 395–427. Luxembourg: CLUDEM, 2011.

Martindale, Jane. "The Nun Immena and the Foundation of the Abbey of Beaulieu: A Woman's Prospects in the Carolingian Church." In *Women in the Church. Papers Read at the 1989 Summer Meeting and the 1990 Winter Meeting of the Ecclesiastical History Society*, edited by W. J. Sheils and Diana Wood, 27–42. Oxford: Basil Blackwell, 1990.

Martine, Tristan. "Les mouvements de réforme monastique en Lotharingie méridionale au Xe siècle: quelles conséquences pour les familles comtales?" *Annales de l'Est*. Forthcoming.

Masai, François. "Deux éditions d'un fragment en onciale d'une règle de moniales." *Scriptorium* 5 (1951): 123–24.

———. "Fragment en onciale d'une règle monastique inconnue démarquant celle de S. Benoît." *Scriptorium* 2 (1948): 215–20.

Masser, Achim. *Lateinische und althochdeutsche Glossierungen der Regula Benedicti im 8. und 9. Jahrhundert*. Innsbruck: Innsbruck University Press, 2008.

Matis, Hannah W. "The Seclusion of Eustochium: Paschasius Radbertus and the Nuns of Soissons." *Church History* 85 (2016): 665–89.

Matzel, Klaus. "Die Namenliste der Metzer Nonnen zu St. Marien." *Beiträge zur Namenforschung*, new ser., 3 (1968): 241–43.

McCall, Leslie. "The Complexity of Intersectionality." *Signs: Journal of Women in Culture and Society* 30 (2005): 1771–1800.

McKitterick, Rosamund. "Glossaries and Other Innovations in Carolingian Book Production." In *Turning Over a New Leaf: Change and Development in the Medieval Book*, edited by Erik Kwakkel, Rosamund McKitterick, and Rodney M. Thomson, 21–78. Leiden: Leiden University Press, 2012.

———. "Women and Literacy in the Early Middle Ages." In *Books, Scribes, and Learning in the Frankish Kingdoms, 6th–9th Centuries*, art. 13:1–43. Aldershot: Variorum, 1994.

McLaughlin, Megan. *Sex, Gender, and Episcopal Authority in an Age of Reform, 1000–1122*. Cambridge: Cambridge University Press, 2010.

McNamara, Jo Ann K. *Sisters in Arms: Catholic Nuns through Two Millennia*. Cambridge: Cambridge University Press, 1996.

BIBLIOGRAPHY

Meens, Rob. *Het tripartite boeteboek: Overlevering en betekenis van vroegmiddeleeuwse biechtvoorschriften (met editie en vertaling van vier "tripartita")*. Hilversum: Verloren, 1994.

Mériaux, Charles. "Fulbert, évêque de Cambrai et d'Arras (933/934 † 956)." *Revue du Nord* 356–57 (2004): 525–42.

———. *Gallia Irradiata: Saints et sanctuaires de la Nord de la Gaule du Haut moyen âge*. Stuttgart: Steiner, 2006.

Mertens, Joseph. "L'église Saint-Michel à Gerpinnes." *Bulletin de la Commission Royale des Monuments et des Sites* 12 (1961): 151–216.

———. "Recherches archéologiques dans l'abbaye mérovingienne de Nivelles." In *Miscellanea archaeologica in honorem J. Breuer*, 89–113. Brussels: Institut royal du patrimoine artistique, Service des fouilles, 1962.

Metz, René. *La consécration des vierges dans l'église romaine: Etude d'histoire de la liturgie*. Paris: Presses universitaires de France, 1954.

Mews, Constant J. "Negotiating the Boundaries of Gender in Religious Life: Robert of Arbrissel and Hersende, Abelard and Heloise." *Viator* 37 (2007): 113–48.

Meyer, Martin. "Ein übersehenes Diplom Heinrichs I." *Neues Archiv der Gesellschaft für Ältere Deutsche Geschichtskunde* 23 (1898): 115–21.

Miller, Maureen. *Clothing the Clergy: Virtue and Power in Medieval Europe, c. 800–1200*. Ithaca, NY: Cornell University Press, 2014.

Moddelmog, Claudia. "Stiftung oder Eigenkirche? Der Umgang mit Forschungskonzepten und die sächsischen Frauenklöster im 9. und 10. Jahrhundert." In *Gestiftete Zukunft im mittelalterlichen Europa: Festschrift für Michael Borgolte zum 60. Geburtstag*, edited by Wolfgang Huschner and Frank Rexroth, 215–43. Berlin: Akademie Verlag, 2008.

Mohlberg, Leo K. *Katalog der Handschriften der Zentralbibliothek Zürich*. Vol. 1, *Mittelalterliche Handschriften*. Zürich: Buchdrückerei Berichthaus, 1951.

Morin, Germain. "Problèmes relatifs à la Règle de S. Césaire d'Arles pour les moniales." *Revue bénédictine* 44 (1932): 5–20.

Müller, Margit. *Am Schnittpunkt von Stadt und Land: Die Benediktinerabtei St. Arnulf zu Metz im hohen und späten Mittelalter*. Trier: Verlag Trierer Historische Forschungen, 1993.

Munt in Limburg: Tentoonstelling ingericht in de tentoonstellingszalen van het Provinciaal Gallo-Romeins Museum, Kielenstraat 15, 3700 Tongeren. 6 maart-3 mei 1981. Sint-Truiden: Provinciaal museum voor religieuze kunst, 1981.

Muschiol, Gisela. *Famula Dei: Zur Liturgie in merowingischen Frauenklöstern*. Münster: Aschendoff, 1994.

———. "Das 'gebrechliche Geschlecht' und der Gottesdienst: Zum religiösen Alltag in Frauengemeinschaften des Mittelalters." In *Herrschaft, Bildung und Gebet. Gründung und Anfänge des Frauenstifts Essen*, edited by Günter Berghaus, Thomas Schilp, and Michael Schlagheck, 19–27. Essen: Klartext Verlag, 2000.

———. "Liturgie und Klausur: Zu den liturgischen Voraussetzungen von Nonnenemporen." In *Studien zum Kanonissenstift*, edited by Irene Crusius, 129–48. Göttingen: Vandenhoeck und Ruprecht, 2001.

———." 'Psallere et legere.' Zur Beteiligung der Nonnen an der Liturgie nach den frühen gallischen Regulae ad Virgines." In *Liturgie und Frauenfrage: Ein Beitrag zur Frauenforschung aus liturgiewissenschaftlicher Sicht*, edited by Teresa Berger and Albert Gerhards, 77–125. St. Ottilien: Eos Verlag, 1991.

———. "Von Benedikt bis Bernhard: Klausur zwischen Regula und Realität." *Regulae Benedicti Studia* 19 (1997): 27–42.

Müsebeck, E. "Die Benediktinerabtei St. Arnulf zu Metz in der ersten Hälfte des Mittelalters." *Jahr-Buch der Gesellschaft für Lothringische Geschichte und Altertumskunde* 13 (1901): 164–244.

Musson, Anthony. *Medieval Law in Context: The Growth of Legal Consciousness from Magna Carta to the Peasants' Revolt*. Manchester: Manchester University Press, 2001.

Nazet, Jacques. "Crises et réformes dans les abbayes Hainuyères du IXe au début du XIIe siècle." In *Recueil d'études d'histoire Hainuyère offertes à Maurice A. Arnould*, edited by Jean-Marie Cauchies and Jean-Marie Duvosquel, 1:461–96. Mons: Hannonia, 1983.

Neiske, Franz. "Réforme clunisienne et réforme de l'église au temps de l'abbé Hugues de Cluny." In *La reforma gregoriana y su proyección en la cristiandad occidental siglos XI–XII*, edited by José Ignacio Saranyana, 335–59. Pamplona: Gobierno de Navarra, Departamento de cultura y turismo, Institución Príncipe de Viana, 2006.

Nelson, Janet L. *Charles the Bald*. London: Longman, 1992.

———. "Early Medieval Rites of Queen-making and the Shaping of Medieval Queenship." In *Queens and Queenship in Medieval Europe: Proceedings of a Conference Held at King's College London, April 1995*, edited by Anne J. Duggan, 301–15. Woodbridge: Boydell Press, 1997.

———. "Women and the Word in the Earlier Middle Ages." In *Women in the Church: Papers Read at the 1989 Summer Meeting and the 1990 Winter Meeting of the Ecclesiastical History Society*, edited by W. J. Sheils and Diana Wood, 53–78. Oxford: Basil Blackwell, 1990.

Niederkorn-Bruck, Meta. "Verschriftlichung von Erinnerung im Kontext der Liturgie: Überlegungen zum ältesten Sakramentar D1." In *Pro remedio et salute animae peragemus. Totengedenken am Frauenstift Essen im Mittelalter*, edited by Thomas Schilp, 163–90. Essen: Klartext Verlag, 2008.

Nightingale, John. "Bishop Gerard of Toul (963–94) and Attitudes to Episcopal Office." In *Warriors and Churchmen in the High Middle Ages: Essays Presented to Karl Leyser*, edited by Timothy Reuter, 41–62. London: Hambledon, 1992.

———. *Monasteries and Patrons in the Gorze Reform: Lotharingia, c. 850–1000*. Oxford: Oxford University Press, 2007.

North, William, and Anthony Cutler. "The Bishop as Cultural Medium: Berthold of Toul, Byzantium, and Episcopal Self-Consciousness." In *The Bishop. Power and Piety at the First Millenium*, edited by Sean Gilsdorf, 75–111. Münster: LIT Verlag, 2004.

Nuns and Sisters in the Nordic Countries after the Reformation: A Female Counter-Culture in Modern Society, edited by Yvonne M. Werner. Uppsala: Swedish Institute of Mission Research, 2004.

Oberste, Jörg. "Papst Leo IX. und das Reformmönchtum." In *Léon IX et son temps: Actes du colloque international organisé par l'Institut d'Histoire Médiévale de l'Université Marc-Bloch, Strasbourg-Eguisheim, 20–22 juin 2002*, edited by Georges Bischoff and Benoît-Michel Tock, 405–33. Turnhout: Brepols, 2006.

O'Brien O'Keeffe, Katherine. *Stealing Obedience: Narratives of Agency and Identity in Later Anglo-Saxon England*. Toronto: University of Toronto Press, 2012.

Ochsenbein, Peter. *Die St. Galler Klosterschule*. In *Das Kloster St. Gallen im Mittelalter: Die kulturelle Blüte vom 8. bis zum 12. Jahrhundert*, edited by Peter Ochsenbein, 95–107. Stuttgart: Theiss, 1999.

Oediger, Friedrich W. "St. Maria im Kapitol und Remiremont: Bemerkungen zu einem Kollektar des 12. Jhs." *Jahrbuch des Kölnischen Geschichtsvereins* 36 (1962): 73–93.

Ohm, Juliane. "Der Begriff 'carcer' in Klosterregeln des Frankenreiches." In *Consuetudines monasticae. Festgabe für Kassius Hallinger*, edited by Joachim F. Angerer and Josef Lenzenweger, 145–55. Rome: Pontificio Ateneo S. Anselmo, 1982.

Orchard, Nicholas. "The Ninth and Tenth-Century Additions to Cambrai, Mediathèque Municipale, 164." *Revue bénédictine* 113 (2003): 285–97.

Oschema, Klaus. "Zur Gründung des Benediktinerinnenklosters Notre-Dame de Bouxières: Eine wiedergefundene Urkunde des 10. Jahrhunderts." *Mitteilungen des Instituts für Österreichische Geschichtsforschung* 110 (2002): 182–90.

Parisot, Robert. *Le royaume de Lorraine sous les Carolingiens, 843–923*. Paris: A. Picard et fils, 1898.

Parisse, Michel. "Une abbaye de femmes en Lorraine. Poussay au moyen âge." *Sacris erudiri* 26 (1983): 103–18.

———. "L'abbaye de Gorze dans le contexte politique et religieux lorrain à l'époque de Jean de Vandières (900–974)." In *L'abbaye de Gorze au Xe siècle*, edited by Michel Parisse and Otto G. Oexle, 51–90. Nancy: Presses Universitaires de Nancy, 1993.

———. "Der Anteil der Lothringischen Benediktinerinnen an der monastischen Bewegung des 10. und 11. Jahrhunderts." In *Religiöse Frauenbewegung und mystische Frömmigkeit im Mittelalter*, edited by Peter Dinzelbacher, 83–98. Köln: Böhlau Verlag, 1988.

———. "Un évêque réformateur: Gauzelin de Toul (922–962)." In *Ad Libros! Mélanges d'études médiévales offerts à Denise Angers et Joseph-Claude Poulin*, edited by Jean-François Cottier, Martin Gravel, and Sébastien Rossignol, 69–79. s.l.: Les Presses de l'Université de Montréal, 2010.

———. "Die Frauenstifte und Frauenklöster in Sachsen vom 10. bis zur Mitte des 12. Jahrhunderts." In *Die Salier und das Reich*, edited by Odilo Engels, Franz-Jozef Heyen, Franz Staub, and Stefan Weinfurter, 3 vols., 2:465–502. Sigmaringen: Thorbecke, 1991.

———. "Généalogie de la Maison d'Ardenne." In *La maison d'Ardenne Xe–XIe siècles: Actes des Journées Lotharingiennes 24–26 octobre 1980*, 9–41. Luxembourg: Publications de la section historique de l'Institut Grand-Ducal de Luxembourg, 1981.

——. "Le 'monachisme' féminin en Alsace des origines au XIIe siècle." In *Religieux et religieuses en Empire du Xe au XIIe siècle*, 224–45. Paris: Picard, 2011.
——. "Les monastères de femmes en Saxe des Carolingiens aux Saliens." In *Religieux et religieuses en Empire du Xe au XIIe siècle*, 141–72. Paris: Picard, 2011.
——. "Noblesse et monastères en Lotharingie du IXe au XIe siècle." In *Monastische Reformen im 9. und 10. Jahrhundert*, edited by Raymund Kottje and Helmut Maurer, 167–96. Sigmaringen: Jan Thorbecke Verlag, 1989.
——. *La noblesse lorraine XIe–XIIIe s.* 2 vols. Lille: Reproduction des thèses / Paris: Librairie Honoré Champion, 1976.
——. "Les notices de tradition de Remiremont." In *Person und Gemeinschaft im Mittelalter: Festschrift für Karl Schmid zum fünfundsechzigsten Geburtstag*, edited by Gerd Althoff, Dieter Geuenich, Otto G. Oexle, and Joachim Wollasch, 211–36. Sigmaringen: Jan Thorbecke Verlag, 1988.
——. "Les possessions des ducs de Haute-Lotharingie (939–1033)." In *La maison d'Ardenne Xe-XIe siècles: Actes des Journées Lotharingiennes 24–26 octobre 1980*, 241–57. Luxembourg: Publications de la section historique de l'Institut Grand-Ducal de Luxembourg, 1981.
——. "Un prélat d'Empire: Saint Gérard, évêque de Toul (963–994)." *Etudes Touloises* 27 (1982): 9–12.
——. "Recherches sur les formes de symbiose des religieux et religieuses au moyen âge. Introduction." In *Doppelklöster und andere Formen der Symbiose männlicher und weiblicher Religiosen im Mittelalter*, edited by Kaspar Elm and Michel Parisse, 9–11. Berlin: Duncker und Humblot, 1992.
——. "Les règlements d'avouerie en Lorraine au XIe siècle." *L'avouerie en Lotharingie: Actes des 2es Journées Lotharingiennes, 22–23 oct. 1982, Centre Universitaire Luxembourg*, 159–73. Luxembourg: Publications de la section historique de l'Institut Grand-Ducal de Luxembourg, 1984.
——. "Les religieuses dans le nord de l'Allemagne du IXe au XIe siècle: Conditions sociales et religieuses." In *Religieux et religieuses en Empire du Xe au XIIe siècle*, 126–40. Paris: Picard, 2011.
——. "Les religieuses bénédictines de Lorraine au temps de la réforme des XIe et XIIe siècles." In *Religieux et religieuses en Empire du Xe au XIIe siècle*, 200–14. Paris: Picard, 2011.
——. "Les religieuses de Lorraine et leurs documents nécrologiques." In *Religieux et religieuses en Empire du Xe au XIIe siècle*, 215–23. Paris: Picard, 2011.
——. "Restaurer un monastère au Xe siècle: L'exemple de Gorze." In *Vita religiosa im Mittelalter: Festschrift für Kaspar Elm zum 70. Geburtstag*, edited by Franz J. Felten and Nikolas Jaspert, 55–78. Berlin: Duncker und Humblot, 1999.
——. "Thierri du Hamaland, évêque de Metz (965–984) et fondateur d'Epinal." *Annales de la Société d'Emulation du Département des Vosges*, new ser., 3 (1985): 101–3.
——. "La tradition du monachisme féminin au Haut moyen âge." In *Religieux et religieuses en Empire du Xe au XIIe siècle*, 115–24. Paris: Picard, 2011.
Parkes, Henry. *The Making of Liturgy in the Ottonian Church: Books, Music and Ritual in Mainz, 950–1050*. Cambridge: Cambridge University Press, 2015.

Partners in Spirit: Women, Men, and Religious Life in Germany, 1100–1500, edited by Fiona J. Griffiths and Julie Hotchin. Turnhout: Brepols, 2012.

Paulmier-Foucart, Monique, and Anne Wagner. "Lire au Haut moyen âge: Un florilège spirituel de l'abbaye Saint-Vanne de Verdun." *Annales de l'Est*, 6th ser., 52 (2002): 9–24.

Paxton, Frederick S. *Anchoress and Abbess in Ninth-Century Saxony: The Lives of Liutbirga of Wendhausen and Hathumoda of Gandersheim*. Washington, DC: Catholic University of America Press, 2009.

Pélagie la pénitente: Métamorphoses d'une légende. Edited by Pierre Petitmengin, Matei Cazacu, and François Dolbeau. 2 vols. Paris: Etudes Augustiniennes, 1981–84.

Perez de Urbel, Justo. *Los monjes españoles en la edad media*. 2 vols. Madrid: Ediciones "Ancla," 1934.

Perrin, Charles-Edmond. *Recherches sur la seigneurie rurale en Lorraine d'après les plus anciens censiers (IXe–XIIe siècle)*. Strasbourg: Commission des publications de la Faculté des Lettres de Strasbourg, 1935.

Philippart, Guy, and Anne Wagner. "Hagiographie des diocèses de Metz, Toul et Verdun 920–1130." In *Hagiographies* 4:585–744. Turnhout: Brepols Publishers, 2006.

Plenevaux, Catherine. "L'abbaye de Munsterbilzen: De sa fondation à sa sécularisation (XIIe siècle)." Unpublished master's thesis, University of Brussels, 1998–99.

Ploegaerts, Théophile. "Le monastère mérovingien d'Orp-le-Grand et le culte de sainte Adèle." *Collectanea Mechliniensia* 21 (1932): 265–82.

Ponesse, Matthew D. "Standing Distant from the Fathers: Smaragdus of Saint-Mihiel and the Reception of Early Medieval Learning." *Traditio* 67 (2012): 71–99.

Pontal, Odette. *Les conciles de la France capétienne jusqu'en 1215*. Paris: Les Editions du Cerf, 2007.

Prinz, Friedrich. *Frühes Mönchtum im Frankenreich: Kultur und Gesellschaft in Gallien, den Rheinlanden und Bayern am Beispiel der monastischen Entwicklung (4. bis 8. Jahrhundert)*. 2nd ed. Darmstadt: Wissenschaftliche Buchgesellschaft, 1988.

Raaijmakers, Janneke. *The Making of the Monastic Community of Fulda, c. 744–c. 900*. Cambridge: Cambridge University Press, 2012.

Rabin, Andrew. "Courtly Habits: Monastic Women's Legal Literacy in Early Anglo-Saxon England." In *Nuns' Literacies in Medieval Europe: The Kansas City Dialogue*, edited by Virginia Blanton, Veronica O'Mara, and Patricia Stoop, 289–305. Turnhout: Brepols, 2015.

Rand, Edward K. *A Survey of the Manuscripts of Tours*. 2 vols. Cambridge, MA: Mediaeval Academy of America, 1929.

Réal, Isabelle. *Vies de saints, vies de famille: Représentation et système de la parenté dans le royaume mérovingien (481–751) d'après les sources hagiographiques*. Turnhout: Brepols, 2001.

Religious Women and Their History: Breaking the Silence. Edited by Rosemary Raughter. Dublin: Irish Academic Press, 2005.

Robles Carcedo, Laureano. "Anotaciones a la obra del Pseudo-Isidoro 'Commonitiuncula ad sororem.'" *Analecta sacra Tarrocensia* 44 (1971): 5–32.

Röckelein, Hedwig. "Die Auswirkung der Kanonikerreform des 12. Jahrhunderts auf Kanonissen, Augustinerchorfrauen und Benediktinerinnen." In *Institution und Charisma: Festschrift für Gert Melville*, edited by Franz Felten, Annette Kehnel, and Stefan Weinfurter, 55–72. Cologne: Böhlau, 2009.

———. "Bairische, sächsische und mainfränkische Klostergründungen im Vergleich: 8. Jahrhundert bis 1100." In *Nonnen, Kanonissen und Mystikerinnen: Religiöse Frauengemeinschaften in Süddeutschland; Beiträge zur interdisziplinären Tagung vom 21. bis 23. September 2005 in Frauenchiemsee*, edited by Eva Schlotheuber, 23–55. Göttingen: Vandenhoeck und Ruprecht, 2008.

———. "Frauen im Umkreis der benediktinischen Reformen des 10. bis 12. Jahrhunderts: Gorze, Cluny, Hirsau, St. Blasien und Siegburg." In *Female "vita religiosa" between Late Antiquity and the High Middle Ages*, edited by Gert Melville and Anne Müller, 275–328. Vienna: LIT Verlag, 2011.

———. "Gandersheimer Reliquienschätze—erste vorläufige Beobachtungen." In *Gandersheim und Essen: Vergleichende Untersuchungen zu sächsischen Frauenstiften*, edited by Martin Hoernes and Hedwig Röckelein, 33–80. Essen: Klartext Verlag, 2006.

———. "Hiérarchie, ordre et mobilité dans le monachisme féminin." In *Hiérarchie et stratification sociale dans l'Occident médiéval (400–1100)*, edited by Dominique Iogna-Prat, François Bougard, and Régine Le Jan, 205–20. Turnhout: Brepols, 2008.

———. "Inklusion - Exklusion: Weiblich - männlich." In *Innovationen durch Deuten und Gestalten: Klöster im Mittelalter zwischen Jenseits und Welt*, edited by Gert Melville, Bernd Schneidmüller, and Stefan Weinfurter, 127–44. Regensburg: Verlag Schnell und Steiner, 2014.

Roitner, Ingrid. "Sorores inclusae: Bistumspolitik und Klosterreform im Geist von Cluny/Hirsau in der Diözese Salzburg." *Revue Mabillon* new ser. 18 (2007): 73–133.

Rose, Valentin. *Verzeichnis der Lateinischen Handschriften der Königlichen Bibliothek zu Berlin*. Vol. 1, *Erster Band; Die Meermann-Handschriften des Sir Thomas Phillips* (Die Handschriften-Verzeischnisse der Königlichen Bibliothek zu Berlin, 12). Berlin: Ascher, 1893.

Rothschild, Jean-Pierre, and Armand Strubel. "Sainte Pélagie dans le *De triumphis Christi Antiochae* gestis de Flodoard. In *Pélagie la pénitente: Métamorphoses d'une légende*. Vol. 2, *La survie dans les littératures européennes*, edited by Matei Cazacu and François Dolbeau, 67–99. Paris: Etudes Augustiniennes, 1984.

Rudge, Lindsay. "Texts and Contexts: Women's Dedicated Life from Caesarius to Benedict." Unpublished PhD dissertation, University of St. Andrews, 2007.

Schaefer, Mary M. *Women in Pastoral Office: The Story of Santa Prassede, Rome*. Oxford: Oxford University Press, 2013.

Schäfer, Karl Heinrich. *Die Kanonissenstifter im deutschen Mittelalter: Ihre Entwicklung und innere Einrichtung im zusammenhang mit dem altchristlichen Sanktimonialentum*. Stuttgart: Ferdinand Enke, 1907.

Scheck, Helene. "Reading Women at the Margins of Quedlingburg Codex 74." In *Nuns' Literacies in Medieval Europe: The Hull Dialogue*, edited by Virginia Blanton, Veronica O'Mara, and Patricia Stoop, 3–18. Turnhout: Brepols, 2013.

BIBLIOGRAPHY

———. *Reform and Resistance: Formations of Female Subjectivity in Early Medieval Ecclesiastical Culture.* Albany: State University of New York Press, 2008.
Schilp, Thomas. "Frauen und Männer: Kanoniker und Kanonikerconvent am Frauenstift Essen." In *Liturgie in mittelalterlichen Frauenstiften: Forschungen zum Liber Ordinarius*, edited by Klaus G. Beuckers, 91–112. Essen: Klartext Verlag, 2012.
———. *Norm und Wirklichkeit religiöser Frauengemeinschaften im frühen Mittelalter.* Göttingen: Vandenhoeck und Ruprecht, 1998.
———. "'Sorores et fratres capituli secularis ecclesie Assindensis': Binnenstrukturen des Frauenstifts Essen im 13. Jahrhundert." In *Reform, Reformation, Säkularisation: Frauenstifte in Krisenzeiten*, edited by Thomas Schilp, 37–65. Essen: Klartext Verlag, 2004.
———. "Überlegungen zur Sakramentarhandschrift D 1 als *Liber vitae* der Essener Frauenkommunität." In *Libri vitae. Gebetsgedenken in der Gesellschaft des Frühen Mittelalters*, edited by Dieter Geuenich and Uwe Ludwig, 203–20. Cologne: Böhlau Verlag, 2015.
———. "Die Vita Hathumodae, der ersten Äbtissin der Frauenkommunität Gandersheim (852–874): Lebensform im Spannungsfeld von Norm und Wirklichkeit." In *Fromme Frauen - unbequeme Frauen? Weibliches Religiosentum im Mittelalter*, edited by Edeltraud Klueting, 1–25. Hildesheim: Olms, 2006.
———. "Die Wirkung der Aachener 'Institutio sanctimonialium' des Jahres 816." In *Frühformen von Stiftskirchen in Europa: Funktion und Wandel religiöser Frauengemeinschaften vom 6. bis zum Ende des 11. Jahrhunderts; Festgabe für Dieter Mertens zum 65. Geburtstag*, edited by Sönke Lorenz and Thomas Zotz, 163–84. Leinfelden-Echterdingen: DRW-Verlag, 2005.
Schmid, Karl. "Ein karolingischer Königseintrag im Gedenkbuch von Remiremont." *Frühmittelalterliche Studien* 2 (1968): 96–134.
———. "Auf dem Weg zur Erschließung des Gedenkbuchs von Remiremont." In *Festschrift für Eduard Hlawitschka zum 65. Geburtstag*, edited by Karl Schnith and Roland Pauler, 59–96. Kallmünz: Verlag Michael Lassleben, 1993.
Schmitz, Gerhard. "Aachen 816: Zu Überlieferung und Edition der Kanonikergesetzgebung Ludwigs des Frommen." *Deutsches Archiv für Erforschung des Mittelalters* 63 (2007): 497–544.
———. "Zu den Quellen der *Institutio Sanctimonialium* Ludwigs des Frommen (a. 816): Die Homiliensammlung des Codex Paris lat. 13440." *Deutsches Archiv für Erforschung des Mittelalters* 68 (2012): 23–52.
Schmitz, Philibert. *Histoire de l'ordre de Saint-Benoît*. 7 vols. Maredous: Les éditions de Maredsous, 1948–56.
Schneider, Jens, and Tristan Martine. "La production d'un espace: Débuts lotharingiens et pratiques de la frontière (IXe-XIe siècle)." *Revue de géographie historique* (2014). Accessed 12 February 2016. http://rgh.univ-lorraine.fr/articles/view/43/La_production_d_un_espace_debuts_lotharingiens_et_pratiques_de_la_frontiere_IXe_XIe_siecle.
Schulenburg, Jane T. *Forgetful of Their Sex: Female Sanctity and Society, ca. 500–1100.* Chicago: University of Chicago Press, 1998.
———. "Strict Active Enclosure and Its Effects on the Female Monastic Experience, ca. 500–1100." In *Medieval Religious Women*. Vol. 1, *Distant Echoes*, edited by

John A. Nichols and Lillian T. Shank, 51–86. Kalamazoo, MI: Cistercian Publications, 1984.

———. "Women's Monastic Communities, 500–1100: Patterns of Expansion and Decline." *Signs: Journal of Women in Culture and Society* 14 (1989): 261–92.

Schuler, Thomas. "'Regula nil impossibile dicit': Regeltreue und Regelabweichung bei den karolingischen Benediktinern." *Regula Benedicti Studia* 10–11 (1981–82): 51–76.

Seibert, Hubertus. *Abtserhebungen zwischen Rechtsnorm und Rechtswirklichkeit: Formen der Nachfolgeregelung in lothringischen und schwäbischen Klöstern der Salierzeit (1024–1125)*. Mainz: Gesellschaft für Mittelrheinische Kirchengeschichte, 1995.

Semmler, Josef. "Corvey und Herford in der benediktinischen Reformbewegung des 9. Jahrhunderts." *Frühmittelalterliche Studien* 4 (1970): 289–319.

———. "Das Erbe der karolingischen Klosterreform im 10. Jahrhundert." In *Monastische Reformen im 9. und 10. Jahrhundert*, edited by Raymund Kottje and Helmut Maurer, 29–77. Sigmaringen: Jan Thorbecke Verlag, 1989.

———. "Iren in der lothringischen Klosterreform." In *Die Iren und Europa im früheren Mittelalter*, edited by Heinz Löwe, 1:941–57. Stuttgart: Klett-Cotta, 1982.

———. "Le monachisme occidental du VIIIe au Xe siècle: Formation et réformation." *Revue bénédictine* 103 (1993): 68–89.

———. "Monachus—clericus—canonicus. Zur Ausdifferenzierung geistlicher Institutionen im Frankenreich bis ca. 900." In *Frühformen von Stiftskirchen in Europa: Funktion und Wandel religiöser Gemeinschaften vom 6. bis zum Ende des 11. Jahrhunderts: Festgabe für Dieter Mertens zum 65. Geburtstag*, edited by Sönke Lorenz and Thomas Zotz, 1–18. Leinfelden-Echterdingen: DRW-Verlag, 2005.

———. "Reichsidee und kirchliche Gesetzgebung bei Ludwig dem Frommen." *Zeitschrift für Kirchengeschichte* 71 (1960): 37–65.

Signori, Gabriela. "Anchorites in German-speaking Regions." In *Anchoritic Traditions of Medieval Europe*, edited by Liz Herbert McAvoy, 43–61. Woodbridge: Boydell and Brewer, 2010.

Skinner, Mary. "Benedictine Life for Women in Central France, 850–1100: A Feminist Revival." In *Medieval Religious Women*. Vol. 1, *Distant Echoes*, edited by John A. Nichols and Lillian T. Shank, 87–113. Kalamazoo, MI: Cistercian Publications, 1984.

———. "French Abbesses in Action: Structuring Carolingian and Cluniac Communities." *Magistra* 6 (2000): 37–60.

Smith, J. A. *Ordering Women's Lives: Penitentials and Nunnery Rules in the Early Medieval West*. Aldershot: Variorum, 2001.

Smith, J. M. H. "L'accès des femmes aux saintes reliques durant le haut Moyen Age." *Médiévales* 40 (2001): 83–100.

———. "The Problem of Female Sanctity in Carolingian Europe c. 780–920." *Past and Present* 146 (1995): 3–37.

Snijders, Tjamke. "Handschriftelijke productie in tijden van hervorming: De kloosterbibliotheek van Sint-Gislenus in het tweede kwart van de elfde eeuw." *Jaarboek voor middeleeuwse geschiedenis* 13 (2010): 6–31.

―――. "Textual Diversity and Textual Community in a Monastic Context: The Case of Eleventh-Century Marchiennes." *Revue d'histoire ecclésiastique* 107 (2012): 897–930.

Sproemberg, Heinrich. "Die lothringische Politik Ottos des Grossen." In *Beiträge zur belgisch-niederländischen Geschichte*, 111–223. Berlin: Akademie-Verlag, 1959.

Steinbach, Sebastian. *Das Geld der Nonnen und Mönche: Münzrecht, Münzprägung und Geldumlauf der ostfränkisch-deutschen Klöster in ottonisch-salischer Zeit (ca. 911–1125)*. Berlin: Dissertation-de, 2006.

Stocker, Bärbel. "Die Opfergeräte der heiligen Wiborada von St. Gallen - Eine Frau als Zelebrantin der Eucharistie?" *Freiburger Diözesan-Archiv: Zeitschrift des Kirchengeschichtlichen Vereins für Geschichte, Altertums- und Literaturkunde des Erzbistums Freiburg mit Berücksichtigung der angrenzenden Bistümer* 111 (1991): 405–19.

Stoepker, Henk. "Archeologisch onderzoek van de Salvatorabdij te Susteren." *Historisch jaarboek voor het land van Zwentibold* 13 (1992): 130–36.

Stofferahn, Steven A. "Changing Views of Carolingian Women's Literary Culture: The Evidence from Essen." *Early Medieval Europe* 8 (1999): 69–97.

―――. "A Schoolgirl and Mistress Felhin: A Devout Petition From Ninth-Century Saxony." In *Women Writing Latin from Roman Antiquity to Early Modern Europe*. Vol. 2, *Medieval Women Writing Latin*, edited by Laurie J. Churchill, Phyllis R. Brown, and Jane E. Jeffrey, 25–35. New York: Routledge, 2002.

Stone, Rachel. "The Invention of a Theology of Abduction: Hincmar of Reims on Raptus." *Journal of Ecclesiastical History* 60 (2009): 433–48.

Tampière, Marc. "L'évangéliaire de la reine Theutberge: Un joyau de l'époque carolingienne vendu à Londres." *Cahiers Elie Fleur* 16 (1997–98): 14–29.

Tanner, Heather J. *Families, Friends and Allies: Boulogne and Politics in Northern France and England, c. 879–1160*. Leiden: Brill, 2004.

Tarlier, Jules, and Alphonse Wauters. *La Belgique ancienne et moderne: Géographie et histoire des communes Belges; Province de Brabant; Arrondissement de Nivelles*. 2 vols. Brussels: A. Decq, 1873.

Taylor, Anna Lisa. *Epic Lives and Monasticism in the Middle Ages, 800–1050*. Cambridge: Cambridge University Press, 2013.

Theys, A.J. *Le Bienheureux Thierry de Leernes, abbé de Saint-Hubert*. Tournai: Casterman, 1910.

Tiefenbach, Heinrich. "Frühmittelalterliche Volkssprache im Frauenstift Essen." In *Essen und die sächsischen Frauenstifte im Frühmittelalter*, edited by Jan Gerchow and Thomas Schilp, 113–28. Essen: Klartext Verlag, 2003.

Tronquart, Martine. "L'église Saint-Maurice et Saint-Goëry d'Epinal au XIe s: Essai de restitution." *Le Pays Lorrain* 75 (1994): 135–40.

Twellenkamp, Markus. "Das Haus der Luxemburger." In *Die Salier und das Reich*, edited by Odilo Engels, Franz-Jozef Heyen, Franz Staub, and Stefan Weinfurter, 3 vols., 1:475–502. Sigmaringen: Thorbecke Verlag, 1991.

Ugé, Karine. *Creating the Monastic Past in Medieval Flanders*. Woodbridge: Boydell Press, 2005.

Unterkircher, Franz. *Zur Ikonographie und Liturgie des Drogo-Sakramentars (Paris, Bibliothèque nationale, Ms. Lat. 9428)*. Graz: Akademische Druck- u. Verlagsanstalt, 1977.

Untermann, Matthias. "Das Nonnenhaus: Traditionen einen klösterlichen Bautyps." In *Gebaute Klausur: Funktion und Architektur mittelalterlicher Klosterräume*, edited by Renate Oldermann, 97–109. Bielefeld: Verlag für Regionalgeschichte, 2008.

Van Cauteren, John. *De abdijkerk te Thorn*. Zutphen: Clavis, 1987.

Van Den Gheyn, Joseph-Marie-Martin. *Catalogue des manuscrits de la bibliothèque royale de Belgique*. 11 vols. Brussels: H. Lamertin, 1901–27.

Van de Perre, Dirk. "De *Vita Sanctae Berlendis* en de *Miracula Sanctae Berlendis*: Teksttraditie, datering, auteurschap en historische kritiek." *Jaarboek voor middeleeuwse geschiedenis* 8 (2005): 7–46.

Van Der Essen, Léon. *Etude critique et littéraire sur les vitae des saints mérovingiens de l'ancienne Belgique*. Louvain: Bureaux du Recueil, 1907.

Van der Eycken, Johan, and Michel Van der Eycken. *"Wachten op de prins . . .": Negen eeuwen adellijk damesstift Munsterbilzen*. Bilzen: Historisch Studiecentrum Alden Biesen, 2000.

Van der Meer, Matthieu. "The *Glosae in regula S. Benedicti*—A Text between the *Liber Glossarum* and Smaragdus' *Expositio in Regvlam S. Benedicti*." In *Dossiers d'HEL* 10 (2016): 305–19.

Vanderputten, Steven. "Debating Reform in Tenth- and Early Eleventh-Century Female Monasticism." *Zeitschrift für Kirchengeschichte* 125 (2014): 289–306.

——. "Un espace sacré au féminin? Principes et réalités de la clôture des religieuses aux IXe-XIe siècles." In *Spazio e mobilità nella 'Societas Christiana': Spazio, identità, alterità (secoli X–XIII). Atti del Convegno Internazionale Brescia, 17–19 settembre 2015*, edited by Giancarlo Andenna, Nicolangelo d'Acunto, and Elisabetta Filippini, 125–40. Milan: Vita e Pensiero, 2017.

——. "Female Monasticism, Ecclesiastical Reform and Regional Politics: The Northern Archdiocese of Reims, circa 1060–1120." *French Historical Studies* 36 (2013): 363–83.

——. "Fulcard's Pigsty: Cluniac Reformers, Dispute Settlement and the Lower Aristocracy in Early-Twelfth-Century Flanders." *Viator* 38 (2007): 91–115.

——. *Imagining Religious Leadership in the Middle Ages: Richard of Saint-Vanne and the Politics of Reform*. Ithaca, NY: Cornell University Press, 2015.

——. "Reconsidering Religious Migration and Its Impact: The Problem of 'Irish Reform Monks' in Tenth-Century Lotharingia." *Revue d'histoire ecclésiastique* 112 (2017): 588–618.

——. "A Miracle of Jonatus in 1127: The *Translatio sancti Jonati in villa Saliacensi* (BHL 4449) as Political Enterprise and Failed Hagiographical Project." *Analecta Bollandiana* 126 (2008): 55–92.

——. *Monastic Reform as Process: Realities and Representations in Medieval Flanders, 900–1100*. Ithaca, NY: Cornell University Press, 2013.

——. "'Reformatorische lichamelijkheid' en de geconditioneerde emoties van twee religieuze vrouwen omstreeks het jaar 1000." *Tijdschrift voor Geschiedenis* 126 (2013): 466–79.

——. "Universal Historiography as Process? Shaping Monastic Memories in the Eleventh-Century Chronicle of Saint-Vaast." In *The Life of Universal Chronicles in the High Middle Ages*, edited by Michele Campopiano and Henry Bainton, 43–64. Woodbridge: York Medieval Press, 2017.

Vanderputten, Steven, and Charles West. "Inscribing Property, Rituals, and Royal Alliances: The 'Theutberga Gospels' and the Abbey of Remiremont." *Mitteilungen des Instituts für Österreichische Geschichtsforschung* 124 (2016): 296–321.

Van Droogenbroeck, Frans J. "Hugo van Lobbes (1033–1053), auteur van de Vita Amelbergae viduae, Vita S. Reinildis en Vita S. Berlendis." *Eigen Schoon en de Brabander* 94 (2011): 649–84.

Van Heijst, Annelies, and Marjet Derks. "Godsvrucht en gender: Naar een geschiedschrijving in meervoud." In *Terra incognita. Historisch onderzoek naar katholicisme en vrouwelijkheid*, edited by Annelies Van Heijst and Marjet Derks, 7–38. Kampen: Kok, 1994.

Van Osselaer, Tine, and Thomas Buerman. "Feminization Thesis: A Survey of International Historiography and a Probing of Belgian Grounds." *Revue d'histoire ecclésiastique* 103 (2008): 497–544.

Van Rhijn, Carine. "The Local Church, Priests' Handbooks and Pastoral Care in the Carolingian Period." In *Chiese locali e chiese regionali nell'alto medioevo (Spoleto, 4–9 Aprile 2013)*, 2:689–706. Spoleto: Fondazione Centro italiano di studi sull'alto Medioevo, 2014.

Van 't Spijker, Ineke. "Een jeugd in de Ardennen: De kindertijd van Theodericus van Saint-Hubert." *Madoc* 11 (1997): 206–11.

Van Waesberghe, Joseph F. A. M. *De Akense regels voor canonici en canonicae uit 816*. Assen: Van Gorkum, 1967.

Van Winter, Johanna M. "The Education of the Daughters of Nobility in the Ottonian Empire." In *The Empress Theophano. Byzantium and the West at the Turn of the First Millenium*, edited by Adelbert Davids, 86–99. Cambridge: Cambridge University Press, 1995.

Venarde, Bruce. *Women's Monasticism and Medieval Society: Nunneries in France and England, 890–1215*. Ithaca, NY: Cornell University Press, 1997.

Verdon, Jean. "Notes sur le rôle économique des monastères féminins en France dans la seconde moitié du IXe et au début du Xe siècle." *Revue Mabillon* 58 (1975): 329–44.

——. "Recherches sur les monastères féminins dans la France du nord aux IXe–XIe siècles." *Revue Mabillon* 59 (1976): 49–96.

——. "Recherches sur les monastères féminins dans la France du sud aux IXe–XIe siècles." *Annales du Midi* 88 (1976): 117–38.

Vestier, Hélène. "Juvigny-sur-Loison, son abbaye, ses reliques." *Bulletin des Sociétés d'Histoire et d'Archéologie de la Meuse* 11 (1974): 155–62.

Voigt, Karl. *Die karolingische Klosterpolitik und der Niedergang des westfränkischen Königtums: Laienäbte und Klosterinhaber*. Stuttgart: Ferdinand Enke, 1917.

Voltz, Eugène. "Historique des bâtiments de l'abbaye Sainte-Glossinde à Metz." *Mémoires de l'Académie Nationale de Metz: Lettres, sciences, arts et agriculture* 143 (1962): 125–56.

Von Mitis, Oskar. "Eine Archivreise nach Verdun 1549 im Kampf der Reichsregierung um die Westgrenze." *Elsaß-Lothringisches Jahrbuch* 19 (1941): 159–204.

Wade, Susan W. "Gertrude's Tonsure: An Examination of Hair as a Symbol of Gender, Family and Authority in the Seventh-Century Vita of Gertrude of Nivelles." *Journal of Medieval History* 39 (2013): 129–45.

Wagner, Anne. "Collection de reliques et pouvoir épiscopal au Xe siècle: L'exemple de l'évêque Thierry Ier de Metz." *Revue d'histoire de l'église en France* 83 (1997): 317–40.

——. "La vie culturelle à Gorze au Xe siècle d'après la 'Vita Johannis Gorziensis' et le catalogue de la bibliothèque de Gorze." In *L'abbaye de Gorze au Xe siècle*, edited by Michel Parisse and Otto G. Oexle, 213–31. Nancy: Presses Universitaires de Nancy, 1993.

Wagner, Heinrich. "Zur *Notitia de servitio monasteriorum* von 819." *Deutsches Archiv für Erforschung des Mittelalters* 55 (1999): 417–38.

Warichez, Joseph. *L'abbaye de Lobbes depuis les origines jusqu'en 1200: Etude d'histoire générale et spéciale*. Louvain: Bureaux du Recueil / Paris: Alphonse Picard et Fils, 1909.

Watt, Diane. *Medieval Women's Writing: Works by and for Women in England, 1100–1500.* Cambridge: Polity, 2007.

Weikert, Katherine, and Elena Woodacre. "Gender and Status in the Medieval World." *Historical Reflections* 42 (2016): 1–7.

Wemhoff, Matthias. *Das Damenstift Herford: Die archäologischen Ergebnisse zur Geschichte der Profan- und Sakralbauten seit dem späten 8. Jahrhundert.* 3 vols. Bonn: Habelt, 1993.

Wemple, Suzanne Fonay. "Female Monasticism in Italy and its Comparison with France and Germany from the Ninth through the Eleventh Century." In *Frauen in Spätantike und Frühmittelalter: Lebensbedingungen - Lebensnormen - Lebensformen. Beiträge zu einer internationalen Tagung am Fachbereich Geschichtswissenschaft der Freien Universität Berlin, 18. bis 21. Februar 1987*, edited by Ursula Vorwerk and Werner Affeldt, 291–310. Sigmaringen: Thorbecke Verlag, 1990.

——. *Women in Frankish Society: Marriage and the Cloister, 500 to 900.* Philadelphia: University of Philadelphia Press, 1981.

Wengler, K. *Kurzer Rückblick auf das adelige Frauenkloster, das St. Marienstift und die uralte Stiftskirche in Pfalzel, anläßl. d. Wiedererwerbung dieses Gotteshauses durch d. Pfarrgemeinde, d. 900-Jahrfeier d. Marienstifts u. d. Wiederkehr d. 400. Gründungsjahres d. Nikolauskapelle.* Trier: Verein Wahrung Berecht. Interessen Pfalzel, 1927.

Werminghoff, Albert. "Die Beschlüsse des Aachener Concils im Jahre 816." *Neues Archiv der Gesellschaft für ältere deutsche Geschichtskunde* 27 (1902): 605–75.

Werner, Matthias. "Der Herzog von Lothringen in salischer Zeit." In *Die Salier und das Reich*, edited by Odilo Engels, Franz-Jozef Heyen, Franz Staub, and Stefan Weinfurter, 1:367–474. Sigmaringen: Thorbecke Verlag, 1991.

West, Charles. "Group Formation in the Long Tenth Century: A View from Trier and its Region." In *Das lange 10. Jahrhundert—struktureller Wandel zwischen Zentralisierung und Fragmentierung, äußerem Druck und innere Krise*, edited by Christine A. Kleinjung and Stefan Albrecht, 167–78. s.l.: Verlag des Römisch-Germanisches Zentralmuseums, 2014.

Wiegand, Wilhelm. "Ein Nonnen-Verzeichnis der Abtei St. Marie in Metz." *Jahr-Buch der Gesellschaft für Lothringische Geschichte und Altertumskunde* 1 (1888–9): 269.

Will, Madeleine. "Die ehemalige Abteikirche St. Peter zu Metz und ihre frühmittelalterlichen Schrankenelemente." Unpublished PhD dissertation, University of Bonn, 2001.

Wilsdorf, Christian. "Remiremont et Murbach à l'époque carolingienne." In *Remiremont, l'abbaye et la ville: Actes des Journées d'études vosgiennes Remiremont 17–20 avril 1980*, edited by Michel Parisse, 47–57. Nancy: Presses Universitaires de Nancy, 1980.

Wischermann, Else Maria. *Marcigny-Sur-Loire: Gründungs- u. Frühgeschichte des 1. Cluniacenserinnenpriorates (1055–1150)*. Munich: Fink, 1986.

Wolters, J. *Notice historique sur l'ancien chapitre impérial de chanoinesses à Thorn dans la province actuelle de Limbourg*. Ghent: F. and E. Gyselinck, 1850.

Wood, Susan. *The Proprietary Church in the Medieval West*. Oxford: Oxford University Press, 2006.

Worm, Andrea. "'You Shall All Live Together in Harmony and Spiritual Unity': Images of Abbesses and Female Religious Communities in the Empire." In *Mulieres religiosae: Shaping Female Spiritual Authority in the Medieval and Early Modern Periods*, edited by Veerle Fraeters and Imke de Gier, 37–85. Turnhout: Brepols, 2014.

Yorke, Barbara A. E. *Nunneries and the Anglo-Saxon Royal Houses*. London: Continuum, 2003.

———. "'Sisters under the Skin'? Anglo-Saxon Nuns and Nunneries in Southern England." In *Medieval Women in Southern England*, edited by Malcolm C. Barber and Keith Bate, 95–117. Reading: Graduate Centre for Medieval Studies, University of Reading, 1989.

Zettler, Alfons. "Fraternitas und Verwandschaft: Verbindungslinien und Wirkkräfte des Austauschs zwischen frühmittelalterlichen Klöstern." In *Vom Kloster zum Klosterverband. Das Werkzeug der Schriftlichkeit: Akten des Internationalen Kolloquiums des Projekts L 2 im SFB 231 (22.–23. Februar 1996)*, edited by Hagen Keller and Franz Neiske, 100–17. Munich: Wilhelm Fink Verlag, 1997.

Zimmer, Theresia. "Das Kloster St. Irminen-Oeren in Trier von seinen Anfängen bis ins 13. Jahrhundert." *Trierer Zeitschrift* 23 (1954–55): 5–180.

Zola, Alan. "Radbertus's Monastic Voice: Ideas About Monasticism at Ninth-Century Corbie." Unpublished PhD dissertation, University of Chicago, 2008.

Index

Aachen synod (816), 4, 12–14, 16–22, 27, 38, 176–77, 204n23
Aachen synod (817), 220n8
Aachen synod (836), 26, 208n84
Adalbero, Archbishop of Reims, 215n68
Adalbero I, Bishop of Metz, 85, 98–100, 102–6, 108–9, 232n83, 238n55
Adalbero II, Bishop of Metz, 93, 120–22
Adalbero III, Bishop of Metz, 117
Adalhard, Courtier, 41, 43, 57, 217n97
Adelheidis, Abbess, 139, 245n12
Adelmann, Inhabitant of Metz, 91–92
Adelphius, Saint, 56, 69, 126, 147, 248n66
Admonitio ad Nonsuindam reclusam, 228n19
Admonitio Generalis, 23, 207n72
Adventius, Bishop of Metz, 63, 121
Aegidius of Orval, Chronicler, 76, 116, 223n56
Albert I, Count of Namur, 153
Aldegondis, Saint, 46, 51–53, 62, 82, 132, 139–42, 145, 216n72, 246n30
Aldeneik: Charles the Bald ownership, 217n105; *Codex Eyckensis II* acquisition, 133; dissolution, 72; Duke Giselbert, role of, 79, 87, 133; geographic location, 60, 101, 113; invasions, 72; *Life of Harlindis and Relindis*, 54–56, 62; list of monastic personnel, 159; manuscript ownership, 210n103; monastic space organization, 47; Otto I, role of, 106, 133; potential audience, 47; restoration, 72; *Rule* allusions, 54, 56; Thorn proximity, 117
Aldetrudis, Saint, 52, 82
Alhedis, Abbess, 240n83
Alsleben, 28
Amalberga, Abbess, 61
Amat, Saint, 38, 56, 69, 126, 147
Amor, Saint, 148–49, 224n84
Andenne, 60, 73, 101, 113, 147, 159, 217n105
Annals of Lorsch, 18
Annegray, 40

Ansegis, Abbot, 213n28
Ansfrid II, Nobleman, 115–17, 146, 253n79
Ansoaldis, Abbess, 137–40, 142–43, 195–97, 244n11
Ansteus, Abbot, 106
Antoing, 60, 72, 74–75, 159, 217n105, 223n47
Archenbald, Abbot, 96, 100
Arles council (813), 204n16
Arnoul, Saint, 122
Arnulf, Count of Chaumontois, 230n57
Arnulf, Nobleman, 125, 145
Arnulf of Carinthia, King of East Francia, 67, 73, 76–78
Arras, 152
Augustine, Saint, 136, 181
Aurelian, Archbishop of Arles, 29
Ava, Abbess of Aldeneik, 47, 50
Ava, Abbess of Denain, 46, 50
Avra, Saint, 137

Baldwin IV, Count of Flanders, 130, 150–51
Bede the Venerable, Monk and author, 136
Begga, Saint, 147, 248n62
Benedict, Abbot, 107
Benedicta, Abbess, 76–77
Benedict of Aniane, Abbot, 13, 20, 29, 32
Benedict of Nursia, Saint, 17, 30, 32, 83, 91, 103, 152–53, 205n33, 235n1. See also *Rule*
Berenger, Bishop of Verdun, 119
Berenger, Nobleman, 225n84
Berlendis, Saint, 136, 147, 245n11
Berno, Nobleman, 59, 61
Bertarius of Saint-Vanne, Chronicler, 119
Bertha, Abbess, 58, 226n111
Bertha, Noblewoman, 225n84
Bertha, Nun, 240n91
Berthold, Bishop of Toul, 102, 122, 227n15
Betta, Noblewoman, 112, 114, 146
Bleurville, 113, 115, 126, 160
Bliesgau, 121
Boniface, Saint, 55

301

INDEX

Bonmoutier, 101, 159, 213n32, 217n105, 222n42
Boso, Count, 58, 81, 83, 86, 99
Bouxières: Bosonid family patronage, 99; charter, 95–97, 100, 103, 120, 145, 229n40, 230n50, 230n55; estate growth, 100, 102, 114, 247n51; financial status, 118, 239n66, 250n89, 251n13; geographic location, 96, 100–101, 113–14; Gozelin of Toul, role of, 95–96, 98–99, 103, 120, 145–46; list of monastic personnel, 160; Odelric, role of, 100, 109, 114, 234n114; original abbess, 93; Otto I, role of, 102, 230n55; political impact, 98–100; reform efforts, 108; status as canonesses, 249n86
Brabant, 115, 125
Bruno, Archbishop of Cologne, 100, 102, 105
Bruno, Bishop of Toul, 102, 114–15, 122, 207n64. *See also* Leo IX, Pope
Bucilly, 228n24
Burgundy, 71, 87, 122
Buxinda, Abbess, 126

Caddroë, Saint, 107, 228n24
Cambrai, 8, 15, 22, 33, 46–47, 129–32, 139
Catalonia, 84, 241n105
Caudry, 60, 94–95, 101, 132, 143, 159
Cecilia, Abbess, 76–77
Cesarius, Archbishop of Arles, 16, 29–31, 33, 140, 181, 205n27, 209n103, 246n38
Chalon-sur-Saône synod (813), 16–17, 21, 26, 33–35, 140, 167–71, 178, 182, 208n84
Charlemagne, King and Emperor, 14, 16, 19, 21, 23–24, 75, 128, 207n72
Charles the Bald, King of West Francia and Emperor, 27, 57, 59, 61–63, 72, 74–75, 77, 130, 150–51, 217n97, 217n105
Charles the Fat, Emperor, 67, 222n42
Charles the Simple, King of West Francia and Lotharingia, 79, 95, 98, 100, 114, 218n116, 219n136, 222n42, 230n45
Charroux, 43
Childeric, King of the Franks, 132, 142, 245n27, 246n32
Chlodulph, Nobleman, 224n84
Chrodegang, Bishop of Metz, 13
Codex Eyckensis I, 55
Codex Eyckensis II, 133, 243n143
Codex regularum, 29
Cologne, 15, 100–102, 105, 120, 173, 219n5, 235n115
Columbanus, Saint, 32
Condé-sur-Escaut, 60, 72, 159, 217n105

Conrad, Count, 69, 78, 102
Conrad, Emperor, 126, 146
Constantin of Saint-Symphorien, Biographer and hagiographer, 121
Cousolre, 46, 62, 142–43, 246n30
Crespin, 217n101
Cunegondis, Abbess, 117
Cyprian, Bishop of Carthage, 205n27, 206n49

Dagobert I, King of the Franks, 77, 128
Deeds of Bishop Walcand of Liège, 15
Deeds of the Bishops of Cambrai, 72, 129–30, 150
Deeds of the Bishops of Toul, 92, 230n41
Denain: charter, 130, 150; Charles the Bald ownership, 217n105; cleric sanctuary, 130; dissolution uncertainties, 72; Ermentrudis, role of, 150; financial status, 150–51, 153, 217n101; Fredesindis, role of, 150–52; geographic location, 113; Gisela, role of, 59, 61; list of monastic personnel, 160; lost property restitution, 62; Marchiennes relocation, 130, 143, 150; monastic space organization, 46, 50, 152; reform transition, 136, 140, 150–53; restoration, 130, 150
Destry, County of, 113
Deurne, 221n30
Doda, Abbess, 174
Doddo, Abbot, 213n32
Donatus, Bishop of Besançon, 29
Douzy council (874), 220n8
Drogo, Abbot and bishop, 43, 45–47, 50, 206n57, 214n43

Eberwin, Abbot, 137, 244n4
Ebroin, Abbot, 72
Echternach, 54
Egbert, Archbishop of Trier, 127–28, 241n103
Egebert, Hagiographer, 148
Eike, 55, 106
Einhard, Abbot and hagiographer, 216n83
Einold, Abbot, 103, 106, 227n11
Emma, Abbess of Sant Joan de les Abadesses, 84
Emma, Nun, 151
Emma, Queen, 130–31
England, 6, 31–32, 36, 68, 75, 84, 93, 118, 206n50, 210n103, 222n41, 223n50
Epinal, 113, 117, 121–23, 153, 160, 239n66, 239n68
Erluin, Bishop of Cambrai, 131–32

INDEX 303

Ermenaidis, Laywoman, 102
Ermengardis, Abbes, 117
Ermengardis, Noblewoman, 72, 222n34. *See also* Ermesindis, Wife of Count Albert of Namur
Ermengardis, Wife of Lothar I, 61
Ermentrudis, Abbess of Denain, 150
Ermentrudis, Abbess of Hasnon, 59, 61
Ermentrudis, Daughter of Charles the Simple, 114
Ermentrudis, Laywoman, 235n116
Ermentrudis, Wife of Charles the Bald, 59, 217n97
Ermesindis, Wife of Count Albert of Namur, 153
Essen, 29, 32, 127, 201n2, 209n92, 211n124, 213n33, 229n25, 234n108, 237n40, 244n5, 247n51
Etrun, 152, 249n83
Eufrasia, Saint, 212n19
Eufrosina, Saint, 212n19
Eugenia, Laywoman, 226n103
Eugenius III, Pope, 152
Eusebia, Saint, 47, 49, 71, 82, 131, 147, 242n127
Eva, Abbess, 238n47
Eva of Chaumontois, Noblewoman, 96, 100, 146

Fingen, Abbot, 119
Flanders, 130
Flémalle, 76
Fleury, 95
Folcuin, Count, 100
Fosse, 78
Franco, Bishop of Liège, 47, 55
Frankfurt council (796), 14
Fredeburga, 90–91, 108, 143, 185–86, 227n10
Fredegand, Saint, 221n30
Frederic, Count of Verdun, 119
Frederic, Duke of Lotharingia, 100, 103, 105, 231n62
Frederic, Nobleman in Toul, 236n17
Fredesindis, Abbess, 150–51
Frothar, Bishop of Toul, 211n4, 219n135
Fructuosus, Saint, 32
Fulbert, Bishop of Cambrai, 243n136
Furseus, Saint, 233n96

Gandersheim, 212n21, 243n143, 247n51
Gebetrudis, Saint, 71
Geisa of Saint-Pierre-aux-Nonnains, 90–92, 139, 143, 185–88

Gelderland, 115
Gengulph, Saint, 100
Geoffrey, Episcopal Count of Metz, 236n34
Gerard, Advocate of Remiremont, 126
Gerard, Bishop of Cambrai, 130, 132, 138–40, 142–43, 150, 153
Gerard, Bishop of Toul, 92–93, 100, 102, 112, 121
Gerard, Count at Metz, 107
Gerard, Count of Metz, 126, 240n91
Gerard, Nobleman, 77
Gerard of Lunéville, Nobleman, 236n33
Gerberga, Abbess of Hessen, 115
Gerberga, Abbess of Thorn, 117–18
Gerberga, Daughter of Henry I, 79
Gerberga, Queen, 85
Gerhard, Count, 69, 78
Gerpinnes, 153, 222n34, 249n71
Gerresheim, 219n5
Gertrudis, Saint, 47, 77, 144–47, 223n59, 236n17, 248n60
Ghislengien, 249n83
Gisela, Abbess of Remiremont, 126
Gisela, Daughter of Lothar I, 61
Gisela, Daughter of Lothar II and abbess of Nivelles, 59, 61, 77–78, 223n58
Gisela, Sister of Charles the Bald, 59, 61, 72
Giselbert, Duke, 71, 79, 85–87, 96, 98–99, 103, 106, 108, 133, 224n75, 230nn56–57
Gisla, Laywoman, 240n83
Gisla/Gisela, Abbess of Remiremont, 126
Gislebert of Mons, Chronicler, 248n65
Gislen, Saint, 73, 82, 146, 247n56
Glandière, 63
Glossinde, Saint, 45–46, 51, 61, 81–84, 90–92, 103, 106–8, 214nn43–44
Godfrey, Duke of Frisia, 59
Godfrey, Palace Mayor, 114
Godfrey of Florennes, Nobleman, 125
Goëry, Saint, 122, 238n59, 239n68
Gorze, 63, 95, 103, 105–6, 108, 226n111, 227n1, 231n62
Gotfrid, Nobleman, 78–79
Gozelin, Bishop of Langres, 98
Gozelin, Bishop of Toul, 85–86, 93, 95–100, 103, 109, 120–21, 145–46, 230n41, 232n89, 247n51
Gozelo, Duke of Upper and Lower Lotharingia, 117, 126, 133, 145
Gregory VII, Pope, 11, 126. *See also* Hildebrand, Archdeacon
Gregory the Great, Pope, 137, 212n19, 225n93, 242n129

INDEX

Grimlaicus, Author, 228n19
Guînes, 249n83
gyrovagae, 93, 119, 237n44

Hadewidis, Abbess, 107–8, 233n99
Hadrad, Nobleman, 230n41
Hadrian, Pope, 21
Haimo, Bishop, 118–21, 238n52
Hainaut, 73, 130
Hamage: Berno, role of, 59, 61; charter, 61, 74; cleric population, 131–32, 142, 242n129; dissolution, 72, 74; Eusebia, role of, 71, 82, 131, 148; financial status, 74, 217n101; geographic location, 60; invasions, 74, 222n44; Marchiennes, connections with, 70, 74, 82, 131, 142; monastic personnel, 159; monastic space organization, 47–50, 222n45; putative reform, 47
Harlindis, Saint, 47, 54–56, 62
Hasnon, 59–61, 72, 161, 217n101, 222n33
Hastière, 99, 101–2, 104–5, 133, 159, 231n73, 232n82
Hathumoda, Abbess, 212n21, 245n11
Hautmont, 217n101
Heiligenkreuz, 115
Henry, Nobleman, 115
Henry I, King of East Francia, 77, 79, 86–87, 98
Henry II, King and Emperor, 27–28, 116–17, 121–22, 128, 133
Henry III, King and Emperor, 125–26, 144–45, 238n52
Henry IV, King and Emperor, 240n89
Herbitzheim, 60, 78, 159, 217n105
Hereswint/Hilsondis, Noblewoman, 115–17, 146
Herford, 214n38
Heribert II, Count of Vermandois, 79
Heribrand, Abbot, 146
Herman of Lunéville, Nobleman, 236n33
Hermentrudis, Abbess, 107
Hersendis, laywoman, 93, 96, 99
Hesse, 113, 115, 161
Hilary, Bishop of Poitiers, 136
Hilda, Noblewoman, 224n84
Hildebrand, Archdeacon, 11–12, 28, 127, 135, 148, 154. *See also* Gregory VII, Pope
Hildemar of Corbie, Monk, 33, 35, 177, 244n7
Hildeward, Bishop of Halberstadt, 214n44
Hildoard, Bishop of Cambrai, 21
Hilwartshausen, 27
Himiltrudis, Abbess, 103, 105–6, 108

Hincmar, Archbishop of Reims, 25, 208n81
Hohenbourg, 15, 217n105
Hohorst, 116
Honnecourt, 101, 159, 229n29
Hucbald of Saint-Amand, Hagiographer, 69–70, 82–83, 131
Hugh of Flavigny, Chronicler, 238n47
Hugo, Abbot of Charroux, 43
Hugo, Count of Bourges, 230n49
Hulindis, Religious Woman, 214n35
Humbert, Hermit, 93, 96
Humbert of Silva Candida, Cleric, 240n95

Ida, Abbess, 83–85
Ida of Boulogne, Noblewoman, 153
Ida of Chièvres, Noblewoman, 249n83
Imma, Abbess, 39, 57
Inden, 40
Indicularius Thiathildis, 41–43
Institutio canonicorum, 13–14, 16, 27, 210n108
Institutio sanctimonialium: ambiguous vision, 17–19; Archdeacon Hildebrand support, 28; Canon, 28, 34; early title, 21, 54; enclosure references, 32, 34, 210n115; geographic location, 60, 101, 113; Jacques De Guise interpretations, 15–16, 28; Louis the Pious, role of, 14–15, 18; Maubeuge compilation extracts, 33–36, 176–77; mixed realities, 19, 22–23; origins, 14–15; partial observance, 28–29, 241n114; propaganda role, 22–23; *Rule* alternative, 15–17; source text citations, 29; surviving copies, 210n108; text length, 16
Irmintrudis, Abbess, 107

Jacques De Guise, Chronicler, 15–16, 28, 172
Jerome, Saint, 205n27, 209n103, 241n114
John IV, Pope, 126
John XIX, Pope, 120, 238n52
John Cassian, Abbot, 33, 182
John of Arles, Author, 29
John of Saint-Arnoul, Biographer and hagiographer, 90–93, 103–4, 108, 209n92, 214n40, 233n96, 238n47
John of Vandières, Priest and monk (later abbot) of Gorze, 32, 90–94, 105, 185–88, 209n92, 227n11
Jonat, Saint, 132, 147, 248n67
Judith, Abbess, 130–31, 144, 147, 242n124, 243n133

INDEX 305

Judith, Empress, 41, 43
Juvigny, 59, 101, 113, 161, 205n33, 231n62, 232n83

Kunigunde, Wife of Henry II, 128

La Capelle, 153
Lambert I, Count of Louvain, 125
Landevennec, 222n45
Landrada, Saint, 148
Leduin, Abbot, 130
Lennik, 108
Leo IX, Pope, 102, 112, 115, 122, 126, 235n14, 236nn17–18, 238n52, 239n71, 240n95
Le Wast, 153
Libellus de rebus Trevirensibus, 129, 242n118
Liber memorialis (Remiremont), 38–40, 43–44, 56–58, 81, 83, 85, 108–9, 114, 212n12, 212n20, 217nn95–96, 217n98, 224n82, 225n87, 234n107
Liber memorialis (Santa Giulia), 207n61
Liège, 8, 15, 47, 60, 72, 75, 78, 101–2, 104–6, 113, 117, 132–33, 139
Liutard, Layman, 223n58
Liutbirg of Wendeshausen, Anchoress, 91, 139, 245n12
Lobbes, 40, 75, 78, 138–39, 221n24, 223n47
Lorraine, 8
Lothar, King of West Francia, 130–31, 144–45, 242n125
Lothar I, King and Emperor, 57, 59, 61
Lothar II, King and Emperor, 57–59, 61–62, 66, 78, 217n98
Louis, Count, 115
Louis II, King of Italy and Emperor, 57
Louis the Child, King of West Francia, 69, 76, 87, 98, 128, 223n58
Louis the German, King of East Francia, 59, 63
Louis the Pious, Emperor: Abbess Thiathildis correspondence, 41–42, 183–84; Archdeacon Hildebrand condemnation, 127; death, 57; female monasticism regulation, 2, 4, 11–13, 23; half brothers, 43, 45; *Institutio sanctimonialium*, role in, 14–15, 18–19; layman status, 12; model monastery vision, 38; Pope, relations with, 18; reform role, 13–15, 18–19, 23; Remiremont, impact on, 38–39, 57; *Rule* imposition, 13, 19, 47
Louvain, 67, 125, 144

Ludolph, Archbishop of Trier, 128
Lunéville, 113, 117, 161, 236n33
Luxueil, 43

Maastricht, 224n84
Madelberta, Saint, 82–83, 140, 142, 225n93
Madon river, 122
Magyars, 66–67
Mainz council (813), 14
Mainz council (847), 23, 26, 171
Mainz council (888), 220n6
Manasses, Count of Guînes, 249n83
Marbach, 40
Marchiennes: Berno, role of, 59, 61; Breton evangeliary, 222n45; charter, 61, 145; cleric population, 129–31; Denain, relocation to, 130, 143, 150; dissolution, 150; financial status, 217n101, 218n125; geographic location, 101; Hamage, connections with, 70, 74, 82, 131, 142; historical documentation, 73; invasions, 69–70, 222n45; *Life* of Saint Rictrudis, 69–71, 82–83, 131; list of monastic personnel, 161; monastic space organization, 61–62; royal institution status, 144–45; *Rule* adherence, 83
Marcigny, 153, 250n96
Maroilles, 217n101
Martha, Saint, 228n19
Martin, Saint, 96, 132, 138
Mary, Saint, 47, 114, 228n19
Matfrid, Count, 77, 78, 105, 240n91
Matfridis, Nun, 240n91
Mathilde, Noblewoman, 115
Mathilde, Queen, 77, 245n13
Maubeuge: Ansoaldis, role of, 137–40; Charles the Bald ownership, 217n105; charter, 132; cleric population, 52–53, 132, 145, 215n68; communal libraries, 29, 89; financial status, 145, 216n74, 217n101; geographic location, 60, 101, 113; inclusiveness, 52; list of monastic personnel, 162; lordship, 213n28; monastic space organization, 46, 62, 73; *Rule* adherence, 139–40, 173; spiritual culture evidence, 137–42, 196–97; reform date, 245n17; theft attempts, 82. See also *Roll of Maubeuge*
Maur, Saint, 120, 238n47
Mauront, Saint, 132, 147, 248n67
Maxellendis, Saint, 94–95, 132, 229n25
Meerbeke, 60, 72, 101, 113, 159, 217n105
Menna, Saint, 122, 239n75

INDEX

Messines, 151–53
Metz, 8, 22, 29, 32, 45–46, 50, 59–61, 67–68, 81, 88–90, 99–110, 121–22, 212n17
Meurthe river, 96
Meuse river, 8, 55, 67, 115, 117
Milan, 237n45
Mixed Pseudo-Bede-Egbert Penitential, 33, 35, 179–81, 210n107, 211n124, 244n7
Mons, 15, 73, 79, 82, 101, 113, 138, 147
Moorsel, 222n32
Mortagne, County of, 113
Moselle region, 8, 67, 122
Moselle river, 38, 69, 96
Moselotte river, 38
Moustier-sur-Sambre, 60, 72, 101, 113, 153, 159
Moyenmoutier, 67, 85
Munsterbilzen: Amor, role of, 148–49, 224n84; charter, 153; coinage, 117, 148–49; commemorative inscription, 154; financial status, 148, 153; geographic location, 60, 101, 113; Gozelo burial hosting, 145; historical documentation, 73, 133; institution status, 117; list of monastic personnel, 162; psalter ownership, 244n7; relic translation, 224–25n84; Thorn proximity, 117
Murbach, 43
Muslims, 66

Nancy, 96, 145
Navarra, 32
Neumünster, 113, 121, 159
Nicholas II, Pope, 11
Niedermünster, 30–31, 140, 233n99, 246nn37–38
Nivelles: Berlendis, role of, 136, 146–47; charters, 73, 77, 108, 125, 144–46, 240n86; financial status, 124, 148; geographic location, 60, 101, 113; Gisela, role of, 59; historical documentation, 73; incorporation, 125; list of monastic personnel, 163; Meerbeke priory, 72, 221n32; monastic space organization, 46–47, 62, 240n86; reform transition, 89, 108–9; Richildis, role of, 59, 61, 218n113; royal institution status, 77, 110, 124–25, 144, 217n105, 240n85; *Rule* adherence, 28, 172–75
Normans, 66–68, 70, 72–74, 87
Notger, Bishop of Liège, 116–17, 133
Noyon, 66

Obermünster, 209n95
Oda, Abbess of Lunéville, 117
Oda, Abbess of Nivelles, 125
Oda, Abbess of Remiremont, 126, 236n34
Odelric, Abbot, 99–100, 109, 114, 230n55, 234n114
Odilia, Saint, 15
Oeren: Louis the German ownership, 217n105; charters, 106, 127–28, 233n92; geographic location, 60, 101; historical documentation, 129; invasions, 69–70; list of monastic personnel, 163; mint, 241n113; ownership transfers, 127–28, 217n105; Pfalzel refugees, 3, 129, 193–94; royal institution status, 77–78, 217n105, 233n92
Ogiva, Abbess, 152, 198–99
Olbert of Gembloux, Hagiographer, 146–47
Orp-le-Grand, 60, 72, 101, 159
Otto, Count of Louvain, 125
Otto I, King of East Francia and Emperor, 27, 79, 87, 98, 100–103, 105–6, 114–15, 127–28, 133, 224n65, 224n75, 230n55, 231n75, 232n79
Otto II, Emperor, 77, 124, 128, 231n77
Otto III, Emperor, 107, 117, 124, 128

Paenitentiale mixtum Pseudo-Bedae-Egberti, 33, 35, 211n124
Paris council (829), 23–24, 43, 208n83
Paschalis II, Pope, 152, 198–99
Paschasius Radbertus, Abbot, 215n63
Pelagia, Saint, 212n19, 227n12
Pfalzel: artistic activities, 127; charter, 127; cleric population, 3–4, 129, 201n6; geographic location, 60, 100, 113; Gotfrid, role of, 78–79; list of monastic personnel, 163–64; Poppo, role of, 3, 128–29, 241n117; *Rule* adherence, 2, 127–29, 140, 192–94; Ruothildis's epitaph, 1–3, 21, 127–29, 137, 140, 201n6, 213–14n35; Sankt Paulin, links to, 128
Pibo, Bischof of Toul, 239n71
Pippin, King of Aquitaine, 213nn33–34
Pippin, King of the Franks, 128
Poppo, Abbot, 119
Poppo, Archbishop of Trier, 3, 128–29, 241n117
Poussay, 113, 122, 150, 164, 239n76
Prüm, 40, 67, 73, 76, 78, 224nn64–65
Pseudo-Athanasius, Author, 205n27
Pseudo-Columbanus, Author, 30

INDEX   307

Quedlinburg, 254Fn1
Quentin, Saint, 79

Radbod, Archbishop of Trier, 67, 77
Radulph, Nobleman, 59, 61
Ragenfredis, Saint, 46, 150–51
Rainard, Count of Toul, 236n17
Rainer of Ghent, Hagiographer, 146
Rambert, Bishop of Verdun, 120
Ratsindis, Abbess, 79
Regino of Prüm, Abbot, 77–78
Regula cuiusdam ad virgines, 29
Regula sanctimonialium, 209n103
Regula solitarium, 228n19
Reims, 25, 35–36, 66, 91, 100, 151, 204n16, 219n5
Reims council (813), 204n16
Relindis, Recluse, 76
Relindis, Saint, 47, 54–56, 62
Remiremont: cleric population, 43–44, 50, 58, 137, 213n33; donation records, 81; enclosure challenges, 38–40, 44; financial status, 57–58, 109, 117, 236n17, 239n66; florilegia, 136–37; founding, 38, 240n95; geographic location, 60, 101, 113; Gerard and his son's ascendancy, 125–26; Giselbert, role of, 79, 87, 224n75; invasions, 67, 69–71, 109, 219n5; *Liber memorialis* testimony, 38–40, 43–44, 56–58, 81, 83, 85, 108–9, 114, 212n12, 212n20, 217n95, 224n82, 225n87, 234n110; list of monastic personnel, 164–65; Louis the Pious, influence of, 38–39, 57; multiple locations, 38–39, 56, 211n4; Odelric, role of, 100, 109, 114; prayer fraternities, 40, 43; Pelagia manuscript of *Life*, 227n12; reform transition, 38–44, 56–58, 109; royal institution status, 38, 40, 57–58, 211n3, 217n98, 217n105; *Rule* influence, 18, 38–40, 56–58, 86, 115; *Theutberga Gospels* ownership, 22, 84, 212n17; Thiathildis, role of, 40–44, 50, 57–59, 183–84
Remlindis, Laywoman, 79, 91, 104
Renier V, Count of Mons, 138, 140, 142–43, 147, 153, 196–97, 245n17, 248n65
Renier of Hainaut, 73, 79, 98
Richard, Abbot, 119–20, 137, 139, 238n47, 244n4
Richard, Duke of Burgundy, 71, 81, 87
Richer, Bishop of Liège, 72, 105
Richildis, Empress, 59, 61, 218n113, 230n49, 232n83

Rictrudis, Saint, 69–71, 82–83, 130–31, 145, 147, 248n67
Ricuin, Count of Verdun, 78–79, 90–91, 98–99, 104–5, 227n10, 232n86
Rolendis, Saint, 153, 249n71, 250n92
Roll of Maubeuge, 33–36, 89, 132, 140–43, 176–82, 209n92, 211n124, 244n7, 245n19
Romano-Germanic pontifical, 22, 207n59
Romaric, Saint, 38, 41, 56, 69, 71, 126, 147, 248n66
Rome synod (1059), 11–12, 135, 145, 198–91
Rothard, Bishop of Cambrai, 132
Rothildis, Abbess, 96, 99, 230nn49–50
Rotlindis, Oblate, 102
Rule: Aldeneik, impact on, 54, 56; communal life template, 2, 4, 14, 19–20, 27, 56; Gozelin of Toul admiration, 96; *gyrovagae* reference, 93, 119, 237n44; Hildemar of Corbie's commentary, 33, 244n7; historical reconstructions, 12; *Institutio sanctimonialium* as alternative, 15–17; leveraging function, 127; *Life* of Saint Aldegondis allusions, 140; local needs, 14; Louis the Pious imposition, 13, 19, 47; Marchiennes adherence, 83; Maubeuge adherence, 139–40; Nivelles adherence, 28; ordination script, 207n60; partial observance, 29, 107–8, 115; Pfalzel adherence, 2, 127–29, 140; redacted copies, 30–32, 209nn94–95; Remiremont, impact on, 18, 38–40, 56–58, 86, 115; rigidity, 16, 28, 56, 111, 128–29, 157; Sigeric proclamations, 114; Smaragdus's commentary, 32; variety of interpretations, 14, 18, 128; vow rituals, 206n53
Ruodbert, Archbishop of Trier, 85, 212n28
Ruothildis, Abbess, 1–3, 5, 21, 127–29, 137, 140, 201n2, 201n6, 241n105, 242n118, 244n5, 253n69

Säckingen, 40
Sains-lès-Marquion, 60, 72, 101, 159
Saint-Amand, 22, 217n101, 221n24
Saint-Amé, 131
Saint-Arnoul, 63, 67, 107, 233n97
Saint-Dié, 67
Sainte-Croix (abbey), 215n63, 212n28, 213nn33–34, 215n63
Sainte-Croix (chapter and church in Verdun), 120

INDEX

Sainte-Glossinde: Adalbero of Metz, role of, 102–6, 108; charters, 63, 103, 238n55, 249n72; enclosure enforcement, 45–46, 106; geographic location, 60, 101, 113; Hastière ownership transfer, 102, 104–5; list of monastic personnel, 162; monastic space organization, 45–47, 81–82; patron saint promotion, 45–46, 106–7, 249n81
Sainte-Marie-aux-Nonnains, 93, 113, 121, 159
Sainte-Radegonde, 40
Saint-Etienne, 213n33
Saint-Evre, 43, 85–86, 95–96, 100, 108, 230n54, 232n89, 250n89, 251n13
Sainte-Waudru, 15, 60, 73, 82, 101, 113, 147, 153, 163, 213n28, 217n101, 243n137, 248n65
Saint-Felix, 107
Saint-Ghislain, 82, 85, 118, 146, 247n56
Saint-Laurent (abbey in Liège), 147
Saint-Léger (church at Champeaux), 40
Saint-Martin, 132
Saint-Mary (church near Metz), 45
Saint-Maur, 113, 118–21, 166, 238n47
Saint-Mont, 38–39, 69, 71, 211n4
Saint-Paul (church at Nivelles), 124
Saint-Peter (church at Maubeuge), 79
Saint-Peter and Saint-Paul (church at Hamage), 49
Saint-Pierre-aux-Nonnains: Adalbero of Metz, role of, 99, 102–5, 108, 121; charters, 103, 105–6, 246n41; intellectual life at, 32, 209n92; criminal activities, 68; Frederic, role of, 105, 231n62; Geisa, role of, 90–92, 139, 143; geographic location, 60, 101, 113; John of Vandières, role of, 90; list of monastic personnel, 162; Louis the German ownership, 217n105; membership levels, 238n56; monastic space organization, 46; patron saint promotion, 46; royal institution status, 77–79; Waldrada, role of, 46, 60; women religious expectations, 90–93
Saint-Pierre d'Avenay, 213n33, 218n111
Saint-Quentin (abbey), 79
Saint-Quentin (church at Maubeuge), 132
Saint-Sulpice, 106
Saint-Symphorien, 122
Saint-Vaast, 22, 130, 221n24
Saint-Vanne, 119–20, 226n103, 228n19
Saint-Vincent, 228n19
Salm, 113–14
Salvus of Albelda, Abbot, 32, 235n1

Sankt Emmeran, 206n49
Sankt Gallen, 236n34
Sankt Maria im Kapitol, 235n115
Sankt Maximin, 22, 69, 78, 85, 128
Sankt Pantaleon, 120
Sankt Paulin, 128–29, 241nn116–17
Santa Giulia, 61, 207n61, 212n15, 217n107
Santa Maria in Via Lata, 84
Sant Joan de les Abadesses, 84
Sarreboug, County of, 113
Saulnois, 113
Saxony, 8, 21, 27, 32, 114, 116, 202n27, 213n28, 216n73, 227n4, 234n104, 237n34, 240n82, 241n105
Scarpe river, 8
Scheldt river, 8, 69
Schienen, 40
Sigeric, Count, 112–14, 146
Siginand, Monk of Prüm, 76
Sigohard, Count, 78
Smaragdus of Saint-Mihiel, Monk, 32, 254Fn1
Solre-Saint-Géry, 142
Sotzeling, 114
Stavelot-Malmedy, 40, 85, 119
Stephen, Bishop of Cambrai, 82
Stephen, Bishop of Liège, 72, 78, 223n58
Stephen, Saint, 214n44
Stephen VIII, Pope, 100
Sulpicius Severus, Hagiographer, 138–39, 243n134, 244n11, 254Innl–2
Susteren, 60, 73, 76–78, 101, 113, 116–17, 133, 165, 217n105, 224nn64–65, 243n142
Symeon, Hermit in Trier, 137

Teilalf, Layman, 79, 91
Teoderic, *Praepositus*, 43, 58
Terentius, Saint, 121, 238n59
Teutbert, Count, 102
Theoderic, Archbishop of Trier, 127–28
Theophanu, Empress, 77, 108, 124
Theudo, Bishop of Cambrai, 131
Theutberga, Queen, 57, 59, 61, 63, 218n111
Theutberga Gospels, 22, 84, 212n17
Thiathildis, Abbess, 40–44, 50, 57–59, 183–84
Thierry, Abbot, 137–40, 143, 244n7
Thierry, Bishop of Verdun, 120
Thierry, Duke of Upper Lotharingia, 232n83
Thierry I, Bishop of Metz, 122, 238n55, 239n64
Thierry II, Bishop of Metz, 93, 233n97
Thorn, 112–13, 115–18, 133, 146, 150, 165–66, 243n142, 247n56

INDEX

Toul, Town and region, 8, 22, 67, 88, 93, 95–102, 108–15, 117, 120–22, 212n17, 227n15
Toul, Urban Nunneries, 92–93, 100, 112, 159, 227n15
Tours council (813), 204n16
Treaty of Meersen, 59, 72, 75, 217n105
Tribur council (895), 220n8
Trier, 1–3, 8, 22, 60, 67, 69, 76–78, 101, 113, 128–29, 137
Trosly council (909), 27, 220n9

Udalrich Milz, Dean, 201n6
Udo, Bishop of Toul, 236n17
Uta, Abbess, 30, 233n99
Utrecht, 116
Uulfrada, Abbess, 39

Vandières, 90
Venantius Fortunatus, Hagiographer, 245n13
Ver council (755), 14, 23–24
Verdun, 60, 67, 78, 90, 93, 98, 101, 113, 118–21, 219n5
Vergaville, 112–14, 146, 150, 166, 247n51
Vero, Saint, 146–47
Vilich, 128

Visions of Flothildis, 91
Vosges, 8, 38, 67
Vregay, 61–62

Walcand, Bishop of Liège, 172
Waldetrudis, Saint, 51, 53, 147, 216n74
Waldrada, Concubine of Lothar II, 217n98, 218n112
Waldrada, Saint, 46, 60
Walo, Bishop of Metz, 46
Warendrudis, Abbess, 201n2, 213n13
Waulsort, 133
Wiborada of Sankt Gallen, Anchoress, 84, 91, 139, 219n5, 227n11, 228n19, 245n12
Wicfrid, Bishop of Verdun, 119
Wigeric, Bishop of Metz, 232n86
Wigeric, Count, 98–99, 104–5
Willibrord, Saint, 55
Winchester council, 31
Worms council (868), 33, 35, 178, 220n8

Zwentibold, King of Lotharingia, 67, 69, 76–78, 98, 116, 128, 145

Also see Appendix A for a list of the known monastic personnel of female institutions in Lotharingia.

CPSIA information can be obtained
at www.ICGtesting.com
Printed in the USA
LVHW03*0142091018
592824LV00006B/161/P